A Census Monograph Series

RURAL AND SMALL TOWN AMERICA

Glenn V. Fuguitt

David L. Brown

Calvin L. Beale

Assisted by Max J. Pfeffer, Robert M. Jenkins,
and Daniel T. Lichter

for the
National Committee for Research
on the 1980 Census

RUSSELL SAGE FOUNDATION / NEW YORK

HB
2385
.F836
1989

The Russell Sage Foundation

The Russell Sage Foundation, one of the oldest of America's general purpose foundations, was established in 1907 by Mrs. Margaret Olivia Sage for "the improvement of social and living conditions in the United States." The Foundation seeks to fulfill the mandate by fostering the development and dissemination of knowledge about the political, social, and economic problems of America. It conducts research in the social sciences and public policy, and publishes books and pamphlets that derive from the research.

The Board of Trustees is responsible for oversight and the general policies of the Foundation, while administrative direction of the program and staff is vested in the President, assisted by the officers and staff. The President bears final responsibility for the decision to publish a manuscript as a Russell Sage Foundation book. In reaching a judgment on the competence, accuracy, and objectivity of each study, the President is advised by the staff and selected expert readers. The conclusions and interpretations in Russell Sage Foundation publications are those of the authors and not of the Foundation, its Trustees, or its staff. Publication by the Foundation, therefore, does not imply endorsement of the contents of the study.

Library of Congress Cataloging-in-Publication Data
Fuguitt, Glenn Victor, 1928–
    Rural and small town America / Glenn V. Fuguitt, David L. Brown,
  Calvin L. Beale.
       p.   cm. — (The Population of the United States in the 1980s)
    Bibliography: p.
    Includes index.
    ISBN 0–87154–272–2
    1. United States—Population, Rural.   2. Rural-urban migration—
United States.   I. Brown, David L. (David Louis), 1945–
II. Beale, Calvin Lunsford, 1923–   III. Title.   IV. Series.
HB2385.F836   1989
304.6'0973'091734—dc20   89—10067
                                                      CIP

 # 19672012

Cover and text design: HUGUETTE FRANCO

10 9 8 7 6 5 4 3 2 1

107712

Foreword

Rural and Small Town America is one of an ambitious series of volumes aimed at converting the vast statistical yield of the 1980 census into authoritative analyses of major changes and trends in American life. This series, "The Population of the United States in the 1980s," represents an important episode in social science research and revives a long tradition of independent census analysis. First in 1930, and then again in 1950 and 1960, teams of social scientists worked with the U.S. Bureau of the Census to investigate significant social, economic, and demographic developments revealed by the decennial censuses. These census projects produced three landmark series of studies, providing a firm foundation and setting a high standard for our present undertaking.

There is, in fact, more than a theoretical continuity between those earlier census projects and the present one. Like those previous efforts, this new census project has benefited from close cooperation between the Census Bureau and a distinguished, interdisciplinary group of scholars. Like the 1950 and 1960 research projects, research on the 1980 census was initiated by the Social Science Research Council and the Russell Sage Foundation. In deciding once again to promote a coordinated program of census analysis, Russell Sage and the Council were mindful not only of the severe budgetary restrictions imposed on the Census Bureau's own publishing and dissemination activities in the 1980s, but also of the extraordinary changes that have occurred in so many dimensions of American life over the past two decades.

The studies constituting "The Population of the United States in the 1980s" were planned, commissioned, and monitored by the National Committee for Research on the 1980 Census, a special committee appointed by the Social Science Research Council and sponsored by the Council, the Russell Sage Foundation, and the Alfred P. Sloan Foundation, with the collaboration of the U.S. Bureau of the Census. This committee includes leading social scientists from a broad range of fields—demography, economics, education, geography, history, political science, sociology, and statistics. It has been the committee's task to select the main topics for research, obtain highly qualified specialists to carry out that research, and provide the structure necessary to facilitate coordination among researchers and with the Census Bureau.

The topics treated in this series span virtually all the major features of American society—ethnic groups (blacks, Hispanics, foreign-born); spatial dimensions (migration, neighborhoods, housing, regional and metropolitan growth and decline); and status groups (income levels, families and households, women). Authors were encouraged to draw not only on the 1980 census but also on previous censuses and on subsequent national data. Each individual research project was assigned a special advisory panel made up of one committee member, one member nominated by the Census Bureau, one nominated by the National Science Foundation, and one or two other experts. These advisory panels were responsible for project liaison and review and for recommendations to the National Committee regarding the readiness of each manuscript for publication. With the final approval of the chairman of the National Committee, each report was released to the Russell Sage Foundation for publication and distribution.

The debts of gratitude incurred by a project of such scope and organizational complexity are necessarily large and numerous. The committee must thank, first, its sponsors—the Social Science Research Council, the Russell Sage Foundation, and the Alfred P. Sloan Foundation. The long-range vision and day-to-day persistence of these organizations and individuals sustained this research program over many years. The active and willing cooperation of the Bureau of the Census was clearly invaluable at all stages of this project, and the extra commitment of time and effort made by Bureau economist James R. Wetzel must be singled out for special recognition. A special tribute is also due to David L. Sills of the Social Science Research Council, staff member of the committee, whose organizational, administrative, and diplomatic skills kept this complicated project running smoothly.

The committee also wishes to thank those organizations that contributed additional funding to the 1980 census report—the Ford Foundation and its deputy vice president, Louis Winnick, the National Science Foundation, the National Institute on Aging, and the National Institute of Child Health and Human Development. Their support of the research program in general and of several particular studies is gratefully acknowledged.

The ultimate goal of the National Committee and its sponsors has been to produce a definitive, accurate, and comprehensive picture of the

U.S. population in the 1980s, a picture that would be primarily descriptive but also enriched by a historical perspective and a sense of the challenges for the future inherent in the trends of today. We hope our readers will agree that the present volume takes a significant step toward achieving that goal.

CHARLES F. WESTOFF

Chairman and Executive Director
National Committee for Research
on the 1980 Census

Acknowledgments

This work was made possible by support from the Russell Sage Foundation through the National Committee for Research on the 1980 Census, and by our respective institutions, the Department of Rural Sociology, College of Agricultural and Life Sciences, University of Wisconsin–Madison; the Office for Research, College of Agriculture, Cornell University; and the Agriculture and Rural Economy Division, Economic Research Service, U.S. Department of Agriculture. We benefited greatly also from use of the computer and library facilities of the Wisconsin Center for Demography and Ecology, funded in part by the Center for Population Research, National Institute for Child Health and Human Development, National Institutes of Health (HD 05876).

Charles F. Westoff, chairman and executive director of the National Committee for Research on the 1980 Census, and David L. Sills of the Social Science Research Council were very patient and supportive throughout the research and writing process. Priscilla Lewis and her staff at the Russell Sage Foundation have been very effective in turning the manuscript into a book. We greatly appreciate the extra efforts by William Butz and James R. Wetzel of the Bureau of the Census in providing us with an STF-4 county extract and a special PUMS file from the 1980 census in a time of severe budget constraint. Paul Zeisset, also of the Bureau of the Census, devoted considerable time to the design of our Special PUMS file.

An Advisory Panel, Larry Long, Peter Morrison, and John Wardwell, along with Charles Westoff, gave us detailed reactions and criticisms of the chapters. In addition, Conrad Taeuber and Jess Gilbert had a number of valuable suggestions for strengthening Chapter 10 as did Richard Forstall for Chapter 12.

Three persons deserve special mention as active collaborators in our project. Robert Jenkins, a graduate assistant at Wisconsin, had the major responsibility for establishing procedures and coordinating the preparation of the necessary extracts and tabulations used by all the authors. Jenkins was assisted by Max Pfeffer, also a graduate assistant, and together they are coauthors along with David Brown of Chapter 9 on industrial structure. (Jenkins and Pfeffer are now on the faculties of Yale and Rutgers Universities, respectively). Daniel Lichter, Pennsylvania State University, was coauthor of Chapter 3, on place and nonplace populations, continuing a research line followed for some time with Glenn Fuguitt.

Chapters 1, 2, 3, 10, and 12 were the initial responsibility of Glenn Fuguitt; Chapters 4, 6, 8, and 13 were first written by David Brown; and Chapters 5, 7, and 11 by Calvin Beale. We collaborated in preparing revisions, however, so that the end result is very much a joint effort.

As the first graduate assistant on the project, Robert Kominski laid the groundwork for much of our analysis with the PUMS file, especially relating to the farm population. Sunghee Nam, a graduate assistant near the end of the project, was particularly valuable in organizing and keeping up with the large number of data files that were generated.

The authors gratefully appreciate the assistance of Anne Cooper, the Data Librarian of the Center for Demography and Ecology and an able consultant on file and tape handling; her staff of assistants, which helped to keep track of a large volume of tapes; and the numerous CDE computer operators, who graciously mounted many tape volumes during the course of data analysis. John Jones and Cheryl Knobeloch also provided valuable programming assistance. Ruth Sandor, CDE Librarian, was very helpful in providing us with needed references and publications.

Much of the file extract and tabulation work was carried out by undergraduate assistants at Wisconsin, including Christine Czarnecki, Janet Dewey, Tom Godfrey, Jeanne Kimble, Brian Klockziem, Wendy Kramer, Kim Kreiwaldt, Rob Summers, Jay Van Cleave, Jennie Vanderlin, and Karen Weed. Also at Wisconsin, Kathy Torok and Diane Venden were very skilled and effective in word processing much of the manuscript through many revisions, and in the very detailed related work required in putting together a single manuscript from chapters written by several authors in different locations. At the U.S. Department of Agriculture, Gwen Coleman, Iris Blount, and Juanita Butler provided excellent word processing service. Margaret Butler prepared several of the maps and gave valued computer assistance.

Finally, Glenn Fuguitt and David Brown wish to express their deep appreciation to their wives, Martha Fuguitt and Nina Glasgow, for their patient support and active encouragement during this extended undertaking.

GLENN V. FUGUITT
University of Wisconsin–Madison

DAVID L. BROWN
Cornell University

CALVIN L. BEALE
U.S. Department of Agriculture

Contents

List of Tables

List of Figures

INTRODUCTION

Rural and Small Town America Today

THROUGHOUT history most of the world has been rural, with the major portion of the population residing in low density settings and dependent on agriculture or other extractive activities for a livelihood. This was also the case in the United States until early in the twentieth century, but it is now commonplace to refer to our nation as an urban and metropolitan society. It is in this context, and indeed because we are predominantly urban and metropolitan, that it is necessary to understand rural America today, and to try to discern some of the future directions for this part of our nation.

Rural and small town America has undergone fundamental economic and social change in recent years. Fewer and fewer residents depend on farming. Absolute numbers began declining drastically in the 1940s, so that today both the number and the proportion are at an extremely low level. Deconcentration around large cities has extended urban and metropolitan influences outward, penetrating deeply into what formerly were entirely rural areas. The continuing centralization of trade, economic, and social relationships has diminished the importance of many small towns, although not necessarily the size of their population. Overall the social and economic situation of people in rural and in urban America appears to become more similar, with the mass media particularly effecting a homogenization of society.

As the mirror image of urban and metropolitan growth, there has always been a net movement of rural people to cities and to areas around cities, and especially to major metropolitan areas. By 1970, however, something new had happened, with the long-term increase in the proportion of the population urban halted, and nonmetropolitan areas growing more rapidly than metropolitan areas. This was not just an extension of deconcentration around large cities, although that was an important element of the new trend. There was a marked deconcentration of industry into many remote areas, particularly in the 1960s, and a growth in recreation activity and retirement settlement. Since 1980, this new nonmetropolitan growth has abated, but it continues to be above the levels of the 1960s.

There has been considerable research and debate on the meaning of the new trends. Much concern has centered on whether these trends are simply an extension of recognizable urban and metropolitan development, or whether they should more aptly be regarded as some kind of discontinuous shift in demographic change and social organization. Writers in the latter vein have emphasized the greater freedom of choice people now have in choosing a place of residence, coupled with widespread preferences for low density living. This perspective has also included intriguing speculations that we are moving toward a service and information society in which traditional economic and social constraints on territorial location will be almost completely removed. More traditional explanations, on the other hand, have emphasized declines in economies of scale leading to shifts of economic activities away from larger cities and at a regional scale away from the industrial heartland. These changes may be attributed to technological advances in production, transportation, and communication, as well as to sectoral shifts away from heavy industry and greater integration with world markets. A more diffuse settlement, with more rapid nonmetropolitan and slowed metropolitan growth as these residence groupings become less distinct and more highly integrated, has been interpreted as the next or possibly equilibrium phase in the ongoing metropolitanization process.[1]

[1]A discussion of these and other perspectives is found in Bourne (1980). Frey (1986) reviews and compares the regional restructuring and deconcentration explanations. A provocative article announcing a "clean break" based on long-term trends in deconcentration patterns is Vining and Straus (1977). Zuiches (1980) discusses the significance of residential preferences. Speculations on the coming "Information Society" include Berry (1970) and Cleveland (1985). More traditional views relating to the decline of major cities and changes in economies of scale include works in Leven (1978) and Carlino (1985). In a similar vein, Vining (1982) considered the reversal since 1970 in migration between "core" and "peripheral" regions in a number of developed countries. Examples of stage, or equilibrium-convergence approaches include Morrill (1979), Wardwell (1977), and Long (1985). More recently Wardwell (1987) reconsiders equilibrium-convergence and residential preference approaches in view of the recent slowdown in nonmetropolitan growth.

Such varied perspectives should be expected in the effort to understand an unanticipated population change of this magnitude, and no doubt future explanations will incorporate elements of these and other approaches.

What is not equivocal, however, is that in recent years something new in rural America has affected its population composition and economic and social structure. This may not make us less of a metropolitan society than before, but it does indicate a change in rural–urban differences and in the structure of social and economic relations between metropolitan and nonmetropolitan America.

Underlying these significant changes are overall societal trends as reflected in rural demographic and economic behavior and, in turn, population composition. The recent trends in fertility decline, the increase in single person households and female headed households, the growing prominence of the elderly, the shift toward employment in the service industries, and the increased proportion of women working have not bypassed rural and small town America, and so need to be assessed.

In sum, recent changes have led to an increased interest in the low density parts of the nation. To better understand American society as well as the dynamics of contemporary settlement trends we need to examine the demographic and economic structures and changes in rural and small town America. This is the objective of the present work.

The Scope of This Volume

This volume draws on recent United States census data to furnish a composite picture of rural and small town America.[2] Its intended audience includes interested nonprofessionals, public officials, planners and others working in public and private agencies, and professional social scientists. The work lies within the fields of demography and rural sociology, but of necessity its scope is broad, and its general purpose is to provide an overview and indicate areas for more intensive analytical work. A basic assumption is that the place where people live is an important dimension of the structure of American society and that rural

---

[2]Unless otherwise indicated, the primary sources of data in figures and tables presented in this work are the 1980 and earlier decennial United States Censuses of Population. In our analysis we have used printed sources from these censuses along with summary tape (Fourth Count and STF) and Public Use Microdata Sample (PUMS) files for 1970 and 1980. A special 1980 PUMS file, including both the rural–urban and metropolitan–nonmetropolitan distinctions was kindly provided by the United States Bureau of the Census.

and small town America, as a diverse and dynamic component of this dimension, deserves our separate attention.

We have examined demographic, socioeconomic, and employment data from the United States Census of Population, looking for variations among communities and residence groupings. But we have not attempted to sort out causal directions in the possible interrelations among residential location and demographic and economic variables. Our fundamental objective rather is to provide a common basis of information and to suggest directions for such further work, by showing the population composition and distribution in rural and small town America and how it is changing today.

In examining trends in demographic and socioeconomic characteristics over the period since 1970 by location and residence groupings, a guiding proposition is the familiar one of rural–urban convergence. As noted above, the spread of urban influence into rural areas and the blurring of distinctions between rural and urban have long been noted. This does not necessarily require a uniform process of convergence as reflected in census data. Greater interdependence does not necessarily mean greater similarity. Selective processes of migration, for example, could widen differences in population characteristics among areas even as certain cultural distinctions identified with residence continue to fade. It is now generally recognized that any convergence of rural and urban is not necessarily through a diffusion from the nearest metropolitan center, but may be reflected differently for different variables in various times and places. Thus simplistic stereotypes and shallow generalizations about rural and small town America need to be replaced by knowledge based on the detailed analysis of type of community and residential distinctions using contemporary data.

Definitions of Rural and Small Town

As is true of most social science concepts, there is far from complete agreement on how to define what is "rural" or when a community is a "small town." The concept of rural as commonly employed may give varying weights to demographic (properties of small size and low density of settlement), economic (importance of extractive occupations), and sociocultural (ways of life, values and beliefs, smaller and less complex social institutions) dimensions. Controversies about interpreting rural America and its changes often rest ultimately on confusion or disagreement about such basic definitions.[3] For example, radical assertions

---

[3]Bealer, Willits, and Kuvlesky (1965); Lang (1986).

that "rural America no longer exists" or that the recent growth in non-metropolitan areas is simply evidence of further urbanization generally are based on sociocultural considerations with the assumption that rural and nonmetropolitan people now pursue "urban ways of life."

Similarly a small town is generally conceived of as a nodal settlement, that is, a cluster of residences and establishments, but just what is small depends strictly on the viewpoint of the observer, ranging from perhaps 500,000 people for some writers with a major metropolitan vantage point, down to villages with fewer than 2,500 people. Sometimes satellites of major centers are included as small towns and sometimes only more "independent" places are; growth may refer to economic activity or to population or to both.

Rural America is very diverse, and has always been interdependent with the urban component of our society. It is fair to say that there is increasing rural and urban interpenetration and a blurring of rural–urban distinctions, though this is hardly a novel insight, having been considered by rural sociologists since the beginning of the twentieth century. Yet it is this very process of change that makes it important to understand what is going on in rural and nonmetropolitan areas in comparison with other parts of our nation.

Our approach is to adopt a less ambiguous and more precise demographic definition of rural and of small town. Then, on the basis of comparing the social and economic characteristics of rural and small town people with those in other settings, we may draw some conclusions about the economic and the sociocultural dimensions of rural and urban. Such a path is most appropriate—if not virtually essential—for a census monograph, and it has a large number of precedents in the literature. The reader should be conscious, however, of the plurality of perspectives surrounding these seemingly simple concepts, concepts that are fundamental to our work.

There is still the question of appropriate demographic definitions. Obviously there are great advantages in adhering to the definitional system employed by the United States Bureau of the Census, and indeed it would be rather difficult to do anything else in any elaborate study resting on census data. There are still choices, however. First there are two basic definitions in current use that relate to our concerns, and these are sometimes confused: urban–rural and metropolitan-nonmetropolitan. The rural definition is the oldest. From 1910 to 1950 rural included all people outside incorporated places having more than 2,500 population, with those living in such places constituting the urban sector.[4]

---

[4]A few densely settled townships also were made urban by special rule at the time of each census. A more detailed discussion of the rural–urban and metropolitan–nonmetropolitan definitions is included in the analysis of population change in Chapter 2.

Since 1950 the definition has been modified to reflect our increasingly decentralized settlement. Now rural is restricted to the population outside incorporated or unincorporated places with more than 2,500 people and/or outside urbanized areas, the latter being defined today as a central city or cities which together with surrounding closely settled territory (density of more than 1,000 persons per square mile) has a minimum population of 50,000.

Concern about monitoring the increasing interpenetration of rural and urban settlement, especially around large cities, led to the establishment of Standard Metropolitan Areas in 1950. These units, county based outside New England where towns are the building blocks, include those counties having major cities along with any adjacent counties closely related to the center. After 1960 a major criterion for including adjacent counties was based on patterns of commuting revealed through census data. The name of these units was changed to Standard Metropolitan Statistical Areas by 1960 and to Metropolitan Statistical Areas after 1980. By 1980 the definition was modified so that MSAs no longer have to include a city or twin cities of a specified size, but simply an Urbanized Area, although if this area does not have a city of more than 50,000, the entire MSA has to have at least 100,000 people.

The underlying metropolitan area concept is of a large city with satellite cities and outlying suburbs. It does not define the entire trade area, or the extent of metropolitan influence, but it should include a zone where residents have daily social and economic contacts with the central city.[5] Of course, this is imprecise and may only be approximated by using counties as building blocks. The metropolitan–nonmetropolitan distinction is widely used in research today, with considerable attention given to the nonmetropolitan segment as a means of considering the lower density periphery of the nation.

Rural and nonmetropolitan, however, are far from synonymous. Nonmetropolitan areas include urban population, and there is considerable rural population inside MSAs. This is shown for 1980 in Table 1.1, which indicates that 13 percent of the urban population is nonmetropolitan, whereas 39 percent of the rural population is metropolitan. (The proportion of the rural population that is metropolitan has increased steadily since 1950 when the smaller number of counties classed as metropolitan only included 22 percent of the rural population. At that time the nonmetropolitan counties contained 36 percent of the urban population.)

Our major focus here will be on (1) the rural population, metropolitan or nonmetropolitan; and (2) the urban nonmetropolitan population. Together, they correspond to what most analysts mean when referring

[5]Shryock (1957).

TABLE 1.1

Population Rural and Urban
by Metropolitan Status, 1980

Residence	Metropolitan	Nonmetropolitan	Total
Urban	145,442,528	21,608,464	167,050,992
Percent	87.1	12.9	100.0
Rural	22,988,095	35,506,718	58,494,813
Percent	39.3	60.7	100.0
Total	168,430,623	57,115,182	225,545,805
Percent	74.7	25.3	100.0
Percent Population Urban	86.4	37.7	74.1

colloquially to "rural and small town America." We also make selected comparisons with the urban metropolitan segment where appropriate.

Making both a rural–urban and a metropolitan–nonmetropolitan distinction is very important because both rural and urban components of metropolitan areas may be expected to differ considerably from those in nonmetropolitan areas. Though the common meaning of the designation "small town" varies widely, we believe that nonmetropolitan urban places, which we have termed small towns, should be considered as part of the more peripheral settlement structure. Many small towns have traditionally served as trade and service centers for their rural hinterlands, and conversely they have represented important sources of employment opportunities for nearby rural people through commutation or migration. Whether the rural metropolitan component is "really rural" according to occupational or sociocultural criteria can be addressed in part through the comparisons made here. Traditional rural areas may be found near the edges of many smaller MSAs, but in general this is a component in transition and as such needs to be included here.

Because the occupational activity of farming is no longer closely identified with the conventional rural residential distinctions, we have not made the rural farm designation of the United States Bureau of the Census a major category for comparison across the chapters of this volume. Rather, farming is given a separate treatment in which three indicators from the population census are compared and interrelated for household units: rural farm residence (which includes all households situated on a unit defined as a farm), households with a member reporting a farm occupation; and households with a member reporting self-employment income from agriculture.

Approaches to the Analysis

Variations within the basic metropolitan–nonmetropolitan and rural–urban distinctions also need to be taken into account. On the nonmetropolitan side, an important dimension is location with respect to a metropolitan area. Indeed this was the major differentiation made in the 1960 Census Monograph on Rural America, which included several variables based on nearness and size of neighboring metropolitan areas. This was consistent with a view prevailing at that time of the settlement structure of the nation as partitioned into an exhaustive set of metropolitan communities; today it is more common to emphasize the interpenetration of metropolitan influence on a regional and even national basis. Work relating to the nonmetropolitan turnaround has shown recent migration and population growth to be notable in many rural areas remote from metropolitan centers. It also has emphasized subregional variations relating to the structure of local economies and the presence of environmental amenities, as well as the role of major metropolitan centers (which are not necessarily the nearest metropolitan centers) as the source of nonmetropolitan migrants.

Accordingly, we will sometimes distinguish nonmetropolitan counties that are adjacent to metropolitan areas from those that are not, but we will also consider subregional groupings of counties along with the four conventional census regions. The latter is particularly significant since recent trends in population redistribution have manifested distinctive regional imprints, a rather consistent downturn of growth throughout most of the Northeast and Midwest states, for example, sharpening the distinction between the North and the South and West.

Except for some of the analyses of change over time, the 1980 definition and county designations are used to distinguish metropolitan and nonmetropolitan, with county equivalents used for Metropolitan Statistical Areas in New England where possible.[6] Similarly the 1980 definition of urban and rural is used, except in 1970 and earlier comparisons. The definitions for 1970 and 1980 are very similar, the difference being that in 1970 an Urbanized Area (all of which is defined as urban) had to

[6]New England metropolitan county equivalents are not available in the PUMS files for 1970 and 1980, the metropolitan designation used there being the official one based on townships in that census division. In 1963, 1974, and 1983 the Office of Management and Budget reclassified counties adjacent to metropolitan areas on the basis of their commuting patterns and other information from the preceding census. The delineations of those dates may be considered a more accurate portrayal of the metropolitan–nonmetropolitan situation at the time of each census than the original designations found in the published census volumes. Although we could have used the updated delineations in aggregating county-level data, we did not do so because a considerable part of our analysis is based on the PUMS files.

have a city or twin cities totaling more than 50,000, and in 1980 it was only necessary for the total thickly settled area delineated to have 50,000 people. Although with county building blocks it is possible to give some attention to the shift of territory over time from nonmetropolitan to metropolitan, the same cannot be done for urban places, which may expand and grow in population through annexation.

Chapters to Come

We begin our study with a consideration of recent trends in metropolitan–nonmetropolitan and in rural–urban population distribution. Chapter 2 is a summary of distributional changes through the period known as the nonmetropolitan population turnaround, brought up to date to include recent post–1980 population estimates. Much of the new nonmetropolitan growth took place outside urban centers, and Chapter 3 reports on the rural–urban components of this change, differentiating urban areas by size and location.

The age and sex structure of rural areas has traditionally reflected patterns of selective migration and settlement so that there has often been an excess of elderly and an excess of men in the working years. Recent trends in age and sex composition are considered in Chapter 4, and reveal differences from the past associated with the more recent changes in population distribution in these areas, as well as with the general experience of the nation reflecting overall trends in fertility and mortality.

The race and ethnic composition of the population is examined in Chapter 5, including a consideration of distribution and changes in the location of blacks, Hispanics, Native Americans, and Asians. A large number of European ancestry groups contributed to the settlement of rural and nonmetropolitan America, along with blacks from Africa and some Asians. Throughout the period rural areas have included Native Americans. The question on ancestry, included for the first time in the 1980 census, makes it possible to identify major concentrations of ancestry groups in rural areas and to compare some characteristics of different ancestry and race groupings by residence.

In a 1950 census monograph, Otis Dudley Duncan and Albert J. Reiss concluded that a major distinction by type of community was the greater prevalence of indicators of familism in smaller and more rural communities.[7] More recently, on a national basis, there have been no-

---

[7]Duncan and Reiss (1956), p. 4.

table changes in family and household composition, with more people living alone or in single parent families, an increased incidence of divorce and alternative living arrangements, and a delay in age of first marriage. In Chapter 6 we have considered the extent to which these overall trends hold true for the rural and small town portions of the United States.

The recent drastic decline in United States fertility is, of course, closely associated with these family changes. Rural areas have traditionally had higher fertility levels than urban, and although this differential has been declining, and may be explained by differences in other population characteristics, high fertility is still found in many rural areas. In Chapter 7 we have monitored the recent decline in fertility, looking at subregional enthnocultural differences and rural–urban and metropolitan–nonmetropolitan location.

Although the recent growth in nonmetropolitan areas has been identified with the preferences of many for residing in low density areas, there has of necessity also been a considerable increase in employment in this part of the nation. This transition has included a marked increase in the proportion of women working even in remote settings. We have considered employment status and change in employment status, as well as the distribution of the employed population by occupation and class of worker, in Chapter 8.

Much of the recent transition in rural and nonmetropolitan America is intertwined with changes in industry. Increased manufacturing employment, especially in the 1960s, helped trigger the turnaround in population numbers and the economies of nonmetropolitan and rural areas. Similarly, and more in common with metropolitan urban areas, there has been a considerable increase in service employment, both public and private. The drop of agricultural employment to a very low level in most areas has meant that population losses associated with this transition have been reduced considerably, and inevitably that the economies of rural America no longer are as closely tied to changes in agriculture as once was the case. In Chapter 9 we consider the overall industrial composition of the population by residence, and how this has changed since 1960. Demographic and economic characteristics are compared for the employed population classed by broad industry groupings, residence, and race. In Chapter 10 we give particular attention to the population associated with farming through residence, employment, and/or source of income. The decreasing correspondence of these three indicators is examined, along with the social and economic characteristics of households differentiated by possible ties to farming.

Although there is evidence of convergence between metropolitan and nonmetropolitan areas for a number of characteristics, serious differences remain, particularly in the area of income and poverty. Income distributions, sources of income, and median income differentials are considered in Chapter 11, along with the association of income with family composition variables. Also included are measures of poverty and the characteristics of persons associated with poverty for the population distinguished by residence and race.

Chapter 12 is a detailed comparison of the population and economic characteristics of metropolitan and nonmetropolitan cities and villages that have been classified by size. Included also in the comparison is the population outside urban areas. The hierarchy of urban places, from major cities down to villages, continues to be an important component in the organization of settlement structure, despite the increased prevalence of community separation of home and work, and the greater deconcentration of residences.

A summary is provided in the final chapter, and major conclusions are drawn regarding convergence, subregional variability, and the prospects for the future of rural and nonmetropolitan areas. We also have included our views of some of the implications of these findings for policy issues at the national and local levels.

2

POPULATION DISTRIBUTION

RURAL AND SMALL town America is an integral part of the highly urban and metropolitan society that is the United States today. To a large degree its place in this society is a consequence of the twin dynamic processes of urbanization and metropolitanization, along with interregional shifts in population and economic activities. We begin the present chapter with a consideration of long-term trends in rural and nonmetropolitan population change. We then take a closer look at the past twenty-five years, the period that included the "turnaround," when nonmetropolitan areas were growing more rapidly than metropolitan areas, and the post-turnaround period since 1980. Finally, since migration has been the major component accounting for recent trends in population redistribution, the analysis is elaborated and extended by comparing 1965–1970 and 1975–1980 metropolitan–nonmetropolitan interregional migration data from the two most recent censuses. The growth and decline of small towns, and place-nonplace population growth differentials are treated in Chapter 3.

Rural and Urban Population Trends Since 1790

Urbanization is usually defined for demographic research purposes as the process that generates a rising proportion of the population living

FIGURE 2.1

Percentage of Population Rural, 1790–1980

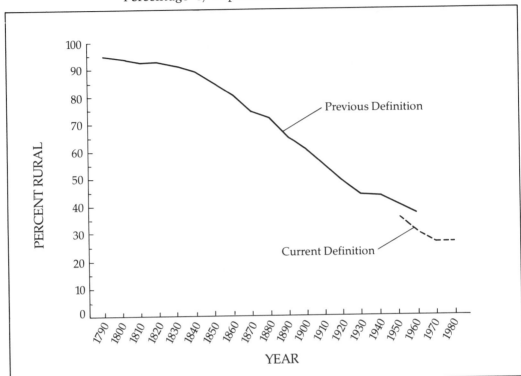

in communities that are cities. It arises both through increase in the size of existing places and through additions of new places to the city roster.[1] The United States increased from 5 to 74 percent urban between 1790 and 1980, and the number of incorporated places with 2,500 or more people blossomed from 24 to almost 8,000. Since a primary interest here is in rural America, we have shown the complementary trend, that is, the proportion rural, in Figure 2.1. The relative decline in the rural proportion was very slow at first, and the United States was still 90 percent rural in 1840, more than fifty years after its founding. The percent rural then dropped about 3 to 7 percentage points in each decade until 1930. The figure shows that for two-thirds of our nation's history—until 1920—the majority of the people lived in rural areas.

In the depression decade of 1930–1940, the proportion rural was almost unchanged at 44 percent, and it was 40 percent in 1950. By that

[1]The classic statement is Tisdale (1942).

14

time, however, it was recognized that the urban definition used since 1910 (and retrojected in Figure 2.1 back to 1790), which with few exceptions included only incorporated places with more than 2,500 people, was becoming less and less meaningful. With a more diffuse settlement pattern, there was an increase in unincorporated places greater than 2,500, and thickly settled areas adjacent to the political boundaries of urban places were physically undistinguishable from the outlying sections of these cities. Accordingly a new urban definition was established in 1950, which included all unincorporated places over 2,500 in addition to incorporated places of this size, as well as all thickly settled areas (1,000 or more persons per square mile), incorporated or unincorporated, delineated around cities with more than 50,000 people. Such cities were termed Central Cities, and they together with their thickly settled peripheries were called Urbanized Areas. By 1960 the Urbanized Area concept was modified to include twin cities, and was changed more substantially for the census of 1980 to include all thickly settled areas with more than 50,000 people whether or not the core city or cities had 50,000 or more. Despite these modifications, however, and following Census Bureau practice, the urban definition used since 1950 will be referred to here as the "current definition" and the earlier one will be termed the "previous definition."[2]

The percent rural according to the current definition is indicated by the dotted line between 1950 and 1980 in Figure 2.1. This line is below the corresponding previous definition line since the effect of the change is to shift population out of rural into urban. An increasing divergence between the two lines is indicated. With the current definition, however, the percent rural is the same within one-tenth of a percent in 1970 and 1980, and indeed the percentage rural would have increased had not the requirement been dropped that central cities of urbanized areas total at least 50,000.[3] In sum, after a 90-year period (1840–1930) of generally rapid urbanization and corresponding decline in the proportion rural, there was a pause during the Great Depression and a resurgence of relative rural decline in the post–World War II period characterized by dif-

---

[2]For each census since 1910 when the previous urban definition was first employed the Bureau of the Census also declared certain minor civil divisions, primarily in New England and the Middle Atlantic states, urban by special rule. Procedures varied somewhat from census to census, and 1940 procedures were followed in preparing "previous urban" designations that appeared in the censuses of 1950 and 1960. Comparable figures are unavailable for 1970 and 1980. Of the 167 million urban in 1980, 23 million were in unincorporated places with more than 2,500 people, and another 13 million were in thickly settled areas around larger cities, so that only 78 percent of the urban population resided in incorporated places having more than 2,500 people.

[3]DeAre and Long (1982).

fuse urban growth outside larger incorporated places. This was followed by another pause in the most recent 1970–1980 decade.

Despite its declining relative importance, the rural population grew from less than four million in 1790 to 50 million in 1910 and to almost 60 million (current definition) by 1980 (Table 2.1). The general trend is a decreasing rate of rural growth, as revealed by the percentage change figures; this was also true of the total and the urban population. The rural population showed an absolute increase over every decade except

TABLE 2.1

Rural and Urban Population, 1790–1980

Year	Population (millions)			Precent Change from Preceding Census		
	Rural	Urban	Total	Rural	Urban	Total
Current Urban Definition						
1980	59.4	167.0	226.5	11.1	11.6	11.4
1970	53.6	149.6	203.3	−0.9	19.5	13.4
1960	54.0	125.3	179.3	−0.8	29.3	18.5
1950	54.5	96.8	151.3	—	—	—
Previous Urban Definition						
1960	66.3	113.0	179.3	8.3	25.4	18.5
1950	61.2	90.1	151.3	6.5	20.6	14.5
1940	57.5	74.7	131.7	6.3	8.0	7.3
1930	54.0	69.2	122.8	4.4	27.5	16.2
1920	51.8	54.2	105.7	3.2	29.0	15.0
1910	50.1	42.0	91.9	9.1	39.2	21.0
1900	46.0	30.2	76.0	12.5	36.7	21.0
1890	40.9	22.1	62.9	13.4	56.5	25.5
1880	36.1	14.1	60.2	25.8	42.7	30.2
1870	28.7	9.9	39.8	13.6	59.3	22.6
1860	25.2	6.2	31.4	28.4	75.4	35.6
1850	19.6	3.5	23.2	29.1	92.1	35.9
1840	15.2	1.8	17.1	29.7	63.7	32.7
1830	11.7	1.1	12.9	31.2	62.6	33.4
1820	8.9	0.7	9.6	33.2	31.9	33.1
1810	6.7	0.5	7.2	34.7	63.0	36.4
1800	5.0	0.3	5.3	33.8	59.9	35.1
1790	3.7	0.2	3.9	—	—	—

SOURCE: U.S. Bureau of the Census (1983a), pp. 1–35.

for the 1950s and 1960s (current definition), when there was a slight decline. The urban population grew more rapidly than the rural, however, in every decade except 1810–1820, and this differential is quite large in some instances.

Regional Trends in the Rural Population

The regional pattern of the proportion rural is one of increasing divergence from 1820 to 1910, particularly between the Northeast and the South, with convergence thereafter. From independence through 1960 the Northeast had the highest levels of urban concentration of any region, and conversely the lowest proportion of population classed as rural (Figure 2.2). Among the other regions, the South emerged as a laggard in urban development after 1820, with the Midwest and West being inter-

FIGURE 2.2

Percentage of Population Rural for Regions, 1790–1980

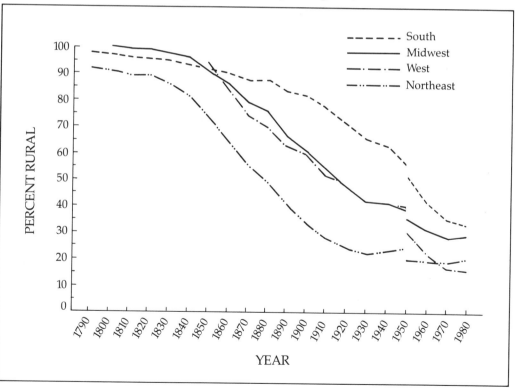

mediate. Although the United States as a whole had become more than 50 percent urban by 1920, this was not yet true for the South thirty years later, in 1950. The difference between the Northeast and the South in the proportion rural peaked in 1910 at 50 percentage points (78 percent for the South versus 28 percent for the Northeast). Proportions for the four regions converged thereafter, reflecting a spread of urbanization throughout the nation particularly following World War I. The South continues to be behind the others. but the West overtook the Northeast in 1970 and now has the lowest rural proportion.

Despite this considerable change in the proportion rural with the spread of urbanization throughout the country, the distribution of the rural population across the four regions has changed relatively little during this century (Figure 2.3). Along with the total population there has

FIGURE 2.3

Distribution of Rural Population by Region, 1900–1980

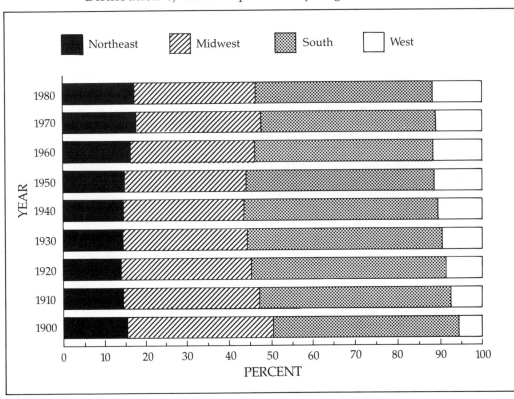

been an increase in the proportion of the rural population residing in the West. This is at the expense of the South and the Midwest, with the Northeast having a higher proportion of the rural population in 1970 and 1980 than in 1960. (The old urban definition is employed for 1900–1940 and the new for 1950–1980 in Figures 2.3 and 2.4). The distribution of the urban population, however, is quite different and indicates that the overall national relative shift of population out of the North was predominantly urban (Figure 2.4). In 1900, almost 50 percent of the urban population was in the Northeast and almost 80 percent was in this region plus the Midwest. By 1980, however, only about 50 percent of the urban population was in the two regions of the North, with a considerable increase in the proportions found in both the South and the West since 1900.

FIGURE 2.4

Distribution of Urban Population by Region, 1900–1980

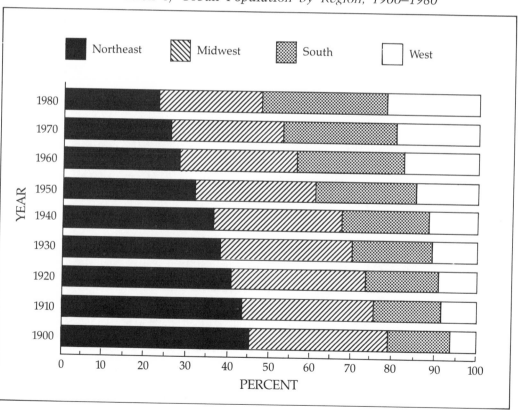

Metropolitan and Nonmetropolitan Trends Since 1900

Trends for the nonmetropolitan population have closely followed those of the rural population. As discussed in Chapter 1, the metropolitan area concept was initiated with the census of 1950 to reflect the increasing interpenetration of rural and urban areas around large cities. Based on county units (outside New England), it is more inclusive than the previous metropolitan district concept of 1910–1940, which was delineated primarily by using smaller minor civil divisions. In this way the entire population in and around large cities, viewed as an integrated social and economic system, is separated from the nonmetropolitan remainder.[4] A distinction based on whole counties must be somewhat arbitrary, however, and in any event does not imply that there are no important interrelations between nonmetropolitan and metropolitan areas. A Metropolitan Statistical Area (MSA) is a county (or counties) that includes a densely settled larger urban core (Urbanized Area). Peripheral counties may be declared a part of the MSA if they meet certain criteria of metropolitan character and interaction with the core. As both the urban and the metropolitan concepts tap related aspects of a major population redistribution process, it is not surprising that long-term trends should be similar, as seen by applying the 1950 metropolitan definition back to 1900. Indeed, the percentage rural and the percentage nonmetropolitan have been very close to each other since 1900, dropping from 60–67 percent in 1900 to about 25 percent in 1980 (Figure 2.5). This is true despite the fact that both rural and urban areas are found in metropolitan and nonmetropolitan sectors of the country.[5]

The metropolitan and nonmetropolitan population totals for 1900 through 1980 are given in Table 2.2. Again, as was true of the rural

---

[4]Shryock (1957).

[5]The metropolitan–nonmetropolitan distinction for 1900–1940 is based on work by Warren Robinson (1968). For 1900 through 1950 all metropolitan areas include a city having more than 50,000 population at the time. For 1960, 1970, and 1980 (previous), twin cities totaling 50,000 population may define a metropolitan area. No additional metropolitan areas would have been defined in this way had the twin-city rule been applied for 1900 through 1950 except for Champaign–Urbana, Illinois; Brownsville–Harlingen–San Benito, Texas; Lewiston–Auburn, Maine; New London–Norwich–Groton, Connecticut; and Muskegon–Muskegon Heights, Michigan, all of which would have been included for 1950. Including these twin-city metropolitan areas in 1950, however, makes a difference of 1 percent or less in the 1940–1950 and the 1950–1960 percent change figures shown in Table 2.2, so the series from 1900 through 1980 (previous) is equivalent to a series using a constant 1958–1971 metropolitan definition. The top line 1980 (current) is based on the current metropolitan definition, which requires that an area include an Urbanized Area without the 50,000 place-size criterion unless the entire area has less than 100,000 people. This series utilizes county-equivalent areas for the New England states although the official delineations there follow township boundaries.

FIGURE 2.5

Percentage of Population Nonmetropolitan and Percentage Rural, 1900–1980

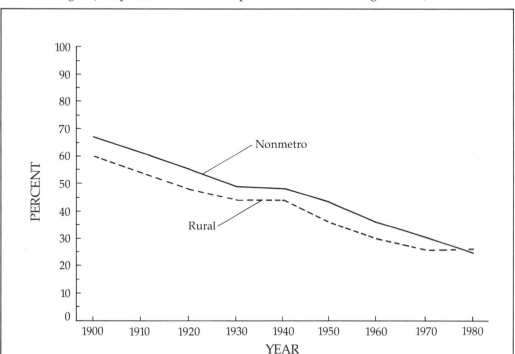

population, the nonmetropolitan numbers are relatively stable, ranging from 51 to 65 million. The metropolitan population, on the other hand, increased sevenfold from 25 to 170 million in the 80-year period. The first two lines of the table are both for 1980, the top one representing the current metropolitan definition, which requires that an MSA include an urbanized area having at least 50,000 people or, if there is no central city of 50,000, that the MSA as a whole have more than 100,000 people. The second line shows what the metropolitan population would be if only those MSAs were included that had an incorporated central city or twin cities with at least 50,000 population. (It was not possible to adjust for changes in the rules for including peripheral counties.) This was the basic metropolitan definition between 1958 and 1971. The difference between the two lines shows that the change to the recent, more liberal definition has resulted in 6.4 million people being transferred from nonmetropolitan to metropolitan status.

TABLE 2.2

Nonmetropolitan and Metropolitan Population, 1900–1980[a]

Census Year	United States	Nonmetro	Population in Millions				Percent Metro Increment Due to Counties Added
				Metropolitan			
			Total	Counties Added[b]	Total Increment[b]		
Current Metropolitan Definition							
1980	226.5	56.1	170.4	17.3	29.6		58
Previous Metropolitan Definition							
1980	226.5	62.5	164.0	10.8	23.2		47
1970	203.3	62.5	140.8	8.1	26.7		30
1960	179.3	65.1	114.1	7.2	28.7		25
1950	151.3	65.9	85.4	3.0	17.1		18
1940	132.2	63.9	68.3	0.8	5.3		15
1930	123.2	60.2	63.0	2.4	15.6		15
1920	106.0	58.6	47.4	2.9	11.7		9
1910	92.0	56.5	35.7	2.7	10.5		26
1900	76.2	51.0	25.2	—	—		—

[a]For explanation of data series and definitions, see text.
[b]Counties added refers to those counties made metropolitan during the previous decade; total increment is change in the entire population classed as metropolitan during the previous decade.

Metropolitanization involves both the growth of population within existing territory designated as metropolitan and the addition of population through transfer of territory from nonmetropolitan to metropolitan status.[6] The latter growth component can be further subdivided to distinguish those counties added to existing metropolitan areas because of their expansion and those representing newly established MSAs. The addition of new territory in both ways is an increasingly important part of the metropolitanization process with the complementary decline in nonmetropolitan population and area. The new counties added to metropolitan status between 1970 and 1980 using the definition current at each time (that is, previous in 1970 and current in 1980) had almost 30 million people, and this number is more than one-half of the population added to the metropolitan total over the period. Even if the definition of metropolitan had not been changed for 1980, one-half of the 1970–1980

[6]For these data the transfer is always from nonmetropolitan to metropolitan status. In 1983, however, the Office of Management and Budget reclassified a number of peripheral metropolitan counties as nonmetropolitan following a change in the rules for including peripheral counties within a metropolitan area.

growth of metropolitan population would have been due to the addition of new areas, whereas this figure was never over 30 percent for other decades since 1900 (right-hand column of Table 2.2).

How important to metropolitanization are new metropolitan areas in contrast to counties added to metropolitan areas already in existence? There has been a considerable increase in the number of metropolitan areas throughout this century. Under the 1950 rules for metropolitan status there would have been 70 MSAs in 1900. There were 168 designated when the concept was first introduced in the 1950 census, with an increase to 318 by 1980. Of the 7.2 million persons in new metropolitan counties as of 1960 two-thirds were in newly designated MSAs that had appeared since 1950, and the remainder in counties added to existing MSAs. This proportion dropped to one-half in 1970 but returned to a little over two-thirds in 1980. The move back in the proportion for 1980 was due to the more liberal rules for admitting new metropolitan areas. Under the old rules about one-half of the new metropolitan counties were in new MSAs in 1980 with the remainder added to the peripheries of older MSAs, which was the same proportion as in 1970.

Regardless of the definition employed, at least one-half of the population in counties that had shifted from nonmetropolitan to metropolitan status over each decade since 1950 lived in counties having small towns that became new metropolitan areas in their own right. This spreading of metropolitanization has had a major impact on nonmetropolitan America, not only in the loss of its more rapidly growing urban components but also in making the remainder more accessible to urban agglomerations of a size qualifying as the cores of MSAs. At the same time, 4 million people in 1960–1970 and over 5 million people in 1970–1980 were shifted from nonmetropolitan to metropolitan by being in a peripheral county that had become increasingly integrated with a nearby metropolitan area so as to achieve metropolitan status. This expansion of metropolitan areas has also had a profound effect on nonmetropolitan America. Social and economic interpenetration continues and is not limited to those adjacent counties changing status in a given period.

The rates of nonmetropolitan and metropolitan population change have varied over time, in part following total United States change. As is true of the total population, the lowest metropolitan percentage change figures were for the 1930–1940 and the 1970–1980 decades (Table 2.3). Nonmetropolitan rates are generally lower than metropolitan, and there is considerable difference depending upon whether the counties that shifted from nonmetropolitan to metropolitan status over the decade are included in the end-of-period totals used in calculating the percentage change. When the county shifts are included, metropolitan growth is more in each decade from 1900 to the present and nonmetro-

TABLE 2.3

Metropolitanization in the United States, 1900–1980[a]

| | | Percent Change from Preceding Census | | | | | |
| | | Current Designation[b] | | Beginning Decade Designation[c] | | Percent Metropolitan | |
Year	United States	Metro	Nonmetro	Metro	Nonmetro	Total	Previous Designation[d]
Current Metropolitan Definition							
1980	11.4	21.2	− 10.4	8.8	17.3	75.3	67.6
Previous Metropolitan Definition							
1980	11.4	16.5	− 0.1	8.8	17.3	72.4	67.6
1970	13.4	23.3	− 4.0	16.2	8.4	69.2	65.3
1960	18.5	33.7	− 1.2	25.2	9.8	63.7	59.6
1950	14.5	25.1	3.1	20.7	7.8	56.4	54.4
1940	7.3	8.4	6.1	7.2	7.4	51.7	51.0
1930	16.2	32.9	2.7	27.9	6.8	51.1	49.1
1920	15.0	32.8	3.7	24.8	8.8	44.7	42.0
1910	21.0	41.6	10.9	31.0	16.1	38.7	35.8
1900	—	—	—	—	—	33.1	—

[a]For explanation of data series and definitions, see text.
[b]Metropolitan–nonmetropolitan county designation at the time of each census.
[c]Metropolitan–nonmetropolitan county designation as of the beginning of each decade for which percent change is calculated.
[d]Metropolitan–nonmetropolitan county designation as of the census previous to the one indicated. This figure shows what the percent metropolitan would have been had no new counties become metropolitan over the preceding ten years.

politan growth is less, with absolute declines in number for each decade after 1950. Using a constant area approach with metropolitan–nonmetropolitan county designation at the beginning of each decade, the largest nonmetropolitan growth in this century is for 1970–1980, and this rate is almost twice as high as the corresponding metropolitan rate. This differential, a primary indicator of the "nonmetropolitan turnaround," is quite a contrast with all previous decades, when metropolitan rates were about twice as large as nonmetropolitan rates except for the 1930–1940 Depression period, when the two rates using the 1930 constant areas are about equal. Yet when the county shifts from nonmetropolitan to metropolitan status are taken into account along with the change from the previous (1970) to the more liberal (1980) metropolitan definition, the nonmetropolitan population actually experienced its most severe decline during the turnaround decade of more than 10 percent![7]

[7]See Beale (1984) for a discussion of recent changes in the metropolitan definition and their implications.

This seeming paradox does not refute the event of the turnaround but underscores the fact that the 1970–1980 resurgence of growth in most nonmetropolitan areas and the slowdown in major metropolitan areas have not moved us away from being a society organized around large-scale population concentrations. We will consider the turnaround and its aftermath in more detail in the next section.

The consequences of this differential growth in terms of the percentage of the total population classed as metropolitan are given in the two right-hand columns of Table 2.3. The difference in the percent metropolitan from one decade to the next may be taken as a measure of metropolitanization. Except for the 1930s the increase has been from about 5 to 7 percentage points over each decade. For the decade 1970–1980 the increase is only 3 percentage points, however (69.2–72.4), if the 1970 metropolitan definition is used for 1980. The shift to the current, more liberal definition of a metropolitan area added another 3 percentage points (72.4–75.3). The last column gives the percent metropolitan if the counties added over the past decade are not included. This means that the differences in the percentages across diagonals of these two columns (going from left to right) give the degree of metropolitanization without the new areas. For example, the percent metropolitan increased from 63.7 to 69.2, or 5.5 percentage points, between 1960 and 1970, but the diagonal difference is from 63.7 to 65.3, or 1.6 points. Growth within the initial area is from about one-half to two-thirds of the total metropolitanization prior to the Depression and a decreasing component thereafter until 1970–1980, when it is negative, indicating demetropolitanization of established areas (69.2–67.6). The 1970–1980 finding, of course, is a consequence of the initial area growth differentials, which favored nonmetropolitan areas. All in all the increasing significance of metropolitan spread through the transfer of nonmetropolitan territory is clearly indicated.

Regional Trends in the Nonmetropolitan Population

Regional patterns in the percentage of the population nonmetropolitan parallel those for the percent rural since 1900, with a general decline and convergence (Figure 2.6). The West dropped below the Midwest by 1930 and moved to a position only slightly above that of the Northeast by 1970. The South continued in 1980 to have the highest proportion nonmetropolitan, but dropped farther in this proportion than any other region during this century.

The nonmetropolitan population remained relatively stable in each of the regions, so that the distribution by region varied little from 1900

FIGURE 2.6

Percentage of Population Nonmetropolitan for Regions, 1900–1980

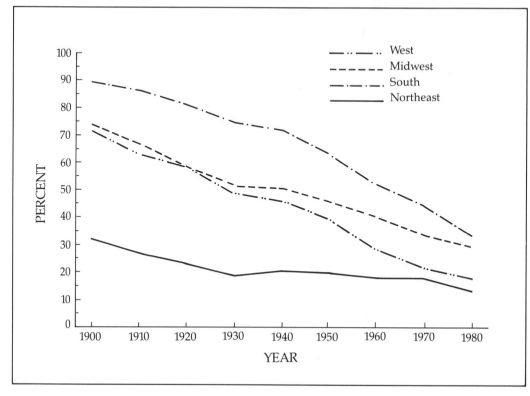

to 1980. Most notable was the West, which increased its proportion of the total nonmetropolitan from about 6 to 13 percent. The South also increased and the Midwest decreased slightly in its share of nonmetropolitan people (Figure 2.7). In contrast, there was an extreme decline in the metropolitan population proportion in the Northeast, which included more than one-half of the metropolitan population in 1900 but only about one-fourth in 1980 (Figure 2.8). This, of course, demonstrates the spread of metropolitan growth across the nation both in existing areas and through the addition of areas newly designated as metropolitan. Results here closely parallel those in Figures 2.3 and 2.4 for the rural and urban population, again showing that although the concepts are different they reflect parallel aspects of the population concentration process taking place in the United States.

FIGURE 2.7

Distribution of Nonmetropolitan Population by Region, 1900–1980

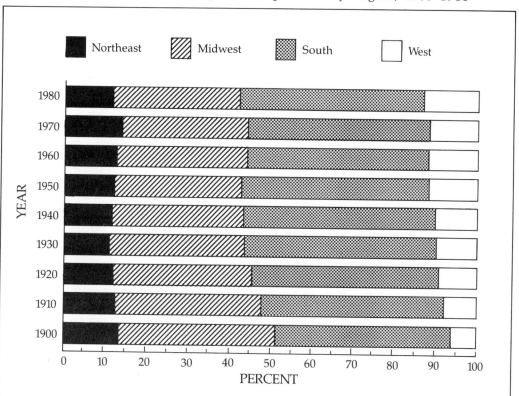

The Nonmetropolitan Turnaround and Beyond

One of the most noted but unforeseen demographic trends in the United States during the 1970s was the revival of population growth in the rural and small town parts of the country. As shown in the preceding section, throughout the twentieth century and most of the nineteenth century as well, urban and/or metropolitan areas had higher growth rates. Especially after the farm population reached its peak during World War I it had been the common experience of a majority of rural counties to have net outmovement of people. In hundreds of counties in any decade from 1920 to 1970 this outmovement exceeded the excess of births over deaths, resulting in population decline. It is not an exaggeration to suggest that the experience of rural demographic decline

FIGURE 2.8

Distribution of Metropolitan Population by Region, 1900–1980

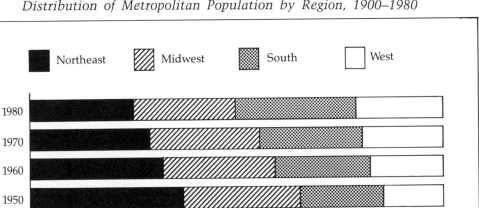

or comparative stagnation was so prevalent and prolonged that it became axiomatic to expect a continuance of this condition, and it was thought to be consistent with theories of urban and regional economics and related views in the social sciences of the urban transformation of modern society. Acceptance of the established trend was so uncritical that there was little foreshadowing in the demographic literature of the late 1960s of the major change that was starting. From the very beginning of the 1970s nonmetropolitan counties began to increase in population collectively at a rate twice that of the metropolitan counties. By contrast, over the 1960–1970 period the nonmetropolitan rate of increase had been one-half as high as that in metropolitan areas, 8.4 percent versus 16.2 percent. Furthermore, this growth was widespread, including many remote rural counties as well as territory at the edge of metropolitan areas in all regions of the country. It also had its parallel in many other industrial nations.[8] Several factors seem to have combined to bring about this dramatic change:

1. During the 1970s there was a major slackening of the exodus from agriculture. Farm employment had dropped by 2 million in the 1960s, but stabilized in the 1970s, falling by only 100,000 for the entire United States.

2. There was major growth of other employment in nonmetropolitan America during the 1970s. Decentralization of manufacturing continued a trend begun in the 1960s. Jobs in professional services rapidly expanded, especially in health and education, and mining revived briefly, spurred largely by the energy crisis of the time.

3. The growing function of many rural areas as recreation and/or retirement communities was notable. This trend was evident in the 1960s but accelerated in the 1970s.

4. Greater residential sprawl around metropolitan areas took many people into communities that were rural in character and nonmetropolitan in official status but that were accessible to metropolitan jobs and services for those tolerant of long-distance commuting. About 20 percent of those moving from metropolitan to nonmetropolitan areas between 1975 and 1980 reported working in metropolitan areas, compared with 6 percent of those living in nonmetropolitan areas at both times.

5. There was both survey and anecdotal evidence indicating that noneconomic quality-of-life reasons were important for many thousands of people who decided either to remain in or move to rural and small town areas. Even though the average family income in nonmetropolitan areas has been about 20 percent less than that in metropolitan areas, there was strong sentiment for the "simpler" life, expressed either in terms of negative perceptions of life in the large cities and their suburbs or in terms of positive conceptions of the merits of living in smaller communities.

6. An important facilitating factor related to all of the above must surely be the modernization of rural communities over the past several decades. Rural electrification and telephone service, technology making indoor plumbing and running water possible, and the spread of all-weather roads greatly decreased the differences between rural and urban areas in housing and other aspects of local life-styles.

In the latter part of the 1970s nonmetropolitan growth began to slow down and post-1980 population estimates revealed that metropol-

---

[8]See, for example, Vining and Kontuly (1978), Wardwell (1980), and Fielding (1982).

itan areas were once again growing faster than nonmetropolitan areas. Although a definitive explanation for the post-1980 decline in nonmetropolitan growth is not yet available, a number of recent economic events no doubt has contributed to this change in the trend. Some of these are of general impact, but for the most part they are related to specific areas of the country and groups of counties. As the decade of the 1970s ended, the United States went into the worst economic slump since the 1930s. For reasons that are partly but not fully clear, the nonmetropolitan economy was more seriously affected in the early 1980s than the metropolitan economy. Employment in timber industries dropped as housing construction declined. Many rural manufacturing plants were linked to the dwindling automotive and steel industries. In addition, the recently revived mining industry underwent severe depression in mining of metal ores and a lesser contraction in coal mining. In the textile, clothing, and leather industries with a large nonmetropolitan base there has been increasing competition and job loss from lower priced imports.

The result was a greater rise in unemployment in rural and small town areas than in cities and suburbs. The nonmetropolitan areas were also more heavily hurt by shortened work weeks (involuntary part-time work) and showed a higher percentage of workers who dropped out of the official labor force because of discouragement and belief that there was no point in looking for jobs. The farm economy suffered badly from the beginning of the 1980s. Overproduction and weak markets drove the annual net income of farm operators from farm sources in 1980–1984 down to less than one-half the average level of the 1970s, adjusting for changes in the value of the dollar.[9] This made it impossible for some commercial farmers to continue and seriously depressed general business conditions in agriculturally dependent areas.

In the 1980–1984 period there were many more declining counties in the central and southern Corn Belt of the Midwest than there had been in the 1970s. This change reflects the agricultural crisis and the low purchasing power of farmers in those years, as well as stagnation in the older metal goods and automotive industrial economy that coexists with farming in many parts of this area. Numerous new or renewed areas of nonmetropolitan population decline include the industry-based Ohio valley, coastal plain districts in the lower South, some of the timber industry areas of the Pacific Northwest, and certain mining counties of the West.

On the other hand, a good many of the small agricultural countries of the western part of the Great Plains that lost people in the 1970s are

[9]Economic Research Service (1984).

estimated to have had some increase in the early 1980s. The source of this growth is not clear, but with few exceptions the newly growing counties are west of the Corn Belt in a region dominated by wheat and cattle agriculture that experienced less farm income loss than did the Corn Belt counties and where oil and gas drilling bolstered the economy.

Recent Nonmetropolitan–Metropolitan Trends

A comparison of recent trends, extending beyond the turnaround, is possible by aggregating county population estimates for 1984 provided by the Bureau of the Census.[10] Annualized population change rates were calculated for 1980–1984 and compared with those for 1960–1970 and 1970–1980.[11] The return to more rapid metropolitan growth is seen for 1980–1984, when the annualized rate per 100 for metropolitan areas was 1.02, above the nonmetropolitan value of .84 (Table 2.4). Comparing the three time periods in the top panel shows that after declining by almost one-half between 1960–1970 and 1970–1980, the metropolitan figure in-

TABLE 2.4

Metropolitan and Nonmetropolitan Annualized Population Change per 100, 1960–1984

Residence	Period		
	1960–1970	1970–1980	1980–1984
Total	1.25	1.08	.98
Initial Designation[a]			
Metropolitan	1.50	.85	1.02
Nonmetropolitan	.81	1.59	.84
1980 Designation[b]			
Metropolitan	1.57	.98	1.02
Nonmetropolitan	.30	1.40	.84

[a]Metropolitan–nonmetropolitan designation of counties at the beginning of each period for comparison of annualized change over that period.
[b]Metropolitan–nonmetropolitan designation of 1980 used throughout.

[10]U.S. Bureau of the Census (1985b).
[11]Shryock and Siegel (1971), pp. 377-380.

creased by one-fifth between 1970–1980 and 1980–1984. In contrast, the nonmetropolitan rate almost doubled between the first two periods, and then dropped back almost to its previous 1960–1970 level. Note, however, that the nonmetropolitan rate was less than two-thirds of the total United States rate in the 1960s but was 85 percent of the total growth level in the 1980s.

These annualized rates do not include the gains or losses of counties to metropolitan and nonmetropolitan areas; rather, successive rates are based on the metropolitan designation current at the beginning of each period. Because of the metropolitanization process, as discussed in the preceding section, this initial area approach should be more appropriate in reflecting the metropolitan–nonmetropolitan situation at each time than one using a constant metropolitan designation across all three time intervals.[12] Nevertheless, it is useful to compare these results with those obtained with the constant 1980 classification of counties as metropolitan, as shown in the bottom panel of Table 2.4. The 1980–1984 growth of counties that were nonmetropolitan in 1980, although only about six-tenths as rapid as in the previous decade, was nevertheless more than twice that of the 1960–1970 period. So overall the growth transition for the current nonmetropolitan area is of considerable magnitude, despite the more recent downturn. This bottom panel shows also that the turnaround of the 1970–1980 period was not just concealed metropolitanization. That is, 1970–1980 nonmetropolitan growth was still considerably above metropolitan growth, although the former group does not include counties that had become metropolitan by 1980.

Population Change and the Metropolitan Hierarchy

The nonmetropolitan turnaround and its aftermath have been part of a more general deconcentration process down the metropolitan size hierarchy and across regions of the country. Figure 2.9 shows the changing growth, differentials by size of metropolitan area designated at the beginning of each period. In the 1960s the most rapidly growing group

---

[12]For example, of counties classed as nonmetropolitan in 1960, the subsets that were also nonmetropolitan in 1980 must include the ones that were the most remote in 1960 and the slowest growing subsequently, since these are the ones that have remained nonmetropolitan for at least twenty years through 1980. Yet many of these same counties may be expected to become metropolitan over the next twenty years. So a metropolitan–nonmetropolitan comparison using these counties will have a different meaning for the 1960s than for the 1980s. Such a comparison may be useful, however, if basically one is interested in the most recent nonmetropolitan designation.

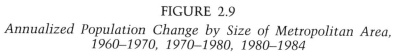

FIGURE 2.9

Annualized Population Change by Size of Metropolitan Area,
1960–1970, 1970–1980, 1980–1984

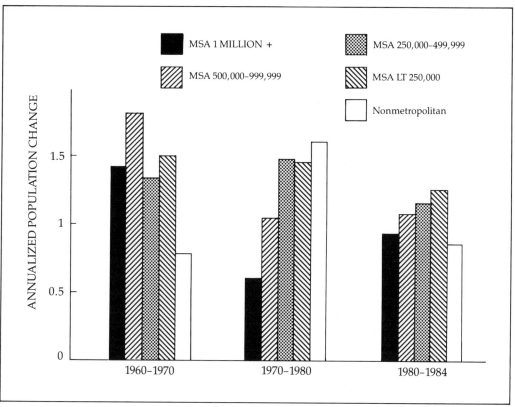

was those MSAs of 500,000 to 1 million, at twice the rate of nonmetropolitan areas. All other metropolitan groups also grew more rapidly
than nonmetropolitan areas, and more rapidly than the United States as
a whole. In the decade of the turnaround that followed, however, there
was an inverse relation between size and growth, with the largest metropolitan areas having the slowest growth overall and nonmetropolitan
areas having the most rapid growth. There continued to be an inverse
relation between MSA size and level of growth in the early 1980s, but
the nonmetropolitan counties together grew more slowly than any metropolitan group. Although the decline in growth for the largest-size metropolitan group was substantial across the first two time periods, this
group showed a notable increase in growth level between 1970–1980

and 1980–1984. The next largest group also increased slightly, but the level of growth for the smaller MSA groups and the nonmetropolitan counties declined. In other words, the change in growth was toward somewhat more concentration in larger metropolitan areas even though deconcentration among the metropolitan groups continued. A further classification showed that the increased growth levels of larger MSAs was restricted to core counties that included Central Cities. Although peripheral counties for all MSA size groups continued to grow considerably faster than core counties, their level of growth in the 1980s was lower than the 1970s. Generally these trends are repeated across the regions, indicating that they are not just due to a possible rejuvenation of major cities in the "rust belt" of the North. A detailed examination of this interesting development is, of course, beyond the scope of a volume concerned with rural and small town America, but its possible relation to changes in nonmetropolitan populations should not be overlooked.

Regional Trends
in Nonmetropolitan–Metropolitan Change

Another major trend of the 1960s and 1970s was the overall decline in growth levels in the Northeast and Midwest states in contrast to increasing or continued high growth levels in the South and the West. As was true in other recent decades, the national growth level of the 1980–1984 period concealed a wide range of regional diversity, with hundreds of nonmetropolitan counties—particularly in the South and West—continuing to attract migrants while others declined in the face of industrial and agricultural conditions. The metropolitan–nonmetropolitan change pattern described above is rather different when considered separately for the four census regions (Table 2.5). In comparing 1960–1970 with 1970–1980, the nonmetropolitan turnaround is clearly seen for the Midwest and West, and although the South showed a similar pattern, the difference between metropolitan and nonmetropolitan growth was small there in the 1970s. In the Northeast nonmetropolitan areas already were growing somewhat more rapidly than metropolitan in 1960–1970. Nonmetropolitan growth in this region was less and metropolitan growth somewhat more in 1980–1984 than 1970–1980, but the nonmetropolitan category was still growing twice as rapidly as the metropolitan. In the Midwest overall growth in both residence categories was essentially zero by 1980–1984.

TABLE 2.5

Metropolitan and Nonmetropolitan Annualized Population Change per 100, for Regions, 1960–1984[a]

	Northeast	Midwest	South	West	United States
1960–1970					
Metropolitan	.88	1.16	1.95	2.44	1.50
Nonmetropolitan	1.16	.54	.72	1.40	.81
Total	.94	.92	1.33	2.15	1.25
1970–1980					
Metropolitan	− .23	.17	1.77	1.94	.85
Nonmetropolitan	1.08	.82	1.88	2.84	1.59
Total	.02	.39	1.82	2.13	1.08
1980–1984					
Metropolitan	.25	.09	1.81	1.86	1.02
Nonmetropolitan	.52	.13	1.08	1.89	.84
Total	.28	.10	1.57	1.87	.98

[a]Metropolitan–nonmetropolitan designation at the beginning of each period.

In contrast to the regions of the North, there was a reversal of the turnaround in the South due to a sharp drop in the nonmetropolitan rate although it was still considerably above that for the 1960s. In the West, after showing a turnaround between the 1960s and 1970s, metropolitan and nonmetropolitan growth were essentially the same in 1980–1984. Nonmetropolitan growth levels declined in all regions, whereas overall metropolitan growth gained only in the Northeast and the South. A regional comparison of metropolitan areas by size reveals, however, that all regions had an increase in growth for the largest metropolitan size group, but in the Midwest and West this was compensated for by the slower growth in the smaller metropolitan size groups.

These diverse results underscore the need to be very cautious about generalizations concerning overall metropolitan–nonmetropolitan growth comparisons. After all, both metropolitan and nonmetropolitan areas are quite heterogeneous, and the fact that one such category is higher than the other is perhaps not as significant as the changes in growth patterns that are taking place within the metropolitan and nonmetropolitan sectors.

Nonmetropolitan County Growth Patterns

All those who have given much attention to nonmetropolitan America have been struck by its diversity in resources, economy, and culture.[13] Although the turnaround and its aftermath were widespread, there were important variations in growth, so that examining the types of areas growing more rapidly than others, and determining whether these associations are changing over time, can contribute to a better understanding of recent trends.

To review the situation, we have associated selected variables with county population change for each of the three time periods considered in this chapter. The county properties we examined were selected on the basis of findings from previous research, most of which compared growth patterns of the first time period and part of the second time period considered.[14] These variables pertain to location with respect to urban centers and transportation networks, employment and economic activities, income, recreation, and climate. This previous research showed population growth to have changed with the turnaround in its associations with a number of these factors, and the findings have been interpreted as indicative of a modification of the structure of population distribution processes. With the slowing of nonmetropolitan growth in the late 1970s and early 1980s a basic question is whether the recent patterns are a reversion toward the situation in the 1960s or a continuation of patterns that became evident in the turnaround decade.

Results are shown in Figure 2.10. Annualized population changes for 1960–1970, 1970–1980, and 1980–1984 are given for nonmetropolitan counties grouped according to levels of the seven different sorting variables. The nonmetropolitan designation and, where possible, subgroup classifications for the independent variables are as of the beginning of each time period. The correlation ratio, *eta*, is also included as a measure of association to summarize the findings for each variable at each time.

The first panel contrasts growth levels for a simultaneous classification of nonmetropolitan counties by whether or not they were adjacent to an MSA and by three categories for size of largest incorporated place in the county. These distinctions are as of the beginning of each time period. There is a very consistent pattern for the 1960s with higher population change rates for adjacent than for corresponding nonadjacent counties and higher rates for counties that include larger cities whether or not they are adjacent. This is the pattern that would be expected for

---

[13]Brown and Beale (1981).
[14]See review in Fuguitt (1985).

FIGURE 2.10

Annualized Growth Rates by Selected Variables for Nonmetropolitan Counties,
1960–1984

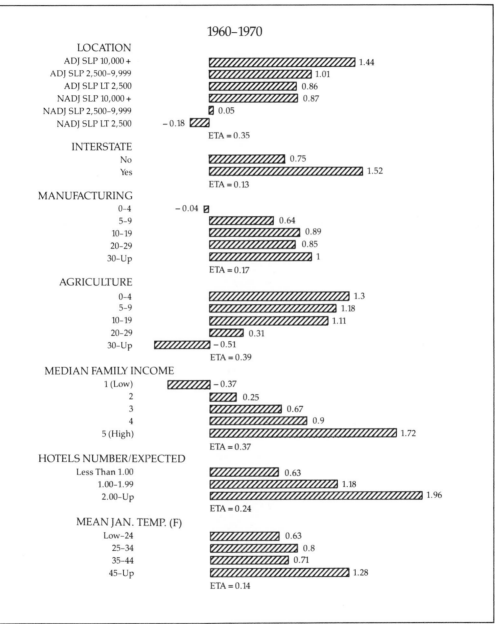

(continued on pages 38 and 39)

FIGURE 2.10 *(continued)*

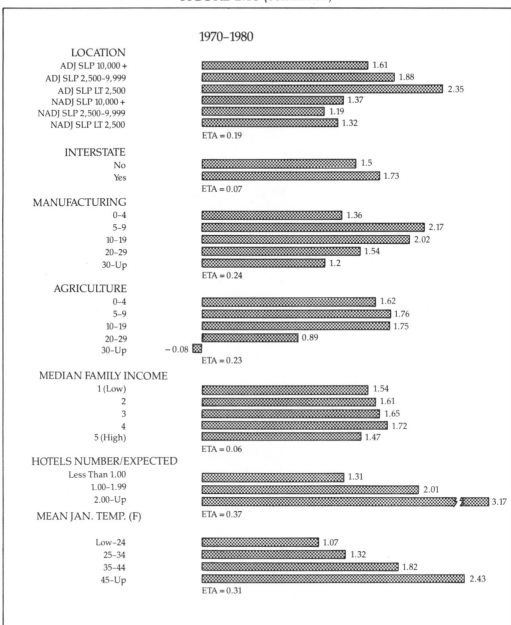

1970–1980

LOCATION
ADJ SLP 10,000 +   1.61
ADJ SLP 2,500–9,999   1.88
ADJ SLP LT 2,500   2.35
NADJ SLP 10,000 +   1.37
NADJ SLP 2,500–9,999   1.19
NADJ SLP LT 2,500   1.32
ETA = 0.19

INTERSTATE
No   1.5
Yes   1.73
ETA = 0.07

MANUFACTURING
0–4   1.36
5–9   2.17
10–19   2.02
20–29   1.54
30–Up   1.2
ETA = 0.24

AGRICULTURE
0–4   1.62
5–9   1.76
10–19   1.75
20–29   0.89
30–Up   – 0.08
ETA = 0.23

MEDIAN FAMILY INCOME
1 (Low)   1.54
2   1.61
3   1.65
4   1.72
5 (High)   1.47
ETA = 0.06

HOTELS NUMBER/EXPECTED
Less Than 1.00   1.31
1.00–1.99   2.01
2.00–Up   3.17
ETA = 0.37

MEAN JAN. TEMP. (F)
Low–24   1.07
25–34   1.32
35–44   1.82
45–Up   2.43
ETA = 0.31

FIGURE 2.10 *(continued)*

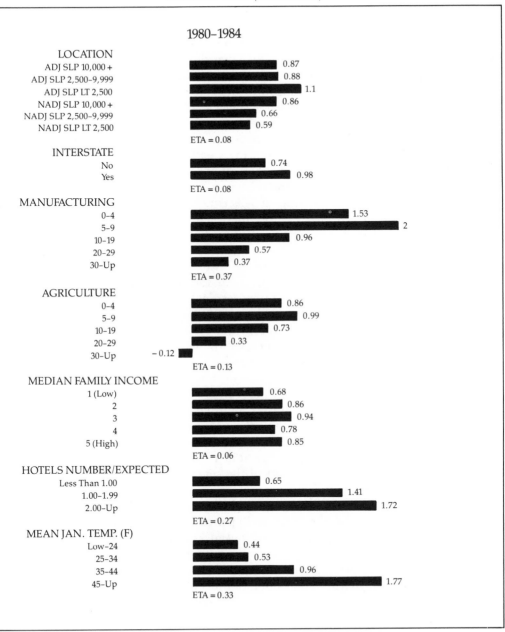

the earlier period with population growth associated with both metropolitan expansion and local level of urbanization. Results were somewhat different, however, in the 1970–1980 turnaround decade. Although adjacent counties continue to grow more rapidly than nonadjacent ones, the highest annualized rate is for adjacent completely rural counties rather than for those with places over 10,000 in size. Furthermore, the counties with the largest absolute increase in growth rates are those that are completely rural and not adjacent to a metropolitan area. The *eta* shows that the overall association of this location variable with population change declines sharply over the three time periods. By 1980–1984 differences between groups were small; the *eta* coefficient is only 0.08. Yet there continues to be a small advantage for counties adjacent to metropolitan areas, and the adjacent completely rural counties are still the most rapidly growing, as was true in 1970–1980. A major component of the new growth in nonmetropolitan areas has been outside established urban places, and this tendency will be considered in detail in Chapter 3.

The presence of an interstate highway is another location variable that has been given some attention in the turnaround literature. Although situated in large part in nonmetropolitan counties this transportation network might be viewed as an essential part of metropolitan America, since it serves to bind together the major and lesser metropolitan centers. Interstates are generally thought to promote growth, although the direction of causation may be in doubt.[15] That is, these roads are generally laid down in major transportation corridors and may in part have followed rather than induced growth. For the 1960–1970 period, we identified the 81 counties on interstate or limited-access highways as of 1960; for 1970–1980, the 524 counties on interstates as of 1970; and for 1980–1984 those 674 counties on the interstate system as projected for completion in the mid-1970s. This variable however, proved to be the least important of the seven under consideration in its association with annualized population change. The correlation ratios (*etas*) indicate that the interstate highway association with population change was largest in the 1960–1970 period, but this value is only 0.13.

Manufacturing has long been viewed as a major component in the economic development of rural and nonmetropolitan areas. Thus, attracting new industry has been promoted as a solution to local problems of economic stagnation and population decline. This has been true despite the fact that metropolitan areas specializing in manufacturing have generally grown more slowly than other metropolitan areas. We classified nonmetropolitan counties by percent of the employed labor

---

[15]Lichter and Fuguitt (1980).

force engaged in manufacturing at the beginning of each decade. A positive association between county growth and percent in manufacturing has generally been found for the pre-turnaround period in previous research, although this association generally was lower during the 1970–1980 turnaround.

In the present analysis, comparison of the three times reveals an orderly transition in the association of population change with concentration of employment in manufacturing. In the 1960s there was a positive association between growth and proportion employed in manufacturing. By the 1970s, according to Figure 2.10, the association had changed with the group of counties having the highest percentage in manufacturing showing the lowest growth, and the group with only 5–9 percent in manufacturing at the beginning of the decade the highest growth. For 1980–1984 the pattern was almost completely inverse, with the 0–4 percent group showing the next-to-highest growth followed by the 5–9 percent group.

The long-standing decrease in labor needs for agriculture has been accepted as a major basis for the decline in population and net migration loss experienced by rural and nonmetropolitan America prior to the 1970s. Noted above as a possible reason for the turnaround, however, is the fact that the exodus from agriculture slowed down in the 1970s, and the proportion employed in agriculture reached a very low level in most parts of the country. On the other hand, the end of the turnaround has been linked in part to a more recent renewal of decline in agricultural employment for those areas still highly dependent upon this economic activity. Thus the search for a better understanding of recent nonmetropolitan population trends should include a comparison of the importance of agricultural employment before, during, and after the turnaround.

Here counties were classified by the percent of employed population in agriculture at the beginning of each period. Figure 2.10 shows a consistent inverse association between growth and concentration of employment in agriculture across the three times. There is, however, a lessening of differences in population change among the five groups of counties, with a decline in *eta* from 0.39 to 0.13. Of perhaps greater significance for this variable is the decline in the proportion of counties at least moderately dependent upon this source of employment. One-half of the nonmetropolitan counties had more than 20 percent employed in agriculture in 1960 but only one in five counties had this high a percentage in 1980. Over the same period, the proportion of counties with less than 10 percent employed in agriculture increased from one in five to more than one in two.

The median income of an area has been given considerable attention in the migration literature as a factor positively associated with migration gain or loss. Consistent with the human resources perspective, population movement may be anticipated from areas of lower to areas of higher median income, as individuals seek out economic opportunities. There was considerable interest, therefore, in the finding reported by some analysts that in the early 1970s this expected positive association was considerably lessened or even reversed in comparison with earlier periods.[16] This contributed to speculation concerning the possible increase in nonpecuniary factors in migration decisions.

Income here shows a positive association with level of population growth in the 1960s, as expected. Consistent with recent research, however, the association of growth and median income is considerably lower in the turnaround decade, with the *eta* coefficient equivalent to that for interstate highway; the pattern of rates peaks at the next-to-highest income group. For 1980–1984 median income again was of minor importance in its association with annualized population change, and the pattern of rates is not regular but peaks at the middle income group.

There is growing recognition that the presence of recreation and resort activities may have an important impact on population trends. In particular many nonmetropolitan counties growing rapidly in the 1970–1980 period in all parts of the country were known to be physically attractive and to include recreation areas. County indicators of recreational activities or "amenities" are, however, not easy to find. As a single indirect measure we have employed here the number of hotels and motels (taken from the 1967 Census of Retail Trade) related to the population in the county. To be specific, counties are classed according to ratio of the number of hotels and motels observed, to the number expected, as predicted by a linear regression on the basis of the 1970 population.[17] Results are in the expected direction, showing greater growth in counties having more hotels than expected. The *eta* for this variable is the largest for the 1970–1980 period.

With the increasing concern about population changes in nonmetropolitan areas, there has been growing recognition of the major demographic and economic growth taking place in the South and West, made more significant by widespread decline in growth taking place in the

---

[16]Beale (1977); McCarthy and Morrison (1979).

[17]We did not calculate this measure separately for the beginning of each decade, but we noted that the three bivariate correlations of the number of hotels and motels in 1962, 1967, and 1972 were 0.95 or above. A concentration of hotels and motels might also be found in nonmetropolitan counties on major transportation routes, even though the area is not particularly attractive for visitors. Our hotel measure, however, correlates less than 0.09 with the interstate highway variable for each time period.

North. This trend continued into the 1980s. As a single measure we have employed a categorization of counties according to average January temperature. Even though we considered only nonmetropolitan counties, we expected this variable to be of increasing importance over time. Although mild temperature is generally considered to be an attractive amenity, we recognize that the growth of the economy and population expansion in areas of mild climate is more than just a reflection of the increased importance of amenities in population movement. Nonetheless, winter temperature does capture an important dimension of recent population trends in the United States. The effect of the temperature variable as seen in Figure 2.10 is in the expected direction throughout the 24-year period. *Etas* are relatively large and increase in importance, particularly between the first and the second time intervals.

In sum, several factors shown in previous research to be associated with variations in nonmetropolitan county population change also have associations for the time periods considered here, but in some cases the magnitudes and patterns of association have shifted.[18] In comparing the first two time periods there has been a decline in the importance of variables associated with local urban development, and an increase in the importance of amenities and temperature. The recent turndown of nonmetropolitan growth in the 1980s was not a return to the "status quo" of the 1960s in terms of growth patterns. Hotels and temperature continued to be among the three most important variables, and percent in manufacturing continued its shift in pattern to an inverse association with level of growth. The further decline in the importance of the location code indicates an increasingly diffuse pattern of nonmetropolitan growth. The turnaround appears to have signaled a major shift in the determinants of population redistribution patterns that continues in the

---

[18]In this presentation results have been reported for each independent variable individually, though, of course, there are interrelations between these that may affect the results. We did a multiple classification analysis following the procedures of Andrews et al. (1973) that shows the effect of each independent variable controlling for all the others. Using unweighted county means, each independent variable has a significant association with population change net of the other variables, with the exception of interstate highway for 1960–1970. The patterns of association also tend to change little upon controlling for all the other variables (Appendix Table 2.1). Exceptions are median income and the location code. Further analysis indicates that because of a negative association with temperature and the fact that the latter variable is more highly associated with growth, median income continues a regular positive association with growth in the two latter time periods net of the other variables. The size-of-largest-place variable shifts to an inverse association with growth upon controlling simultaneously for the agriculture, manufacturing, and temperature variables. To the extent possible, further work should include causal modeling with variables such as these over successive time periods. Nevertheless, the simple results reported here are a necessary first step for understanding the shifting patterns of county population change.

1980s, even though overall the metropolitan–nonmetropolitan growth differential has turned around for the most recent period considered.

Metropolitan–Nonmetropolitan Migration Streams

Explanations of metropolitan–nonmetropolitan population redistribution usually have been based on assumptions about, or analysis of, migration streams and differentials. Natural increase, the difference between births and deaths, is the other basic component of population change. Traditionally population shifts favoring urban and metropolitan areas, however, were due to a net migration gain, which more than made up for higher natural increase levels in rural nonmetropolitan areas. In the 1970s, when the metropolitan–nonmetropolitan growth differential was reversed, overall differences in natural increase between the two residence types had reached a low level, and they remain minimal. Local variations in nonmetropolitan natural increase do exist, in some instances due to differences in fertility associated with ethnic and cultural minorities. Differences may also in part be a consequence of migration patterns. That is, areas experiencing high levels of inmigration of younger people may as a result have lower mortality and higher fertility levels than other areas. Conversely, areas losing younger migrants—the traditional experience of much of rural America—may as a consequence have lower fertility and higher mortality, sometimes to the extreme of posting a natural decrease in population.[19] Nevertheless, it is fair to say that migration is the major basis of the differential growth patterns examined in this chapter, and in the present section we consider this more directly through data on metropolitan–nonmetropolitan migration streams and differentials.

The recent metropolitan–nonmetropolitan trends can be traced through the Current Population Surveys carried out by the Bureau of the Census. In March of each year this survey includes direct questions on migration so that data are obtained for a large national sample of the population. By determining place of residence at a previous time, these data allow the tabulation of movers between metropolitan and nonmetropolitan areas over one- through five-year time intervals beginning in 1973. The 1970 metropolitan definition was employed through March 1984, the most recent survey considered here. A major finding of the first of these surveys to carry metropolitan–nonmetropolitan origin and destination, which helped to announce the turnaround, was that more

---

[19]Beale (1969). Also see Chapter 4.

TABLE 2.6

Metropolitan–Nonmetropolitan Migration Streams, 1970–1984

Period	Interval Years	All Ages[a]			Aged 20–29		
		Metro to Nonmetro (000)	Nonmetro to Metro (000)	Net to Nonmetro (000)	Metro to Nonmetro (000)	Nonmetro to Metro (000)	Net to Nonmetro (000)
1970–1973	3	4,680	3,736	944	1,332	1,415	−83
1970–1974	4	5,965	4,121	1,844	1,549	1,614	−65
1970–1975	5	6,721	5,127	1,594	1,723	2,058	−335
1975–1976	1	2,477	2,081	396	846	811	35
1975–1977	2	3,805	3,202	603	1,285	1,241	44
1975–1978	3	5,321	4,220	1,101	1,615	1,581	34
1975–1979	4	6,691	5,171	1,520	1,882	2,061	−179
1975–1980	5	7,337	5,993	1,344	1,781	2,423	−642
1980–1981	1	2,350	2,156	194	791	843	−52
1981–1982	1	2,366	2,217	149	850	893	−43
1982–1983	1	2,066	2,088	−22	721	867	−146
1983–1984	1	2,258	2,609	−351	725	990	−265

SOURCES: U.S. Bureau of the Census, *Current Population Reports*, series P-20, Nos. 262, 273, 285, 305, 320, 331, 353, 368, 377, 384, 393. *Geographical Mobility*, Washington, D.C.: U.S. Government Printing Office, 1974–1984.

[a]Aged 5 and over for 1970–1975 and 1975–1980; aged 4 and over for 1970–1974 and 1975–1979; aged 3 and over for 1970–1973 and 1975–1978; aged 1 and over for 1975–1976, 1980–1981, 1981–1982, 1982–1983, 1983–1984.

domestic migrants had moved into nonmetropolitan areas than were leaving them over the 1970–1973 period.

This pattern held up across ten surveys using different time intervals between 1970 and 1982 (Table 2.6), but there was a slowdown in this trend by the early 1980s as seen by comparing the one-year interval surveys of 1975–1976 with 1980–1981 and 1981–1982. The net direction of the flow was essentially balanced for 1982–1983, and then a decided net movement back into metropolitan areas of more than 300,000 occurred in 1983–1984.

If one compares the two five-year intervals of 1970–1975 and 1975–1980, or the two four-year intervals of 1970–1974 and 1975–1979, the balance favoring nonmetropolitan areas was less in each of the latter periods, although the reverse was true comparing the earlier three-year interval of 1970–1973 with 1975–1978. These data are subject to sampling variation, but they indicate that the turnaround began slowing at least by 1978. This is consistent with the finding of Richter using annual county estimates of net migration.[20] She found the annualized non-

[20]Richter (1985).

45

metropolitan net migration rate per 100 to be 0.88 for 1970–1974, 0.92 for 1974–1977, and 0.60 for 1977–1980.

Throughout most of the 1970–1984 period young adults aged 20–29 continued on balance to leave rural small town communities for the cities and suburbs. The only exceptions are for the three surveys covering the interval from 1975 through 1978, which may be further evidence that the turnaround peaked at that time. The excess of departures of young people to metropolitan areas presumably reflects such factors as the need for higher education, the desire for a metropolitan life experience, and continued economic advantages there, particularly for those in the career initiation stage. For all other broad age groups, the net interchange was toward the nonmetropolitan communities until the very early 1980s, although by 1984 this was true only for those 45 years and over.

An important point revealed by these survey results and confirmed by the 1970 and 1980 census migration data is that metropolitan–nonmetropolitan migration is definitely a two-way movement. Among all the pairs of streams in Table 2.6 the least amount of overlap in magnitude for all over 5 was in 1970–1974, when the movement to metropolitan areas was only 69 percent of the countermovement. The overlap is generally in the 80–90 percent range, and tends to be greater for young adults. In terms of migration streams, then, the turnaround did not mean (as sterotypical views sometimes implied) a movement all in one direction changed to a movement all in the other; rather there was a relatively small shift in the balance of two rather large movements. Another way to put this is to note that even for 1970–1974, when results showed the least overlap, more than 10 million moves in both directions were required to result in a net gain of 1.8 million people in nonmetropolitan areas. A five-year migration question also was included in the 1970 and 1980 censuses, by which one can compare residence in 1975 with 1980 and 1965 with 1970. Because of its comparability with other work presented here and larger sample size, a more detailed analysis of migration rates for these two time intervals follows.

The inmigration, outmigration, and net migration rates for the flows between metropolitan and nonmetropolitan areas are presented in Table 2.7, along with the inmigration rates from abroad.[21] Rates of outmigration to residences abroad cannot be obtained, and so total net mi-

---

[21]Net migration is the difference between in- and outmigration. Rates in this and subsequent migration tables have as their base the total population at the time of the census minus the number of migrants from abroad and minus the net migration for the age group considered. Although this approach is customary in migration research, inmigration rates are not "true" rates in the sense that the denominator does not represent those exposed to the risk of being inmigrants.

TABLE 2.7

In-, Out-, and Net Migration Rates by Age and Residence,
1965–1970 and 1975–1980

	1965–1970				1975–1980			
	Abroad in	Between Metro & Nonmetro			Abroad in	Between Metro & Nonmetro		
Age and Residence[a]		In	Out	Net		In	Out	Net
5 Years and Over								
Metropolitan	1.90	4.88	4.65	.23	2.29	3.58	4.27	−.69
Nonmetropolitan	.75	9.91	10.39	−.48	.85	12.88	10.81	2.07
0–19								
Metropolitan	1.65	4.78	4.84	−.06	2.53	3.53	4.48	−.95
Nonmetropolitan	.66	9.97	9.84	.13	.89	12.98	10.23	2.57
20–29								
Metropolitan	4.01	12.15	8.60	3.55	3.86	7.27	6.37	.90
Nonmetropolitan	1.54	15.52	21.93	−6.41	1.63	19.90	22.71	−2.81
30–54								
Metropolitan	2.01	3.51	3.81	−.30	2.28	2.77	3.86	−1.09
Nonmetropolitan	.78	8.85	8.15	.70	.88	12.83	9.21	3.62
55 and Over								
Metropolitan	.57	1.85	2.78	−.93	.70	1.53	2.63	−1.10
Nonmetropolitan	.13	5.28	3.52	1.76	.12	6.93	4.03	2.90

[a]Metropolitan–nonmetropolitan designation of 1970 used for 1965–1970 migration and designation of 1980 for 1975–1980 migration.

gration also is unavailable. A comparison of each pair of inmigration rates, however, shows that residents from abroad make up an increasing proportion of inmigrants to metropolitan areas. The abroad rates have changed little, but with the decline in the movement from nonmetropolitan areas across these two times the proportion of metropolitan inmigrants from abroad increased from 28 to 39 percent overall. On the other hand, the proportion of nonmetropolitan inmigrants from abroad was only about 7 percent for both times. Although the most recent Current Population Survey report shows that the net balance of metropolitan–nonmetropolitan migrants has now shifted to favor the metropolitan side once again, an important component of the current metropolitan growth advantage is no doubt due to higher rates of inmigration from abroad.

The turnaround favoring nonmetropolitan areas is clearly evident in Table 2.7 in the changing signs of the net rates, as well as in the decline in metropolitan and the increase in nonmetropolitan inmigration rates across the two times. Outmigration rates, however, declined slightly for metropolitan areas and increased slightly for nonmetropolitan areas, which is contrary to expectations and previous research.[22] This earlier work showed the increase of nonmetropolitan net migration to be almost equally due to an increased retention (decline in outmigration) and to increased attraction (gain of inmigration). Behaviorally, the two are quite different, of course. This discrepancy in results is probably due primarily to the different metropolitan designations for 1970 and 1980. If the 1965–1970 rates in Table 2.7 are compared with those of the Current Population Survey for 1975–1980 (which also has the 1970 metropolitan definition), more than one-third of the increase in nonmetropolitan net migration appears to be due to increased retention.[23]

One point that bears emphasis is the fact that throughout the turnaround era, the probability that a nonmetropolitan resident would move to a metropolitan area was greater than the probability of a move by a metropolitan resident to a rural or small town community. This anomaly, shown by comparing the outmigration rates of the table, is explained by the disparity in the size of the base populations. Generally the metropolitan bases are about twice the size of the corresponding nonmetropolitan bases.

Migration and Age

The age differentials in the migration rates are given in the remaining panels of Table 2.7. They show, as expected, greater tendency to move among young adults with all of the in-, out-, and net migration rates highest for the 20–29 year group. Even in 1975–1980 the net rates for young adults continued to favor metropolitan areas though at a lower level than in 1965–1970. The net migration differential favored nonmetropolitan areas for all other age groups, however, in *both* 1965–1970 and 1975–1980, though nonmetropolitan net rates were consider-

---

[22]Tucker (1976); Brown (1981); Fuguitt, Pfeffer, and Jenkins (1985).

[23]Because of differences in universes and in sampling, the two sources are only approximately comparable, but both have the 1970 metropolitan distinction. The nonmetropolitan outmigration rate declined from 10.4 to 9.5 and the inmigration rate increased from 9.9 to 11.6. The increase in the net migration of 2.6 is equal to the difference in the inmigration rates (1.7) minus the difference in the outmigration rates (−.9); 0.9 is 35 percent of 2.6.

ably higher and metropolitan rates considerably lower in the latter time period for all age groups. Thus in terms of migration streams the turnaround had begun in the late 1960s, but it was not until the 1970s that the comparative migration advantage for nonmetropolitan areas was sufficient to outweigh the continued tendency of young adults to turn to the city. Since the moves of young people more often tend to be related to jobs and the pursuit of higher education, this tendency, seen throughout the Current Population Survey series, at least suggests a greater importance of noneconomic motivations for movers to nonmetropolitan than for movers to metropolitan areas.[24] As noted above, however, the post-1980 Current Population Survey findings included evidence that the most recent trend favoring metropolitan areas affects a wider range of ages than was true in the late 1960s, with the exception of older groups.

Migration and Size of Metropolitan Area

The previous analysis of overall population growth trends showed a deconcentration of population from large to small metropolitan areas as well as to nonmetropolitan areas over the 1960–1980 period. With census migration data it is possible to examine streams between large metropolitan (greater than 500,000), small metropolitan, and nonmetropolitan areas for 1975–1980 and 1965–1970. As before, the definition of metropolitan and the size classification of metropolitan areas is that current at each census. The number of migrants (in thousands) between these residence groups is given in Table 2.8. In the 1965–1970 period over 2,344,000 persons moved from large to small metropolitan areas and about the same number (2,414,000) moved in the opposite direction. Similarly more than 3 million moved from large metropolitan to nonmetropolitan areas, and this was approximately balanced by a countermove, whereas less than 2 million moved from small metropolitan to nonmetropolitan areas with a somewhat larger number going in the opposite direction.

For 1975–1980 the outmovement streams from large metropolitan areas (top row) are considerably larger than those from small metropolitan areas (second row). The movement from nonmetropolitan to large metropolitan areas, on the other hand, declined from about 3.5 million to 2.9 million, although the corresponding movement from nonmetropolitan to small metropolitan areas increased slightly. Such compari-

---

[24]Tucker (1976); Bowles (1978); Zuiches and Brown (1978).

TABLE 2.8

Number of Migrants Between Large and Small Metropolitan Areas and Nonmetropolitan Areas, 1965–1970, 1975–1980[a] (in thousands)

Residence Five Years Before	Residence in 1970			Residence in 1980		
	Large Metro	Small Metro	Nonmetro	Large Metro	Small Metro	Nonmetro
Large Metropolitan	—	2,344	3,469	—	4,232	4,030
Small Metropolitan	2,414	—	1,989	3,754	—	2,517
Nonmetropolitan	3,460	2,349	—	2,947	2,562	—

[a]Large metropolitan are MSAs with more than 500,000 population: Small Metropolitan are other MSAs. Metropolitan and size of metropolitan designation of 1970 used for 1965–1970 migration and designation of 1980 used for 1975–1980 migration.

sons across the two time periods can be misleading, however, since in 1980 the metropolitan population bases were larger and the nonmetropolitan smaller than in 1970. Above all, this table shows that there is a substantial amount of moving between these major residence groupings. In each decade almost 10 percent of the base population (total minus those coming from abroad) made such a shift, which included more than 16 million persons for 1965–1970 and more than 20 million for 1975–1980.

The net result of these streams is given in Table 2.9. The top panel shows that for 1965–1970 all the moving around had very little net redistributive effect. Large metropolitan areas were gaining slightly from smaller metropolitan areas and were essentially balanced with nonmetropolitan areas; small metropolitan areas were losing slightly to larger metropolitan areas but gaining substantially (one-third of a million people) in their interchange with nonmetropolitan areas. The net gains and losses were rather larger in the 1975–1980 period, when large metropolitan areas lost almost half a million people in the interchange with small metropolitan areas and over 1 million to nonmetropolitan areas. In addition to this net gain from larger areas, the smaller metropolitan areas gained a small amount from nonmetropolitan areas. In other words, the net gain to nonmetropolitan areas was entirely from larger metropolitan areas in the late 1970s.

Interpreting changes over time in these migration stream numbers is difficult because the total population increased and both metropolitan groups gained, in large part by area redefinition between the 1970s and the 1980s. Net migration rates for the three residence groups are given in the bottom panel of Table 2.9. The total rates are decomposed into

TABLE 2.9

Net Migration Decomposition for Large and Small Metropolitan Areas and Nonmetropolitan Areas, 1965–1970, 1975–1980[a]

Residence Category[b]	1965–1970				1975–1980			
	Total Net Migration	Net migration with			Total Net Migration	Net migration with		
		Large Metro	Small Metro	Non-metro		Large Metro	Small Metro	Non-metro
Net Migration Numbers (000s)								
Large metropolitan	61	–	70	–9	–1,561	–	–478	–1,083
Small metropolitan	290	–70	–	360	523	478	–	45
Nonmetropolitan	–351	9	–360	–	1,038	1,083	–45	–
Net Migration Rates per 100								
Large metropolitan	.07	–	.08	–.01	–1.40	–	–.43	–.97
Small metropolitan	.94	–.22	–	1.16	1.19	1.09	–	.10
Nonmetropolitan	–.63	.01	–.64	–	2.01	2.10	–.09	–

[a]Number and rate rows are additive for each period.
[b]Large metropolitan are MSAs with more than 500,000 population: Small Metropolitan are other MSAs. Metropolitan and size of metropolitan designation of 1970 used for 1965–1970 migration and designation of 1980 used for 1975–1980 migration.

additive components for each interchange by this procedure. Overall large metropolitan areas went from essentially zero to a substantial negative net migration rate, nonmetropolitan areas shifted from negative to strongly positive, and small metropolitan areas increased their relative net gains. The net migration components further show a shift in the pattern of interchanges among the three residence groups. In the 1960s large metropolitan areas were essentially in migration balance with the other two residence groups, and the gain of small metropolitan and loss of nonmetropolitan areas was due to the unequal interchange between these two residence types. By the 1970s two-thirds of the large metropolitan area net migration loss was with nonmetropolitan areas and the other third with small metropolitan areas; these large MSAs were the source of virtually all of the net gain for both of the other residence groups. From the nonmetropolitan perspective, one could conclude that the turnaround was due to a shift of balance of the substantial interchange with both large and small metropolitan areas; with the former from essentially zero to strongly positive, and with the latter from negative to almost zero.

Regional Migration

The nonmetropolitan and metropolitan rates of net migration by region are a result of movements both within and among these groups of states. The four regions differ not only in levels of net migration but also in the patterns of movement underlying them. Furthermore, these levels and patterns have changed between the 1960s and the 1970s. Metropolitan and nonmetropolitan net migration rates are shown by regional components in Table 2.10, with the numbers on which these rates are based given in Appendix Table 2.2. In the first time period (1965–1970) for metropolitan areas there were appreciable negative net migration rates in the Northeast and Midwest and appreciable positive net migration rates in the South and West (line 4). The nonmetropolitan rate for the Northeast was rather high and positive, showing (as was seen also in Table 2.5) that the turnaround was already present there, but the negative rate for the Midwest was greater than the metropolitan negative rate there, and negative nonmetropolitan rates also were found for the South and West (line 8).

By 1975–1980 metropolitan net migration rates continued to be negative and were considerably larger than in 1965–1970 in both regions of the North, and continued positive at about the same level in the South and West (line 12). The nonmetropolitan rate had dropped to a

TABLE 2.10

Net Migration Rates by Metropolitan–Nonmetropolitan Regional Components,
1965–1970, 1975–1980

Components	Northeast	Midwest	South	West	Total
1965–1970					
Metro in Region Indicated with:					
Metro in other regions	−1.58	−1.19	1.50	2.05	—
Nonmetro in other regions	−.15	−.07	.60	.80	.24
Nonmetro in same region	−.92	.15	.65	.21	−.02
Total Metro	−2.65	−1.11	2.75	3.06	.22
Nonmetro in Region Indicated with:					
Nonmetro in other regions	−.35	−.44	.36	.28	—
Metro in other regions	−1.10	−1.16	.01	.01	−.52
Metro in same region	3.57	−.30	−.80	−.75	.04
Total Nonmetro	2.12	−1.90	−.43	−.47	−.48
1975–1980					
Metro in Region Indicated with:					
Metro in other regions	−3.49	−2.59	3.07	3.46	—
Nonmetro in other regions	−.49	−.48	.47	.41	−.04
Nonmetro in same region	−.62	−.54	−.50	−.96	−.63
Total Metro	−4.60	−3.61	3.04	2.91	−.67
Nonmetro in Region Indicated with:					
Nonmetro in other regions	−.76	−.47	.39	.62	—
Metro in other regions	−2.50	−1.06	1.39	1.28	.1C
Metro in same region	3.65	1.37	.99	4.60	1.91
Total Nonmetro	.39	−.16	2.77	6.50	2.01

low but continued positive level in the Northeast, the corresponding
rate increased from strongly negative to only slightly negative in the
Midwest, and the rate shifted from a negative to a strongly positive level
in the South and West (line 16). Though calculated from the smallest
base the nonmetropolitan 1975–1980 net migration rate for the West at
6.5 is the largest in either direction in the table.

These results parallel the annualized population change rates given
in Table 2.5. With the migration data, however, it is also possible to
consider the contribution of various streams summarized as components in Table 2.10. On the metropolitan side, the table shows the im-

portance of intermetropolitan movement between regions. This component contributes more than one-half of the net loss for the two northern regions, and similarly more than one-half of the net migration gain of the South and West between 1965 and 1970. The contribution of the nonmetropolitan-to-metropolitan movement is slightly greater for the South than for the West in this earlier period. In the South this is about evenly divided between net gains within and among regions, whereas in the West 80 percent of the net gain is from other regions, particularly from the Midwest.

On the nonmetropolitan side in 1965–1970, the net losses to both metropolitan and nonmetropolitan areas in other regions are important components of the overall nonmetropolitan net migration rates for the Northeast and Midwest. The positive rate of net migration for the interchange with metropolitan areas within the region is quite high in the Northeast, whereas there was a smaller net loss for this migration stream in the Midwest. For nonmetropolitan areas of the South and the West, on the other hand, the 1965–1970 gain from nonmetropolitan areas in other regions offsets up to one-half of the losses to metropolitan areas in the same region. At that time, the movements from nonmetropolitan areas of the South and West to metropolitan areas in other regions were evenly balanced by the corresponding countermovements.

By 1975–1980 the net migration loss for metropolitan areas of the North had increased considerably. This was due primarily to increases in the losses through interchange with metropolitan areas of the South and West. The interchange with nonmetropolitan areas contributed only about one-fourth of the loss in the most recent period, and this was almost evenly divided between nonmetropolitan areas within the regions and those in the South and West. For the South and West, on the other hand, metropolitan areas had net migration gains overall at about the same rates as in the preceding period. The increase in the gains from metropolitan areas in other regions tended to be offset by lower net gains from nonmetropolitan areas of other regions and the turnaround to net loss with nonmetropolitan areas of the same region. The net component for loss to nonmetropolitan areas of the same region is largest in the West, as is the corresponding component of net migration gain for nonmetropolitan areas of this region.

The smaller nonmetropolitan total net migration gain in the Northeast for 1975–1980 (0.39 as compared with 2.12 for 1965–1970) is due to the fact that although the net gain from metropolitan areas in the region is at about the same level as in 1965–1970, this component is now almost offset by a doubling of the rate of loss to both metropolitan and nonmetropolitan areas of other regions. For the nonmetropolitan Midwest, the shift to a net gain from metropolitan areas within the region from $-.30$ to 1.37 does not quite offset the interregional loss, although the two interregional components are approximately the same as previously. Nonmetropolitan areas of the South and the West gained from all three components in the latter period. Only about 10 percent of this gain was from nonmetropolitan areas of other regions. In the South one-half was from metropolitan areas outside the region and one-third from metropolitan areas inside the region, whereas in the West 70 percent was from inside the region. Of the South's overall net migration gain to nonmetropolitan areas from metropolitan areas, 42 percent is in the interchange within the South, 28 percent with the Northeast, 26 percent with the Midwest, and 4 percent with the West.

These results for broad regional and residence categories underscore the geographic complexity of recent trends in regional and metropolitan–nonmetropolitan migration.[25] The nonmetropolitan turnaround appears to have had less impact on metropolitan areas than increases in regional shifts between the North and the South and West during the same period. For nonmetropolitan areas the increased net migration growth levels have been based in part on shifts in regional migrant interchanges. Although overall most migrants from metropolitan to nonmetropolitan areas are within the same region, a substantial proportion in the South are from the two northern regions. Regional shifts favoring the South and West continued in the early 1980s even with the reversal of the turnaround and diminution of nonmetropolitan population growth. Yet the interrelations of these two aspects of population redistribution are evident in our analysis, and further efforts to understand and explain the turnaround and its aftermath should be closely related to a consideration of forces behind the change in regional population redistribution.

Overview and Conclusion

Rural and nonmetropolitan areas have included a declining proportion of the nation's population, and the absolute size of their population overall has changed little during this century. These simple facts are nonetheless the consequence of the major transformation of our society from one based largely on agriculture to one based on manufacturing and later trade and services. This transformation has had far-reaching implications in terms of technology, economic production, trade, and social relationships. Population residential distribution traditionally has been closely tied to economic production and trade. This has meant that

---

[25]This complements the findings of earlier research, including McCarthy and Morrison (1979) and Brown (1981).

after initial settlement, with declining labor needs in extractive industries, and the expansion of trade and manufacturing found mostly in urban concentrations, many rural areas and small towns experienced a downward spiral in total population numbers. Other such areas, however, were stationary or continued to grow. With the increased dispersion of settlement and economic activity in the proximity of large centers, however, the basic unit of concentrated settlement by 1950 had shifted from the urban place to the metropolitan area.

A major aspect of both urban and metropolitan growth has been the further spread of this form of settlement through the establishment of new cities and metropolitan areas. Consequently the slow growth or decline of the nonmetropolitan population as a whole has in large part been due to the growth of many subareas and their consequent transition to metropolitan status as new freestanding areas, along with the transfer of others, to become peripheral parts of already existing metropolitan areas.

The growth of the metropolitan population has continued to the present, but in the 1970–1980 decade this growth was entirely due to the transfer of territory to metropolitan status. For the first time metropolitan areas, without benefit of such transfers, grew more slowly than nonmetropolitan areas. This unexpected finding, termed the "nonmetropolitan turnaround," led to a substantial amount of research, theorizing, debate, and policy discussion. On the nonmetropolitan side increased growth was widespread beginning in the 1960s; it intensified in the early and middle 1970s and tapered off at the end of the decade. Research has shown several factors to be associated with this dramatic increase in growth, including a slowdown in the exodus from agriculture, which had ceased to be a major component in the economies of many rural areas; growth in other extractive industries and in manufacturing and services; an increased importance of rural areas for recreation and retirement residence; and greater residential sprawl around metropolitan areas and so evidence of an increased importance of quality-of-life considerations in migration decisions.[26] The bases for the more recent downturn in nonmetropolitan population growth are not yet clear,

---

[26]Almost all of the direct evidence on the last-named factor comes from noncensus sources, and so we have not included migration decisions in our analysis. Surveys have shown the importance of antiurban sentiments among the reasons given by metropolitan migrants for their moves to nonmetropolitan areas. There was fragmentary evidence also of a decline in preferences for living in metropolitan areas in the 1970s, particularly among those growing up in nonmetropolitan areas. But some other evidence runs counter to the view that there has been more emphasis on noneconomic factors in migration decisions. Although we believe there has been an increase in quality-of-life considerations in migration, made possible in part because of more widespread economic opportunities, the issue is far from settled. See discussion in Fuguitt (1985).

but they include the economic stress in agriculture and diminished employment in manufacturing, and the passing of the short boom in extractive industries related to energy. The general economic downturn after 1980 seemed to affect nonmetropolitan more than metropolitan areas.

An examination in this chapter of county characteristics associated with variations in nonmetropolitan growth was consistent with most of the above explanations. Though there was a turndown of growth in 1980–1984 compared with 1970–1980, county patterns did show a continuation of a trend toward more deconcentrated settlement. By the early 1980s concentration in manufacturing had shifted to become inversely associated with county growth. Although growth levels in amenity/recreation areas were lower in the early 1980s than in the 1970s, these counties continue to be the fastest growing nonmetropolitan group.

Both the 1970s turnaround and its aftermath were surprises, making evident the need to move beyond these approximate reasons toward a better understanding of the underlying population processes. Yet empirical work continues to reveal the complexity of the task. The major distribution trends considered here derive primarily from migration flows, but this is a two-way movement, and the countermove is 80 to 90 percent of the dominant one before, during, and after the turnaround. Young adults on balance favored metropolitan areas throughout the period (except for a few years in the mid-1970s), and the older age groups continually favored nonmetropolitan areas. Thus the timing of the trend, as measured by the stream that is larger for all ages, is due to a balancing of different tendencies for different age groups. Furthermore the likelihood of a metropolitan person moving to a nonmetropolitan area was always less than the likelihood of a nonmetropolitan person moving to a metropolitan area, so that in an absolute sense the former stream was greater than the latter in the 1970s, due to the larger metropolitan base population. These qualifications do not rule out the existence of a turnaround, but they suggest paying less attention to balance and relative size of metropolitan–nonmetropolitan rates and more to the fact that nonmetropolitan areas did experience renewed widespread growth in the 1970s when major metropolitan areas were experiencing slower growth or decline. The disaggregations by stream and age illustrate the challenge to be met in seeking to fathom these trends from the standpoint of migrant characteristics or decision-making processes, and developing theoretical propositions to explain them. Not only is it essential to consider different stages of the life cycle, it is also necessary to focus on the counterstreams as well as dominant streams, and on nonmigrants as well as migrants.

To put our metropolitan–nonmetropolitan analysis in a broader context we examined trends by size of nonmetropolitan area and by region. Results showed the nonmetropolitan turnaround to be closely interrelated with changes in growth and migration across the metropolitan hierarchy and among regions of the country. By the 1970s population growth differences were inversely related to size of metropolitan area, with the smallest metropolitan size group exceeded in growth only by nonmetropolitan areas in that decade and the fastest growing group of all for 1980–1984. Nevertheless, the overall increased metropolitan growth in the most recent period is due to a slight resurgence in growth for the core counties of major metropolitan areas in all regions. Migration streams between large and small metropolitan and nonmetropolitan areas show considerable movement in all directions, but a general shift down the hierarchy is found in comparing the net flows for 1965–1970 with 1975–1980.

There was a complex pattern of inter- and intraregional migration interchanges, and shifts in this pattern between the late 1960s and the late 1970s reflected both the greater movement to the South and West and the nonmetropolitan turnaround. Regional and other subarea variations in metropolitan–nonmetropolitan population trends point up the need to learn more about these interrelations and to concentrate attention on particular subareas because of regional diversity.

Some more general explanations of the turnaround have been couched in terms of fundamental processes of urbanization and metropolitanization, with the nonmetropolitan shifts a part of recent changes in growth across the metropolitan hierarchy and among regions.[27] Growth patterns favoring smaller metropolitan areas as well as nonmetropolitan areas, and patterns favoring parts of the country away from the industrial heartland of the Northeast and Midwest, have been viewed as a continuation, at different levels of aggregation, of deconcentration first noted at the peripheries of large cities. With the spread of metropolitan areas through all regions of the country we may be close to a ceiling or "equilibrium" in the metropolitanization process. Technological advances in transportation and communication as well as organizational and political changes may have muted the previous advantages of large agglomerations, and indeed larger agglomerations may have reached limits in their efficiency. The restructuring of our nation's industrial base, with the preponderant shift from heavy industry to high technology and services also has been related to regional population trends and changes in metropolitan structure.

[27]Recent work includes Frey (1986), Greenwood (1985), Hugo and Smailes (1985), Long (1985), Wardwell (1980), and Wilson (1988). See also footnote 1 of Chapter 1.

The post-1980 trends need to be reconciled with overall explanations and theory about changes in settlement patterns. Growth favoring the South and the West continued into the 1980s, but there was a relative decline in levels of growth for nonmetropolitan and small metropolitan areas and increased growth for major metropolitan centers. The latter relative increase has been attributed to the continuing role of the major metropolitan areas as "control centers" or as centers of high-technology innovation with the initial decline due to industrial change beginning to run its course.[28] An important point is that the deconcentrated settlement pattern by region and size of metropolitan area evident in the 1970s has continued, and that deconcentration among nonmetropolitan subareas is still the rule. This latter point will be elaborated in Chapter 3, in which growth of places and the nonplace population are compared.

The nonmetropolitan turnaround is sometimes compared with the post–World War II baby boom in being both unexpected and unprecedented. Perhaps a further analogy is apt: Even if the decline in nonmetropolitan growth extends and deepens to become like the present "baby bust," population distribution and change in nonmetropolitan areas will have been transformed, just as most aspects of fertility patterns today are quite different from the 1930s, when overall levels were also low. Similarly, just as the baby boom cohort continues to reverberate through our population structure, so the impact of the new nonmetropolitan growth of the 1970s will be long-lasting in the affected communities, perhaps for years or decades to come.[29] The nature of this impact, as seen in the present situation, and the character of recent changes in demographic and economic structure, are the subjects of the remainder of this volume.

[28]See, for example, Noyelle and Stanback (1983). This interpretation has been questioned by Frey (1986), however, in an empirical study in which he relates the recent growth of large metropolitan areas to their economic functions. Detailed data to relate pre-1980 and post-1980 trends to general explanations about changes in settlement structure are not yet available.

[29]In counties classed as nonmetropolitan in 1980 the population would have been 5.8 million less than reported in 1980 had the 1960–1970 growth continued over 1970–1980. On the other hand, had the 1970–1980 growth continued into the 1980s, the 1984 population of these counties would have been about 1.4 million greater than estimated.

Multiple Classification Analysis of Weighted Annualized Growth Rates with Selected Independent Variables, Nonmetropolitan Counties, 1960–1970, 1970–1980, 1980–1984

Variable and Category	Means			Adjusted means		
	1960–1970	1970–1980	1980–1984	1960–1970	1970–1980	1980–1984
Location Code						
Adj SLP 10,000+	1.44	1.61	.87	.93	1.35	.73
Adj SLP 2,500–9,999	1.01	1.88	.88	1.14	2.03	.99
Adj SLP 2,500	.86	2.35	1.10	1.32	2.63	1.24
Nadj SLP 10,000+	.87	1.37	.86	.59	1.06	.63
Nadj SLP 2,500–9,999	.05	1.19	.66	.45	1.45	.76
Nadj SLP 2,500	-.18	1.32	.59	.82	2.14	1.05
Eta/Beta	.35	.19	.08	.17	.28	.12
Interstate Highway						
No	.75	1.50	.74	.79	1.50	.78
Yes	1.52	1.73	.98	1.01	1.74	.93
Eta/Beta	.13	.07	.08	.04	.08	.05
Percent in Manufacturing						
0–4	-.04	1.36	1.53	.60	1.94	1.78
5–9	.64	2.17	2.00	.85	2.15	1.83
10–19	.89	2.02	.96	1.10	2.02	.98
20–29	.85	1.54	.57	.86	1.47	.58
30–up	1.00	1.20	.37	.56	1.16	.36
Eta/Beta	.17	.24	.37	.13	.25	.36
Percent in Agriculture						
0–4	1.30	1.62	.86	1.12	1.71	.82
5–9	1.18	1.76	.99	.97	1.81	1.00
10–19	1.11	1.75	.73	1.02	1.59	.80
20–29	.31	.89	.33	.54	.71	.41
30–up	-.51	-.08	-.12	-.02	-.10	-.37
Eta/Beta	.39	.23	.13	.24	.25	.13

APPENDIX TABLE 2.1 (continued)

Variable and Category	Means			Adjusted means		
	1960–1970	1970–1980	1980–1984	1960–1970	1970–1980	1980–1984
Median Family Income						
1 (low)	-.37	1.54	.68	-.19	1.17	.37
2	.25	1.61	.86	.21	1.32	.67
3	.67	1.65	.94	.65	1.54	.86
4	.90	1.72	.78	.94	1.76	.92
5 (high)	1.72	1.47	.85	1.65	1.73	1.14
Eta/Beta	.37	.06	.06	.34	.13	.16
Hotels Number/Expected						
1 less than 1.00	.63	1.31	.65	.71	1.36	.69
2 1.00–1.99	1.18	2.01	1.41	.88	2.07	1.38
3 2.00–up	1.96	3.17	1.72	1.42	2.76	1.43
Eta/Beta	.24	.37	.27	.12	.29	.21
Mean January Temperature						
Low–24	.63	1.07	.44	.47	.96	.21
25–34	.80	1.32	.53	.51	1.34	.52
35–44	.71	1.82	.96	1.01	2.00	1.19
45–up	1.28	2.43	1.77	1.51	2.28	1.75
Eta/Beta	.14	.31	.33	.24	.32	.39
Grand Means	.81	1.59	.84			
Number of Counties	2,741	2,627	2,384			
Multiple R Squared				.283	.359	.338
Multiple R				.532	.599	.581

NOTES:
Income 59: 1. Low–2,499; 2. 2,500–3,499; 3. 3,500–4,499; 4. 4,500–5,499; 5. 5,500–up.
Income 69: 1. Low–5,499; 2. 5,500–6,499; 3. 6,500–7,499; 4. 7,500–8,499; 5. 8,500–up.
Income 79: 1. Low–12,999; 2. 13,000–14,999; 3. 15,000–16,999; 4. 17,000–18,999; 5. 19,000–up.

APPENDIX TABLE 2.2

Net Migration Numbers by Metropolitan–Nonmetropolitan Regional Components, 1965–1970, 1975–1980

Components	Northeast	Midwest	South	West	Total
1965–1970					
Metro in Region Indicated with:					
Metro in other regions	−5,277	−3,829	4,417	4,689	0
Nonmetro in other regions	−534	−223	1,780	1,838	2,861
Nonmetro in same region	−3,069	489	1,907	477	−196
Total Metro	−8,880	−3,563	8,104	7,004	2,665
Nonmetro in Region Indicated with:					
Nonmetro in other regions	−301	−739	864	176	0
Metro in other regions	−944	−1,931	10	4	−2,861
Metro in same region	3,069	−489	−1,907	−477	196
Total Nonmetro	1,824	−3,159	−1,033	−297	−2,665
1975–1980					
Metro in Region Indicated with:					
Metro in other regions	−14,034	−10,276	13,638	10,672	0
Nonmetro in other regions	−1,978	−1,912	2,088	1,266	−536
Nonmetro in same region	−2,504	−2,162	−2,214	−2,954	−9,834
Total Metro	−18,516	−14,350	13,512	8,984	−10,370
Nonmetro in Region Indicated with:					
Nonmetro in other regions	−522	−740	866	396	0
Metro in other regions	−1,718	−1,680	3,112	822	536
Metro in same region	2,504	2,162	2,214	2,954	9,834
Total Nonmetro	264	−258	6,192	4,172	10,370

3

SMALL TOWN GROWTH
AND POPULATION DISPERSAL

FOR MANY DECADES urban growth in the United States has been accompanied by the spread of population settlement. In his international study of the growth of cities in the nineteenth century, Weber noted this movement in the United States and other countries.[1] With the coming of the automobile population deconcentration around large cities increased in relative importance as settlements spread widely into formerly rural areas. The prevalence of this growth led to the adoption of the metropolitan area as a unit of demographic and economic analysis beginning in 1950, as discussed in Chapters 1 and 2. By means of this concept one may generalize that at least until 1970, the settlement process of the nation can be succinctly described as one of population concentration into metropolitan areas and deconcentration within these areas.

The long-term data series in Chapter 2 revealed an ever-increasing relative concentration in urban and metropolitan areas. The population displaced by the mechanization of agriculture and the excess fertility in rural areas, as well as the expansion of urban economic opportunities, contributed significantly to the rapid growth of cities and towns. Major metropolitan cities not only acted as magnets for the indigenous popu-

---

[1]Weber (1895).

This chapter was written by Glenn V. Fuguitt and Daniel T. Lichter.

lation seeking jobs but also for migrants from abroad. The industrial revolution and the factory mode of production required a large labor pool in a relatively small geographic space. This dense pattern of population settlement and economic activities was beneficial in promoting further economies of scale, contributing to differential growth up the urban size-of-place hierarchy.

As the metropolis grew ever larger in size, however, more efficient modes of short distance transportation including streetcars, buses, and automobiles came into widespread use, allowing workers to increase the separation of places of work from places of residence. More recently there has been a further extended growth at the peripheries of large cities fueled by the deconcentration of economic activities (Kasarda, 1980). New industrial plants and even financial institutions and corporate headquarters are often attracted to peripheral settings providing more space, cheaper land, and greater access to automobile and air travel facilities. This was accompanied by the decentralization of retail trade and personal services to be more accessible to consumers in the rapidly growing periphery.

Deconcentration within the metropolitan region was characterized by the emergence and rapid growth of many smaller towns and cities under the umbrella of the metropolitan center. At the same time the growth of many of the older larger metropolitan cities has waned as net outmigration was further compounded by low natural increase, brought about by the era of low fertility in the 1970s. There has been some resurgence of migratory growth since 1980, although much of the renewed metropolitan growth has been found outside places in unincorporated territory. A part of this is thickly settled at the peripheries of major cities and is a major element in the revised urban definition of 1950 (see Chapter 2), but this nonplace population is also scattered widely with a rural–urban fringe of mixed land use found around all major cities.

Population patterns within nonmetropolitan areas have also gone through a number of recent changes. Historically, differential growth has occurred in larger nonmetropolitan cities, many of which "grew up" to be reclassified along with their counties as metropolitan. As with the metropolitan sector, nonmetropolitan urban growth was fueled by rural to urban migration as farm workers were displaced by mechanization and consolidation of agricultural production. Consequently rural open-country areas tended to grow much more slowly, and many sections experienced absolute population declines. Such changes generated considerable concern about the "dying" rural farming community that depended on agriculture for its economic livelihood. The actual situation, however, is quite diverse. In general, small towns in nonmetropolitan America serve as employment centers and provide goods and services for vast areas. They contain almost one-half of the population living outside metropolitan areas and include places varying in size from fewer than 100 up to 50,000 people.

For at least 100 years there has been considerable concern about the fate of the declining village or small town bypassed by trade routes or industry. In terms of their primary function of providing trade and services, the negative effect of a declining clientele was compounded by increased tendencies of remaining residents to turn to nearby larger cities and suburban shopping centers for their needs, to take advantage of wider selections and often lower prices. To some extent the widespread belief that smaller towns are dying is based on impressions gained from their business trends. Johansen and Fuguitt (1984) have shown that for 1950–1970 nonmetropolitan villages of fewer than 2,500 people had an average decline of nearly one-third in the number of consumer business establishments.[2] Such losses have a visible impact on the physical fabric of towns, yet most of the same places actually increased in population. Thus trends in the residential functions of many small nonmetropolitan towns often have taken a course contrary to their business functions. Business decline does not preclude population growth in an era when there are more retired people and greater propensity to live in one place and work or shop in another.

Much of the concern about village and rural decline was laid to rest at least for a time by reports in the 1970s that nonmetropolitan areas were growing more rapidly than metropolitan areas and for the first time were experiencing net migration gains at the expense of metropolitan areas. As indicated in Chapter 2, further work showed that the new nonmetropolitan growth was widespread, and not just an extension of peripheral metropolitan growth or part of the establishment of new metropolitan areas. Of equal importance, and the topic of the present chapter, was the finding that within nonmetroplitan areas the growth was not primarily nodal in character, so that the population outside of and even remote from cities tended to grow more rapidly than the cities themselves.[3] Thus the 1970s were characterized not only by redistribution toward nonmetropolitan areas but also by deconcentration down the urban hierarchy within the nonmetropolitan sector.

In the early 1980s there was once more a turndown in nonmetropolitan growth and a renewal of concern about small towns, particularly those in areas economically dependent upon agriculture. So the question is raised whether the reversal of the turnaround led to a shift back to

---

[2]Johansen and Fuguitt (1984).

[3]Works include J. Long (1981); Fuguitt, Lichter, and Beale (1981); Lichter and Fuguitt (1982); and L. Long and DeAre (1982).

population concentration within nonmetropolitan areas. Using 1984 population estimates for incorporated cities we show that overall these places are not growing as rapidly as in the 1970s but that deconcentration within the nonmetropolitan sector continues.

In this chapter we consider the changing distribution of incorporated places by size and the growth of places contrasted with the population outside places over the 1960–1980 period. Metropolitan–nonmetropolitan comparisons are made throughout, and we have extended the analysis by giving special attention to the growth and decline of small nonmetropolitan towns. Population change for such places is considered, perhaps too uncritically, to be an important indicator of community well-being and vitality. We have compared the distributions of places by their growth and decline for the three time periods, and have considered how these patterns have varied by type of community and how they relate to changes in the urban-size hierarchy.

Using 1984 population estimates, it is also possible to contrast the growth of cities over 2,500 with the remainder of the population for 1980–1984. By so doing, our time series covers the period before, during, and after the nonmetropolitan turnaround of the 1970s. In this analysis we differentiated types of nonmetropolitan counties by level of urbanization and region of the country for 1960–1970, 1970–1980, and 1980–1984. Next, counties as units of analysis are classed by type of concentration or deconcentration for each of the three time periods to assess the spread across the nation of deconcentration tendencies at the local level. This extension of a more deconcentrated local settlement pattern from metropolitan to nonmetropolitan areas has important community and regional implications, and is part of the backdrop for interpreting the social and economic characteristics considered in the remainder of the book.

Procedures

The basic data for this chapter are the populations of incorporated places and counties found in the censuses of 1960, 1970, and 1980 along with estimates prepared by the Bureau of the Census for 1984, published in their *Current Population Report* series.[4] Counties have been designated as metropolitan or nonmetropolitan in two ways across the time series. For the successive comparisons of 1960, 1970, and 1980 (Tables

[4]U.S. Bureau of the Census (1985, 1986). Because of questions concerning the quality of population estimates for very small places, the 1984 estimates for incorporated centers having less than 2,500 people are not considered here.

3.1–3.4), the metropolitan designation is first shown as of the year in question and then by the designation for 1980. For the remainder of the chapter the emphasis is on growth across successive time intervals, and the designation generally is as of the beginning of each time, although the first two change tables (Tables 3.5–3.6) also include a comparison of rates of change using a constant 1980 metropolitan–nonmetropolitan county designation. As discussed in Chapter 2, we believe that the initial designation is preferable in comparing growth across successive time intervals. Given the continuous transfer of counties from nonmetropolitan to metropolitan status, this approach should yield a more accurate portrayal of the situation prevailing at each time. There is some interest, however, in tracing changes for the contemporary nonmetropolitan territory back in time, hence selected results using the constant 1980 county designation also are given.

With either approach to metropolitan county designation, incorporated places are classed by size as of the year indicated or where change over time is measured, by the initial year for each time interval. Since in part of the analysis we make comparisons among two ten-year and one four-year time intervals, annualized population growth rates have been used in all population change comparisons.[5]

Comparing the population in incorporated places having more than 2,500 people with the remainder is essentially the same as a rural–urban comparison under the previous urban definition employed by the Bureau of the Census prior to 1950. With the definition used since then, however, much territory outside such cities also is counted as urban, particularly in metropolitan areas. The percentage of the urban population (current definition) that lived in incorporated places having more than 2,500 people was 82 in 1960 and dropped to 76 in 1980. Conversely, only a little more than one-half of the people not living in incorporated cities were rural in 1960, and about four out of ten were rural in 1980. The fit is much better in nonmetropolitan areas, where the percentage of the urban population living in incorporated places greater than 2,500 ranges from 93 to 89 between 1960 and 1980, and the percentage of the population not living in such incorporated places that is classed as rural by the census ranges from 96 to 93. In other words, our distinction between those living inside and outside incorporated places over 2,500 in size

---

[5]The formula is:

$$\text{Rate of population growth} = \frac{P2 - P1}{K(1/2)(P2 + P1)}(100)$$

where $P1$ and $P2$ are the population of a unit at the beginning and the end of the period, and K is the length of the time interval, either 10 or 4-1/4 (Shryock and Siegel and Associates, 1971:378-80). One-fourth is added to the latter interval because the 1984 estimates are as of July 1 and the census dates are April 1.

comes reasonably close to the current rural–urban distinction for non-metropolitan areas but not for metropolitan areas (see Appendix Table 3.1). Nevertheless, in both types of areas, by comparing changes in the urban place population with the remainder we are considering evidence of population concentration in cities or a tendency for dispersion from them.

In both metropolitan and nonmetropolitan areas the population not living in an incorporated place includes (1) the densely settled fringe around cities (whether captured by the urbanized area definition or that around smaller places); (2) residents of unincorporated places of any size; and (3) the open country consisting of population dispersed or in linear or other patterns not usually identified as villagelike or nodal. In addition to these three elements, the population outside cities (i.e., not living in places of 2,500 and more) includes those villages that are incorporated and have less than 2,500 people. In 1980 incorporated villages formed about 18 percent of the nonmetropolitan population outside cities of 2,500 and if as much as an equal population were found in unincorporated places, villages would be 36 percent of the total outside cities. Unfortunately, the population residing in the fringe around nonmetropolitan cities, or that in the open country balance may not be generally distinguished since the thickly settled territory around cities that does not total at least 50,000 population is not delimited in census reports. Less than 1 percent of the nonmetropolitan population living outside places of greater than 2,500 is found in officially designated urban fringes in 1980. (The comparable figure for metropolitan areas is 23 percent). The important point here is not to consider the other population or the population outside cities simply as rural "open country," even in nonmetropolitan areas.

In calculating growth rates places are classed by size at the beginning of each time interval. Consequently, the population outside cities may include places which are under 2,500 at the beginning of this period but over 2,500 by the end, and the population considered in places over 2,500 may include cities that have declined to under 2,500 by the end of the period. By following the same places over time, however, we avoid the problem of including growth or decline due to the reclassification of places. Using the initial metropolitan designation, about one-third of the growth classed as outside cities for 1960–1970 was actually in places that were over 2,500 by 1970, in both metropolitan and nonmetropolitan areas, due to the establishment of new incorporated centers and the growth of places across the 2,500 threshold. This tendency was diminished in 1970–1980, when corresponding percentages were 22 for metropolitan and 11 for nonmetropolitan areas.

Although county areas remain constant over time in these comparisons the place areas do not, since much of the population growth of cities is associated with the annexation of new territory. This variable we cannot control over the time periods examined. If growth is accompanied by political annexation during an interval it represents city growth by our analysis. On the other hand, growth in any peripheral area that is not annexed is part of the growth in the other population. An earlier study showed that annexation is the most common way cities grow in both metropolitan and nonmetropolitan areas outside of the northeastern United States.[6] Part of the greater difference between nonplace and place growth in the Northeast is no doubt due to the fact that annexation is extremely difficult there.

Yet if we had data to adjust for annexation there would be ambiguity in interpreting the results. Most growth after all must occur at the outer edges of places so there is a question about when this peripheral growth is extraordinary. The answer would appear to lie in the extent to which growth outside places is not restricted to the thickly settled areas around these places. By failing to adjust for annexation, at least a part of this thickly settled growth is excluded from the other population. As we shall see, the recent upturn in nonmetropolitan growth outside cities is not explained entirely by city fringe development, since much is in counties that have no cities. Also in many parts of the country field studies have pointed to the dispersed nature of much of the new nonmetropolitan settlement.[7]

The results reveal remarkable recent changes in the growth patterns and the distribution of population both outside and inside incorporated places of different sizes. The evidence of a shift toward deconcentration even in remote rural areas, although lacking in the rigor we would like, nevertheless is based on conventional procedures and is consistent with other evidence of recent trends in population distribution. The findings based on the data and analytical tools at our disposal hardly appear to be artifactual or entirely an extension of conventional urban growth.

The Distribution of Places and Population

The total number of incorporated places in the United States increased modestly by about 4 percent in each decade from 1960 to 1980. In 1980 there were approximately 19,000 places, 53 percent of which were classified as metropolitan. The number classed as metropolitan in previous years, however, depends upon the date of designation. In the

[6]Klaff and Fuguitt (1978).
[7]Appalachian Regional Commission (1980); Voss and Fuguitt (1979); Hart (1984).

first three columns of Table 3.1 metropolitan–nonmetropolitan status is as reported in the census for each time. This shows that the number of metropolitan places increased from 4,000 to 7,000, or almost 75 percent, whereas the number of nonmetropolitan places declined more than 10 percent. This shift, however, was almost entirely due to the reclassification of places from nonmetropolitan to metropolitan. The three right-hand columns of the table show that when using a constant 1980 metropolitan designation the number of metropolitan places grew about 11 percent and the number of nonmetropolitan places grew at about 7 percent. These increases are due to the addition of newly incorporated centers net of the small number of losses through disincorporation, consolidation, or failure to be reported separately for other reasons.

An increase in the number of places was found for every metropolitan size category and a decline for every size category of nonmetropol-

TABLE 3.1
Number of Incorporated Places by Size, 1960–1980

Size of Place and Metro Status	Current Metropolitan[a]			1980 Metropolitan		
	1960	1970	1980	1960	1970	1980
Metropolitan						
250,000+	50	55	55	50	55	55
50,000–249,999	259	327	363	259	327	363
25,000–49,999	198	284	415	290	361	415
10,000–24,999	456	627	803	591	710	803
2,500–9,999	1,063	1,366	1,840	1,500	1,680	1,840
1,000–2,499	822	991	1,376	1,334	1,337	1,376
500–999	524	705	966	963	984	966
LT 500	662	782	1,189	1,312	1,190	1,189
Total Metro	4,034	5,137	7,007	6,299	6,644	7,007
Nonmetropolitan						
25,000+	167	170	113	75	93	113
10,000–24,999	515	499	453	380	416	453
2,500–9,999	1,968	1,930	1,746	1,531	1,616	1,746
1,000–2,499	2,666	2,552	2,392	2,154	2,206	2,392
500–999	2,685	2,564	2,417	2,246	2,285	2,417
LT 500	5,554	5,456	4,965	4,904	5,048	4,965
Total Nonmetro	13,555	13,171	12,086	11,290	11,664	12,086
Total United States	17,589	18,308	19,093	17,589	18,308	19,093

[a]Metropolitan designation current at the time of each census.

itan places using the metropolitan designation current at each time. Using the fixed 1980 definition, however, all size categories grew except for the two less than 1,000 categories for the metropolitan population. In general, the increase in numbers is greater for larger than for smaller places, the only exception being for metropolitan places over 250,000. This largest group gained only 10 percent in number, less than the growth for all metropolitan places as classed in 1980. In contrast, the largest nonmetropolitan size category, for places 25,000 and over, increased 51 percent in number over the 20-year period, whereas all nonmetropolitan places grew only 7 percent in number. This greater growth in the larger places is due to a shift of places from smaller to larger size categories. Although some places move in the opposite direction, the prevailing tendency is for growth and in the process movement from one size category to a larger one.

The number of people (in thousands) living in incorporated places classed by size is shown in Table 3.2 for each of the time periods, again both by current and by constant 1980 metropolitan–nonmetropolitan designations. In addition, the population not living in any incorporated place is shown, so that the total for each column in the table is the entire United States population at that date. There is a consistent increase in population numbers in each size category for metropolitan and decline for nonmetropolitan using the metropolitan designation current at each time. On the other hand, all population size groups increased in number of people except for those under 500 using the constant 1980 designation. This is generally consistent with the trends in the number of places in Table 3.1. The population outside places also increased considerably over this interval. Using the 1980 definition across the 20-year span, the metropolitan other population increased from 38 to 56 million and the nonmetropolitan other population from 25 to 30 million. As was true for places, however, the nonmetropolitan other population declined when using the metropolitan designation current at each time, due to the substantial number of counties transferred from nonmetropolitan to metropolitan status between 1960 and 1980.

The numbers in Table 3.2 show clearly that we are still a society dominated by large cities. The population residing in metropolitan places over 250,000 was 39 million in 1960, increased to almost 42 million in 1970, and declined to 40 million in 1980. Although almost stationary in size, this largest size-of-place category included the greatest share of the United States population at each census date considered.

By combining the information in Tables 3.1 and 3.2 one can calculate the mean place size for each group. Using the metropolitan designation current at each time, the metropolitan mean place size declined

TABLE 3.2

Population by Size of Place, 1960–1980 (in thousands)

Size of Place and Metro Status	Current Metropolitan[a]			1980 Metropolitan		
	1960	1970	1980	1960	1970	1980
Metropolitan						
250,000+	39,066	41,868	40,223	39,066	41,868	40,223
50,000–249,999	23,873	29,961	33,817	23,872	29,961	33,817
25,000–49,999	6,860	9,840	14,706	10,237	12,686	14,706
10,000–24,999	7,110	9,952	12,826	9,180	11,244	12,826
2,500–9,999	5,586	7,063	9,560	7,770	8,706	9,560
1,000–2,499	1,349	1,648	2,249	2,143	2,186	2,249
500–999	376	515	704	696	718	704
LT 500	188	225	332	373	337	332
All Places	84,408	101,072	114,417	93,337	107,706	114,417
Other Population	29,773	39,688	56,076	38,732	46,878	56,076
Total Metro	114,181	140,760	170,493	132,069	154,584	170,493
Nonmetropolitan						
25,000+	5,836	5,867	3,734	2,459	3,022	3,734
10,000–24,999	7,845	7,576	6,873	5,776	6,284	6,873
2,500–9,999	9,611	9,438	8,461	7,428	7,795	8,461
1,000–2,499	4,179	4,012	3,791	3,385	3,474	3,791
500–999	1,924	1,837	1,731	1,604	1,632	1,731
LT 500	1,455	1,374	1,240	1,270	1,262	1,240
All Places	30,851	30,104	25,829	21,922	23,469	25,829
Other Population	34,295	32,438	30,224	25,336	25,249	30,224
Total Nonmetro	65,146	62,542	56,053	47,258	48,718	56,053
Total United States	179,327	203,302	226,546	179,327	203,302	226,546

[a]Metropolitan designation current at the time of each census.

from 28,000 to 24,000, and the nonmetropolitan mean place size declined from 4,800 to 4,600. Both trends appear to be due, however, to the transfer of places from nonmetropolitan to metropolitan status over the 20-year period, with those transferring tending to be among the larger of the nonmetropolitan but among the smaller of the metropolitan centers they joined. With the constant 1980 definition, both metropolitan and nonmetropolitan mean place size increased over the 20-year period. Although there has been a recent increase in the number and proportion of both metropolitan and nonmetropolitan people living outside urban places, there has also been an increase in the overall mean size of cities for both residence categories using the constant 1980 metropolitan designation. Deconcentration is indicated, however, by the decline in the mean size of incorporated places having populations of 250,000 or more for both current and constant designations, from 781,000 to 731,000.

Perhaps the easiest way to assess the changing geographic distribution of population is to calculate the relative share of the nation's population in each size-of-place category. In Table 3.3, observe that the largest percentage of population resides in metropolitan areas, having increased from 63.7 to 69.2 to 75.3 over the 20-year period using the metropolitan designation of each census. With the constant 1980 metropolitan designation of counties, the proportion metropolitan increased

TABLE 3.3

Percentage Distribution of Population by Size of Place, 1960–1980

Size of Place and Metro Status	Current Metropolitan[a]			1980 Metropolitan		
	1960	1970	1980	1960	1970	1980
Metropolitan						
250,000+	21.8	20.6	17.8	21.8	20.6	17.8
50,000–249,999	13.3	14.7	14.9	13.3	14.7	14.9
25,000–49,999	3.8	4.8	6.5	5.7	6.2	6.5
10,000–24,999	4.0	4.9	5.7	5.1	5.5	5.7
2,500–9,999	3.1	3.5	4.2	4.3	4.3	4.2
1,000–2,499	0.8	0.8	1.0	1.2	1.1	1.0
500–999	0.2	0.3	0.3	0.4	0.4	0.3
LT 500	0.1	0.1	0.1	0.2	0.2	0.1
All Places	47.1	49.7	50.5	52.0	53.0	51.0
Other Population	16.6	19.5	24.8	21.6	23.1	24.8
Total Metro	63.7	69.2	75.3	73.6	76.1	75.3
Nonmetropolitan						
25,000+	3.3	2.9	1.6	1.4	1.5	1.6
10,000–24,999	4.4	3.7	3.0	3.2	3.1	3.0
2,500–9,999	5.3	4.6	3.7	4.2	3.8	3.7
1,000–2,499	2.3	2.0	1.7	1.9	1.7	1.7
500–999	1.1	0.9	0.8	0.9	0.8	0.8
LT 500	0.8	0.7	0.5	0.7	0.6	0.5
All Places	17.2	14.8	11.4	12.3	11.5	11.4
Other Population	19.1	16.0	13.3	14.1	12.4	13.3
Total Nonmetro	36.3	30.8	24.7	26.4	23.9	24.7
Total United States	100.0	100.0	100.0	100.0	100.0	100.0

[a]Metropolitan designation current at the time of each census.

from 73 to 76 between 1960 and 1970, and then fell back to 75 in 1980. The latter decline was the result of the "turnaround" in growth rates between metropolitan and nonmetropolitan areas in the 1970–1980 period. By adding percentages one can also show that the majority of the population (about 60 percent) resides in incorporated places of over 2,500 in each distribution. Although the percentage of the population residing in the very largest places over 250,000 in size has declined over time it is obvious that recent trends have not dramatically altered the size-of-place distribution of population in the United States.

The results in Table 3.3, however, do provide some revealing indicators of demographic change. Using the metropolitan designation current at each time, which allows places to shift from nonmetropolitan to metropolitan status over a decade, there was a decline in the share of residents in the largest metropolitan size group, a gain in the proportion in other size groups over 2,500, and stability in proportion in smaller place size groups. The largest percentage point change in the table, however, is the increase in the proportion in the "other population" living outside incorporated centers. On the nonmetropolitan side, the proportion living in all place sizes and in the other population category declined between 1960 and 1980, as the total population residing in nonmetropolitan areas dropped from 36 to 25 percent. Yet with a constant 1980 definition, the proportion living in nonmetropolitan cities and villages changed little, and the proportion in the other population dropped between 1960 and 1970 and rose again between 1970 and 1980.

These deconcentrating tendencies are seen more clearly in Table 3.4, which gives the relative distribution of population within metropolitan and nonmetropolitan areas. Within metropolitan areas, large cities are strongly declining in relative importance, middle-sized cities are gaining, and the other population is showing the largest increase in proportionate share. Villages under 2,500 are a very small part of the total throughout. Within nonmetropolitan areas, places over 25,000 gained in their proportionate share between 1960 and 1970, but over 1970–1980 they declined using the current designation and gained using the constant 1980 designation. The decline using the current designation is no doubt because many rapidly growing larger places that were nonmetropolitan in 1970 had become metropolitan by 1980. With both designations, however, the proportion of people residing in all nonmetropolitan places increased and the proportion outside places declined over the 1960–1970 decade, but the reverse was true in the 1970–1980 decade. This is a clear indication that the nonmetropolitan turnaround was accompanied by a shift to deconcentrated settlement in nonmetropolitan areas, a process that was already established and prevailed through the 20-year period for metropolitan areas.

TABLE 3.4

Percentage Distribution of Population by Size of Place, Within Metropolitan and Nonmetropolitan Areas, 1960–1980

Size of Place and Metro Status	Current Metropolitan[a]			1980 Metropolitan		
	1960	1970	1980	1960	1970	1980
Metropolitan						
250,000+	34.2	29.7	23.7	29.6	27.1	23.7
50,000–249,999	20.9	21.3	19.8	18.1	19.4	19.8
25,000–49,999	6.0	7.0	8.6	7.8	8.2	8.6
10,000–24,999	6.2	7.1	7.5	6.9	7.3	7.5
2,500–9,999	4.9	5.0	5.6	5.9	5.6	5.6
1,000–2,499	1.2	1.2	1.3	1.6	1.4	1.3
500–999	0.3	0.3	0.4	0.5	0.5	0.4
LT 500	0.2	0.2	0.2	0.3	0.2	0.2
All Places	73.9	71.8	67.1	70.7	69.7	67.1
Other Population	26.1	28.2	32.9	29.3	30.3	32.9
Total Metro	100.0	100.0	100.0	100.0	100.0	100.0
Nonmetropolitan						
25,000+	9.0	9.4	6.7	5.2	6.2	6.7
10,000–24,999	12.0	12.1	12.3	12.2	12.9	12.3
2,500–9,999	14.8	15.1	15.1	15.7	16.0	15.1
1,000–2,499	6.4	6.4	6.8	7.2	7.1	6.8
500–999	3.0	2.9	3.1	3.4	3.4	3.1
LT 500	2.2	2.2	2.2	2.7	2.6	2.2
All Places	47.4	48.1	46.1	46.4	48.2	46.1
Other Population	52.6	51.9	53.8	53.6	51.8	53.8
Total Nonmetro	100.0	100.0	100.0	100.0	100.0	100.0

[a]Metropolitan designation current at the time of each census.

Differential Growth by Size of Place

These shifts in population distribution are based on differentials in growth across the various size-of-place categories. In Table 3.5 we present annualized growth rates by metropolitan and nonmetropolitan size-of-place groups for the 1960s and the 1970s. Places are classified by size at the beginning of each time period and, as before, the metropolitan distinction is made in two ways. In the first two columns places are metropolitan or nonmetropolitan according to their status at the beginning of each time, and in the second two columns they are listed according to their status in 1980.

TABLE 3.5

Annualized Population Change per 100 by Initial Size of Place, 1960–1980

Initial Size of Place and Metro Status	Initial Metropolitan[a]		1980 Metropolitan	
	1960–1970	1970–1980	1960–1970	1970–1980
Metropolitan				
250,000+	.22	−.45	.22	−.45
50,000–249,999	1.19	.54	1.19	.54
25,000–49,999	2.06	.53	1.94	.72
10,000–24,999	2.63	1.46	2.43	1.43
2,500–9,999	3.31	2.01	2.96	1.97
1,000–2,499	3.63	2.56	3.11	2.48
500–999	4.22	2.61	3.67	2.57
LT 500	5.20	5.00	3.92	4.27
All Places	1.20	.42	1.26	.49
Other Population	2.30	1.86	2.27	2.01
Total Metro	1.50	.85	1.57	.98
Nonmetropolitan				
25,000+	1.06	.88	.11	.43
10,000–24,999	.95	.76	.64	.64
2,500–9,999	1.04	1.09	.73	.94
1,000–2,499	.94	1.24	.64	1.08
500–999	.94	1.30	.65	1.15
LT 500	.52	1.56	.21	1.47
All Places	.97	1.02	.58	.86
Other Population	.66	2.09	.06	1.88
Total Nonmetro	.81	1.59	.30	1.40
Total United States	1.25	1.08	1.25	1.08

[a]Metropolitan designation of 1960 for 1960–1970 and 1970 for 1970–1980.

With either metropolitan classification the results yield several interesting conclusions. First we note the now familiar metropolitan-to-nonmetropolitan turnaround discussed at length in Chapter 2. The decline in metropolitan and increase in nonmetropolitan annualized rates over the two decades are substantial, so that the overall metropolitan–nonmetropolitan population growth differential is reversed. Using the initial designations, nonmetropolitan areas grew at about one-half the rate of metropolitan in the 1960–1970 period, but they grew at almost twice the rate in 1970–1980. With the 1980 designation the earlier differential is much greater. Nonmetropolitan areas grew only one-fifth as rapidly as metropolitan areas in 1960–1970 but they grew almost one and one-half times as rapidly in 1970–1980.[8]

The 1970s also were a period when, for the first time, metropolitan places larger than 250,000 population were together experiencing absolute population decline. Moreover, only those metropolitan places of less than 25,000 population were experiencing growth rates above the national figure of 1.08. Although the level of metropolitan growth outside places ("other population") was somewhat less in the 1970s, it was exceeded only by the levels for smaller places using either each initial or the 1980 metropolitan designations. The overall differential favoring nonplace growth relative to place growth increased over the two times, with nonplace growth shifting from about twice to more than four times the overall place annualized rate. This intensification of within-metropolitan deconcentration was due in large part to the absolute population declines observed in the very largest metropolitan places.

Within nonmetropolitan areas, size-of-place groups over 500 were growing at about 1 percent a year in 1960–1970 using the initial (1960) metropolitan designation. During the 1960–1970 period places still nonmetropolitan in 1980 were growing more slowly than those nonmetropolitan in 1960, since the latter group included centers that became metropolitan over the subsequent 20 years. This was particularly true for the 25,000-and-over category, since the growth of such places to become the center of an urbanized area having more than 50,000 usually will cause their counties to be reclassified as metropolitan. Note that with either the initial or the 1980 designation villages over 500 in size (but under 2,500 since at that point they are termed cities here) were growing about as rapidly as other nonmetropolitan places. Previous research has shown that serious population decline is typical of only the very smallest incorporated villages.[9] In the 1960–1970 period the population outside incorporated places was gaining substantially less than the incorporated place population. This was particularly true for those counties that remained nonmetropolitan through 1980.

The pattern of nonmetropolitan rates of growth by size of place completely shifted in 1970–1980. For both metropolitan designations there was a highly consistent inverse association between size of place

---

[8]The counties nonmetropolitan in 1980 were the most remote and slowest growing subset of all those classed as nonmetropolitan in 1960, being counties that did not switch to metropolitan status over the succeeding twenty years. In contrast we can expect that many of these will become metropolitan over the next twenty years, as nonmetropolitan growth leads to metropolitan territorial expansion. See the analysis and discussion in Chapter 2.

[9]Fuguitt and Beale (1976); Johansen and Fuguitt (1984).

and growth paralleling that found for metropolitan places over both decades. It was the villages of under 500 in size that grew most rapidly among nonmetropolitan incorporated places, and this rate was exceeded only by the growth of the other population. In the 1970s the nonmetropolitan population outside incorporated places was growing at twice the rate of the incorporated place population. Indeed, nonmetropolitan places as a whole continued to grow more slowly than the total United States population in the 1970s, and with the 1980 metropolitan designation more slowly than the total metropolitan population as well. Regardless of metropolitan designation, it is clear that the metropolitan–nonmetropolitan turnaround was based chiefly on the remarkable surge in growth in largely rural areas outside incorporated places. The urban and nodal growth characteristic of the past in nonmetropolitan areas has been replaced by a more dispersed pattern of settlement.

Although the growth rates just presented illustrate a pattern of deconcentration in both metropolitan and nonmetropolitan areas during the 1970s, metropolitan and place growth may still be contributing larger shares to the absolute amount of population growth. That is, we may have relative deconcentration but absolute concentration. Although the rapidity of growth may have important implications, the changing numbers of people is more significant for many local institutions.[10] What is the spatial distribution of absolute growth in the United States during the 1960–1980 period? This question is addressed by the data presented in Table 3.6.

Despite higher growth rates in nonmetropolitan than in metropolitan areas, metropolitan areas nevertheless contributed more than one half of the absolute United States growth during the 1970s. This is still a significant decline from 1960–1970, when metropolitan areas captured more than three-fourths of the absolute growth. This decline was due in part to the absolute losses of population (1.8 million) in metropolitan places above 250,000 in population.

But perhaps the most interesting insight provided from the data presented in Table 3.6 is that most of the absolute growth in the United States during the 1970s took place outside incorporated places. One-third or more of the growth in both decades was in metropolitan areas outside incorporated places, with a small increase for 1970–1980. The overall importance of the other population in nonmetropolitan areas increased from 10 percent to one-third across the two time periods using the initial metropolitan designation and from about zero to almost one-quarter of the growth using the 1980 metropolitan designation. Altogether, then, metropolitan and nonmetropolitan population growth in

---

[10]Lichter, Fuguitt, and Heaton (1985).

78

TABLE 3.6

Percentage Distribution of Absolute Growth by Initial Size of Place,
1960–1970, 1970–1980

Initial Size of Place and Metro Status	Initial Metropolitan[a]		1980 Metropolitan	
	1960–1970	1970–1980	1960–1970	1970–1980
Metropolitan				
250,000+	3.7	−8.0	3.7	−8.0
50,000–249,999	12.6	7.2	12.6	7.2
25,000–49,999	6.6	2.3	9.2	4.1
10,000–24,999	9.0	6.7	10.6	7.5
2,500–9,999	9.2	6.8	11.3	8.2
1,000–2,499	2.5	2.1	3.3	2.6
500–999	0.8	0.6	1.1	0.9
LT 500	0.5	0.6	0.7	0.8
All Places	44.9	18.5	52.5	23.3
Other Population	32.3	35.0	41.4	45.1
Total Metro	77.2	53.5	93.9	68.4
Nonmetropolitan				
25,000+	2.7	2.3	0.1	0.6
10,000–24,999	3.3	2.6	1.6	1.8
2,500–9,999	4.4	4.7	2.3	3.3
1,000–2,499	1.7	2.3	0.9	1.7
500–999	0.8	1.1	0.5	0.8
LT 500	0.3	1.0	0.1	0.9
All Places	13.2	14.0	5.5	9.1
Other Population	9.6	32.5	0.6	22.5
Total Nonmetro	22.8	46.5	6.1	31.6
Total United States	100.0	100.0	100.0	100.0
(000s)	23,975	23,244	23,975	23,244

[a]Metropolitan designation of 1960 for 1960–1970 and 1970 for 1970–1980.

the territory initially outside of incorporated places was about two-thirds of the total absolute growth in 1970–1980 using either the initial or the 1980 metropolitan designation. Within the nonmetropolitan category, about 70 percent of the absolute growth took place outside incorporated places in this most recent decade. Thus, deconcentration within nonmetropolitan areas is not only apparent in a relative sense based on differential growth rates but in an absolute sense as well.

As we have illustrated, both relative and absolute population deconcentration are characteristic of the 1970s across metropolitan and nonmetropolitan areas. Not only is relative growth more rapid in nonmetropolitan areas and outside incorporated places in the 1970s than in the 1960s but by the 1970s a substantial proportion of the absolute United States growth also was found there. Rural growth is not an artifact of growth rates computed on small population bases.

The Growth and Decline of Nonmetropolitan Cities and Towns

In addition to considering the aggregate growth of groups of cities and towns, it is important to compare growth trends with the place as the unit of analysis. Concern about small towns is usually expressed in terms of what happens to individual places. Even though towns of a given size group may collectively be growing at a moderate rate, some may decline as others grow rapidly. Here the annualized change in population per 100 has been computed for every place over each of the two decades. Comparisons are then made either of the distributions of places by percentage change or of the proportion of places growing among various size and location groupings.

Distributions of places by annualized population change groups are given in Table 3.7 for nonmetropolitan cities and villages grouped by size at the beginning of each decade. The metropolitan–nonmetropolitan designation of 1960 is used for the 1960–1970 period, and the designation of 1970 is used for 1970–1980. During the first time period larger places are more likely to be found in the higher change columns. About one out of four places in the 25,000-and-over category grew more than 2 percent a year, compared with 17 percent of the places less than 500. Conversely, one-third of the places under 500 in 1960 lost population at a rate of 1 percent or more a year during 1960–1970, whereas this was true of only 15 percent of the places 25,000 and over.

This growth tendency is summarized in the last two columns, the first giving the percentage of places growing. There is almost no difference in this measure between different size groups over 1,000 for 1960–1970, with almost two-thirds growing in each group. Only one-half of the places under 500 grew during that period, however. The right-hand column is the percentage of places growing more than the United States as a whole. Such cities and towns experienced a relative concentration of population across the United States settlement structure; that is, the proportion they were of the total population was larger at the end of the decade than at the beginning. Overall, only about one-third of the nonmetropolitan places grew more than 1.25 percent per year, the figure for

TABLE 3.7

Percentage Distribution of Nonmetropolitan Places by Level of Annualized Population Change, 1960–1970, 1970–1980[a]

Initial Size of Place	Rate of Annualized Population Change						Percent Growing	
	Loss			Gain				
	−1.00+	−.99−−.01	.01–.99	1.00–1.99	2.00+	Total	All	GT U.S. Rate
1960–1970								
25,000+	15	18	29	15	23	100	67	37
10,000–24,999	9	27	28	17	19	100	65	41
2,500–9,999	10	23	29	18	20	100	67	40
1,000–2,499	12	24	29	17	18	100	65	36
500–999	16	23	27	17	17	100	61	32
LT 500	32	19	19	13	17	100	49	28
Total	21	22	25	15	17	100	58	34
1970–1980								
25,000+	8	31	27	20	14	100	61	27
10,000–24,999	8	29	33	15	15	100	64	34
2,500–5,999	6	23	34	20	17	100	71	38
1,000–2,499	7	21	30	20	22	100	72	42
500–999	10	21	28	18	22	100	69	40
LT 500	20	17	21	16	26	100	63	41
Total	13	20	26	18	23	100	67	39

[a]Places in counties classed as nonmetropolitan in 1960 for 1960–1970 panel and as of 1970 for 1970–1980 panel.

the United States as a whole. Again, the smallest villages have the lowest percentage in this column, but the highest percentages are for large places less than 25,000 rather than for the largest size group.

As expected, in the 1970–1980 decade the distribution of places by annualized change reflects the generally higher nonmetropolitan growth that prevailed then in comparison with 1960–1970. Fewer places suffered heavy losses and more experienced rapid gains than in the previous decade. The overall proportion of places growing increased from 58 to 67 percent, and with this higher overall growth came a shift in the size–growth relationship. In terms of the percentage of places growing, the relation had become like an inverted U, that is, middle-sized places 1,000 up to 10,000 were the ones most likely to grow. The smallest places were still most likely to have experienced declines of more than 1 percent a year. Yet at the other extreme, the smallest places also were most likely to have experienced rapid growth exceeding 2 percent over 1970–1980. Although the proportion declining rapidly was considerably lower for the smallest places in the most recent decade, there was still a hard core of rapid decliners in this group. The proportion of rapid growers (greater than 2 percent a year), however, increased by half across the two decades. As a result, the population change for these smaller places was more variable in the most recent decade than before.

Recall that Table 3.5 showed that aggregate population change shifted from a more-or-less positive to an inverse association with initial size. The somewhat different results found here illustrate the need to consider both an aggregate and a distributive approach to obtain a more complete picture of place change patterns. Evidently among the smaller places the population increases for those rapidly growing are sufficient to make their aggregate rate highest among the size groups, despite the fact that a higher proportion also was declining more rapidly than was true for other size groups.

The proportion of places growing more rapidly than the United States as a whole is little different for the two decades. One-third of the nonmetropolitan incorporated places were growing faster than the United States as a whole (1.25 percent a year) in 1960–1970, and this was true of four out of ten places growing faster than 1.08 during 1970–1980. This proportion is somewhat lower for places in groups above 2,500 and higher for smaller places in the most recent decade, when the overall pattern was inverse by size. In 1960–1970 there was a positive association between size and this percentage so that the smallest proportions were for places under 1,000 in 1960–1970. Thus a higher proportion of villages than cities in nonmetropolitan America increased their proportionate share of the United States population during the turnaround decade.

The relation between size of place and growth is explored further in Figure 3.1. Here the percentage of places growing is the summary measure, and incorporated places are distinguished by whether or not they are in counties adjacent to a metropolitan center at the beginning of the decade, as well as by region of the country. To provide more background on recent trends we have also included results for 1950–1960 in this figure. In the 1950s there was a comparatively strong positive association between growth and initial size of place in nonadjacent counties. In contrast, except for the two smaller size groups, there was virtually no association in adjacent counties during the period. In 1960–1970 larger nonadjacent places were considerably less likely to be growing than in the 1950s, so that relationship had become almost nonexistent there as well. In the turnaround decade (1970–1980) all the nonadjacent place-size groups had a higher proportion growing than in 1960–1970, but increases were greater for smaller sized centers. Adjacent places followed a similar transition, except that by 1970–1980 those greater than 10,000 in size were less likely to grow than in either previous decade, so that the beginning of an inverse association is evident. A comparison of the adjacent and nonadjacent graphs shows that the greater likelihood of growth for adjacent than nonadjacent places, particularly those of smaller size, that was evident in the 1950s was less so in the 1960s and virtually disappeared in the 1970s.

The major regional differences are between the Northeast and the other regions. Already in 1950–1960 the Northeast showed the pattern closely resembling the US as a whole for 1970–1980, with little difference by metropolitan adjacency. For 1960–1970 the likelihood of growth declined, and the pattern shifted further to an inverse relation, so that the larger size groups were less likely to grow than the smaller ones. In the turnaround decade all size groups but two were less likely to grow than previously, indicating that in the Northeast the resurgence of growth was almost entirely outside places. In nonadjacent counties there was some evidence of improvement for larger places and less of an inverse relation there than in 1960–1970.

The other three regions all began the three-decade series with at least as strong a positive association between size and growth as the United States as a whole. By 1970–1980 all these had disappeared except in the West where this pattern was still evident particularly for places in adjacent counties. The Midwest appeared to be moving closer to the Northeast than the other regions, with the beginnings of an inverse distribution in adjacent counties and a suggestion of an inverted-U distribution in nonadjacent counties by 1970–1980.

To sum up the size–growth analysis, first recall that a positive association indicates population concentration into larger places. It is the

FIGURE 3.1

Percentage of Nonmetropolitan Places Growing by Size of Place (log scale), Metropolitan Adjacency, and Region, 1950–1960, 1960–1970, 1970–1980

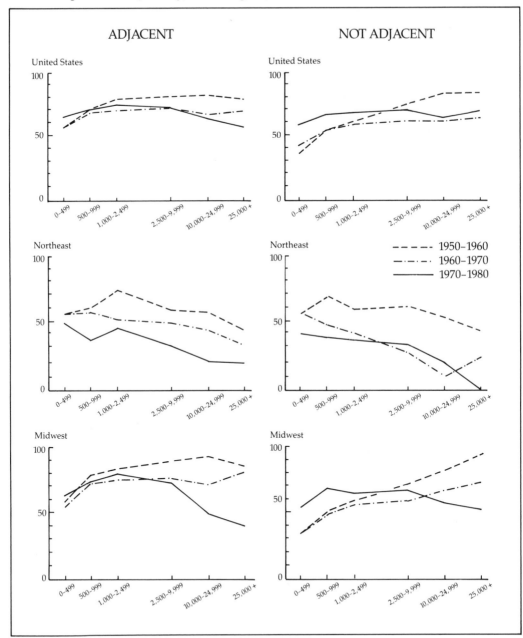

FIGURE 3.1 *(continued)*

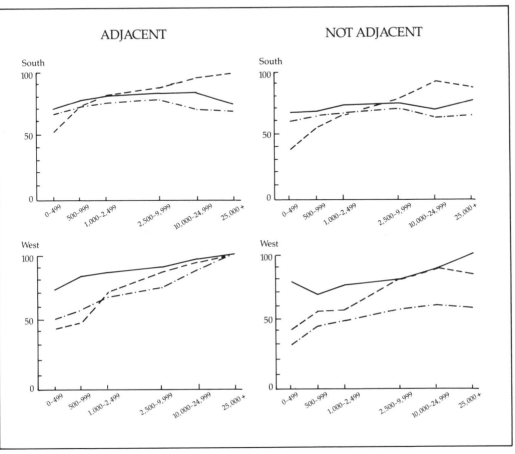

kind of association one would expect under the older regime of population redistribution, under which people were leaving open-country areas, and smaller towns, which served largely as trade centers for this population, also tended to grow slowly or lose residents because of a decline in clientele and increased competition from larger places. In the overall transition of nonmetropolitan population change, which culminated in the turnaround decade, these positive associations have generally shifted to ones that are almost zero or even inverse, as is consistent with a uniform or deconcentrating pattern of change. The exception is the West. Less deconcentration into smaller places there might be due in part to lower densities and greater distances between places. The location of places could therefore be more consistent with a classic "central place hierarchy" of centers according to the number and variety of services offered. Figure 3.2, discussed in the next section, also shows that although the West had more rapid nonmetropolitan growth outside than inside places of 2,500 and over in 1970–1980, such places were growing more rapidly there than in any other region.

In a number of instances (Chapter 2) the Northeast stood out as the vanguard of urbanization and industrialization trends. The patterns of growth by size of place are no exception, with this region generally two decades ahead of the others in an indication of deconcentration among places. The reversal of the turnaround in the early 1980s, however, lends caution to anyone wishing to jump to the conclusion that in two decades the rest of the country will show a deconcentration pattern like that for 1970–1980 in the Northeast. The findings discussed in the following section show a shift back in the direction of concentration into larger places, during the early 1980s, but not to the extent that it was true in the 1950s or even the 1960s.

Beyond the Turnaround: Trends Through 1984

After 1980, the nonmetropolitan turnaround halted, and once more metropolitan areas are growing more rapidly than nonmetropolitan areas. To extend the analysis in Chapter 2, some information about the place-nonplace dimensions of this most recent trend may be obtained using 1984 place estimates along with 1984 county population estimates and earlier census data. Because estimates for very small places are assumed to be unreliable, only aggregate totals for groups of cities having more than 2,500 population are considered here. Annualized growth rates were calculated for 1960–1970, 1970–1980, and 1980–1984 for various population groupings of places over 2,500 and outside cities, using the current metropolitan–nonmetropolitan designation.

Metropolitan and nonmetropolitan growth rates between 1960 and 1984 are summarized for the United States and the four census regions in Figure 3.2. Results for the first two decades in the top panel parallel those of Table 3.5. The 1960–1970 growth dominance of the metropolitan smaller city and outside-city population segments made for concentration into metropolitan areas but deconcentration within them. During this period there also was concentration into cities within nonmetropolitan areas. This had changed by the 1970s when the outside-city nonmetropolitan segments were the fastest growing in both metropolitan and nonmetropolitan areas, and large cities had begun to

FIGURE 3.2

Annualized Population Change for Urban Places and Other Territory in Metropolitan and Nonmetropolitan Areas, 1960–1970, 1970–1980, 1980–1984

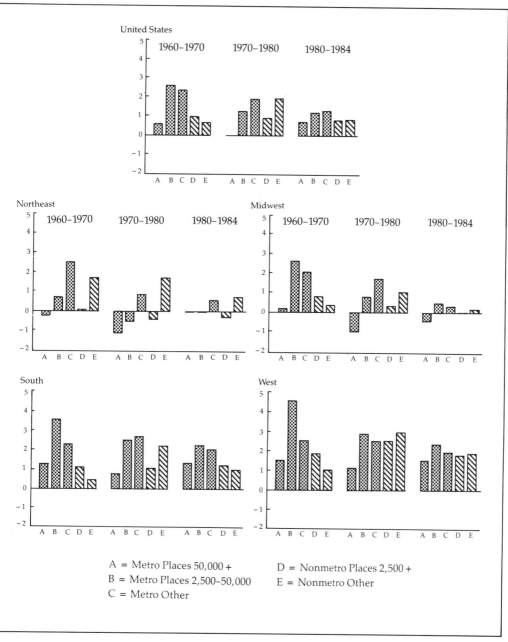

A = Metro Places 50,000 +
B = Metro Places 2,500–50,000
C = Metro Other
D = Nonmetro Places 2,500 +
E = Nonmetro Other

decline absolutely.[11] The early 1980s showed a decline in all growth segments except places over 50,000, which overall had bounced back to grow faster than in the 1960s. The metropolitan population outside cities was no longer growing much faster than the smaller places, and the nonmetropolitan population outside cities was just barely growing faster than the nonmetropolitan population in incorporated places having more than 2,500 population.

There are regional variations in these trends, however. The Northeast in 1960–1970 already was showing the deconcentration pattern not found for the nation until 1970–1980, and the metropolitan and nonmetropolitan outside-city population groupings were the only segments with even a low level of growth after 1980. The three other regions, however, generally followed the United States pattern for the first two time periods.

The major observation to be made from the 1980–1984 regional classification is the sharp decline in rates in the Northeast and Midwest regions, a trend considered also in Chapter 2. In all regions places over 50,000 declined less or grew more than they did in 1970–1980, and indeed in the South and West the growth level was above that for 1960–1970. Except for the Northeast, the most rapidly growing segment was incorporated places less than 50,000 in size. Within nonmetropolitan areas, the slight tendency for deconcentration found for the United States as a whole was a balance of a strong differential in the Northeast, a weak differential continuing in the Midwest and West, and a shift from deconcentration back to a low degree of concentration in the South. For the South this was after the most marked nonmetropolitan shift from a substantial loss outside cities in the 1950s to a gain more rapid than that in cities in the 1970s. Thus overall nonmetropolitan deconcentration, though much reduced and overshadowed by regional shifts away from the North, was still continuing in three out of four United States regions in 1980–1984.

The next issue to be addressed is where nonmetropolitan concentration and deconcentration have been occurring within each broad region. The first specific question is whether deconcentration is found only near metropolitan areas. If this is the case, then deconcentration would be simply extended metropolitan growth. Nonmetropolitan counties are distinguished in Figure 3.3 by whether or not they were physically adjacent to counties that were classed as metropolitan at the beginning of each time period. In the 1960s the United States pattern was one of deconcentration in adjacent counties and concentration in nonadjacent

[11]From Table 3.5 we know that the decline in the population in places over 50,000 is due to the predominant size of the larger places over 250,000. Metropolitan places 50,000 to 250,000 were growing, but not nearly as rapidly as smaller ones.

FIGURE 3.3

Annualized Population Change for Urban Places and Other Territory in Adjacent and Nonadjacent Nonmetropolitan Counties, 1960–1970, 1970–1980, 1980–1984

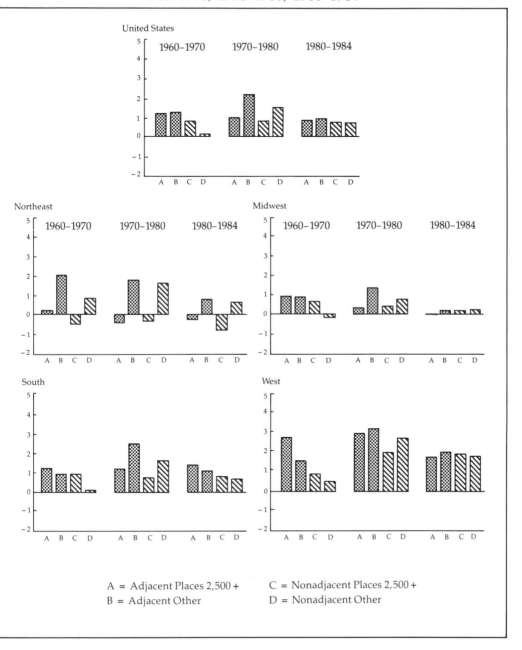

A = Adjacent Places 2,500 +   C = Nonadjacent Places 2,500 +
B = Adjacent Other   D = Nonadjacent Other

counties, strongly suggesting an important suburbanlike growth process. Within regions, however, this particular pattern was found only in the Northeast where nonadjacent counties also showed deconcentration to a high degree. The adjacent city and outside-city segments were almost equal in the Midwest, but there was concentration in the two other regions, and particularly the West, in both adjacent and nonadjacent subareas.

In the 1970s, however, deconcentration occurred uniformly across all regions in both adjacent and nonadjacent counties, a truly remarkable shift, particularly for counties away from metropolitan centers.

For 1980–1984 in the United States as a whole there was very little difference between places over 2,500 and the other population in adjacent areas, and rates were only slightly smaller in nonadjacent areas. Again overall growth levels were much lower in the Northeast and particularly in the Midwest, though in the former region a strong deconcentrating trend still prevailed. In the South there was concentration both adjacent and not adjacent to metropolitan centers, but this region also had the strongest evidence of an adjacency effect favoring growth near metropolitan centers. Nonmetropolitan rates were by far the highest in the West in 1980–1984, ranging upward to 2 percent a year. There was little difference between segments in the graph for this region, but there was some deconcentration in adjacent areas and a smaller differential favoring concentration in nonadjacent areas.

Was the deconcentration in nonadjacent counties in the 1970–1980 period due to the development of what might be termed "incipient metropolitan areas"? That is, is it basically peripheral growth around the larger cities in nonadjacent counties and so a continuation of the previous pattern of metropolitanization? This may be examined by dividing counties not adjacent to metropolitan areas according to the size of the largest place in the county at the beginning of each time period. For each portion of Figure 3.4 the first bar represents the incorporated places over 2,500 in counties having at least one such place over 10,000 in size, and the second bar is the other population in such counties. These counties could become metropolitan through the growth of the largest place or, in the most recent metropolitan definition, the largest place and its environs, to exceed 50,000 (see discussion of metropolitan definitions in Chapter 2). The next two bars are for places over 2,500 and for the other population in counties with largest place between 2,500 and 10,000, and the last bar is for the rate of population change in counties having no place over 2,500.

In 1960–1970 for the United States as a whole there was population concentration into nonmetropolitan counties with larger cities. In such counties, however, the population outside cities was growing as rapidly

FIGURE 3.4

Annualized Population Change for Urban Places and Other Territory in Nonadjacent Nonmetropolitan Counties by Size of Largest Place in County

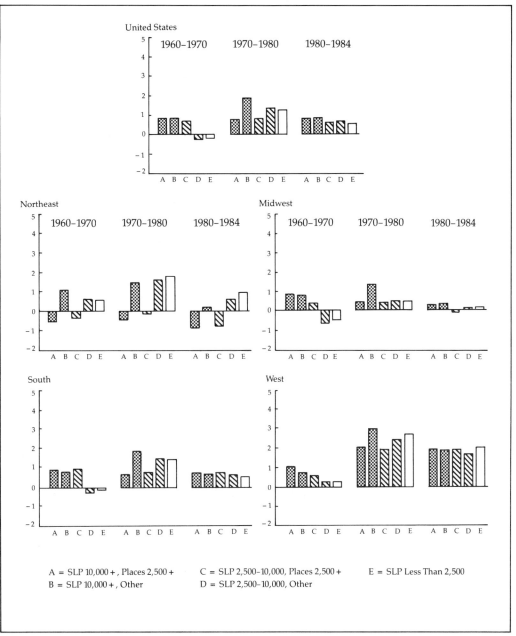

A = SLP 10,000 +, Places 2,500 +   C = SLP 2,500–10,000, Places 2,500 +   E = SLP Less Than 2,500

B = SLP 10,000 +, Other   D = SLP 2,500–10,000, Other

91

as that in places over 2,500 in size. Places over 2,500 in other counties were growing almost as rapidly, but the outside-city population in these counties was declining, as was the population in counties having no cities. As before, the Northeast is quite different, already showing strong deconcentration with absolute decline in both place categories. Recall that incorporation is difficult in the Northeast and annexation by cities unusual. The results for other regions are generally consistent with the United States as a whole.

The shift to deconcentration across all regions during the turn-around decade is dramatic. There was deconcentration both around larger places and around places 2,500 to 10,000, with outside-city rates higher than those for cities. Furthermore, in all regions completely rural nonadjacent counties, the segment presumably most removed from conventional urban influence, were growing more rapidly than either non-adjacent place segment. The rapid growth of completely rural counties is known to be associated with recreation, retirement, and geographic amenities found in many parts of the country. On the other hand, outside the more densely settled Northeast the most rapid growth sector in the 1970s shown here was for the areas outside cities in counties having cities over 10,000 population. Deconcentration around the larger cities, including those away from existing metropolitan areas, is an important component of this deconcentration process.

In the post-1980 period the United States rates were quite uniform across the nonmetropolitan nonadjacent segments. In particular the rate for the other population in counties having large cities once more had dropped to a level equal to that of cities. The other three segments were only slightly lower. Again the Northeast stands out as continuing the deconcentration pattern, with substantial absolute decline for both urban place categories, and the largest growth (though at only about one-half the level of 1970–1980) found for the completely rural counties. All rates were quite low in the Midwest, and the only segments showing even a small amount of growth are those for counties with cities over 10,000, so what little overall nonadjacent growth there is in the Midwest displays a slight concentrating pattern. Growth in the South is higher and more uniform across the segments, and the same is true for the West, where rates are generally twice the size of those in the South.

In summary, within nonadjacent counties the Northeast experienced deconcentration over the entire 24-year period, but other parts of the country underwent a transition from one supporting concentration into "incipient metropolitan area" counties and into places elsewhere, to one with major growth outside urban places in all locations during the 1970s. The 1980s have brought back a more subdued pattern of almost uniform growth across the city and outside-city segments. Consequently, the most recent situation is one of lowered growth, particularly in areas that underwent the most change between the 1960s and the 1970s, which contributed to a more undifferentiated pattern of population change.

Deconcentration Within Nonmetropolitan Counties

To assess more completely the extent of deconcentration in nonmetropolitan America we have extended our analysis to the county level. The aggregate rural and urban population change compared in a preceding section (Figures 3.1–3.3) showed a general shift toward deconcentration with greater growth outside places over 2,500 population. Such aggregate rates give greater weight to counties having larger populations, however, and do not necessarily reveal the "typical" population changes experienced by individual nonmetropolitan counties. Nonmetropolitan areas may be experiencing faster urban than rural growth in the aggregate, but the majority of nonmetropolitan counties could nonetheless be experiencing faster urban growth. If rural and urban growth rates are calculated for each nonmetropolitan county, we can determine the percentage of counties that grew in their rural and urban sectors, and those that deconcentrated by experiencing faster rural than urban growth. This has been done for the three time intervals 1960–1970, 1970–1980, 1980–1984 with urban defined as before as the population in places 2,500 or more at the beginning of each decade. These places are then followed across the time interval to indicate the amount of urban growth or decline. Change in the balance of the county population (i.e., the difference between county and urban place population) is for convenience termed here rural growth or decline.

The percentage of nonmetropolitan counties with total, urban, or rural growth is shown in Table 3.8.[12] Only about one-half of all nonmetropolitan counties grew over 1960–1970. By 1970–1980, eight out of ten counties grew, and two-thirds did so during 1980–1984. Counties considered here to be completely rural (i.e., no place 2,500 or more at the beginning of a decade) showed a similar trend, from less than 40 percent growing in the 1960s to more than 70 and back to 63 percent growing in 1980–1984. Totally rural counties may be compared with the rural parts of urban counties. The fact that more than one-half of the

[12]Of the 2,741 counties nonmetropolitan in 1960, 1,001 had no urban population as measured here. Of the 2,627 in 1970, 920 had no urban population and of the 2,384 nonmetropolitan in 1980, 820 had no urban population. The total number of counties with urban populations by largest place in county is given in Table 3.10.

TABLE 3.8

Percentage of Nonmetropolitan Counties With Urban or Rural Growth by Largest Place in County, 1960–1984[a]

Type of County and Urban, Rural Segment	1960–1970	1970–1980	1980–1984
All Nonmetro Counties	52	82	68
All Rural Counties	38	72	63
All Urban Counties			
Rural part	53	84	72
Urban part	68	73	61
Largest Place 10,000+			
Rural part	69	90	76
Urban part	68	70	66
Other Urban Counties			
Rural part	31	81	70
Urban part	69	75	58

[a]Urban in this table refers to incorporated places having more than 2,500 people at the beginning of a time interval; rural refers to other places and the nonplace population. This classification of places and the largest place and nonmetropolitan designations were as of 1960 for 1960–1970, 1970 for 1970–1980, and 1980 for 1980–1984. Zero change is regarded as growth.

rural parts of urban counties grew over 1960–1970 whereas less than 40 percent of the completely rural counties did so suggests some deconcentration around nonmetropolitan cities in that period. Indeed, fully two-thirds of the rural parts grew in counties having places with 10,000 people or more in 1960, whereas the rural parts of other urban counties were less likely to be growing than totally rural counties.

By 1970–1980, however, more than 80 percent of the rural parts of urban counties were growing and the differential by whether or not there was a major center in the county had almost disappeared. During this decade the proportion of rural parts growing in urban counties was higher than the proportion for the urban parts, and the completely rural counties were about as likely to grow as the urban parts of urban counties. The downturn in the 1980–1984 interval affected all segments of the table, but completely rural counties and the rural parts of other urban counties continued to be well above the 1960–1970 level in likelihood of growth. The rural parts of both types of urban counties, moreover, continued the 1970–1980 pattern of higher growth proportions than corresponding urban segments.

Although the approach is different, the results here closely parallel those previously presented, which compared aggregate growth rates. The turnaround decade was one in which the likelihood of rural growth greatly increased in all three county settings and exceeded corresponding urban segments. In this way the differences by a conventional indicator of concentration related to urban places (size of largest place in the county) almost disappeared. Once again, the 1980–1984 period is revealed as one of retrenchment but not a return to the pre-turnaround 1960–1970 pattern of population concentration.

But what about urban–rural concentration or deconcentration within individual nonmetropolitan counties? Here we restrict attention to counties having cities of 2,500 and over at the beginning of a decade, and show the proportion of counties in which rural growth exceeded urban growth. Because deconcentration has always been considered more characteristic around large cities, the tabulation is shown here separately by whether or not the county includes a place of 10,000 population or more at the beginning of each period, and also by whether or not the county is adjacent to a county classed as metropolitan at the beginning of the decade.

During the 1960–1970 period only about four out of ten nonmetropolitan counties with cities could be classed as deconcentrating (top panel of Table 3.9). This is, however, a percentage larger than that reported for the 1950s, when 22 percent experienced urban–rural deconcentration (Lichter and Fuguitt, 1982). As expected, this percentage was even smaller in less urbanized counties, where only 32 percent had differential rural growth, and larger in counties with cities of 10,000 and over, one-half of which were deconcentrating. Similarly, regardless of size of largest place, counties that were not adjacent to metropolitan counties were considerably less likely to be deconcentrating than adjacent counties. Overall, the 1960–1970 period can be characterized as one of nonmetropolitan population concentration within counties, particularly in more rural and remote settings.

By 1970–1980, however, this pattern had shifted substantially. More than two-thirds of the counties were deconcentrating overall, with six out of ten deconcentrating in counties without large cities and more than three-quarters doing so where large cities were present. The absolute increase in this percentage across the two decades, however, is larger in more rural counties and largest in the nonadjacent counties without a city of 10,000 or more. Since these are the groups of counties that had the lowest proportion deconcentrating, the effect is to move toward a more uniform rate across counties distinguished by nearness to metropolitan areas and local urbanization. It seems remarkable that in the 1970–1980 period more than one-half of the more rural nonadjacent counties experienced faster rural than urban growth.

TABLE 3.9

Percentage of Nonmetropolitan Counties Deconcentrating by Size of Largest Place in County, Adjacency to a Metropolitan Area, and Region, 1960–1984[a]

| | 1960–1970 | | | 1970–1980 | | | 1980–1984 | | |
| | | Largest Place | | | Largest Place | | | Largest Place | |
	Total	10,000	Other	Total	10,000	Other	Total	10,000	Other
United States									
Total	38	52	32	68	79	63	61	63	59
Adjacent	47	59	39	74	84	68	63	64	62
Not adjacent	32	46	26	61	71	57	58	61	57
Northeast									
Adjacent	87	88	86	96	100	89	93	92	94
Not adjacent	92	93	92	100	100	100	100	100	100
Midwest									
Adjacent	47	63	40	72	86	65	62	66	60
Not adjacent	26	40	19	48	63	42	62	68	60
South									
Adjacent	37	52	31	72	80	68	61	59	62
Not adjacent	29	43	22	64	71	62	54	60	52
West									
Adjacent	44	37	51	72	77	67	52	57	47
Not adjacent	43	51	40	75	81	73	51	39	55

[a]Urban in this table refers to incorporated places having more than 2,500 people at the beginning of a time interval; rural refers to other places and the nonplace population. This classification of places, and the largest place, nonmetropolitan, and adjacency designations were as of 1960 for 1960–1970, 1970 for 1970–1980, and 1980 for 1980–1984. A county is deconcentrating if its rural growth exceeds its urban growth, it has rural growth and urban decline, or rural decline less than urban decline. Zero change is regarded as growth.

For 1980–1984 there was a modest decline in the proportion of counties deconcentrating to about 60 percent but also a further convergence in differences by nearness to a metropolitan area and level of local urbanization. That is, most of the shift back to concentration occurred in counties having cities of 10,000 or more, and among the other counties, those not adjacent to metropolitan areas retained the same percentage (57) as in 1970–1980. Across the three time periods between 1960 and 1984 there was overall a 23 point increase in the percent of all nonmetropolitan counties deconcontrating, from 38 to 61. For counties having large cities at the beginning of a time period, however, the percentage point increase was 11, and in other counties with any city it was 27. The latter difference was larger (31) for counties in nonadjacent settings. The increased prevalence of deconcentration was most marked in more rural and remote counties between the 1960s and the 1970s, but the decline in this prevalence between the 1970s and the early 1980s was zero or less there. Consequently, the differences between these four county groups in the likelihood of deconcentration had almost disappeared by 1980–1984.

The remaining panels of Table 3.9 give the results for the four regions of the United States. Almost all of the counties in the Northeast have deconcentrated since 1960, but the proportions were higher in the last two time periods, when in fact 100 percent of the nonadjacent county groups had higher rural than urban growth. In the highly urban and metropolitan Northeast, however, this has included a very small and continuously declining set of counties.

The results for the three other regions were similar to each other and to the United States as a whole, as discussed above. All county groups in all three regions had a higher proportion deconcentrating in 1970–1980 than in 1960–1970, and since this also was true in the Northeast the extreme pervasiveness of this trend is underscored. Similarly, the proportion deconcentrating was less in the 1980s than in the 1970s in all groups outside the Northeast except for those not adjacent to a metropolitan area and located in the Midwest. These proportions, however, still remained above the 1960–1970 period for all groups except two that were in the West.

Type of County Concentration and Deconcentration

The patterns of rural and urban growth may take on a variety of forms. Counties may concentrate by experiencing (1) faster urban than rural growth; (2) urban growth with decline in rural areas; and (3) slower urban decline than rural decline. Conversely, deconcentrating counties undergo either (1) faster rural than urban growth; (2) rural growth and urban decline; or (3) slower rural than urban decline. The distributions of these various combinations of growth have exhibited some rather substantial changes for nonmetropolitan counties over the 24-year period from 1960 to 1984, as is seen by comparing the columns of Table 3.10.

In the 1960s the dominant county pattern was one in which cities were growing and areas outside cities were declining in population. This was particularly true for counties in which there was no larger city. In the 1970s the mode was the first deconcentration category, which included counties with rural growth greater than urban growth. This was true of 45 percent of the counties, the highest percentage in the table. By 1980–1984 this category was still the mode but it stood out less from the others and the percentage had dropped to 28. Even when counties were concentrating after 1970, more than one-half were doing so in conjunction with rural growth. In the 1960s twice as many counties were experiencing urban growth and rural decline as were undergoing urban decline and rural growth, but the situation almost exactly reversed for the next two time periods.

The largest decline in a deconcentration category in the transition from 1970–1980 to 1980–1984 was for rural growth greater than urban growth, the same category that increased the most between 1960–1970 and 1970–1980. Rural growth with urban decline was somewhat less likely to be found in counties having large cities in the later time period, but in both types of county there was a countervailing increase in the percentage of counties having rural decline less than urban decline. Obviously, differential city and noncity growth and decline have undergone a significant change in many parts of nonmetropolitan America, but the deconcentration within counties became much more prevalent in the 1970s and is still widespread.

These results are generally found for each region of the country outside of the Northeast (data not shown). The increase between the early 1980s and the 1970s in the percentage of counties having rural decline less than urban decline was concentrated in the Midwest, however, where the more rural counties had an absolute increase in the percentage deconcentrating for this region. In the most recent time period this was the pattern for about one-third of the deconcentrating counties in the Midwest, whereas this was true for less than 10 percent of the deconcentrating counties in other regions.

The Northeast differed from the others in that almost all of the nonmetropolitan counties were classed as deconcentrating (see Table 3.9). The major deconcentration type for this region, however, was rural

TABLE 3.10

Percentage Distribution of Nonmetropolitan Counties Having Urban Population by Type of Population Concentration/Deconcentration, 1960–1984[a]

| | 1960–1970 | | | 1970–1980 | | | 1980–1984 | | |
| | | Largest Place | | | Largest Place | | | Largest Place | |
	Total	10,000	Other	Total	10,000	Other	Total	10,000	Other
Concentrating Counties									
Urban growth GT rural growth	20	21	19	18	13	21	23	22	23
Urban growth, rural decline	29	20	34	11	7	12	11	11	11
Urban decline LT rural decline	13	7	16	3	1	4	6	4	7
Subtotal	62	48	69	32	21	37	40	37	41
Deconcentrating Counties									
Rural growth GT urban growth	19	21	16	45	50	42	27	33	25
Rural growth, urban decline	14	27	10	21	27	18	22	21	22
Rural decline LT urban decline	5	4	6	2	2	3	11	9	12
Subtotal	38	52	32	68	79	63	60	63	59
Total	100	100	100	100	100	100	100	100	100
No. of Counties	1,740	583	1,157	1,707	578	1,129	1,564	510	1,054

[a]Urban in this table refers to incorporated places having more than 2,500 people at the beginning of a time interval; rural refers to other places and the nonplace population. This classification of places, and the largest place and nonmetropolitan designations were as of 1960 for 1960–70, 1970 for 1970–80, and 1980 for 1980–84. Zero change is regarded as growth.

growth with urban decline, but the modal and often major type for the other regions, except for the Midwest in 1980–1984, was rural growth greater than urban growth. Consequently, unlike previous periods, within-nonmetropolitan county deconcentration is occurring largely in the context of both urban and rural growth for most parts of the United States.

Conclusions

In the 1970s there was widespread population deconcentration within the United States, taking place at several territorially based levels. This included population decline in the nation's largest cities, a continuing pattern of metropolitan suburbanization, more rapid growth in smaller than larger Metropolitan Statistical Areas, population redistribution away from the densely settled North, and a reversal in growth patterns between metropolitan and nonmetropolitan areas. These trends were discussed in Chapter 2, but in addition we documented in the present chapter a dramatic change from concentration to deconcentration within nonmetropolitan areas. Here we have shown widespread growth favoring areas outside urban nonmetropolitan centers throughout most areas of the country and most types of counties. Since 1980, furthermore, this urban–rural deconcentration within counties continued, despite a diminution in overall levels of nonmetropolitan growth, increased growth levels in the central counties of major metropolitan areas, and a massive regional population shift away from the North. Although the proportion of counties deconcentrating was at a somewhat reduced level compared with the 1970s deconcentration, this was still the rule for a majority of counties in all parts of the country, which was a distinct contrast with the earlier 1960–1970 decade. Also deconcentration was more pervasive in the sense that the proportions were almost identical for groups of counties distinguished by proximity to a metropolitan area or local urbanization, and this also was true on a regional basis except for the West.

In comparing the last two time periods, we did find differences in the type of deconcentration being experienced. Of considerable interest is the increase in the proportion of deconcentrating counties in the slow-growing Midwest, which was due to a shift to slower rural decline than urban decline that accompanied the increase in numbers of counties losing population overall. This also is in contrast to the 1960s and before, when declining nonmetropolitan areas were experiencing more drastic losses in rural population, with accompanying urban growth the most common pattern.

Aggregate changes do give evidence of a return to a concentrating pattern in the South and more remote areas of the West after 1980, though differences between levels of overall urban and rural growth there are far from the extremes of the 1960s. Consequently, the picture is mixed, but the conclusion seems valid that since 1970 population redistribution patterns in nonmetropolitan America are no longer supporting rapid concentration into cities, and indeed deconcentration into rural areas may well prevail in most local settings on a long-term basis.

There has been concern about the dying small town for at least 100 years. Except for very small, usually unincorporated places, however, growth to larger size has been more likely than decline over any decade, with actual disappearance a relatively rare event. During the turnaround decade of 1970–1980 nonmetropolitan places generally increased their rates of growth, but the recent economic and population downturn, particularly in areas highly dependent on agriculture, have once more turned the spotlight on the plight of these places. Detailed, reliable post-1980 data are not available for very small places, but overall 1980–1984 growth levels for nonmetropolitan incorporated places are generally somewhat below levels for the preceding decade.

The changing growth patterns reported here for 1950–1980 give some evidence of a transition in the role of the small town within the organization of nonmetropolitan areas. In earlier times, there was a strong tendency for larger places to grow more rapidly than smaller ones, which was consistent with their greater importance in economic production and trade as part of a hierarchy of urban centers. By the 1970s, however, villages and smaller urban centers, even in remote settings, were growing about as rapidly or more rapidly than larger cities. With a greater dispersion of trade and manufacturing activity within nonmetropolitan America, and the expansion of complex patterns of commuting by residents, community size no longer gives a growth advantage, and may no longer be a good indicator of functional importance within the settlement structure. One reason for the continuing controversy about "dying small towns," particularly at the lower size range, is that many such places are losing trade establishments and other economic activity but are gaining residents who work elsewhere. Some have argued that with an expanded "urban field" of diffuse activity, the question can be raised whether places are still meaningful units of analysis, particularly around larger metropolitan centers. The shift from a positive to a virtually nonexistent flat size–growth relationship between 1950 and 1980 is evidence of movement in that direction in nonmetropolitan America, although some retrenchment back toward a more positive relationship may be revealed when the 1990 census results are analyzed. In Chapter 12 we examine the urban size hierarchy in more detail with a consideration of differentials in population characteristics by place size, and how they have changed over the 1970–1980 decade.

Differential growth (or decline) favoring rural areas may signal a halt to the long-standing pattern of centralization in many parts of non-metropolitan America, but these intracounty growth differentials remain an issue of continuing policy concern. For example, the trend toward deconcentration may exacerbate fiscal pressures especially for nonmetropolitan urban centers as their tax bases deteriorate at a time when they may be subjected to growing demands of residents in surrounding rural areas who make use of various community services. In the past, such concerns have usually been limited to discussions of the impact of suburbanization in metropolitan areas, but they have now taken on added importance in many nonmetropolitan regions of the United States.

Another policy concern often expressed is that differential rural growth in nonmetropolitan areas may contribute to more rapid conversion of prime agricultural land for residential purposes. There is little evidence to support this premise, but it points up the need to relate land use to population changes at the local level in future research.[13] A parallel problem is possible pressure on other environmental resources, particularly those related to recreational amenities. Population densities remain very low in most nonmetropolitan rural areas, but in many parts of the country available prime scenic property is becoming scarce through rapid settlement.[14]

Although appropriate data are not available for a detailed analysis of rural and urban migration streams between nonmetropolitan and metropolitan areas, it seems safe to say that the population changes reported in this chapter are primarily due to differential migration.[15] Selectivities in movement and retention should lead to a more heterogeneous rural population and to decreased rural–urban differences in population composition. Unfortunately we cannot be more precise at this time about the possible effects of this migration, but the remainder

---

[13]Brown and Beale (1980); Kasarda (1980).

[14]As an example, real estate agents in a northern Wisconsin county that was part of the national nonmetropolitan turnaround because of its attractive amenities have asserted that although since the late 1970s the demand for new housing has lessened, this is not true for lakefront property, which has continued to increase in value.

[15]Elsewhere we have shown that the correlation between county net migration and county population change was about .95 for 1960–1970 and 1970–1980; Lichter, Heaton, and Fuguitt (1986), p. 25. Our PUMS file does make it possible to compare migration streams between metropolitan and nonmetropolitan areas by size of place of origin and destination. The proportion of metropolitan to nonmetropolitan migrants going to rural areas increased from 50 to 56 percent between 1965–1970 and 1975–1980.

of the book will consider residence differences in population composition and how this has changed in the most recent census decade.

Improvements in transportation and communication technology have allowed but not required population and economic activity to be more dispersed than previously. Problems of congestion, new processes of production, the declining population dependent upon agriculture, as well as the preferences of many people for living in low density areas have undoubtedly helped to fuel the deconcentration process that extends from the regional to the local county level of analysis. At a more general level, changes in industrial structure, as America becomes a more interdependent part of the world economy, undoubtedly have played a part in these residence shifts. Although population deconcentration, which became so prevalent in the 1970–1980 decade, continues throughout nonmetropolitan America, some concentration tendencies are nevertheless evident, and the present decade will not simply be a repeat of the one before that. Our difficulties in making more confident predictions about the future of population redistribution tendencies are based in large part on the interdependence, not yet well understood, of this process with many interrelated aspects of our economy and society.

APPENDIX TABLE 3.1

Comparison of Urban and Rural Population with the Population Living in Places 2,500 or More and Other Territory by Metropolitan Status, 1960–1980[a]

	Metropolitan			Nonmetropolitan		
Residence	1960	1970	1980	1960	1970	1980
Population (000s)						
Urban	100,212	123,600	145,922	25,062	25,733	21,133
Rural	13,968	17,159	24,571	40,086	36,809	34,920
Places 2,500+	82,495	98,683	111,132	23,274	22,881	19,067
Other Terr.	31,685	42,076	59,361	41,874	39,661	36,986
Total	144,180	140,759	170,493	65,148	62,542	56,053
Percentage						
Urban	87.8	87.8	85.6	38.5	41.1	37.7
Places 2,500+	72.2	70.1	65.1	35.7	36.6	34.0
Urban and in Places 2,500+	82.3	79.8	76.2	92.9	88.9	90.2
Rural and not in Places 2,500+	44.1	40.8	41.4	95.7	92.8	94.4

[a]The metropolitan county designation is that current at each date indicated.

4

AGE–SEX COMPOSITION

THE AGE–SEX composition of a population shapes community needs and demands for goods, services, and economic opportunities, as well as patterns of consumption, life-style, and social behavior. It is through changes in age–sex composition that demand shifts associated with population growth or decline are most clearly articulated. The age–sex composition of a community imposes requirements and limitations on each of its institutions. This is true in both urban and rural areas, but adaptation to changes in age–sex composition are especially difficult in rural areas where small size, geographic isolation, sparse settlement, or some combination of these factors act as limiting forces. Public policymakers, business leaders, and program managers increasingly realize that information on demographic composition, and particularly sex and age, in addition to that on population size and change is essential for carrying out their responsibilities and planning for the future.

In addition, age–sex composition shapes the fundamental demographic processes of future change—fertility, mortality, and migration. Together these processes determine a population's age–sex composition, and in turn age–sex composition affects the current and future levels of fertility, mortality, and migration. The size of each age–sex cohort in a population is determined by the number and distribution by sex of persons born into the cohort, the year-by-year death rates the cohort experiences as it moves through the life course, and its geographic mobility.

Rural birthrates have exceeded those of urban areas throughout American history, leading to a younger population in rural areas. The impact of higher rural fertility has been moderated somewhat by rural to urban migration, which siphoned off excess young persons of child-bearing years from the rural population. And, because high rural fertility in the context of declining opportunities in agriculture and sluggish economic development outside of agriculture has contributed to a rural labor surplus, it has been an indirect cause of rural-to-urban migration. Rural–urban fertility differences have been great enough, and of such duration, that every United States census in which age data were available by residence has shown the rural population to have a broader base of children less than 15 years of age. The migration of young adults from rural areas has been selective of women, in part because employment opportunities have tended to be in jobs usually held by men. This is a major reason why rural and nonmetropolitan populations have traditionally had a higher ratio of men to women than urban and metropolitan populations.

Recent decades, and especially the 1970s, have witnessed important changes in the demographic and economic patterns of nonmetropolitan and metropolitan areas that are associated with residential differences in age–sex composition. Nonmetropolitan fertility still exceeds metropolitan fertility, but the difference has diminished substantially (see Chapter 7), and net migration at all ages except 20–24 was toward nonmetropolitan areas during the 1970s.[1] Migration to nonmetropolitan areas in 1975–1980 was especially great (and different from that expected on the basis of prior age-specific migration rates for 1965–1970) in the youngest age groups (5–14), the middle family age groups (35–44), and among the elderly. In addition, the industrial composition of the nonmetropolitan and metropolitan economies has become more similar with a dramatic decline in extractive—traditionally male-oriented—industries. Also, female labor force participation increased throughout the nation, but was especially rapid in nonmetropolitan areas.

In light of these demographic and economic changes, we examine here the age–sex structures of the metropolitan and nonmetropolitan populations in 1980, and analyze changes since 1960. As suggested earlier, persistence of metropolitan–nonmetropolitan or urban–rural differences and the emergence of new patterns of difference have important implications for service needs, for economic opportunities, and for targeting public assistance. Diminished differentiation, on the other hand, would lead to a reconsideration of the need for special attention to the

---

[1]See Chapter 2 and Zuiches and Brown (1978).

age and sex related needs of the nonmetropolitan (or metropolitan) population.

Historical Trends in Age–Sex Composition

The classification of persons by age and sex has been an aspect of every United States census, but the amount of detail on age and sex has increased markedly over time.[2] In the first census, conducted in 1790, only the free white population was differentiated by sex, and age (less than 16 or 16 and older) was reported only for males. Black people were not distinguished by sex or age. By 1850, five-year age distributions up to age 20 were available for the entire population, and by 1890 quinquennial age distributions by sex were published for the total population and for principal race and nationality groups. The quality of these earlier data was adversely affected by reporting errors, and changes in enumeration procedures have affected their comparability over time. A reasonably accurate account of changes in the nation's age–sex composition can nevertheless be assembled from about 1820 to the present.

Age Composition

Donald Bogue and Conrad and Irene Taeuber have published historical accounts of the changing age composition of the United States population.[3] Their studies show that the nation's population was very young in the late eighteenth and early nineteenth centuries. In fact, the country's median age did not reach 20 years until after the Civil War, and by the turn of the twentieth century it was only 22.9 years (Table 4.1). Since then, with a brief interruption during the high fertility years of the 1950s and early 1960s, median age has increased continuously. In 1980, the median stood at 30 years, almost twice as high as in 1820 (16.7 years), and almost a decade older than 100 years ago in 1880. By 1987 it had increased further to 32.1 years.

These increases in median age are associated with a diminished proportion of children and an increasing proportion of elderly persons. The data in Figure 4.1 show that infants and youths less than 18 years comprised 44 percent of the nation's population in 1880, and elderly persons accounted only for about 3 percent. A century later, in 1980, the infant

---

[3]Bogue (1985); Taeuber and Taeuber (1958).
[2]U.S. Bureau of the Census (1975).

TABLE 4.1

Median Age and Sex Ratio
of the United States Population, 1820–1980

Date	Median Age	Sex Ratio
1980	30.0	94.5
1970	28.0	94.8
1960	29.5	97.1
1950	30.2	98.6
1940	29.0	100.7
1930	26.5	102.5
1920	25.3	101.7
1910	24.1	106.0
1900	22.9	104.4
1890	22.0	105.0
1880	20.9	103.6
1870	20.2	102.2
1860	19.4	104.7
1850	18.9	104.3
1840	17.8	103.7
1830	17.2	103.1
1820	16.7	103.3

SOURCE: Bogue (1985).

and youth component of the population had declined to 28 percent and over one in ten Americans was age 65 or older.

The demographic factors behind this long-term increase in median age are reduced fertility, mortality, and international immigration (which tends to be selective of younger persons), although reduced fertility is the principal factor over the long term.[4] As Weller and Bouvier have pointed out, the average age of a population is the average age of living persons, not the average age at death.[5] Accordingly, because much of the twentieth century mortality decline in the United States has been among infants, it has tended to increase the number of young persons more than of older persons, which in itself would lower the median age. Lower fertility, on the other hand, has been the principal factor contributing to aging the United States population. United States fertility has fallen continuously during this century except during the baby boom of the 1950s and early 1960s. As shown in Chapter 7, the number of children under 5 years of age per 1,000 white women 20–44 years old fell from about 1,300 in 1800 to about 400 in 1980. This long-term decline

[4]Coale (1964).
[5]Weller and Bouvier (1981).

FIGURE 4.1

Age Composition of the Population, 1880–1980

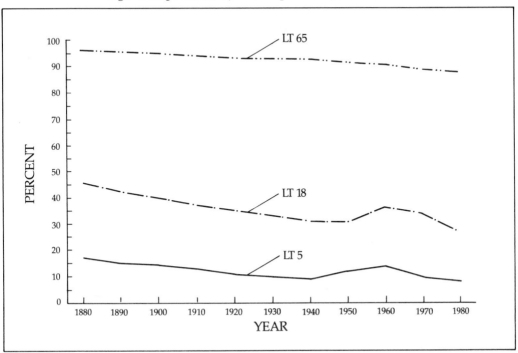

SOURCE: U.S. Bureau of the Census (1983a), table 42.

was interrupted only during the 1950s and 1960s when the child–woman ratio rose from about 450 in 1940 to over 700 in 1960 (equivalent to the level in 1890) before declining again thereafter. The effect of these fertility trends on age structure is clearly demonstrated in Figure 4.1. The number of younger persons declined continuously from 1880 to 1940, rose during the baby boom years, and then declined again. Median age (Table 4.1), which had increased throughout the 1880–1940 period, declined during the 1950s and 1960s before increasing again in 1980. Median age in 1980 was about the same as in 1950, before the effects of high fertility had become noticeable.

Sex Composition

Throughout most of its history the United States has had a preponderance of males in its population (Table 4.1). During the nineteenth century the sex ratio (males per 100 females) fluctuated between 102 and 106. The ratio remained at 102 or higher through the first third of this century, and then began its steady decline. In 1940 the sex ratio was essentially even (100.7) and by 1950 for the first time in its history the United States population had more women than men (sex ratio = 98.6). Today women outnumber men by almost 6.5 million, and the sex ratio has declined to 94.5, ten points less than it was 100 years ago.

The sex ratio is affected by numerous demographic and societal factors, and in recent years there is evidence that it has been marginally diminished by underenumeration of males (particularly young black males). Sex differences in mortality are the principal factors affecting the long-term decline in the United States sex ratio. The sex ratio at birth is above 100, but mortality is higher for males from conception onward. As the population has aged, older cohorts have become a larger percentage of the total population, and since they tend to be heavily weighted with females, they tend to depress the sex ratio.

Immigration had an important influence on the sex ratio until about 1910 when legislation tightly reduced the flow of foreign nationals into the United States. The great waves of nineteenth and early twentieth century European immigrants to the United States were heavily male and contributed to the high sex ratio of the time. In recent decades immigration has once more become important absolutely and as a proportion of the total growth, although current legal immigration is disproportionately female and so contributes some to the low sex ratio in contemporary America.

Residential Differences in Age–Sex Composition

Residential differences in age–sex composition have been clearly documented throughout the twentieth century. A number of analysts have found a regular decrease in the median age from rural farm to urban areas or a similar inverse association by city size. Similarly, residential differences in the sex ratio have also been pronounced during this century, being inversely related to the level of urbanization.[6]

The reasons for these residential differences can be briefly summarized. Traditionally, the rural population has been characterized by higher birthrates than the urban population, and internal migration has subtracted young adults from the rural population and added them to

[6]Hagood (1949); Bogue (1959), pp. 99-104, 158-161; Duncan and Reiss (1956), p. 103. Duncan and Reiss concluded that the differences among city size groups had become more marked in recent decades (up to 1950) and more clearly related to city size.

urban areas. Both of these factors—a larger proportion of children because of higher fertility and a smaller proportion of young adults because of selective outmigration—have created a younger population in rural compared with urban areas (even though rural areas have had a larger proportion of elderly persons). The higher sex ratio in rural areas is thought to be associated with the labor force needs of traditional resource-based industries, the higher proportion of the rural population that is married (requiring a nearly even sex ratio at marriageable ages), and the fact that farm wives tend to move to town after the death of a spouse while men appear more likely to remain on the farm.

Narrowing residential differences in fertility began to break down traditional urban–rural differences in age composition by about 1960 (Table 4.2). As discussed in Chapter 7, urban areas experienced much greater fertility increases during the baby boom than was true of rural areas. Fertility differentials were thus diminished, and they have continued to shrink during the last couple of decades. Largely as a result of this, the median age of the urban and rural nonfarm populations are now essentially the same. The rural farm population, however, has become decidedly older than the other two groups. A major reason for this must be a decline in the number of young families beginning and continuing to farm (Table 4.2).

In contrast with the situation for age, residential differences in sex composition have increased over time because the sex ratio in more urbanized areas has declined while that in more rural locales has remained essentially the same (Table 4.3). Apparently, the industrial factors asso-

TABLE 4.2

Median Age by Urban–Rural Residence, 1920–1980[a]

| | | | Rural | |
Date	Total	Urban	Nonfarm	Farm
1980	30.0	29.9	29.8	35.8
1970	27.9	28.1	27.2	32.0
1960	29.2	30.3	26.8	29.6
1950	30.2	31.6	27.9	26.3
1940	29.0	31.0	27.7	24.4
1930	26.5	28.4	25.8	21.6
1920	25.3	27.4	25.1	20.7

SOURCES: 1920–1950: Bogue (1959), p. 103; 1960–1980: various United States censuses of population.

[a]Previous urban and rural definition employed before 1950. See Chapter 2 for these definitions and Chapter 10 for discussions of farm definitions used at various dates.

TABLE 4.3

Sex Ratio by Urban–Rural Residence, 1920–1980

Date	Total	Urban	Rural Nonfarm	Farm
1980	94.5	92.8	99.3	108.1
1950	98.6	94.6	103.6	110.1
1920	101.7	100.4	106.5	109.1

SOURCES: Bogue (1959); and U.S. Census of Population (1980).

ciated with a higher sex ratio in the most rural locales, while diminished, are still in force today, while other factors such as the female balance in legal immigration are more effective in reducing the sex ratio of urban areas.

Nonmetropolitan Age Composition

We have used an urban–rural residential distinction in describing historical trends in age–sex composition because generally comparable historical data are available for urban and rural populations but not for metropolitan and nonmetropolitan areas. In the present section we will take a more detailed and residentially disaggregated look at current age–sex composition. County level data and the metropolitan–nonmetropolitan residential schema are more appropriate for such analyses.

Metropolitan–nonmetropolitan and urban–rural are both concepts that deal with population concentration, but they are not equivalent. Indeed, urban and rural areas are both imbedded in metropolitan and nonmetropolitan counties. As discussed in Chapter 1, we use both residential classifications in this book. In general, we focus on urban–rural differences to measure residential differentiation within the metropolitan and nonnmetropolitan aggregates. This is consistent with recent research showing that differences within the metropolitan and nonmetropolitan categories are as important as gross differences between them.[7]

Marked rural–urban differences are often translated into metropolitan–nonmetropolitan differences because of the differing urban–rural composition of these categories. For the United States as a whole, the nonmetropolitan population is 62 percent rural, whereas the metropoli-

[7]McGranahan, Hession, Hines, and Jordan (1986); Hines, Brown, and Zimmer (1975).

tan population is only 15 percent rural. For this reason it is necessary to distinguish the rural and urban components of both metropolitan and nonmetropolitan areas. In some cases, metropolitan–nonmetropolitan differences may be explained in large part by rural–urban differences; in other cases both the rural and urban portions of metropolitan areas may differ from their nonmetropolitan counterparts. The importance of considering urban–rural composition on the differential attributes of metropolitan and nonmetropolitan areas is a recurring theme in this and other chapters focusing on population composition.

In 1980 the median age of the nonmetropolitan population was 30.1 years. The population can be characterized as having a relatively narrow base because of low current fertility, a substantial bulge at the adult ages as the baby boom cohorts push their way through the age distribution, and a rather noticeable bulge at ages 55 and older (Figure 4.2 top).

The median age of the nonmetropolitan population is essentially the same as the United States and metropolitan totals (30.0), but closer inspection shows a pattern of residential differences similar to the rural–urban differences previously discussed in which nonmetropolitan counties have a higher proportion of children, relatively fewer young adults and middle-aged persons, and a larger proportion of the elderly than do metropolitan counties. These residential differences are accounted for by a higher level of fertility in nonmetropolitan areas, continued net outmigration of young adults to metropolitan areas (even during the nonmetropolitan population growth turnaround of the 1970s), and both inmigration of older persons and aging in place.

Two summary measures of these differences are presented in Table 4.4, along with the distributions for three broad age groups. Again, they show that the median ages of the metropolitan and nonmetropolitan populations are essentially the same. Nonmetropolitan counties have a substantially higher dependency ratio (58.0 vs. 49.1), with a greater concentration of the population less than 15 and 65 and over. The dependency ratio is generally considered to show the relationship between the economically active (15-64) and inactive (less than 15 and 65+) components of the population. Its social significance has probably diminished recently because public income maintenance programs, investments, and private pensions are providing more adequate incomes for elderly persons than was true in the past. Income aside, the dependency ratio does identify populations that have a greater than average need of such services as education, health care, and personal transportation.

Similar rural–urban differences are also found within both metropolitan and nonmetropolitan categories (Table 4.4 and Figure 4.2 middle and lower panels). Rural areas, regardless of metropolitan or nonmetropolitan status, have a greater representation of children, relatively fewer

FIGURE 4.2

Age Distribution of the Metropolitan and Nonmetropolitan Populations by Urban and Rural Residence, 1980

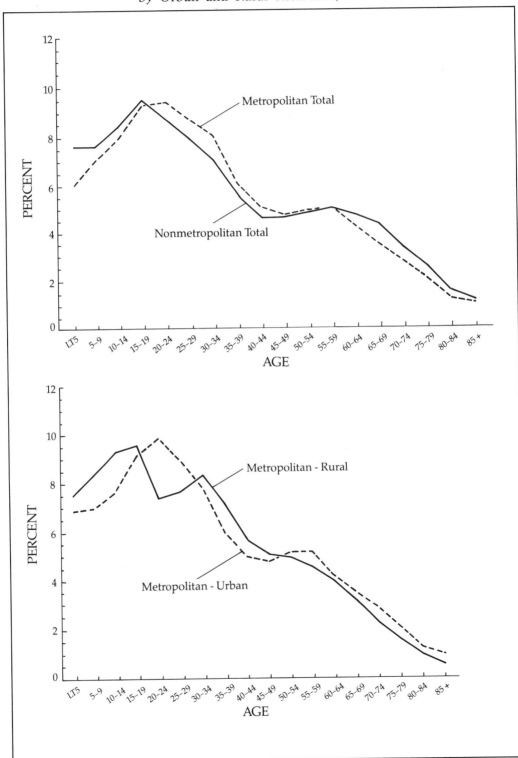

FIGURE 4.2 *(continued)*

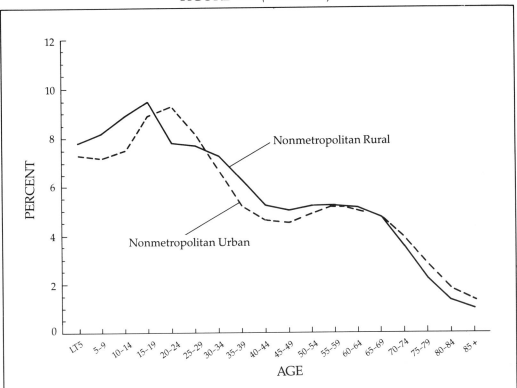

young adults, a greater proportion of middle-aged persons, and relatively *fewer* elderly persons. This latter point is somewhat counterintuitive and difficult to explain. Donald Bogue and others have commented that farm wives tend to move to town after the death of a spouse, and as demonstrated in Chapter 6 the old age institutional population tends to be disproportionately located in urban-nonmetropolitan areas.[8] This is a circumstance where metropolitan–nonmetropolitan differences do not parallel rural–urban differences. Although (as shown in Figure 4.2) urban areas have higher concentrations of the elderly in both metropolitan and nonmetropolitan areas, it is also true that nonmetropolitan areas have higher proportions of the elderly than metropolitan areas in both urban and rural settings. Residential differences in age composition are consistent across the four census regions, although the South and West, and

[8]Bogue (1959), p. 161.

TABLE 4.4

Age Composition by Metropolitan–Nonmetropolitan Residence, 1970, 1980[a]

	Metropolitan			Nonmetropolitan		
	Total	Urban	Rural	Total	Urban	Rural
1980 Percent						
LT 15	22.7	21.8	25.2	23.7	22.0	24.7
15–64	66.0	67.3	65.8	63.3	63.7	63.0
65+	11.3	10.9	9.0	13.0	14.3	12.3
Total	100.0	100.0	100.0	100.0	100.0	100.0
Median Age	30.0	30.0	29.9	30.1	29.8	31.4
Dependency Ratio[b]	51.2	48.7	51.8	58.0	57.0	58.6
1970 Percent						
LT 15	28.6	27.9	31.4	28.7	26.8	29.8
15–64	61.5	62.6	60.2	59.6	61.0	58.8
65+	9.9	9.5	8.4	11.7	12.2	11.4
Total	100.0	100.0	100.0	100.0	100.0	100.0
Median Age	28.1	28.1	27.0	28.6	29.3	28.8
Dependency Ratio[b]	62.6	59.7	66.1	67.8	63.9	70.1

[a]Fixed 1980 metropolitan designation; urban and rural territory within metropolitan and nonmetropolitan categories is not fixed, but rather reflects delineation current at time of each census.

[b]Population less than 15 and 65 and over divided by the population 15–64 times 100.

116

each of their residential components, are slightly younger than the other two regions.

Recent Changes in the Nonmetropolitan Age Composition

Changes in the age composition of the nonmetropolitan population from the end of the baby boom (1960) to 1980 are displayed in Figure 4.3. The high proportion of children in 1960 is clear evidence of more than a decade of high fertility. In contrast, the deficit of young adults is an outcome of heavy nonmetropolitan to metropolitan migration of this age group (especially in the South) during the 1950s, and it is a residue of low fertility experienced during the Great Depression of the 1930s.

The number of children in the nonmetropolitan population is much lower in 1970 than in 1960 because the baby boom came to an end during the ensuing decade (Figure 4.3 top). Young adults, on the other hand, comprise a much higher proportion of the nonmetropolitan population in 1970 than a decade before because the large baby boom cohorts had begun their movement into these age groups. Middle-aged persons are generally underrepresented in the nonmetropolitan population in 1970 compared with 1960 because individuals entering this age group over the decade were members of the small Depression-era birth cohorts. Finally, the proportion of older nonmetropolitan persons is larger in 1970 than in 1960 in large part because of reduced mortality among older people.

Substantial alterations in the age structure of the nonmetropolitan population also took place during the 1970s. The lower section of Figure 4.3 shows the marked effects of nearly two decades of very low fertility. Effects of the "baby bust" of the late 1960s and 1970s are clearly demonstrated by the deficit of infants and young children in the nonmetropolitan population in 1980. In fact, the nonmetropolitan population less than 15 years of age in 1980 is only 85 percent as large as it was in 1960 (13.3 million vs. 15.3 million).

Other substantial changes during the 1970s are also evident in Figure 4.3. It was during this decade that the large baby boom cohorts moved into young adulthood. Accordingly, the nonmetropolitan population age 15–34 years grew by 36 percent. The increase of this age group is also associated with reduced outmigration at these ages (see Chapter 2). The nonmetropolitan elderly also increased in number and as a proportion of the population (1.6 million—28 percent increase). David McGranahan has determined that about one-third of this increase is due to reductions in mortality.[9] Net inmigration from metropolitan areas

[9]McGranahan (1985).

FIGURE 4.3

*Age Distribution of the Nonmetropolitan Population, 1960–1970, 1970–1980**

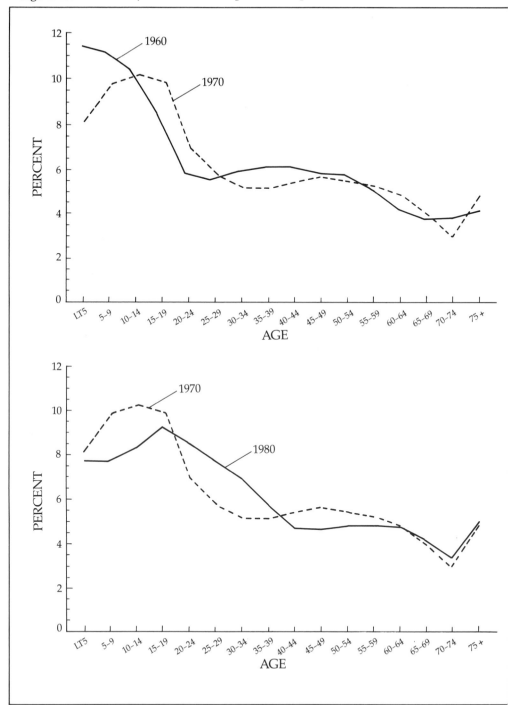

*Fixed 1980 designation of Metropolitan Statistical Areas.

was also a notable factor in growth of the elderly population during the 1970s, although it makes a greater contribution in some areas than in others.

The effects of demographic trends on changes in the age composition of the metropolitan and nonmetropolitan populations between 1960 and 1980 can be seen in Figure 4.4. The decline in the population proportion under 15 years of age is pronounced in both residential categories, and is associated with the current prolonged period of low (by historical standards) fertility. Nonetheless, the nonmetropolitan population in 1980 still has a slightly larger proportion of infants and children than is true in metropolitan areas. Because of aging in place and net inmigration of elderly persons from metropolitan counties, the nonmetropolitan population appears to have aged more than its metropolitan counterpart. This is in contrast with the working age population, which grew somewhat more rapidly in metropolitan areas because the baby boom was more dramatic there, and because metropolitan areas are still gaining young labor force age migrants from the nonmetropolitan population. These same patterns of change also characterize the four census regions except that the proportion of infants and children did not decline in the South and West. These regions gained population at all ages in all residential categories.

Residential Differences in the Sex Ratio

In 1980 there were 94.5 men for every 100 women in the United States, a decline from 97.1 in 1960. Throughout the 1960–1980 period nonmetropolitan ratios have been somewhat higher than metropolitan, though the relative differential has declined (Table 4.5). Writing in 1959, Bogue commented that the major declines in the sex ratio had taken place in more highly urbanized areas. The metropolitan–nonmetropolitan data presented in Table 4.5, however, suggest that this does not characterize the situation since 1960. The relative decline in the nonmetropolitan ratio of −3.2 percentage points is greater than the corresponding decline in the metropolitan ratio of −2.4 percentage points. The declining nonmetropolitan sex ratio is probably related to the reduced importance of traditionally male-oriented extractive industries in much of nonmetropolitan America and to a declining outmigration of nonmetropolitan women related to their increased labor force participation.[10] Both of these changes took place throughout the entire 1960–1980 period, but the decline of extractive industries was more rapid dur-

[10]Brown and O'Leary (1979); also see Chapter 8.

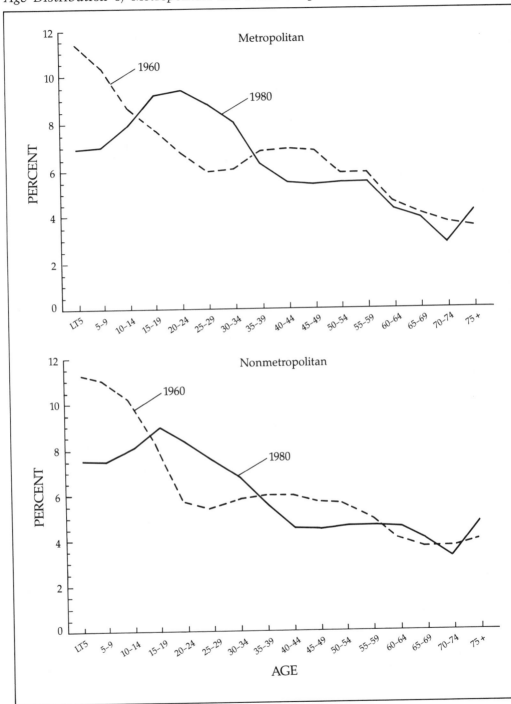

FIGURE 4.4

Age Distribution of Metropolitan and Nonmetropolitan Populations, 1960–1980*

*Fixed 1980 designation of Metropolitan Statistical Areas.

120

TABLE 4.5

Sex Ratio by Metropolitan–Nonmetropolitan Residence, 1960–1980[a]

Year	Total	Metropolitan	Nonmetropolitan
1980	94.5	93.9	96.1
1970	94.8	94.3	96.7
1960	97.1	96.3	99.3

[a]Fixed 1980 metropolitan designation.

ing 1960–1970 than in 1970–1980. Women's labor force participation increased at about the same pace in both decades.

Demographic factors are also involved in these changes. The elderly population is disproportionately female, and since the nonmetropolitan age distribution is becoming older, with a higher proportion of persons at the oldest ages, the effect should be to lower the sex ratio. The greater prevalence of husband-wife households in nonmetropolitan areas is another factor supporting a higher nonmetropolitan sex ratio (see Chapter 6), although this type of household has become less typical in both residence groupings.

The female orientation of current international immigration (at least legal immigration) would tend, on the other hand, to reduce the metropolitan sex ratio more than the nonmetropolitan, because most current immigration is destined for metropolitan areas.

We do not have comparable urban–rural data on the sex ratio for 1960–1980, but the 1980 data in Table 4.6 show that the higher sex ratio in nonmetropolitan areas in 1980 is entirely due to the fact that a much higher proportion of the nonmetropolitan population is rural (62 percent vs. 15 percent). That is, *within* both rural and urban areas the nonmetropolitan sex ratio is actually lower than the metropolitan ratio. Since rural sex ratios are higher than urban in both residential categories but

TABLE 4.6

Sex Ratio by Residence and Region, 1980

	Total	Metropolitan			Nonmetropolitan		
		Total	Urban	Rural	Total	Urban	Rural
United States	94.5	93.9	92.7	101.0	96.1	90.8	99.4
Northeast	91.5	91.1	89.7	99.2	94.6	89.5	98.1
Midwest	94.6	93.8	92.3	102.0	96.6	90.4	101.0
South	94.3	94.2	92.9	100.0	94.6	89.1	97.7
West	98.0	97.4	96.6	106.0	101.0	97.1	105.0

TABLE 4.7

Sex Ratio by Age, Residence, and Region, 1980

Region and Age Group	Total	Metropolitan			Nonmetropolitan		
		Total	Urban	Rural	Total	Urban	Rural
United States							
Age 15–44	99.1	98.3	97.6	103.0	102.0	99.3	103.0
65+	67.4	65.2	63.1	82.1	72.9	60.8	82.5
Northeast							
Age 15–44	96.0	95.3	94.4	101.0	100.0	97.1	102.0
65+	64.0	63.0	61.3	77.0	69.7	59.3	78.1
Midwest							
Age 15–44	98.9	97.3	96.3	103.0	103.0	100.0	104.0
65+	66.9	64.0	61.4	82.8	72.4	58.5	83.0
South							
Age 15–44	99.2	98.8	98.1	102.0	100.0	97.8	101.0
65+	68.2	66.2	63.8	81.1	71.4	59.7	78.0
West							
Age 15–44	103.0	103.0	102.0	109.0	105.0	103.0	107.0
65+	71.5	68.8	66.9	95.8	84.3	72.3	98.2

the rural population is concentrated in nonmetropolitan areas, the total nonmetropolitan ratio is higher than the overall metropolitan ratio. This is also true for the census regions except the West, where the pattern is mixed.

In general the sex ratio is highest in rural parts of the West and North Central regions, regardless of metropolitan–nonmetropolitan classification, and lowest in the most highly urbanized parts of the Northeast. This is primarily because of the heavy dependence on agriculture, mining, timber, and ranching in the rural Plains and West.[11] Also the rural population in the West and Midwest is mostly white (the white population has a higher ratio). As the nation's frontier, the West has traditionally had a higher sex ratio than the other three regions. Even in 1980, some parts of the West still had a sex ratio of 105, equivalent to the total United States level at the turn of the century.

The residential and regional differences mentioned above are also evident in Table 4.7 where sex ratios are presented by age. The ratio hovers around 100 in the prime working ages, being somewhat higher in less highly urbanized areas in all four regions and in the West in all

[11]Bender, Green, Hady, Kuehn, Nelson, Perkinson, and Ross (1985).

metropolitan–nonmetropolitan and urban–rural categories. The sex ratio of the elderly population (age 65 and over) is much more variable,
ranging from near unity in the rural component of the nonmetropolitan
West to only 58.5 in the urban-nonmetropolitan part of the North Central region. The elderly sex ratio in the rural parts of both metropolitan
and nonmetropolitan categories is much higher than in the urban parts
in all four census regions. This is partly due to a higher proportion of
very old persons (age 75 and above) among the elderly in urban areas,
since women account for two-thirds of the population at these ages.
Also, there is evidence that single farm men are more likely to stay on
the farm than are farm women, who more generally move to town.[12]

The Elderly Population

The elderly are the most rapidly growing age group in the United
States population (Table 4.8). Between 1970 and 1980 the population 65
and over grew by 26.8 percent, over twice the rate of growth of the entire population (11.5 percent). Although the elderly comprise only 11.3
percent of the population, they accounted for almost one-quarter of the
decade's population growth. As a consequence, during the 1970s the elderly population grew 5.4 million to a total of 25.5 million and as a
percentage of the population from 9.9 percent to 11.3 percent. The female elderly population grew more rapidly than the male (30.6 percent
vs. 21.6 percent), and within both gender groups growth rates differed by
age (Table 4.9). Among elderly males, the younger age groups grew most
rapidly, but the opposite was true among women—growth was directly

TABLE 4.8

Population Change by Age, 1970–1980[a]

Age Group	Total		Metropolitan		Nonmetropolitan	
	Number (000s)	Percent	Number (000s)	Percent	Number (000s)	Percent
Total	23,333	11.5	15,981	10.3	7,351	15.1
Youth (LT 20)	−4,792	−6.2	−4,602	−7.9	−191	−1.0
Adult (20–64)	22,279	21.5	16,788	20.5	5,940	24.6
Elderly (65 +)	5,397	26.8	3,794	26.3	1,602	28.1

Fixed 1980 designation of metropolitan and nonmetropolitan counties.

[12]Bogue (1959), p. 161.

TABLE 4.9

Growth of the Elderly Population by Age, Sex, and Residence, 1970–1980[a]

Age/Sex	Total			Metropolitan			Nonmetropolitan		
	Number (000s)		Percent Change 1970–1980	Number (000s)		Percent Change 1970–1980	Number (000s)		Percent Change 1970–1980
	1970	1980		1970	1980		1970	1980	
Male 65 and up	8,438	10,263	21.6	5,923	7,185	21.3	2,514	3,077	22.4
65–69	3,113	3,881	24.7	2,210	2,748	24.3	902	1,133	25.6
70–74	2,320	2,860	23.3	1,638	1,990	21.5	681	869	27.6
75+	3,005	3,522	17.2	2,075	2,447	17.9	930	1,075	15.6
Female 65 and up	11,644	15,236	30.6	8,484	11,013	29.8	3,182	4,222	32.7
65–69	3,879	4,887	26.0	2,833	3,540	25.0	1,045	1,348	29.0
70–74	3,129	3,963	26.7	2,294	2,858	24.6	834	1,045	32.5
75+	4,657	6,386	37.1	3,354	4,617	37.7	1,303	1,769	35.9

[a]Fixed 1980 designation of metropolitan and nonmetropolitan counties.

associated with advancing age. All of these trends and differences characterize both the metropolitan and nonmetropolitan populations, although growth of the elderly populations was slightly more rapid in nonmetropolitan areas except after age 75.

The social and economic implications of a growing elderly population, in number or percent, can be substantial for rural communities. Smaller community size, greater geographic distance, sparse settlement patterns, and more specialized economic structures in such areas can constrain effective adaptation to changes in age composition. Communities facing an aging population may have to adapt their commercial and trade structures and reduce their per capita dependence on local public resources. An aging population still generally translates into increased public sector responsibilities, even though small rural communities may be less able to contend with such demands than many other residential units. Accordingly, since aging-related issues are so critical nationally and at the local level, we give the elderly population special attention in this chapter.

Components of Change in the Elderly Population

Increased absolute and relative size of the elderly population is the outcome of a complex set of demographic processes. Lichter and his colleagues have examined the effects of net migration and natural increase of those aged 0–64 and 65 or older on the number and percent of elderly persons in a population.[13] Although they concluded that the relative importance of these four components varied across residential categories, they were able to arrive at some general conclusions.

They found that natural increase in the numbers 65 and over (residents attaining 65 years in the places where they live minus deaths) is the dominant component in elderly population change over each of the three time periods (Table 4.10). Net migration of those 65 and over, however, has become an increasingly important component of change in both the absolute and the relative size of the nonmetropolitan elderly population. Natural increase of the less than 65-year-old group (births minus both deaths and movement out of the group to older ages) is important in slowing the increase in the proportion that is elderly by adding to the denominator of that proportion. This component declined in importance for nonmetropolitan areas over the three time periods, no doubt reflecting the general decline in fertility. The net outmigration of persons less than 65 served to increase the proportion over 65 in the

---

[13]Lichter, Fuguitt, Heaton, and Clifford (1981).

TABLE 4.10

Components of Numerical and Relative Change in the Elderly Population for Nonmetropolitan Areas, 1950–1975[a]

Components	1950–1960	1960–1970	1970–1975
Numerical Change Elderly (000s)			
Additive components:			
Natural increase 65+	1,130	635	1,059
Net migration 65+	−109	159	454
Total numerical change 65+	1,021	794	1,513
Percentage due to net migration	−10.7	20.0	30.0
Annual rate of population change:			
65 and over	20.8	13.7	21.7
Less than 65	1.1	3.1	10.8
Change in Percentage Elderly			
Additive components:			
Natural increase 65+	2.01	1.07	1.62
Net migration 65+	−.19	.27	.69
Natural increase less than 65	−1.26	−.92	−.50
Net migration less than 65	1.17	.61	−.65
Total change in percentage 65+	1.71	1.03	1.16
Percentage of population 65+ (beginning of period)	8.72	10.43	11.46

SOURCE: Lichter, Fuguitt, Heaton, and Clifford (1981).

[a]Fixed 1974 nonmetropolitan designation was employed.

[b]To provide comparability across time periods, adjusted components are computed on the basis of th figures implied if the annualized rates of net migration and population change for 1970–1975 were o served throughout the entire decade of the 1970s. See Shryock and Siegel (1971, p. 387–390) for annualize change formulas.

1950–1960 and 1960–1970 decades, again through the denominator. In the 1970s, with the nonmetropolitan population turnaround, the net in-migration of younger people to nonmetropolitan areas was a negative component of change in the percent over 65 that was almost as large as the positive component of elderly net inmigration.

Geographic Location of the Nonmetropolitan Elderly

The regional distribution of the nation's elderly population closely resembles the regional distribution of all persons in both metropolitan and nonmetropolitan areas (Table 4.11). That is to say, elderly nonmetropolitan persons are concentrated in the South and Midwest states, whereas the metropolitan elderly are more evenly distributed across the regions.

TABLE 4.11

Geographic Distribution of the Elderly Population, 1980

| | Population Distribution by Region | | | | Percent Population Nonmetropolitan | |
| | Metropolitan | | Nonmetropolitan | | | |
	Total	Age 65 +	Total	Age 65 +	Total	Age 65 +
nited States	100.0	100.0	100.0	100.0	24.7	28.5
Northeast	25.1	28.5	11.3	11.8	12.9	14.1
Midwest	24.5	23.5	30.6	33.4	29.1	36.3
South	29.5	28.9	44.6	44.3	33.2	38.2
West	20.9	19.1	13.5	10.6	17.5	18.0

Not only do the South and Midwest states contain three-quarters of the nation's nonmetropolitan elderly but older persons are more decentralized in these regions than is true of the general population. Almost 40 percent of elderly persons in the South and Midwest states live in nonmetropolitan counties compared with about 30 percent of the total population. Only about one-sixth of the elderly population in the Northeast and West are nonmetropolitan residents, about the same proportion as the total population in these regions.

Within regions the proportion of elderly persons varies widely throughout the country. In over 500 nonmetropolitan counties, elderly persons account for one-sixth or more of the population and in 178 of these counties the proportion exceeds one-fifth, almost twice the national percentage (Figure 4.5). Net elderly migration to nonmetropolitan counties has become an increasingly important factor in determining age composition of nonmetropolitan areas since 1970. About one in five nonmetropolitan counties experienced at least 15 percent inmigration of elderly persons during 1970–1980, as shown in Figure 4.6. In most cases this elderly inmigration did not result in a substantial aging of the population because population growth at younger ages was also rapid. As a group these "retirement inmigration counties" grew by 33.5 percent during the 1970s, compared with a growth rate of 14.6 percent for all nonmetropolitan counties. Some nonmetropolitan retirement counties do have very old age structures, however, as can be seen by comparing Figures 4.5 and 4.6. A county can have a high proportion of elderly because of past outmigration of young persons and not increase this proportion in the turnaround era if both young and old persons move in on a net basis. This is particularly true in the Ozarks and the hill country of Central Texas. In contrast, the bulk of retirement inmigration counties do not have particularly old age distributions and are spread throughout

FIGURE 4.5

Nonmetropolitan Counties with a High Percentage of Older Persons, 1980

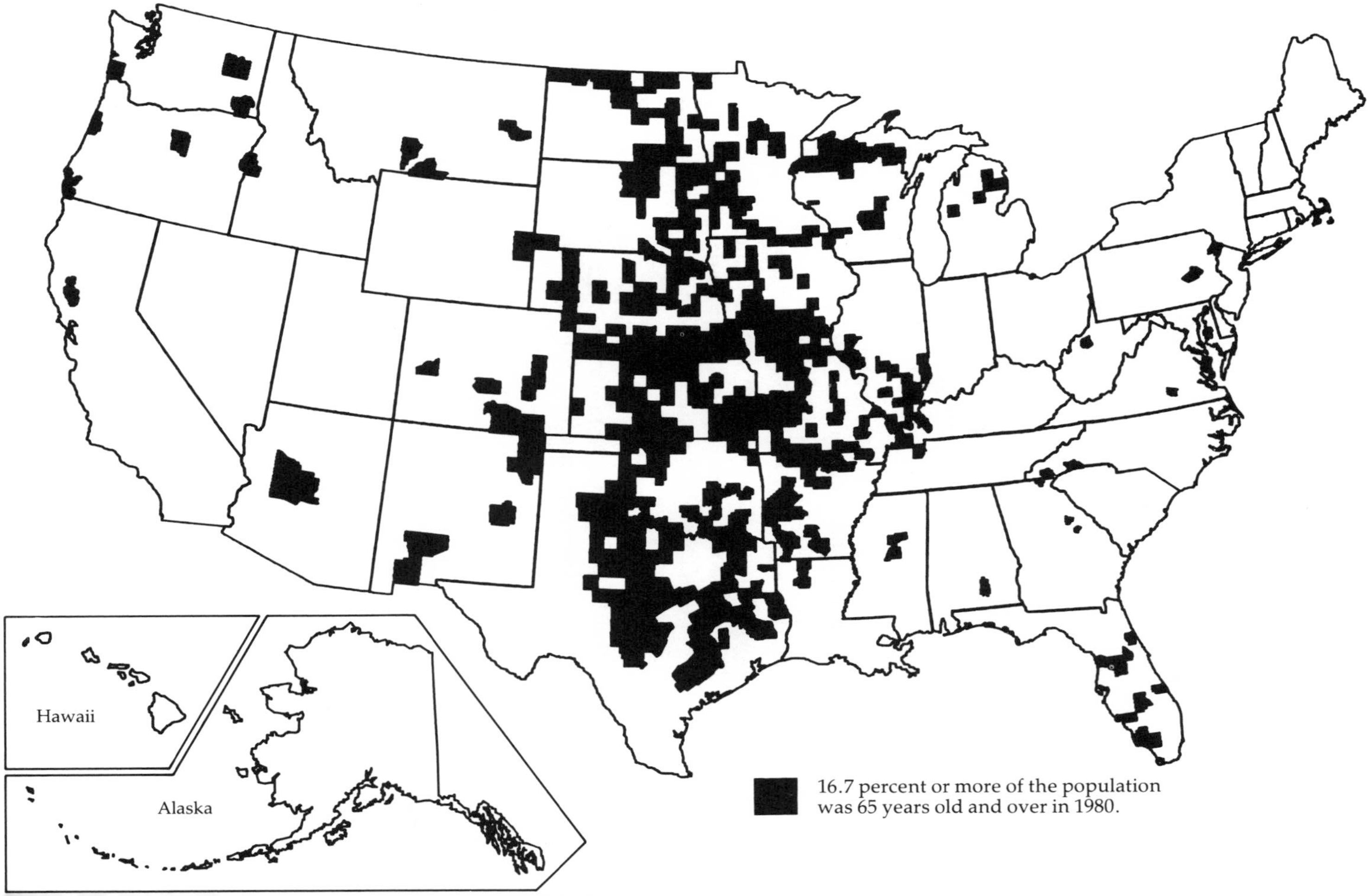

16.7 percent or more of the population was 65 years old and over in 1980.

Alaska

Hawaii

FIGURE 4.6

Nonmetropolitan Retirement Counties, 1970–1980

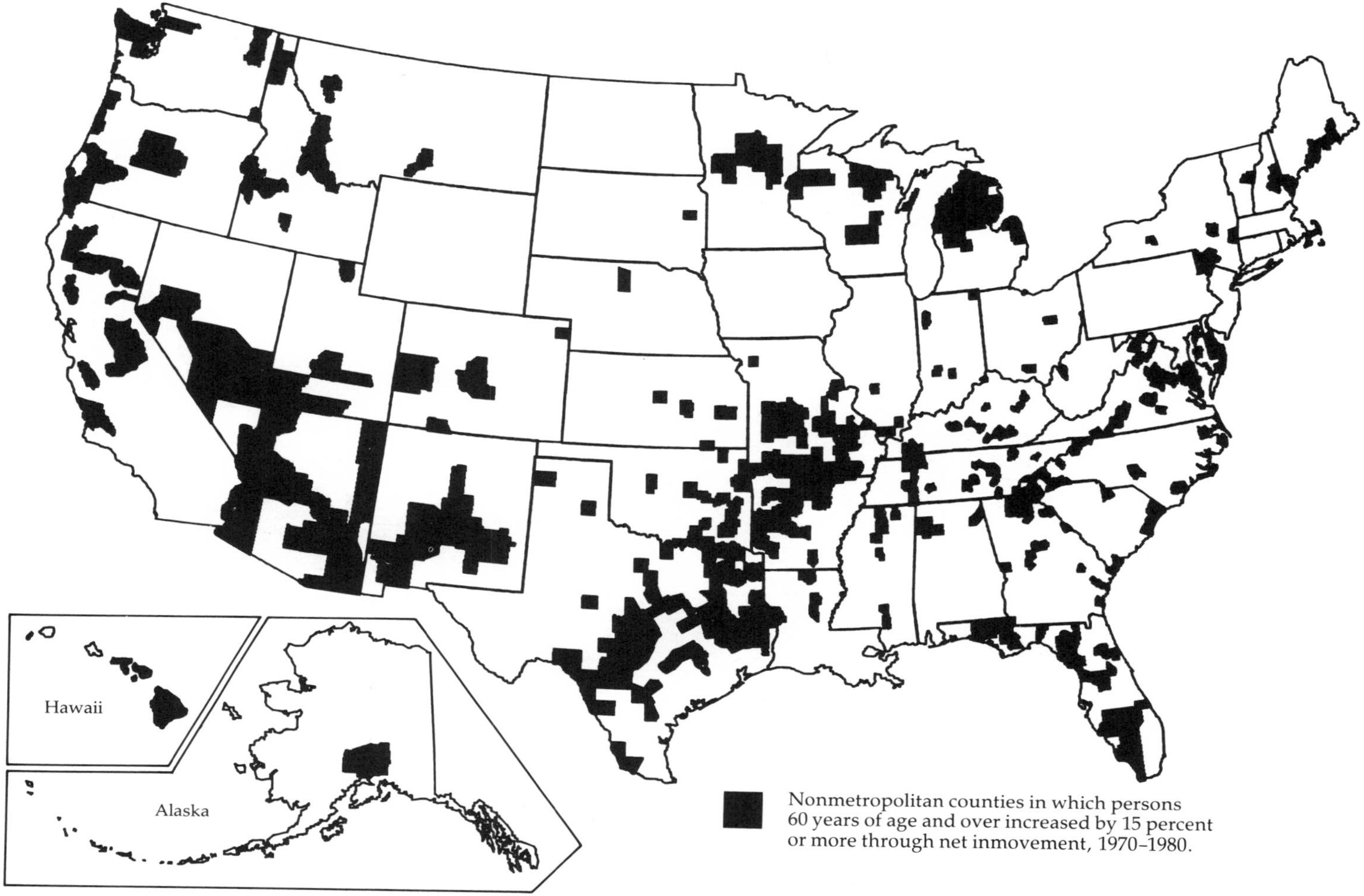
Hawaii
Alaska
Nonmetropolitan counties in which persons 60 years of age and over increased by 15 percent or more through net inmovement, 1970–1980.

the country with notable concentrations in these two areas and in Florida, the Upper Great Lakes, Appalachia, the Southwest, and northern California–southwest Oregon.

Extreme aging of the population because of a past history of heavy outmigration of couples of childbearing age may be associated with natural population decrease. Calvin Beale showed that in 1966, 271 counties had fewer births than deaths. These counties were typically rural and agricultural, located in marginal Corn Belt areas of Missouri, Kansas, Nebraska, and Iowa and in Central Texas.[14] He projected a substantial extension of the natural decrease phenomenon to include over 500 counties by 1970 because of low fertility and the rural outmigration of persons in the childbearing years. The expected extension, however, did not occur. In fact, there were only 144 natural decrease counties in 1980, far fewer than in 1966. The low fertility of the late 1960s has continued, but we suspect that nonmetropolitan counties in the Plains and Corn Belt must have retained more of their baby boom era young people than anticipated. As can be seen in Figure 4.7, the core of natural decrease continues to be situated in Missouri, Kansas, and Central Texas.

Natural decrease in these counties is not caused by insufficient fertility rates. In fact, the number of children ever born to women age 20–44 in these 144 counties (2.86) is equal to the ratio for all nonmetropolitan counties, and is higher than the ratio for white women in nonmetropolitan counties (2.76). Rather, natural decrease is brought about by a distorted age distribution with an insufficient number of couples in the childbearing ages in relation to the proportion of elderly persons. The age distribution of natural decrease counties is compared to that of the total nonmetropolitan population in Figure 4.8. The deficit of persons in the childbearing ages is clearly evident, as is the excess of elderly persons, especially women.

Selected demographic characteristics of the elderly are displayed in Table 4.12. Both metropolitan and nonmetropolitan populations are disproportionately female, having sex ratios well below 100, and are concentrated between the ages of 65 and 74. However, the female elderly population is substantially older than the male, with a much greater percentage falling in the 75–84 and 85+ age groups. Older nonmetropolitan persons are predominantly white, although in the South about one out of six is black.

About three out of four elderly nonmetropolitan men are married and only 14 percent are widowed. In contrast, because of sex differences in mortality at the older ages, a much higher proportion (over half) of

[14]Beale (1969).

FIGURE 4.7

Counties in which Average Deaths Exceeded Births, 1980–1982

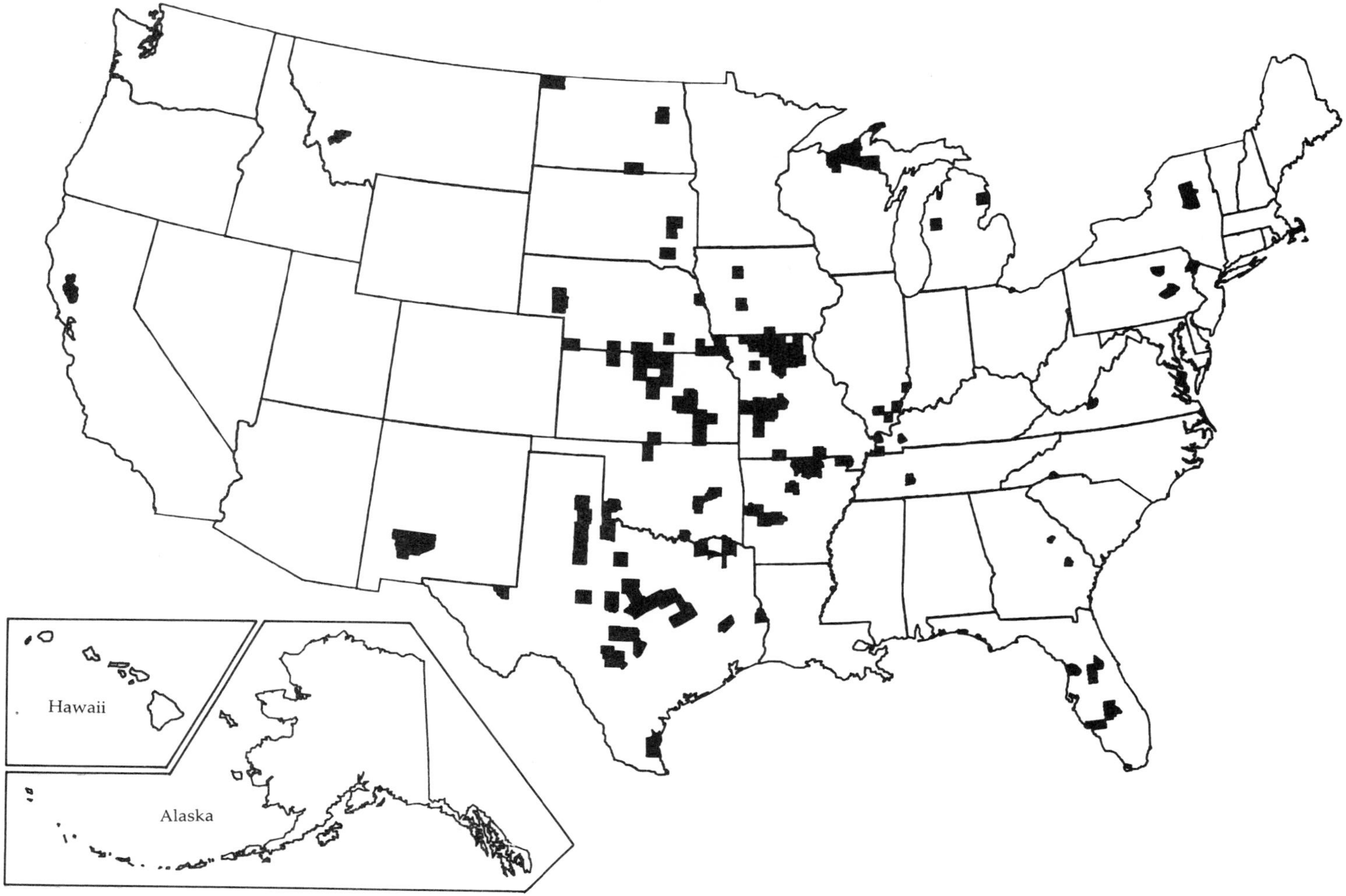

FIGURE 4.8

Age Distribution of Natural Decrease Counties, 1980

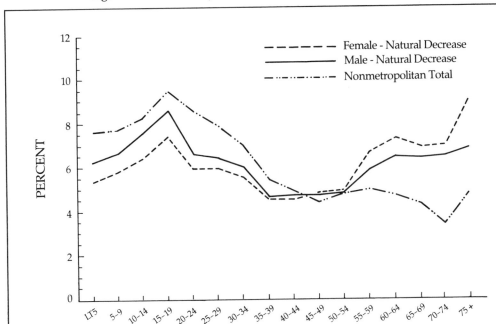

nonmetropolitan elderly women are widowed and conversely a much lower proportion are married with spouse present.

The demographic profiles of metropolitan and nonmetropolitan elderly persons are quite similar. Only the sex ratio clearly differentiates the two populations. The metropolitan population has a somewhat greater representation of women than is true of nonmetropolitan areas.

In contrast, the socioeconomic characteristics of the metropolitan and nonmetropolitan elderly are markedly different (Table 4.13). Elderly nonmetropolitan persons have attained substantially lower levels of formal education, they have lower median family income (about 25 percent lower), and a higher percentage are in poverty. Labor force participation is about the same in both residential categories, and hence the proportion receiving income from wages and salaries is similar. But as Nina Glasgow has demonstrated, metropolitan elderly who are employed are

TABLE 4.12

Characteristics of the Population Aged 65 and Over by Residence, 1980

Characteristics	Metropolitan	Nonmetropolitan
Age–Sex		
Sex ratio	65.2	72.9
Age distribution		
Males	100.0	100.0
65–74	65.8	64.9
75–84	27.7	28.5
85 +	6.5	6.6
Females	100.0	100.0
65–74	57.9	58.4
75–84	32.0	31.5
85 +	10.1	10.1
Race		
Percentage nonwhite		
United States	10.7	8.5
South	15.0	16.6
Marital Status		
Males		
Married-spouse present	74.3	75.4
Single-divorced-separated	10.9	10.4
Widowed	14.8	14.2
Females		
Married-spouse present	34.2	39.6
Single-divorced-separated	13.3	9.0
Widowed	52.5	51.0

more likely to have higher status occupations and their wages are about 30 percent higher than those of nonmetropolitan elderly.[15]

A higher percentage of nonmetropolitan elderly receive income from farm self-employment, Social Security, and public assistance, but average income received from Social Security and public assistance is lower in nonmetropolitan than in metropolitan areas. The proportion receiving income from interest, dividends, and rents is considerably higher in metropolitan areas. Higher wages and salaries, receipt of higher benefits from Social Security and public assistance, and a greater proportion of persons receiving income in the form of dividends and interest account for the higher family income of elderly persons living in metropolitan areas. Of course, lower educational attainment, older age distributions, and higher proportions of nonmetropolitan elderly living alone are also important factors in their lower family income.

[15]Glasgow (1988).

RURAL AND SMALL TOWN AMERICA

TABLE 4.13

*Selected Socioeconomic Characteristics of the Population
Aged 65 and Over, 1980*

Characteristics	Metropolitan	Nonmetropolitan
Educational Attainment		
Percentage 8 years or less	40.6	49.2
Percentage at least one year		
college	15.8	12.9
Labor Force Participation		
Percentage males in labor force	19.6	18.8
Percentage females in labor		
force	8.3	7.6
Income and Poverty		
Percentage families below		
poverty, householder 65 +	6.8	13.4
Median family income,		
householder 65 +	$13,421	$10,157
Percentage receiving income		
from selected source:		
Wages and salary	14.8	15.1
Farm self-employment	1.0	4.8
Interest, dividends, net rental	42.6	36.6
Social security	80.1	82.0
Public assistance	8.5	10.9

age distributions, and higher proportions of nonmetropolitan elderly living alone are also important factors in their lower family income.

Metropolitan–nonmetropolitan differences in the socioeconomic status of elderly persons tend to be somewhat larger than differences for younger persons. For example, the median family income of nonmetropolitan households with an elderly householder is only 76 percent of comparable metropolitan households. In contrast, the median family income of nonmetropolitan households ranges from 79 to 98 percent of the corresponding metropolitan median for each householder age group between 15 and 44 (Table 4.14). Accordingly, income differences between the metropolitan and nonmetropolitan elderly account for a disproportionate amount of the overall income difference between the two residential sectors.

Succeeding chapters will include detailed examinations of metropolitan–nonmetropolitan differences in income distribution, employment, labor market activity, and household and other aspects of demographic structure for the population of all ages.

TABLE 4.14

Median Family Income by Age of Householder and Residence, 1980

Age of Householder	Metropolitan	Nonmetropolitan	Metropolitan/ Nonmetropolitan
15–24	$12,440	$12,229	.98
25–34	19,327	17,014	.88
35–44	23,829	20,284	.85
45–54	27,076	21,376	.79
55–64	23,517	17,416	.74
65+	13,300	10,157	.76
All Households	17,159	14,040	.82

Conclusions

Like the rings of trees that show variations in climate, the nonmetropolitan population's age–sex composition records most of the major demographic events of the twentieth century. The effects of the post–World War II baby boom and the current prolonged period of low fertility are not as clearly etched in the nonmetropolitan population structure as in metropolitan areas, but they have nonetheless had a marked impact on the composition of the nonmetropolitan population. In both residence categories the large baby boom cohorts have created noticeable bulges in the young adult age groups while the infant and youth age groups are now substantially smaller than two decades ago.

In contrast, both internal and international migration have influenced metropolitan and nonmetropolitan areas differently. Legal immigration from abroad, because it was capped early in this century and because it has generally been destined for large cities, has had most of its twentieth-century impact on metropolitan areas. In contrast, internal migration has transferred millions of young adults from nonmetropolitan to metropolitan areas. Even today the age profiles of metropolitan and nonmetropolitan counties show the effects of this internal population transfer. As shown in Figure 4.2, metropolitan counties have a relative surplus and nonmetropolitan areas a relative deficit of persons in the young adult and middle ages. Elderly migration, in contrast, has been toward nonmetropolitan areas since at least the 1960s and is an increasingly important factor in the aging of the nonmetropolitan population.

Increased longevity has contributed to the aging of population (in both metropolitan and nonmetropolitan areas), and because of sex differences in mortality at the older ages it is the major factor reducing the sex ratio of the United States population. In fact, at age 65 and older there were fewer than 70 males per 100 females in 1980.

These trends and changes in age and sex composition affect every aspect of the nation's social, economic, demographic, and political life. Perhaps the most dramatic impact is on population growth itself. Were it not for the large numbers of baby boom cohort women now in the childbearing ages, given the current low fertility rate (less than 70 live births per 1,000 women age 15–44) the nation's population would be growing much more slowly. Births are up even though the fertility rate is low because there are so many of these women. In fact, in 1980 the 53 million women of childbearing age gave birth to 3.6 million babies. By comparison during the 1950s, at the peak of the baby boom, about the same number of babies was born each year to about 36 million mothers.[16]

Different age groups have different needs, hence changes in age composition are likely to translate into changes in the demand for goods and services. For example, today's low fertility society contains relatively fewer children, and hence fewer new parents, than was true twenty-five years ago. This has direct implications for the demand for furniture, diapers, baby food and clothing, pediatric health care, and day care services, since new parents' purchasing habits are likely to change quickly in response to their new infant's needs. A much higher proportion of infants in the 1980s are first children than was true in the 1960s, however, and research has shown that infant-related purchases are much higher for first children than for subsequent births.[17] Of course, as infants grow into young children their needs change. The demand for baby-related goods and services changes to textbooks, teachers, schoolrooms, tapes and records, and athletic paraphernalia.

Adapting to changes in age–sex composition can be especially difficult in a rural environment. These communities typically have fewer fiscal resources at their disposal for providing essential public services, and they lack the institutional capacity for managing change and planning for the future. Because they are smaller communities, they frequently lack some services and facilities of particular interest to youth and the elderly (such as specialized health and educational services and facilities), and the distances separating rural communities from each other and from larger centers impose logistic constraints and increased costs with respect to the provision of goods and services.

[16]Robey (1982).
[17]Olson (1983).

Much has been made in this chapter about the absolute and relative growth of the elderly population in nonmetropolitan America. These increases translate into changes in consumption patterns and have direct implications for public priorities. The demands for hospital care, other medical services and pharmaceutical products, and group housing arrangements advance with age. This is a critical issue in rural communities as is the provision of transportation services for the elderly. Rural communities generally lack mass transportation and are overwhelmingly dependent on the private automobile for personal mobility. Accordingly, some communities are now experimenting with innovative technologies and organizational structures to provide mobility for older residents.

Programs principally oriented toward the elderly (Social Security, Supplemental Security Income, Medicare) have grown from 19 percent of the federal budget in 1969 to nearly one-fourth in the 1980s; they have generally been credited with improving the economic status of older persons.[18] Cross-sectional data from the University of Michigan's Panel Study of Income Dynamics (PSID) show that total cash income of elderly families rose 26 percent (in constant 1982 dollars) between 1968 and 1982 whereas average cash income of families containing children actually declined from $29,800 to $29,100.[19] Longitudinal analysis of these same data shows that individual children gained in economic status between 1968 and 1982 and that the economic status of older persons declined. The elderly as a group have gained because new cohorts entering the older age groups are more affluent than their predecessors. The older elderly, in contrast, have experienced declining real cash income. The oldest population is disproportionately located in nonmetropolitan areas, and the nonmetropolitan elderly have only three-quarters of the income of their metropolitan counterparts. Accordingly, income maintenance for elderly persons can be expected to be a big ticket item in nonmetropolitan America throughout the remainder of this century.

In conclusion, whether our focus is on the declining proportion of children, the movement of the baby boom cohort into young adulthood and middle age, or the swelling of the elderly age groups, changes in the relative numbers of persons at different ages in a community have broad-based public and private sector effects. Accurate information of the determinants and consequences of changing age–sex composition is essential for conducting public and private activities and for planning for the future.

[18]Weller and Bouvier (1981).
[19]Duncan, Hill, and Rogers (1986).

5

RACE AND ETHNICITY

THE RACIAL and ethnic composition of rural and small town America has never been an exact replica of urban America, but the nature of the differences between them has gradually changed. The tenor and origin of most of the Eastern seaboard settlements were English, but well before the Revolutionary period there was a leavening of other people. Some were other British, such as the Welsh or Scotch–Irish who came in through Philadelphia. Others had settled independently before the British had extended their hegemony, such as the Dutch of New York or the Swedes in the lower Delaware Valley. French Huguenots were common in South Carolina and a variety of Germans were attracted to Pennsylvania, from which they fanned out in the Shenandoah and Tennessee valleys and parts of the Piedmont. Among them were the conservative Mennonite, Old Order Amish, and Brethren groups with their strong attachment to agriculture. In Louisiana, the French were firmly planted and in the southwest the Spanish had moved far up the Rio Grande and the California coast. Simultaneously, from the early years of European settlement blacks from Africa had been brought in, usually as slaves. With the exception of minor numbers in the Hudson Valley and southern New Jersey, their use in farming—and thus their rural location—was southern.

In the wave of immigration of the mid- and late nineteenth century, large numbers of German agriculturists permeated the Midwest, along with Scandinavians and western Slavs. Given the reputation of the Catholic Irish as city dwellers today, there were surprisingly large numbers of Irish farm settlements. Rural and small town mining districts attracted a wide variety of nationalities, including southern Slavs, Hungarians, Finns, Italians, and Cornish, as well as most of the other groups mentioned above. And, throughout the period there existed the indigenous Indian peoples. Some were settled and in close contact with the white population; others were leading traditional lives and not even enumerated in the census until the latter part of the century. All but a comparative few were rural.

By World War I, the period of rural settlement was essentially over. There were few suitable unoccupied lands still to be cultivated and the era of uncontrolled immigration had nearly ended. Rural population exceeded 50 million for the first time in 1920, and today it is still under 60 million. Racially, 85 percent of rural people were white in 1910, shortly before the slowdown in rural growth occurred. All but a small minority of the rest were black. At that time, just a little more than half (52 percent) of all whites lived in rural areas, but blacks were still heavily rural (73 percent).

The Black Population

In a manner perhaps unexpected at the time, the black rural population reached its peak count of 7,143,000 in 1910 and then began to diminish. The lure of urban jobs during World War I, the early depredations of the boll weevil on cotton farming, and increasing erosion of older cotton lands were factors leading to an outmovement of blacks that lowered the black rural population by about a quarter million by 1920. The white population, however, continued a slow rural increase. From that time until 1940, a similar pattern occurred. After 1940 an unprecedented exodus of rural blacks began, associated first with job opportunities of the World War II period but fostered thereafter by the radical modernization of southern farming, the abandonment of the tenant farming system that had long been the main support of rural blacks, and the sheer momentum of the movement away from the poverty and social suppression that was the common black experience in the rural South. A drop of one-half million in the number of rural blacks from 1910 to 1940 was followed by a reduction of 4.7 million from 1940 to 1980, despite a high rate of natural increase that would have produced rapid growth in the absence of outmigration. It was common in the 1950s and 1960s for decade county net outmigration rates to range from

50 to 65 percent for blacks reaching age 20 in the decade. As a result of these trends, the rural black population numbered only 3,901,000 by 1980. And, whereas blacks comprised 14.3 percent of the total rural population in 1910 when their number was at its highest, they had declined to 6.6 percent of the total by 1980.

The regional location of rural blacks is still essentially what it was after the Civil War. In 1880, 94 percent of rural blacks lived in the South; in 1980, 93 percent still did so. The vast migration of blacks out of the South to the North and West was almost exclusively to urban places.[1] There has been some dispersal of blacks into rural areas outside of metropolitan cities or associated with military bases or other institutions, but it is distinctly minor. Rural blacks are concentrated in the Coastal Plain from Maryland to eastern Texas and, to a lesser extent, in the Piedmont. There were still 81 nonmetropolitan counties in 1980 in which blacks comprised a majority of the population, although this is only about three-tenths as many as the number at the beginning of the century. At the extreme, there were eight nonmetropolitan counties in 1980 in which blacks were over 70 percent of the population.

Many of the conditions that led to the departure of rural blacks—such as mechanization of cotton and other row crop farming or legal racial segregation—have ended or else have greatly improved, such as political participation or access to occupations not previously open to blacks. The rate of decrease in the southern rural black population in the 1970s (7.5 percent) was less than half that of the 1960s (17.0 percent), although it is possible that some of the reduced loss is the result of better enumeration in the 1980 census. Some growth in the movement of blacks into nonmetropolitan communities from metropolitan areas has taken place. Whereas the 1980 census showed 354,000 nonmetropolitan blacks who had lived in a metropolitan area five years earlier, the 1970 census showed 234,000.[2]

The discussion of historic trends is presented for the most part in terms of urban and rural, for these categories can be applied to the earlier censuses. The nonmetropolitan black population of approximately 5.0 million in 1980 was considerably larger than the rural population of 3.9 million (see Table 5.1). Particularly in the South and the Midwest, the number of blacks living in nonmetropolitan urban places is larger

---

[1]In 1910 the black population was 27 percent urban and the total population was 46 percent urban. By 1960 blacks were more urban than the total population (73 percent vs. 70 percent).

[2]Strict comparability of these numbers is not possible because metropolitan areas were more extensive and somewhat more liberally defined in 1980 and because nonresponses to the migration question were not allocated in 1970. These differences work in offsetting ways, however, and we believe that the indicated trend is real.

than the number in outlying rural districts. This is not true of whites except in the West. This difference reflects a greater propensity for blacks to urbanize, even in small cities, plus the overwhelming presence of whites among people who disperse into the still rural but incipiently suburban territory around large urbanized areas. Expressed another way, within the total universe of nonmetropolitan and/or rural population, black representation is greatest in the nonmetropolitan urban population (10.1 percent), next greatest in the nonmetropolitan rural population (8.0 percent), and least among metropolitan rural residents (4.5 percent). The corresponding figure for the metropolitan urban population is 14.5 percent.

TABLE 5.1

Race and Spanish Origin of Population, 1980

Race or Spanish Origin	Metropolitan			Nonmetropolitan		
	Total	Urban	Rural	Total	Urban	Rural
Population (000s)						
Total	169,431	145,443	23,988	57,115	21,608	35,507
White	138,064	115,719	22,335	50,307	18,602	31,705
Black	21,478	20,405	1,073	5,017	2,189	2,828
Indian, Eskimo, Aleut	696	558	138	724	182	542
Asian and Pacific Islander[a]	3,198	3,087	111	302	175	127
Other[b]	5,994	5,674	321	764	459	305
Spanish Origin[c]	12,795	12,084	711	1,814	1,050	764
Percentage of Total						
Total	100.0	100.0	100.0	100.0	100.0	100.0
White	81.5	79.6	93.1	88.1	86.1	89.3
Black	12.7	14.0	4.5	8.8	10.1	8.0
Indian, Eskimo, Aleut	.4	.4	.6	1.3	.8	1.5
Asian and Pacific Islander[a]	1.9	2.1	.5	.5	.8	.4
Other[b]	3.5	3.9	1.3	1.3	2.1	.9
Spanish Origin[c]	7.6	8.3	3.0	3.2	4.9	2.2

[a]Japanese, Chinese, Filipino, Korean, Asian Indian, Vietnamese, Hawaiian, Guamanian, Samoan.
[b]Predominantly persons who wrote in any of various Hispanic entries in the race item. Also includes Asian and Pacific Islanders such as Thai, Pakistani, or Cambodian not listed in footnote *a*.
[c]Persons of Spanish origin may be of any race.

In the 1970s, overall population growth rates were higher in every southern state than they were in the United States as a whole, reflecting much improved economic conditions (including those in rural areas) and the perceived attractiveness of much of the region as a place to live. These trends could not help but have a stabilizing influence on the number of blacks present in the traditional southern rural heartland. In the 1980s by contrast, the East South Central States in particular lost ground in the recession of the early years of the decade. Alabama, Mississippi, and Tennessee all had nonmetropolitan job growth and population increase well below the national average, as did neighboring Arkansas. And in the Southeast as a whole, problems in textile employment have come only a decade or so after blacks finally gained access to this work. But, it is not evident that rural and/or nonmetropolitan blacks have been affected any worse than the white population, and a resumption of earlier levels of black rural outmovement is not likely to occur.

The Hispanic Population

In the 1930 census, a decision was made to treat Mexicans as a separate racial category. It was an effort that caused enough resentment to preclude its reuse in 1940. Furthermore, the count was limited to persons of Mexican birth or parentage. Thus it was incomplete, for there were numerous people of early Mexican origin whose families had been in the United States for several generations by 1930, such as most of the "Hispanos" in the Upper Rio Grande Valley.

By 1950, there was sufficient new interest in this population that census schedules in the five southwestern states of Arizona, California, Colorado, New Mexico, and Texas were inspected to identify white persons of Spanish surname. Although minor clusters of Mexicans were known to exist outside of these states—often associated with industrial, railroad, or farm employment—it was commonplace knowledge that the five states contained the vast majority of persons of Mexican background. Some 770,000 rural Hispanics were identified in this manner, accounting for a little more than 1 percent of the total rural population but 12.6 percent of the rural population of the five states.

By 1970, the rapidly growing size and diversified character of Hispanics in the United States resulted in inclusion in the census of a separate nationwide sample question on Spanish origin. This approach counted 1,160,000 such persons in rural areas, of whom 692,000, or 60 percent, were in the five southwestern states. Although statistical procedures in the 1950 and 1970 censuses differed, it is likely that the lower count of rural Hispanics in the Southwest in 1970 reflected at least some real decrease in population. Many of the rural and small town counties having large numbers of Hispanics in 1950 had heavy outmigration over the next twenty years. There was a surge of urbanization among southwestern Hispanics, much like that of blacks in the same period. Some of the rather surprisingly high proportion of rural Hispanics counted in other states appears invalid, associated with response problems stemming from schedule design, affecting people in the southern and central states. But much of it is a product of the gradual diffusion of Mexican-Americans into other regions, and of the rapid entry of Hispanics other than Mexicans into the country in the 1950–1970 period.

In 1980, the same technique of obtaining data on the Hispanic population by asking about Spanish origin was used in the census, but on a complete count basis. A similar problem of spurious entries arising from misunderstanding of the question arose, giving somewhat inflated results in some areas, but this problem is negligible in the national context. A total of 1,475,000 rural Hispanics was enumerated in 1980, an implied increase of 27 percent, far above the growth of 11 percent in the total national rural population. But, despite their rapid growth in the rural setting in the 1970s, Hispanics were still only 2.5 percent of all rural residents. Ninety percent of all Hispanics were urban, making them one of the most urban elements of the American people. Much Hispanic growth has come from immigration in recent years. Although the presence of Mexican immigrants in farm work is well known—especially as migratory laborers—Hispanic immigrants as a whole go in heavily disproportionate numbers to metropolitan urban areas. Ninety-four percent of Hispanics coming into the country in 1975–1980 lived in urban areas in 1980, and 93 percent were in metropolitan areas.

Despite the fact that they comprise only 2.5 percent of the rural population, Hispanics are still concentrated enough that they make up a majority of the population in thirty-two nonmetropolitan counties, with two-thirds of these in southern and southwestern Texas. At the extreme, their dominance of local populations is very high, reaching more than 90 percent in three counties—a higher degree of "minority" racial dominance than is found in any of the black majority counties in the southeast.

As with blacks, the nonmetropolitan population of Hispanics was larger than the rural population in 1980. Nonmetropolitan Hispanics numbered approximately 1.8 million, and rural Hispanics 1.4 million. In the dry Southwest, people of all races are typically more concentrated in towns than in the open county, but within these states, this pattern

144

is more true of Hispanics than of other races. Their comparative lack of participation in farming as operators surely contributes to this pattern, although it is not a full explanation.

The Hispanic rural and/or nonmetropolitan population is distinctive for its continued high involvement in agricultural work. Some 28 percent of employed rural Hispanic men were in agriculture in 1980, far higher than the 12 to 13 percent found among whites and blacks. However, only 8 percent of the Hispanic men in agriculture were operators; the vast majority were hired laborers.

Rural Hispanics are also distinctive among racial and ethnic groups in that nearly half of them live in metropolitan areas. Many of the Hispanics live in large agricultural counties where either small metropolitan cities have developed because of the sheer volume of employment generated by the local scale of intensive farming or where large farming districts still survive around growing nonagricultural urbanization. The Fresno, Greeley, Phoenix, and Yakima areas are examples.

Two-thirds of the growth in the Hispanic rural population from 1970–1980 took place in California and Texas, which also had a majority of the increase in urban Hispanics. Some of the increase almost certainly derives from improved enumeration, but both states have had a heavy influx of Hispanic immigrants, both legal and illegal.

Nationally, Puerto Ricans and Cubans are the largest Hispanic population groups after Mexicans, amounting to nearly one-fifth of all Spanish-origin persons. They are extraordinarily urban people, however, with only 3 percent living in rural areas. As a result, they comprise only 5 percent of all rural Hispanics.

Given the concentration of rural and/or small town Hispanics in a rapidly developing region (the Southwest), the continued economic and demographic pressure for emigration from Mexico, and the adjacency of that country to the southwestern United States, it would seem almost certain that the number and importance of Hispanics in the rural and related population will grow further.

Indians and Alaskan Natives

In 1910, when a special Indian schedule was included in the census, 254,000 rural Indians were counted, representing an astonishing 95 percent of the total Indian population. Indians were then and continue to be today the most rural major racial group in America. In the century after the Revolution, the assignment of Indian tribes to reservations and the forcible movement of many of them from the East and South to locations west of the Mississippi led to a greater degree of concentration of Indians in certain localities—or even states—than otherwise would have occurred. But, little urbanization occurred. The way of life was rural and often traditional.

Indians seem rarely to have been enumerated at similar levels of completeness in any two consecutive censuses in recent history, but since 1970 their number has risen rapidly, especially in the cities. Their total count in 1980 was 72 percent higher than that of 1970, making it all too obvious that improved enumeration procedures, or heightened positive image of Indian origin, or other factors had produced a statistical increase that was far beyond the realm of reality. The excess of births over deaths among Indians from 1970 to 1980 was very high (27 percent), but equal to only three-eighths of the purported total Indian growth. Immigration was insignificant, with only 2 percent of the Indian population being foreign born in 1980. Most of the enumerated increase was in urban areas, where a doubling of Indians is implied. As a result, over one-half of all Indians (53 percent) were found to be urban—the first census to show an urban majority. A growth rate of 48 percent is implied in rural areas, however, where the Indian population rose from 437,000 in 1970 to 645,000 in 1980. This, too, is well beyond that possible from natural increase.

A large amount of the enumerated increase in rural Indians from 1970 to 1980 occurred in states that have no reservations or other established Indian communities. For example, in Arkansas persons counted as Indians in rural areas rose nearly sixfold from 862 to 4,993. In Georgia they quadrupled from 731 to 2,854.

Four states reported at least 50,000 rural Indians. Arizona was first with 105,000, and the combination with neighboring, third-ranking New Mexico (75,000) gave the pair 28 percent of the national total. These states contain most of the reservation area of the largest tribe, the Navajo, as well as several other sizable groups, such as the Apache, Papago, and the various Pueblo tribes. There is a wide range in degree of acculturation or proximity to the white-dominated urban culture in these states. But, in general, the major reservations contain rather few non-Indians and the people continue use of the native languages. For instance, 95 percent of the 100,000 residents of the Navajo reservation are Indian and 92 percent of them employ the Indian language at home.

Oklahoma has the second largest number of rural Indians, with 85,000. Although some tribes in Oklahoma were native to that area at the time of white intrusion, Oklahoma in its prestatehood days had the distinction of being the principal territory where tribes or portions of tribes were relocated from states to the east. It is perhaps best known as the home of five southeastern tribes—the Cherokee, Chickasaw, Choctaw, Creek, and Seminole. There were many smaller groups, though. Some of the resettled groups had much white and, to a lesser extent, black admixture. Unlike the large tribes of the Southwest, their lands were ultimately opened to general settlement and ownership, after the Indian families were allotted homestead-sized parcels in individual ownership. Thus the major tribes lost collective tribal ownership of their former "nations," and the Indians lived in much greater propinquity to the rest of the population than was generally true in the Southwest or the Northern Plains.

In North Carolina, the fourth state in number of rural Indians (50,000), the situation is different from either Oklahoma or the Southwest. Here the majority are people of uncertain origin, living in the Coastal Plain, whose tradition of Indian ancestry is strong, but who lost the language, religion, and other cultural identifiers generations ago. The largest group is the Lumbee. Their existence was essentially unknown, except locally, until the Civil War and Reconstruction period when they came in conflict first with Confederate and then with Union authorities. Until the early 1950s they lacked any federal recognition. Their livelihood was based on farming, but, like other people in the area, most have now gone into other work.

Other principal locations of rural Indian settlement are the Northern Plains states (South Dakota, Montana, and North Dakota), with 76,000 in total, and California and Washington. Eleven United States counties have Indian majorities, with five of these being in South Dakota, where the rural Sioux presence continues to grow. Other native minorities are the Eskimo and Aleut in Alaska, both of whom are still predominantly rural, and the Hawaiians in Hawaii. The rural Eskimos and Aleuts are both concentrated along the coasts. The Hawaiian population has become largely urban, by about a four to one margin.

Asians

Americans of Asiatic descent are exceptionally urban. Although much of the early immigration was for agricultural work, especially in Hawaii, by 1980 all of the six groups of Asian and Pacific origin who numbered more than 250,000 people each in the United States were more than 90 percent urban. These are the Japanese, Chinese, Filipinos, Koreans, Asian Indians, and Vietnamese. (With the exception of the Japanese, they were also more than 90 percent metropolitan). Only in Hawaii do Asians have any significant rural demographic presence, where the Japanese and Filipinos, in combination with Hawaiians, account for nearly 55 percent of the rural population.

Ethnic Stock of the White Population

In the 1980 census a question on ancestry was included for the first time, primarily to obtain the nationality background of whites, most of whom have immigrant antecedents too far back in the past to be ascertained any longer merely on the basis of place of birth of parents. In addition, some nationalities are not distinguishable simply by knowing country of origin. For example, knowledge that a person's ancestors came from Russia does not tell whether he or she is ethnically Russian, Ukrainian, German, or some other of the various nationalities present in that country. The question asked was simple: "What is this person's ancestry?" If respondents followed the instruction guide they were told to report the group with which the person "identifies," and that "Ancestry (or origin or descent) may be viewed as the nationality group, the lineage, or the country in which the person or the person's parents or ancestors were born before their arrival in the United States." More than one group could be reported, in the case of mixed origin. About 11 percent of the white population in each residence category did not provide an answer to the nationality question, or gave a response that was not usefully classifiable.

The largest group of single ancestry was the English, who numbered 8.9 million, or 15 percent of the rural white population (Table 5.2). The English were followed by Germans, with 6.2 million persons, or 10.4 percent. The groups who came from Great Britain, however, essentially became a common stock, along with the Scotch-Irish. If the English, Scottish, and Welsh are combined along with those who report themselves as British, or as a dual mixture of any of the above, or as Scotch-Irish, or who report a three-way combination of English, Scottish, and Welsh, then the British-descended group that formed the bulk of the Colonial American stock amounted to 10.5 million persons, or 19.5 percent of the rural total. Irish and British mixtures provide another 1.8 million.

The German stock did not all originate in Germany. In the Great Plains states in particular, there are many communities of Germans from Russia—people whose ancestors settled in Russia by invitation, especially at the time of Catherine the Great, but who emigrated to America during and after the 1870s as they felt their situation deteriorating. Other Plains Germans came from Hungary, Rumania, or what is now Czechoslovakia.

A revealing feature of the data on ancestry is that the people who reported themselves simply as "American" (or in some cases "United States") are the third largest (5.3 million) and most rural white ancestry group. Forty-one percent of them were rural and 38 percent nonmetropolitan compared with 29 and 27 percent, respectively, for the entire

TABLE 5.2

White Population of Single Ancestry by Residence, 1980 (in thousands)

	Metropolitan			Nonmetropolitan		
Ancestry	Total	Urban	Rural	Total	Urban	Rural
Total	74,415	62,674	11,741	29,148	10,644	18,504
English	14,542	11,505	3,037	8,550	2,866	5,684
Welsh	226	190	36	84	36	48
Scottish	869	738	131	307	124	183
Scotch-Irish	2,159	1,812	347	853	360	493
Other British	94	82	12	25	11	14
Irish	7,606	6,526	1,080	2,701	1,040	1,661
Dutch	967	745	222	448	165	283
Belgian	107	86	21	36	13	23
French	2,352	1,975	377	1,094	481	613
German	12,346	9,773	2,573	5,659	2,047	3,612
Swiss	163	129	34	74	24	50
Austrian	287	265	22	38	16	22
Norwegian	745	631	114	495	179	316
Swedish	875	752	123	407	163	244
Danish	287	245	42	161	65	96
Finnish	161	131	30	105	34	71
Scandinavian	175	150	25	78	33	45
Hungarian	662	597	65	75	32	43
Czech	577	502	75	205	68	137
Slovak	312	274	38	41	15	26
Polish	3,321	2,996	325	455	194	261
Other Slavic, except USSR	454	416	38	56	22	34
Russian	1,313	1,268	45	62	32	30
Ukrainian	350	318	32	42	17	25
Lithuanian	300	276	24	42	18	24
Portuguese	500	450	50	89	51	38
Spaniard, Spanish	814	779	35	150	81	69
Spanish-American[a]	4,890	4,616	274	642	405	237
Italian	6,249	5,849	400	603	323	280
Greek	561	537	24	48	32	16
Other European	662	621	41	62	31	31
Arabic nations	370	352	18	32	22	10
Canadian, except French	180	163	17	42	18	24
American	7,930	6,097	1,833	4,931	1,472	3,459
All other	1,009	828	181	456	154	302

[a]Includes Spanish-American, Hispanic, and all country-specific Latin American nationalities.

white population. Does this frequent use of "American" represent a greater degree of philosophical nativism on the part of rural and small town people, or is there some other explanation? An inspection of the geographic distribution of nonspecific entries, of which "American" is the most common, shows that they were relatively far more numerous in the southern states, amounting to better than 20 percent of all non-metropolitan whites in Alabama and Georgia. In a number of counties of southern Appalachia the figure runs to 25 percent or more. By contrast, in typical states of the Northeast, Midwest, or Northwest, the nonspecific responses are just 5 to 10 percent. Thus the phenomenon is strongly regional. In almost every instance the incidence of such entries was higher in nonmetropolitan counties than in metropolitan areas. So it is also residentially associated. Basically the use of "American" is most common in those states where the population is most derived from the Colonial stock, which in turn was predominantly British and to a much lesser extent German. The location of the "Americans" implies that the population of British descent is considerably more understated in the nominal statistics than that of people of more recent immigration background, and that people of Colonial British origin are less likely than others to think of themselves in European nationality terms.

The only other rural white group to exceed 1 million was the Irish, with 2.7 million. The rural Irish cannot be thought of as simply a curious minority of the large Catholic Irish population that is so commonly associated with northern cities. There was, indeed, a rural and small town component of the huge inpouring of Irish immigrants from the late 1840s until the beginning of World War I. Some came to work on railroads or canals or in mines. Others began to farm, individually or in colonies. But the location of many of the rural people who reported themselves as Irish in the 1980 census ancestry question makes it clear that a large block of them are of quite different background. Thirty-six percent of all rural single-ancestry Irish are located in ten southern states that make up the core of the Protestant South.[3] These states have only 29 percent of the total rural population; thus the Irish are even overrepresented in them. This population has to be descended from the large Protestant immigration from Ireland that took place primarily in the eighteenth century. Many would be Scotch-Irish, the descendants of the Scots who were settled in Northern Ireland after the British conquest of the island was completed, largely in the seventeenth century. Although the term "Scotch-Irish" is still used (and there were 800,000 rural persons reported as such in 1980), it was not uncommon for this population to be referred to in early America simply as Irish, and it is most probable that many of the southern rural "Irish" are Scotch-Irish.[4]

As an indication of how little the southern Irish have to do with the period of classic nineteenth-century Irish immigration into the

[3]Alabama, Arkansas, Georgia, Kentucky, Mississippi, North Carolina, South Carolina, Tennessee, Virginia, West Virginia.
[4]Jones (1980).

United States, one can note that in 1910 when the number of persons of Irish birth or parentage was nearly at its peak nationally, less than 8 percent of the rural Irish stock identified by birth or parentage was in the 16-state census South. Compare this with the 36 percent of Irish by ancestry in 1980 who were in the ten-state southern core cited above. Because of the large southern component among them, the Irish are the third largest group in the farm population, as well as in the white rural population as a whole.

Rural persons of single-ancestry French descent numbered 1.0 million. The majority had ancestors who either came under American sovereignty when Louisiana was purchased in 1803 or who settled in the northern United States from Canada. Other single-ancestry rural populations with 500,000 or more members are Italians (700,000), Polish (600,000), and Dutch (500,000). The Dutch are one of the most rural white nationality groups. A majority of those who are rural are outside of metropolitan areas, and within nonmetropolitan territory they are almost twice as likely to live in rural settings as in small cities.

Among the single-ancestry white population, persons of Italian descent are the fourth largest nationally, numbering nearly 7 million people. But they are one of the most urban groups, with 90 percent living in urban territory. Despite this urban propensity, their rural minority of almost 700,000 is one of the largest white rural ancestry groups. Italians participated very little in agricultural settlement during their main period of immigration. The lateness of their arrival surely contributed to this, for most of the land had already been taken by the time they came. This does not appear to be a full explanation, however, for there were other populations arriving in the quarter-century before World War I who sought more participation in farming. In 1980 only 4 percent of rural Italians were living on farms. Much of the Italian rural population has developed around large cities, with the result that nearly three-fifths of it is in metropolitan areas. Somewhat over one-half of all rural Italians live in the Middle Atlantic states and Southern New England.

Slavic rural settlement began before the Civil War, with agricultural settlements of Poles and Czechs (then typically referred to as Bohemians). For the most part these people located in the Midwest and Texas. Many Poles who entered as logging or industrial laborers later acquired land when they could. Like Italians, rural people of Polish descent today are somewhat more likely to live within metropolitan areas than outside of them.

These two western Slavic groups were the only Slavic immigrants to enter farming in a significant way. Later Slavic immigration was strongly focused on industrial and urban work, plus mining. The rural Russians, Ukrainians, Slovaks, Slovenes, Serbs, Croatians, and Bulgarians combined do not equal either the Poles or less numerous Czechs today.

Of the individual Scandinavian populations (Norwegians, Swedes, Danes, and Finns), none numbers as much as one-half million in the rural setting, although the Norwegians do in nonmetropolitan areas. Collectively, however, these groups of common heritage who tended to settle in the Upper Midwest came to 1.1 million rural persons of single Scandinavian descent and 200,000 of dual Scandinavian nationalities or who simply reported themselves as Scandinavian.[5] Nearly a third of all single-descent Scandinavians lived in rural areas, making them one of the most rural ethnic groups.

With the passage of time, the growth of American-born generations, and the high rate of both social and physical mobility in our society, there has, of course, been much intermarriage between ethnic groups. Of white persons giving ancestry answers in the 1980 census, about 40 percent of the urban population and about 36 percent of rural people reported multiple ancestry, if "American" is treated as a single ancestry in light of the discussion of this group above. In all but a few states the degree of multiple ancestry is somewhat higher in the more heterogeneous rural areas around metropolitan cities than it is in more remote counties.

Among white rural people of multiple origin, the most common combination is that of German crossed with British or Irish, numbering 4.4 million (Table 5.3). These were followed in number by 1.9 million persons of mixed Irish and British ancestry (exclusive of Scotch-Irish entries). Some 1.2 million people reported ancestry of triple origin, drawn from combinations of English, Dutch, French, German, Irish, and Scottish, the major white nationalities of Colonial times. An additional 1.0 million rural whites of any of these same six northwestern European ancestries reported partial American Indian descent. This population is the most rural of all of the multiple origin groups (along with Germanic combinations). Thirty-six percent lived in rural communities in 1980. This degree of rurality is not surprising given the almost total location of Indians in rural areas in the past and the resulting necessity for white-Indian mixtures to have originated in a rural setting.

Altogether, the Colonial nationalities of northwestern Europe, plus combinations of these nationalities and "Americans," comprised three-fourths of the white rural population that reported an ancestry in 1980. In urban America, where immigration from Eastern and Southern Eu-

---

[5]Single Scandinavian descent includes Finns but excludes Icelanders and Lapps. Dual Scandinavian nationalities or those who simply reported themselves as Scandinavian include Icelanders and Lapps.

TABLE 5.3

White Population of Multiple Ancestry by Residence, 1980 (in thousands)

Multiple Ancestry Combinations	Metropolitan			Nonmetropolitan		
	Total	Urban	Rural	Total	Urban	Rural
Total Multiple Ancestry	50,126	42,155	7,971	15,185	5,912	9,260
British comb.	1,620	1,378	242	491	212	279
British-Irish	5,416	4,591	825	1,731	680	1,051
Germanic comb.[a]	1,427	1,096	331	607	203	404
British-German and Irish-German comb.	11,822	9,761	2,061	3,850	1,479	2,371
Scandinavian comb.	376	324	52	169	57	112
German-Scandinavian	1,394	1,165	229	636	236	400
German-French[b]	1,702	1,410	292	550	231	319
French-British[b]	1,499	1,253	246	526	211	315
Slavic comb.	810	741	69	80	34	46
3-Origin comb. of English, Dutch, French, Irish, German, Scottish[c]	3,233	2,673	560	995	389	606
British, Dutch, French, German, or Irish with American Indian	1,878	1,455	423	886	308	578
All other multiple origin ancestries	18,949	16,308	2,641	4,664	1,885	2,779
None, not classified[d]	14,185	11,489	2,696	6,215	2,155	4,060

[a]Including Dutch, Belgian, Luxemburger, Alsatian, as well as German, Austrian, and Swiss.
[b]Includes French Canadian.
[c]Except English-Irish-Scottish, which is included under British combinations.
[d]Not included in above totals.

rope was more common, they still accounted for three-fifths of the white population. This is indicative of ancestral origin only and does not necessarily imply descent from immigrants of the Colonial period. Many British, Irish, Dutch, French, and German immigrants did not come to the United States until the nineteenth century or later.

Conclusion

Like urban residents, rural Americans are of diverse racial and national origins. They differ most significantly from urban people in that rural areas contain a much smaller percentage of each of the three largest racial or ethnic minorities (blacks, Hispanics, and Asians and Pacific Islanders). These three groups combined (including a negligible amount of double counting of Hispanics with the others) amounted to just 9 percent of the rural population and 13 percent of the nonmetropolitan population, whereas they made up 19 percent of all urbanites and 22 percent of the metropolitan population. Further, the disparity is growing as blacks continue to show loss or no growth in rural and small town settings, and as Hispanics and Asians increase but not nearly so rapidly as in urban areas. Thus social and economic issues related to the progress of these groups do not, on average, have the same proportionate immediacy and salience in rural and small town communities as they do in larger areas. But the geographic distribution of these minorities is so uneven that in most of the southern third of the nation, blacks and Hispanics comprise large fractions or even majorities of the rural populace. Thus, there are many other areas where they are almost totally absent. Hispanics seem to be making more of a gradual penetration of rural and/or nonmetropolitan areas beyond their original hearth land than do blacks.

The Indian population is a major exception to the dominant metropolitan urbanism of racial minorities. For the first time, in 1980, a slight majority of Indians lived in urban places, and this proportion is almost certain to grow. But the existence of reservations and the rural—even isolated—character of most of them ensures a continued rural base for Indians. It can still be said that a majority (about 60 percent) of Indians live in rural and/or nonmetropolitan America, whereas none of the other three minorities noted above has as much as 20 percent of its numbers outside of metropolitan urban communities.

Within the white population, the major urban–rural ethnic difference is the derivation of a much higher percentage of the rural population from the countries of Northern and Western Europe and, correspondingly, a pronounced underrepresentation of people whose ancestors came from Eastern and Southern Europe (with the exception of the Spanish component of Mexican-American Hispanics) or elsewhere. Among whites of single ancestry, 92 percent of those in rural nonmetropolitan territory were of Northern and Western European origin (including "American"), compared with 67 percent in metropolitan urban places. Among both metropolitan rural and nonmetropolitan urban people the comparable percentage was 86. Rural and small town America, therefore, is the locus of the population most heavily comprised of descendants of the Anglo colonial stock and of the groups who were the core of the "old" immigration of the first three-quarters of the nineteenth century. Their relative dominance is increased by the comparative underrepresentation of nonwhite minorities in rural areas. The data of Table 5.3 do not show as much dominance of Northern and Western European ancestry combinations among rural nonmetropolitan white persons reporting multiple ancestry, with 69 percent reporting combinations of Northern and Western European origin, compared to 59 percent for urban metropolitan residents.

To the extent that ancestral culture of origin is still residually associated with differences in attitudes, values, affiliations, and ways of living, the rural and small town white population is the longest removed in time from immigrant influences. Religious affiliation may be the most obvious measurable characteristic still derived from the immigrant period. Recent polls confirm that the rural population is disproportionately Protestant.[6] In another area, recent research has found that ethnic origin is still a partial determinant in agriculture of persistence of families from one generation to another, variation in land ownership and inheritance, patterns of family cooperation, and the structure of farming.[7]

It would be foolish to think that ethnic identity within the white population is as significant in shaping rural society and providing the norms of conduct as it was for earlier generations during the immigration period and the more isolated conditions of the previous century. Further, it is not the purpose of this chapter to examine the extent to which ethnic social differences persist. The demographic data do make it clear, however, that with all the melding of population groups that has occurred, there are still major regional differences in the ethnic composition of the rural population and between that of urban and rural areas. And as will be demonstrated repeatedly in other chapters, the largest rural and small town racial minorities consistently live in the context of serious social and economic disadvantage, compared either with urban members of the same groups or with local whites.

[6]Rosten (1975).
[7]For example, Salamon (1985).

HOUSEHOLD GROWTH
AND STRUCTURE

THE STRUCTURE of American society has undergone rapid and pervasive change during the last quarter-century, and few institutions have changed more than the family. Age at first marriage has increased, the number of children couples have reached an all-time low in the 1970s and persists today at a low (by historical standards) level, the average number of persons who live together has declined, single parent households—especially those maintained by women—are increasingly common, couples not married to each other sharing a household are twice as common as in the 1970s, and it has been estimated that almost one-half of persons now marrying will eventually divorce.[1]

These trends and changes have caused concern about family viability in the United States. Yet, most social scientists believe that the family is a lasting institution, but one that is changing its configuration. Young people today may want some different things from marriage and family life, but there is evidence that marrying and having children continue to be the nearly universal aspirations for young people entering adulthood.[2]

Indeed, the viability of the family institution is demonstrated in the

[1]Weed (1980).
[2]Taeuber and Sweet (1976).

very demographic data that are for some a cause for concern. For example, while it is true that the lifetime proportion divorcing for marriage cohorts has risen in a regular pattern during the past century,[3] about five of six men and three of four women remarry after divorce.[4] Although the remarriage rate is now declining, this leads to some complex family structures, especially where children are involved, but nonetheless most persons who ever marry tend to live in a married state for a large (albeit declining) portion of their adult lives.

Andrew Cherlin argues that many current family trends, while markedly different from the 1950s, are in line with longer-term trends and changes and therefore are not a cause for alarm. He argues that the 1950s were atypical and a poor reference for present experience. Current trends, then, are a continuation of changes that had been occurring prior to the 1950s. Cherlin is most sanguine on this argument with respect to entering into marriage and childbearing. A great majority of Americans eventually marry, although the age at first marriage varies from era to era, and the cohort total fertility rate has declined steadily (except for the baby boom cohorts) for 150 years.[5] In contrast, the current rise in the divorce rate, while a continuation of a long-term trend, has been more rapid than expected from previous experience. And, the increase in single parent, female headed households with children, is, in our estimation, a cause for concern. In general, however, demographic data do not suggest a breakdown of the American family, but rather point to significant changes in its structure and function in American society.

Household growth, size, and structure have traditionally been different for urban and rural areas in response to demographic, economic, and social conditions. Higher rural fertility, earlier age at marriage in rural areas, chronic rural outmigration of couples in the childbearing ages, economic dependence on farming and other extractive industries, and more traditional rural attitudes concerning families are just a few of the factors associated with household size, growth, and structure that have differentiated rural and nonmetropolitan areas from their urban and metropolitan counterparts. However, many of these residential differences have converged substantially during recent decades, leading to the question of whether metropolitan–nonmetropolitan or urban–rural residence is significantly related to differences in household attributes in present-day America.[6] Residential differences in family structure, while real, were never as dramatic as portrayed in popular stereotype. Indeed, the content of these popular images of rural families—stronger

---

[3]Preston and McDonald (1979); Weed (1980).
[4]Cherlin (1981).
[5]Ryder (1980).
[6]Ford (1978).

marital and kinship ties, less stressful lives, more harmonious family relationships in general—have been called into question by empirical analysis.[7]

The prevailing opinion among family scholars is that rural and urban families are following parallel but different courses—moving in the same direction but remaining on distinctly separate paths.[8] Persistence of rural–urban differences is thought to be associated with more traditional rural attitudes toward marital stability, premarital sex, and labor force participation of married women, with remaining residential differences in economic and institutional structure, and with geographical isolation and small community size.[9] In contrast, traditional rural industries including farming have declined in importance, the effects of distance and isolation have been diminished by advances in transportation and communication, major rural institutions have become more similar to their urban counterparts, and public policy affecting the family has permeated the entire nation. Hence, it is not surprising that changes in rural family structure parallel urban changes.

This chapter provides a comparative analysis of household attributes within and between metropolitan and nonmetropolitan areas in 1970 and 1980 to determine whether rural and nonmetropolitan areas have participated in the secular trends and changes in family and household structure and to evaluate the continuing importance of residence as a determinant of differences in household size, structure, and growth in the United States. Although we use a demographic definition of rural–urban and metropolitan–nonmetropolitan residence in our analysis, we believe that this analytical schema represents an important source of cultural and economic differentiation in American society. The particular substantive focuses of this chapter are on (1) growth in the number of households in relation to the rate of general population change; (2) family versus nonfamily living arrangements of households; and (3) the family life course distribution of households.

---

[7]Lee (1986).
[8]Coward and Smith (1981).
[9]Glenn and Hill (1977); Larson (1978); Coward and Smith (1981).

Growth in Population and in the Number of Households

Growth in the Number of Households Relative to Population Change

Growth in the number of households in the United States has exceeded the rate of population growth in each decade since 1900, because the average size of households has fallen. This trend has recently accelerated, however, and the rate of growth in the number of households between 1970 and 1980 (26.5) is the highest of any decade in this century, more than twice as high as the growth rate of population (11.5 percent). Household growth exceeded population growth in all residential categories displayed in Table 6.1, but the difference was greater in metropolitan areas (about 2.5:1) than in the nonmetropolitan counties, where the number of households grew at about twice the rate of population. This metropolitan–nonmetropolitan difference reflects the slightly more rapid decline in the number of persons per household in metropolitan areas (−11.9 percent) compared with nonmetropolitan counties (−11.1 percent).

TABLE 6.1

Population and Household Change and Household Size by Residence, 1970–1980[a]

	Total (000s)	Metropolitan (000s)	Nonmetropolitan (000s)
1970 Population	203,213	154,512	48,700
1980 Population	226,546	170,493	56,053
1970–80 Change	23,333	15,981	7,352
Percentage Change	11.5	10.3	15.1
1970 Households	63,638	48,560	15,078
1980 Households	80,467	60,915	19,552
1970–80 Change	16,830	12,355	4,474
Percentage Change	26.5	25.4	29.7
Household Change/ Population Change	2.3	2.5	2.0
No. of Persons per Household			
1970	3.19	3.18	3.23
1980	2.82	2.87	2.98

[a]Fixed 1980 metropolitan designation.

Substantial variation between residential categories in the rate of growth in population and in the number of households is indicated in Table 6.1. The number of households grew by 30 percent in nonmetropolitan areas, exceeding the growth of 26 percent in metropolitan areas. Population change followed the same general pattern—evidence of the now widely known nonmetropolitan population turnaround of the 1970s,[10] but the nonmetropolitan population grew 1.5 times as fast as the metropolitan population while the number of households grew only 1.2 times as fast.[11] These residential patterns of 1970–1980 growth in population and in the number of households are quite similar in all four census regions. In each region, regardless of residence, the number of households grew faster than population, and in all regions but the South both population and the number of households grew faster in nonmetropolitan areas than in metropolitan areas (Figure 6.1). However, the 2 or 2.5:1 ratio between the household and population growth rates did not hold in all regions. In fact, the metropolitan population in the Northeast actually declined by about 1.5 percent during the decade, while the number of households increased by almost 10 percent. And, in the midwestern region, the metropolitan population growth rate was 2.5 percent, but the number of households grew by almost one-fifth (18.1 percent). Again, this is an expression of the substantial decline in average household size in such areas (3.2 in 1970 to 2.8 in 1980 in metropolitan counties of the Midwest, for example).

Persons per Household

As mentioned earlier, the number of persons per household has declined continuously during American history. Frances Kobrin has identified the demographic factors associated with this decline.[12] She observed that declining fertility diminished the number of large households; falling mortality increased the number of husband-wife households that survive past childbearing, thus increasing the number of small units; fertility and mortality decline have acted together to increase the number of small units by lowering the age at which couples bear their last child and lengthening the "empty nest" period; separated and divorced persons decreasingly opt to live with their parents, choosing instead to set up their own (smaller) household; and finally, since

[10]See Chapter 2 and Fuguitt (1985).

[11]A fixed 1980 metropolitan designation is used in Table 6.1. Urban and rural comparisons could not be made because of changes over the decade in urban territory through annexation, new urban places, and Urbanized Area delineation.

[12]Kobrin (1976).

FIGURE 6.1

Population Change and Change in Number of Households, 1970–1980

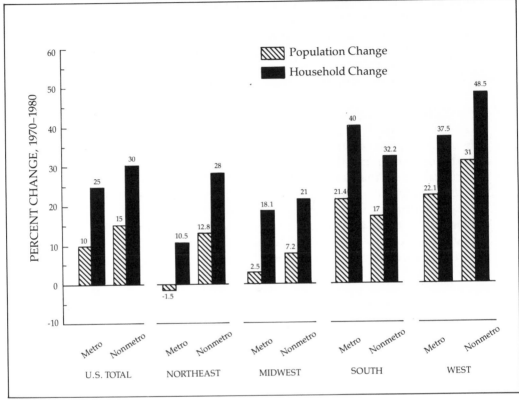

1950 there has been a rise in nonfamily households and especially single person households—particularly those maintained by young men or elderly women. Accordingly, the decline in household size is inextricably tied with changes in household type. As we shall see later in this chapter, the majority of household growth during the 1970s was accounted for by nontraditional family households, and by nonfamily households. These units tend to be smaller than the more traditional husband-wife-with-children unit.

Very little difference in the number of persons per household between metropolitan and nonmetropolitan areas is evident in either 1970 or 1980, although household size was somewhat larger in the rural component of both metropolitan and nonmetropolitan areas in both decades. A more detailed analysis of the size distribution of households (data not shown here) indicated that these urban–rural differences are accounted for by a larger percentage of one-person households in urban areas, and conversely by a larger percentage of households with four or more persons in rural areas. These differences reflect the lower level of urban fertility and a greater propensity to live alone, especially among younger persons in such areas. Conversely, higher fertility and a greater proportion of married couple households account for larger household size in rural areas. The data also showed that all regional and residential county types experienced a decline in the number of persons per household between 1970 and 1980. Smaller household size was brought about by substantial declines in the number of children in households because of the lower fertility of cohorts now in the childbearing ages, a trend toward living alone, particularly among young men and among elderly women, and an increase in the proportion of single parent households, particularly those maintained by women.

Although 83 percent of all United States counties experienced growth both in population and in the number of households during the 1970s, 15 percent of all counties (466) had population decline but an increase in households, and only 72 counties (2.3 percent) had declines in both population and households (Table 6.2). The vast majority of counties with an increase in the number of households but declining population were located in the nonmetropolitan Midwest. The small number of counties with declines in both population and households were also concentrated in nonmetropolitan areas, but the regional distribution of such counties was split almost evenly between the Midwest and Southern regions. Compared with counties that lost population but gained households, these "double losers" have substantially higher rates of population decline. These areas of overall decline are probably associated with an older age structure in midwestern areas (see Chapter 4) with a heavy dependence on agriculture, and with continued black outmigration from some areas of the deep South.

That 15 percent of all United States counties experienced population decline but had an increase in the number of households underscores the fact that the American population is reconstituting itself into more but smaller household units. For example, most divorces create two new households from one original with no population increase. Similarly, the number of households grows, with no population increase, when young adults leave their parental home to establish their own household. Where these trends take place in a generally declining environment, as in parts of the nonmetropolitan Midwest where outmigration continues and an old age structure contributes to low or negative natural increase, change in the number of households can be positive while population declines. The irony of this situation is that demand for housing and household related goods and services—utilities,

TABLE 6.2

*Patterns of Population Change in Comparison with Change
in Number of Households by Residence and Region, 1970–1980*

Population and Household Change	Northeast	Midwest	South	West	United States
All Counties					
1970–1980 growth:					
Both population and					
households	78.8	70.0	91.3	87.2	82.6
Only households	18.9	26.8	6.8	11.2	15.1
Neither	2.3	3.2	1.9	1.6	2.3
Total	100.0	100.0	100.0	100.0	100.0
(Number of counties)	(217)	(1,055)	(1,387)	(429)	(3,088)
Metropolitan Counties[a]					
1970–1980 growth:					
Both population and					
households	67.3	85.1	95.6	96.2	88.2
Only households	28.2	13.9	3.8	3.8	10.5
Neither	4.5	1.0	.6	1.0	1.3
Total	100.0	100.0	100.0	100.0	100.0
(Number of counties)	(110)	(201)	(315)	(78)	(704)
Nonmetropolitan Counties					
1970–1980 growth:					
Both population and					
households	90.7	66.4	90.1	85.2	80.9
Only households	9.3	29.9	7.6	12.8	16.4
Neither	0	3.7	2.2	2.0	2.6
Total	100.0	100.0	100.0	100.0	100.0
(Number of counties)	(107)	(854)	(1,072)	(351)	(2,384)

[a]Fixed 1980 designation of metropolitan and nonmetropolitan counties.

roads, et cetera—is increasing in such areas at the very time the community is losing residents and, in many instances, tax base. Accordingly, financing of public services can be seriously exacerbated in this type of demographic environment.

Family Living Arrangements of Households

Perhaps the most obvious difference among households is whether or not they contain a family, defined by the census as a group of persons who are related to the householder (head) by birth, marriage, or adoption. In contrast, nonfamily households are housing units occupied by a single person living alone, or a householder living with one or more persons, none of whom are related to the householder by birth, marriage, or adoption.

Family households can be further subdivided into married couples, one–parent families with either a male or a female householder, and households characterized by other family relationships, say, siblings or cousins. In addition, these subgroups can be classified according to the presence of minor children. Nonfamily households are classified by the sex of the householder in single person situations, and a residual category of persons living with other unrelated individuals (this category includes the so-called cohabitors). Disaggregating the household data in this fashion permits one to describe the family-type living arrangements of households, and it also sheds light on questions such as the determinants of change in household size raised earlier in the chapter.

Family households have been the modal type throughout American history. However, the proportion of households that include a married couple has declined from 90 percent in 1940 to 74 percent in 1980. Most of this change has occurred since 1960. The only major change during the 1950s was an increase in the proportion of married couple households with minor children because of the baby boom.

Since 1960 the family-type living arrangements of American households have changed dramatically. Married couple households, and especially those with young children, have declined as a percentage of all households. In contrast, because of the persistence of low fertility since 1960, married couples without minor children have increased as a percentage of all households. Nonfamily households also increased (from 15 to 26 percent). One-person households maintained by men increased rapidly, as did those maintained by women (by 78 and 55 percent, respectively, since 1960). And cohabitation (unmarried couples sharing the same dwelling unit) grew from 1.3 million in 1970 to 3.1 million in 1980.[13]

1980 Composition

Three-fourths of all households included a family in 1980, and the proportion was slightly higher in nonmetropolitan than in metropolitan areas (Table 6.3). Rural–urban differences are much greater, however, within the metropolitan and nonmetropolitan categories themselves.

[13]Sweet and Bumpass (1987).

TABLE 6.3

Households by Living Arrangement and Residence, 1980

Family-Type Living Arrangement	Total	Metropolitan			Nonmetropolitan		
		Total	Urban	Rural	Total	Urban	Rural
Family Households	73.6	72.5	70.9	83.4	76.7	71.1	80.3
Married couples	60.9	59.2	56.9	74.7	66.0	58.7	70.8
Children LT 18	30.8	30.0	28.3	41.3	33.5	28.6	36.7
No children LT 18	30.1	29.3	28.7	33.4	32.5	30.1	34.1
One-parent families	7.0	7.5	7.9	4.6	5.7	7.0	4.8
Mother-child	6.1	6.5	7.0	3.7	4.8	6.2	3.8
Father-child	.9	1.0	.9	.9	.9	.8	1.0
Other family households	5.6	5.8	6.1	4.0	5.0	5.5	4.8
Nonfamily Households	26.4	27.5	29.1	16.6	23.3	28.8	19.7
Total Households (percent)	100.0	100.0	100.0	100.0	100.0	100.0	100.0
Total Households (000s)	80,467	60,915	52,923	7,992	19,522	7,689	11,863

The family household component exceeds 80 percent in the rural parts of both metropolitan and nonmetropolitan areas, while it is only 71 percent in urban locales. The basic metropolitan–nonmetropolitan difference here is therefore attributable to the urban–rural balance within the two county-based residence categories. In 1980, only 14 percent of the metropolitan population was rural compared with 62 percent in nonmetropolitan counties. Thus, the rural component of the nonmetropolitan population has a much greater effect on the nonmetropolitan total than is true in metropolitan areas. The high proportion of family households in the rural-metropolitan population has little effect on the metropolitan total, but in the nonmetropolitan category the high rural figure contributes importantly to the total. Most of the metropolitan–nonmetropolitan difference in the proportion of households that are family households, then, is attributable to the high proportion of such units in the rural-nonmetropolitan category.

Family Households. Married couples account for eight of every ten family households, and these married couple units are about evenly split between those with and without minor children. The remainder of family households is about evenly split between one-parent families and other family arrangements. Most single-parent families are comprised of mother-child units. The composition of family households does not differ much between metropolitan and nonmetropolitan areas. In contrast, there are marked differences in the composition of family households between the urban and rural components of both the metropolitan and nonmetropolitan sectors. Rural areas, regardless of metropolitan designation, have more "traditional" family-type living arrangements—a higher proportion of married couple households with minor children, and a smaller proportion of single-parent families. However, similar to urban places, the vast majority of single-parent families in rural areas (eight out of ten) are mother-child arrangements.

Nonfamily Households. About one-quarter (26.4 percent) of all households are nonfamily units. Metropolitan areas have a higher proportion of nonfamily units, but the difference is not great. However, once again the urban and rural components of these two residence categories are markedly dissimilar. A much lower proportion of all rural households are nonfamily units.

The great preponderance of nonfamily households is comprised of persons living alone (Table 6.4). In every residence category, more than eight of ten nonfamily units are single person households, and about three-fifths of these people are women. Less highly urbanized areas have a somewhat higher proportion of single person nonfamily households than more urbanized locales—nonmetropolitan areas exceed metropolitan, and within both of these residence categories rural areas have a

167

TABLE 6.4
Characteristics of Nonfamily Households by Residence, 1980

Household Characteristic	Total	Metropolitan			Nonmetropolitan		
		Total	Urban	Rural	Total	Urban	Rural
Nonfamily Households (000s)	21,276	16,635	15,340	1,295	4,642	2,273	2,390
Percentage with One Person	85.5	84.4	84.1	87.6	89.4	87.7	91.0
Of One-Person Households, Percentage with Female Householder	61.1	60.3	60.8	55.5	63.5	67.6	59.8
Of Two+-Person Households, Percentage with Unmarried Couple Cohabitating	44.1	44.0	43.2	55.3	44.8	36.8	55.4
Age of Householder							
Median age	51.4	48.8	48.0	55.8	61.0	58.9	63.0
Percentage less than 30 years	25.7	27.1	27.7	20.2	20.5	24.5	16.6
Percentage 65+ years	34.2	31.0	30.5	38.0	45.4	43.3	47.4
Marital Status of Householder							
Single	36.8	39.1	39.8	29.9	28.6	31.7	25.5
Divorced-separated	26.3	27.4	27.4	27.7	22.5	22.2	23.0
Widowed	34.9	31.6	30.9	41.2	46.7	43.9	49.1
Married, spouse absent	2.0	1.9	1.9	2.2	2.2	2.2	2.4
Total	100.0	100.0	100.0	100.0	100.0	100.0	100.0

higher proportion than urban. This difference is attributable to the older age distribution of nonfamily household members in rural settings, and is related to the much higher proportion of widowed persons in such areas. It should be noted that a smaller proportion of single-person households in rural areas in both metropolitan and nonmetropolitan areas is maintained by women. The opposite residential difference is true when comparing metropolitan and nonmetropolitan counties; that is, a slightly higher proportion of nonmetropolitan nonfamily households is headed by women. This appears to be a genuine metropolitan–nonmetropolitan difference because the proportion of nonfamily households headed by women is higher in both the urban and the rural components of the nonmetropolitan category. Accordingly, the metropolitan–nonmetropolitan difference is *not* due to the rural–urban composition of these residential aggregates. Although nonmetropolitan counties have a higher proportion of women among one-person households, the most rural locales in both metropolitan and nonmetropolitan counties appear to retain a greater proportion of elderly men than women.

Much has been made of the increase in cohabitation in the United States. The data in Table 6.4 show that four of ten nonfamily households with two or more members contain an unmarried couple. This number, however, is only 6 percent of all nonfamily households, or 2 percent of all households, family and nonfamily, with more than one person. There is virtually no metropolitan–nonmetropolitan difference in the percentage, but it is more prevalent in rural areas. This somewhat counterintuitive finding may be associated with a greater prevalence of common-law marriages in rural settings, or it may be that the social contexts in which one would expect to find noncohabiting nonfamily households—college roommates or young working people sharing a dwelling, for example—are less likely in rural communities.

The nonfamily householder population is relatively old with a median age of over 51 years. Nonmetropolitan nonfamily householders are substantially older than metropolitan, and within each of these two residence categories rural nonfamily householders are older than their urban counterparts. These residential differences in median age are consistent with the other age data in Table 6.4, which show a lower percentage less than 30 years old and a higher percentage over 65 years old in nonmetropolitan and rural areas than in more highly urbanized settings.

Nonfamily householders are concentrated among the single and widowed marital statuses with a substantial proportion also in the divorced and separated category. Marital status differs substantially among the residential groups. Nonmetropolitan and rural areas have a much higher representation of widowed nonfamily householders, consistent with their older age distribution, and greater proportion of one-person households. As Christensen and Slesinger have shown, a high proportion of widows who live alone are poor.[14] This is not an extremely large part of the population, but it is one worthy of both research and policy attention.

1970–1980 Change in Composition

The number of nonfamily households grew at a much faster rate than the number of family households between 1970 and 1980—70 and 16 percent, respectively (Table 6.5). As a consequence, more than one-half of the 17 million new households added during the decade were nonfamily households, and they increased from 20 to 26 percent of all households. Family households grew by only 16 percent, but because of their large base in 1970 they accounted for 49 percent of the decade's growth. Two-thirds of the family household numerical growth was

TABLE 6.5

Change in Family-Type Living Arrangements, 1970–1980

Family-Type Living Arrangement	Percent Distribution		Change 1970–1980		Distribution of Absolute Change
	1980	1970	(000s)	Percent	
Total Households (000s)	80,467	63,444	17,023	26.8	100.0
Total Households (%)	100.0	100.0	—	—	—
Family Households	73.6	80.3	8,278	16.2	48.6
Married couple	61.0	68.8	5,436	12.5	31.9
With children LT 18	30.9	38.6	375	1.5	2.2
No children LT 18	30.1	30.2	5,061	26.4	29.7
One-parent families	7.0	5.8	1,952	53.0	11.5
Mother-child	6.1	4.9	1,799	57.9	10.6
Father-child	.9	.9	153	26.7	.9
Other family households	5.6	5.7	890	24.6	5.2
Nonfamily Households	26.4	19.7	8,745	70.0	51.4
Persons living alone	22.6	17.6	7,019	62.9	41.2
Men	8.8	6.2	3,147	80.0	18.5
Women	13.8	11.4	3,872	53.5	22.7
Other nonfamily households	3.8	2.1	1,726	129.6	10.2

[14]Christensen and Slesinger (1986).

among those married couples without minor children. As a result, married couple households with minor children declined from 39 percent of all households in 1970 to 31 percent in 1980. This is largely a function of delayed marriage and continued low fertility, especially delayed first births, during the 1970s. Another one-fifth of the decade's growth in the number of family households was among one-parent, principally mother-child, units. Both of these trends contributed importantly to declining average household size during the decade.

Most of the new nonfamily households were persons living alone. The number of females living alone exceeded males and contributed more to the decade's growth in the number of households, but the rate of growth in the number of males living alone, because of their small base in 1970, exceeded that of females (80 percent and 54 percent, respectively). The growth of single person nonfamily households was disproportionately among younger persons and among singles. Older persons and widows, although representing a high proportion of all nonfamily households, accounted for less of the growth (Table 6.6).

This type of components-of-change analysis cannot be conducted for the various residence categories of interest in this chapter. The metropolitan and urban definitions used in the public use microsample data

TABLE 6.6
Change in Nonfamily Households, 1970–1980

Household Characteristic	Change 1970–1980		Distribution of Absolute Change
	(000s)	Percent	
Total Nonfamily Households	8,799	70.5	100.0
Household Size			
1 person	7,037	63.1	80.0
Male	3,156	80.0	35.9
Female	3,881	53.5	44.1
2+ persons	1,762	133.2	20.0
Age of Householder			
LT 30 years	3,621	196.0	41.1
30–64 years	3,130	57.9	35.6
65+ years	2,048	39.2	23.3
Marital Status of Householder			
Single	4,112	110.6	46.7
Divorced-separated	2,976	113.6	33.8
Widowed	1,673	29.1	19.0
Married, spouse absent	39	10.1	0.5

were different in 1970 and 1980, which introduced an unmeasured component of change into the analysis. However, a comparison of metropolitan and nonmetropolitan family-type living arrangement distributions in 1970 and 1980, keeping in mind that the changed census geography could be a source of difference, indicated that the proportion of family households declined (especially married couples with children), the proportion of married couples without children remained constant, and the proportion of persons living alone increased in all residence categories.

To summarize, metropolitan and nonmetropolitan counties were relatively similar in family-type living arrangements in both 1970 and 1980, but the urban and rural components of these residence categories remained markedly different. Rural areas, regardless of metropolitan–nonmetropolitan county location, continued to have a higher proportion of married couple households with minor children, a smaller proportion of single parent families, and a much lower proportion of persons living alone. Hence, a more traditional family structure persists in the most rural parts of America. On the other hand, all of the residence categories experienced similar changes in family-type living arrangements during the 1970s. Analysis of county level data showed that even in the most rural counties there was an increase in the proportion of persons living alone, and a decrease in the proportion of married couples with minor children. Persons living alone in rural areas tend disproportionately to be elderly widows and widowers.

The Family Life Course

The family life cycle is a useful analytic framework for discerning commonalities among families according to several predetermined developmental statuses—marriage, childbearing, childrearing, and dissolution through death of a spouse. The life course, in contrast, emphasizes important family-related transitions without assuming predetermined stages. Hence, the life course concept can encompass such events as premarital pregnancy and divorce.[15] This section describes and compares the life course composition of householders in different residential areas, but it should be noted that the essence of life cycle (or life course) analysis is understanding the transition among statuses—the number, timing, and sequencing of these important events as they are influenced by social, economic, and demographic factors. Such analysis is beyond the scope of this chapter.

[15]Teachman, Polonko, and Scanzoni (1982).

Similar to the situation for family-type living arrangements, the family life course distribution of households has changed dramatically since World War II with the most dramatic changes occurring since 1970. The analysis by Sweet and Bumpass of Census Public Use Microsample files from 1940 to 1980 indicates that households maintained by never-married persons under 30 years of age increased from only 1 percent in 1940 to over 7 percent in the most recent census.[16] In fact, between 1970 and 1980 this type of unit accounted for over one-fifth of the growth in all households. This growth is attributable to the aging of the baby boomers, delayed marriage, and the increasing prosperity of young adults, enabling them to establish their own households prior to marriage.

In contrast, married couple households with children, which had increased by over 50 percent during the 1950s because of the baby boom, decreased as a proportion of all households in both the 1960s and the 1970s. These units comprised 40 percent of all households in 1960 and only 31 percent in 1980. This reflects delayed childbearing and a reduced number of children per couple.

Despite the rapid increase in divorce, households with children maintained by a formerly married person are still a small part of the total number of such households (4 percent in 1940 and 6 percent in 1980). The major increase in such households was among those maintained by a person at least 30 years of age and with no children present.

Elderly households, both married couples and households of formerly married persons, have increased continuously since 1940. In each decade the number of such households rose by at least one-fifth. It should be noted that living alone in old age is more a female than a male phenomenon because of women's greater life expectancy and because of the older average age of husbands than wives. The increase in elderly households is associated with both social and economic factors. There has been a noticeable shift away from including nonnuclear kin in the household and an increase in the preference for independent living among the elderly.[17] Of course, this latter preference is not independent of the increased economic ability to maintain a household with the advent of the Social Security, Supplemental Security Income, and Medicare programs (although many elderly persons, and especially the oldest old, are economically disadvantaged). Furthermore, as life expectancy has increased, the number of older widowed persons has increased, but as fertility has continued at a low level they have fewer sons and daughters, nieces and nephews with whom to live should they choose to do so. Bianchi and Spain have estimated that the net effect of having one

[16]Sweet and Bumpass (1987).
[17]Kobrin (1976); Beresford and Rivlin (1966).

adult child is a decline of 25 percent in the probability of living alone for elderly women and a decline of 17 percent for elderly men.[18]

1980 Composition

The 1980 family life course distribution of householders is shown by residence in Table 6.7. Married householders under age 65 account for over one-half of all households, never-married and formerly married householders of this age for 11 and 17 percent each, and elderly householders for about 17 percent. Metropolitan and nonmetropolitan counties differ markedly with respect to life course composition of householders. Metropolitan householders are more likely to be never-married or formerly married. In contrast, nonmetropolitan householders are more likely to be married, especially with children present, and elderly, regardless of marital status. The metropolitan excess in never-marrieds is largely explained by a greater proportion of younger persons (under 30), and the greater proportion of formerly marrieds in metropolitan areas is largely attributable to widowed, divorced, or separated persons over age 30 with no children present. Most of the higher proportion of married couple householders in nonmetropolitan areas is accounted for by the greater presence of couples with children.

Many of these metropolitan–nonmetropolitan differences are due to the higher proportion of rural population in nonmetropolitan areas. Indeed, the nonmetropolitan total is always more similar in householder characteristics to its rural component than to its urban one, and rural-nonmetropolitan areas have a low proportion of never-married, formerly married, and elderly householders and a relatively high proportion of married householders. Rural-metropolitan areas have these same characteristics, but they are such a small part of the metropolitan population that they have little effect on the total. Household units with elderly householders are more concentrated in both rural and urban nonmetropolitan areas, although in both situations the proportion is higher in urban than in rural settings.

Some rural–urban differences are quite large. For example, almost 70 percent of rural-metropolitan householders are married, compared with only one-half of those in urban-metropolitan areas. Most of this difference is accounted for by the extremely high proportion of married couples with children in rural areas (41.3 percent in metropolitan and 37 percent in nonmetropolitan areas). The larger proportion of formerly married elderly householders in urban areas accounts for the higher proportion of elderly households in urban than in rural areas.

[18]Bianchi and Spain (1986).

TABLE 6.7

Family Life Course Status Distribution of Householders by Residence, 1980

Family Life Course Stage of Householder	Total	Metropolitan			Nonmetropolitan		
		Total	Urban	Rural	Total	Urban	Rural
Never Married	11.1	12.3	13.4	5.3	7.2	9.9	5.5
Age LT 30	6.8	7.5	8.2	3.0	4.5	6.9	3.0
30–64	4.2	4.8	5.2	2.3	2.6	3.0	2.4
Married Couple with							
Children Present	30.7	30.0	28.3	41.3	33.5	28.6	36.7
Youngest LT 6	14.0	13.5	12.9	17.8	15.5	13.8	16.7
6–18	16.8	16.5	15.4	23.5	18.0	14.8	20.1
Married Couple with							
no Children Present	23.5	23.3	22.7	27.0	24.3	22.4	25.6
Age LT 30	4.8	4.9	4.8	5.1	4.5	4.6	4.4
30–64	18.8	18.4	17.9	22.0	19.8	17.8	21.2
Formerly Married with							
Children Present	5.9	6.2	6.5	4.3	5.0	6.0	4.3
Youngest LT 6	1.7	1.7	1.8	1.1	1.5	1.9	1.2
6–18	4.2	4.5	4.7	3.2	3.5	4.1	3.1
Formerly Married with							
no Children Present	11.2	11.9	12.5	7.9	9.2	10.7	8.2
Age LT 30	1.3	1.4	1.5	.9	1.0	1.3	.9
30–64	9.9	10.5	11.0	7.0	8.1	9.5	7.3
Elderly (Age 65+)	17.5	16.4	16.7	14.2	20.9	22.4	19.9
Never married	1.2	1.1	1.2	.7	1.2	1.4	1.1
Married couple	6.5	6.0	6.0	6.4	8.2	7.7	8.5
Formerly married	9.9	9.2	9.5	7.1	11.5	13.3	10.3
Total	100.0	100.0	100.0	100.0	100.0	100.0	100.0
Total Population (000s)	80,470	60,552	52,758	7,794	19,918	7,869	12,049

1970–1980 Change in Composition

Households with young never-married householders (under age 30) accounted for over one-fifth of the growth in the number of United States households during the 1970s (Table 6.8). In contrast, households containing married couples with children under six years of age declined during the decade. Other life course statuses that accounted for a substantial proportion of the decade's growth include households containing middle-aged married couples without children present (aging of the

TABLE 6.8

*Change in Number of Households by Life Course Status
of Householder, 1970–1980*

Family Life Course Status of Householder	Change 1970–1980		Distribution of Absolute Change
	(000s)	Percent	
Never Married			
Age LT 30	3,696	208.1	21.7
30–44	1,140	119.8	6.7
45–64	−44	−3.3	−0.3
Married Couple with Children Present			
Youngest LT 6	−661	−5.5	−3.9
6–18	940	7.5	5.5
Married Couple with no Children Present			
Age LT 30	1,008	35.3	5.9
30–44	655	35.6	3.8
45–64	1,912	17.8	11.2
Formerly Married with Children Present			
Youngest LT 6	226	19.8	1.3
6–18	1,159	52.2	6.8
Formerly Married with no Children Present			
Age LT 30	602	135.6	3.5
30–44	1,301	136.7	7.6
45–64	1,335	30.5	7.8
Elderly (Age 65 +)			
Never married	141	17.1	0.8
Married couple	1,361	35.2	8.0
Formerly married	2,257	39.5	13.2
Total	17,026	—	100.0

parents of the baby boom generation), households headed by formerly married persons at least 30 years old without children, and households maintained by elderly formerly married persons. Married couple elderly households also grew substantially and accounted for 8 percent of the decade's growth in households.

All of the major demographic trends of the last decade—the aging of the baby boom, persistent low fertility, delayed marriage, the increased divorce rate, and increased longevity especially among women—are reflected in these changes in the life course distribution of householders. The outcome of these components of change is to alter the life course status composition of householders. Never-married units increased from 6 to 11 percent, married couple households with children declined from 39 to 31 percent, and formerly married and elderly households increased slightly. Again, the reclassification problem constrains the formal analysis of components of change for residential categories, but an inspection of 1970 and 1980 distributions by residence indicates that most types of area experienced similar changes in composition by life course status. Rural areas, whether or not they are found inside a metropolitan area, are an exception. Their life course composition is essentially unchanged in 1980 compared to a decade earlier. Only the proportion of households containing a married couple with children changed noticeably (it declined); the distribution among other statuses is only slightly different. In contrast, the urban component of both metropolitan and nonmetropolitan areas experienced the full range of changes notable at the national and metropolitan–nonmetropolitan levels.

To summarize, the life course composition of United States households is changing in most types of residential areas. Households with never-married and formerly married householders are becoming more prevalent because of the rising age at first marriage, the increased divorce rate, and increases in longevity, especially among women. In addition, the movement of the baby boom cohorts into early adulthood, given their later age at first marriage and low fertility rates, contributes importantly to the decline in the proportion of households comprised of a married couple, especially those with children. And the proportion of households maintained by elderly persons has increased slightly. While these trends have affected most types of areas, metropolitan–nonmetropolitan, and especially urban–rural, differences are still very prominent for this aspect of population composition.

Households Maintained by Women

The increase of households maintained by women is one of the most important demographic events of the last two decades. Increasingly, such households include young women with minor children. Indeed, female-maintained households with children under 18 increased one and one-half times as fast as all households during the 1970s.[19] Female-maintained households tend to be economically disadvantaged. Since 1960, the economic position of households maintained by women has declined relative to all other households. In 1979, households with a female householder were over five times as likely as other households to have an income below the poverty line. In 1959, the ratio was three to one. And, female households with minor children are particularly disadvantaged.[20]

Data presented in Table 6.9 show that the trend has been diffused throughout the settlement structure. By 1980, one in every ten American households (8.2 million) was maintained by a woman. Among the female-maintained households 60 percent include minor children. Similar to the pattern we have seen throughout this chapter, metropolitan and nonmetropolitan areas are not dramatically different in the proportion of households with a female householder, or in the proportion of such households that include children. But within metropolitan and nonmetropolitan counties rural areas have a lower proportion of female-maintained households, and among these households a lower percentage have children.

Increased marital separation and divorce was the major contributor to the growth in female-maintained households with minor children, followed by increased illegitimacy.[21] Widowhood, on the other hand, has declined over time as a mechanism of growth in the number of households with a female householder.

There are substantial racial differences in the prevalence of households with a female householder. The number of nonwhite female-maintained households has grown more rapidly than that of white households maintained by women.[22] Our consideration of race is restricted to the South because almost all blacks who live outside of metropolitan counties are located in this region. Over one-quarter of all southern black households are headed by a woman with no spouse present, compared with only 7.7 percent of white and other nonblack households. The metropolitan–nonmetropolitan and urban–rural patterns described above hold for both blacks and other races in the South.

The marital status of female householders, no spouse present, by

[19]Teachman, Polonko, and Scanzoni (1982).
[20]United States Bureau of the Census (1981).
[21]See Ross and Sawhill (1975) for discussion of the first point; Masnick and Bane (1980) for the second.
[22]Bianchi (1981).

TABLE 6.9

Female Householders, No Spouse Present, by Presence of Children, Marital Status, and Residence, 1980

Family Life Course Status of Householder	Total	Metropolitan			Nonmetropolitan		
		Total	Urban	Rural	Total	Urban	Rural
Total Number of Households (000s)	80,467	60,915	52,923	7,992	19,552	7,689	11,863
With Female Householder (000s)	8,194	6,516	6,021	496	1,677	817	860
Percentage of Total	10.2	10.7	11.4	6.2	8.6	10.6	7.3
Of female householders, percentage with own children LT 18 years old	59.9	60.8	61.1	57.8	56.5	59.5	53.6
Marital Status of Female Householders (percent distribution)							
With own children LT 18 years old							
Single	16.7	17.8	18.6	6.7	12.3	14.1	10.3
Divorced-separated	68.0	68.0	67.6	72.3	67.6	70.3	64.6
Widowed	11.8	10.8	10.4	16.5	16.1	12.1	20.6
Married, spouse absent	3.5	3.4	3.4	4.5	4.0	3.5	4.5
Total	100.0	100.0	100.0	100.0	100.0	100.0	100.0
Without any children LT 18 years old							
Single	15.7	16.6	17.2	10.0	12.4	13.9	11.2
Divorced-separated	27.3	29.5	30.3	20.6	19.5	23.3	16.4
Widowed	55.3	52.1	50.7	67.5	66.5	61.4	70.7
Married, spouse absent	1.7	1.8	1.8	1.9	1.6	1.4	1.7
Total	100.0	100.0	100.0	100.0	100.0	100.0	100.0

the presence of minor children is shown in Table 6.9. About two-thirds of female householders with minor children are divorced or separated. In contrast, divorced and separated householders comprise only about one-quarter of female-headed units without children. These latter households are most likely to be maintained by widows (55 percent).

Residential differentiation in the marital status distribution of households with female householders is most marked among those that do not have a minor child. In these instances nonmetropolitan and rural householders are substantially more likely to be widowed than is true of householders in more urbanized locales, and less likely to be single, separated, or divorced. In female-maintained households containing a child, those located in more urbanized locales are slightly more likely to have a divorced, separated, or single householder, but the differences are not dramatic.

These same residential patterns hold in the South for both black and nonblack female-maintained households. Patterns of residential differentiation appear to be similar regardless of race, but there are some dramatic black–nonblack differences in marital status of female-maintained households in the South in the various residence groups. Fully three-quarters of nonblack female-maintained households, no spouse present, containing a minor child are headed by a divorced or separated person, compared with only half of comparable black households. Conversely, almost one-third of black female-maintained households with a child are maintained by a single person, compared with less than 5 percent of comparable nonblack households. The marital statuses of black and nonblack female-maintained households not containing a minor child are very similar.

One shortcoming of our approach is that while few blacks live in nonmetropolitan areas outside of the South, blacks are an important component of the urban-metropolitan population in those regions. Hence, the fact that nonmetropolitan areas outside of the South do not have many blacks does not eliminate race as a possible basis for residential differentiation in household structure. Indeed, this makes race a prime candidate.

In summary, about one-tenth of United States households (about one-quarter of black households in the South) are maintained by a woman with no spouse present. The majority of these units include at least one minor child. Residential differentiation among these households is not great, but they are somewhat more prevalent in more highly urbanized contexts. Female-headed households in less urbanized settings are more likely to be maintained by widows and less likely to be maintained by separated or divorced persons.

Group Quarters Population

The population not living in households is said to live in group quarters. These living arrangements include correctional institutions, homes for the aged, mental hospitals, military quarters, and college dormitories. The group quarters population is not large, about 5.7 million persons, or 2.5 percent of the United States total, and its regional distribution mirrors that of the general population—22 percent in the Northeast, 26 percent in the Midwest, 34 percent in the South, and 18 percent in the West.

Although the metropolitan–nonmetropolitan distribution of the group quarters population is about the same as that of the general population (73 and 75 percent metropolitan, respectively), it is more highly urbanized than the general population, especially within the nonmetropolitan category. Ninety percent of the nation's metropolitan group quarters population is urban, compared with 85 percent of the general metropolitan population. Two-thirds of the nonmetropolitan group quarters population is urban, compared with only 38 percent of the general nonmetropolitan population.

Looked at somewhat differently, the group quarters population accounts for almost 5 percent of the urban-nonmetropolitan population, twice the percentage of the urban-metropolitan population, and three to four times the percentage in the rural components (Table 6.10). Accordingly, the presence of the group quarters population is proportionately most important in urban-nonmetropolitan settings. The largest component of the group quarters population nationwide includes those persons living in college dormitories (35 percent) and in homes for the aged (25 percent). Correctional institutions account for 14 percent, followed by military quarters (12 percent), and homes for the mentally ill (4 percent).

The composition differs substantially among the residential categories. Compared with the national composition, the nonmetropolitan group quarters population has a higher percentage of persons in correctional institutions, homes for the aged, college dormitories, and a lower percentage in military quarters and mental hospitals. Because it accounts for 73 percent of the nation's entire group quarters population, the composition of the metropolitan group quarters population mirrors that of the entire nation.

Persons living in college dormitories and in homes for the aged comprise the majority of the group quarters population in urban areas in both metropolitan and nonmetropolitan counties. Persons living in homes for the aged account for almost one-quarter of the group quarters population in both of these residence categories, and residents of college

TABLE 6.10

Group Quarters Population by Residence, 1980

Type of Group Quarters	Total	Metropolitan			Nonmetropolitan		
		Total	Urban	Rural	Total	Urban	Rural
Total Population (000s)	226,546	170,493	145,922	24,571	56,053	21,135	34,920
Group Quarters Population (000s)	5,738	4,189	3,774	415	1,549	1,038	511
Percentage of Total	2.5	2.5	2.5	1.7	2.8	4.9	1.3
Type of Group Quarters (percent distribution)							
Correctional institutions	14.3	13.3	11.1	33.5	17.0	10.3	30.5
Homes for aged	24.9	23.7	23.9	22.2	28.0	25.3	33.6
Mental hospitals	4.3	4.7	4.4	7.1	3.3	2.6	4.6
Military quarters	11.7	13.3	13.9	7.9	7.4	9.4	3.3
College dormitories	34.7	33.8	35.8	15.0	37.2	47.4	16.6
Other group quarters	10.1	11.2	10.9	14.3	7.1	5.0	11.4
Total	100.0	100.0	100.0	100.0	100.0	100.0	100.0

dormitories account for over one-third in both instances. In fact, the college dormitory population represents almost one-half (47 percent) of the group quarters population in urban-nonmetropolitan areas, according to the data in Table 6.10. This underscores the importance of colleges and universities to the economic base of such areas.

Persons living in homes for the aged are also a substantial part of the rural group quarters population in both metropolitan and nonmetropolitan counties (22 and 34 percent, respectively). Inmates of correctional institutions are the other major component, accounting for over 30 percent in both instances.

The group quarters residents seldom comprise a large part of a local population. Nonetheless, because of their concentration among homes for the aged, college dormitories, and correctional institutions, the group quarters population can represent an important aspect of the local economy. Residents of old age homes frequently bring money into a community from health care and social service providers and/or from younger relatives. Similarly, correctional institutions often have state or federal funding. Institutions of higher education attract financial resources from the students' parents, and students patronize local trade and service establishments. All three of these types of facility generate employment opportunities for the local labor force. As pointed out earlier, these issues appear to be most salient in urban-nonmetropolitan areas because the group quarters population accounts for about 5 percent of that category's population base.

Conclusions

This chapter has demonstrated that residence continues to be an important factor for explaining variations in household growth and composition. Although residential differences are converging, and most areas, regardless of location, seem to be experiencing similar demographic trends and changes, metropolitan–nonmetropolitan and especially urban–rural differences appear to be quite persistent.

Rural areas continue to be characterized by more traditional household structures, in terms of both family living arrangements and life course composition of householders. The most traditional household structure, in fact, appears to be in the rural component of metropolitan areas. This is the classic suburban situation. Rural parts of nonmetropolitan areas appear to have more heterogeneity overall. Since most types of areas have been affected by similar trends and changes during recent decades, there is little question that these residential differences in household structure will be further moderated in the future. In the meantime, however, residence remains an important factor affecting variations in household composition and growth in the United States.

These changes in household structure are of critical importance at the local community level. For example, since the family is the institutional unit in which childbearing is expected and condoned, the reduction of married-couple households has important implications for childbearing and for goods and services associated with children. On the other hand, the increased prevalence of single-parent, mostly female-headed, households with children implies that the need for public assistance to such householders and their children is growing. Day care, income maintenance, and special educational programs become increasingly necessary. Although the most rural areas continue to lag somewhat behind their more urban counterparts in experiencing these alterations in household structure, the data presented here indicate a diffusion of change throughout the urban hierarchy. Accordingly, public and private officials in all communities, regardless of size or location, need to be aware of the changing nature of family and household living arrangements in managing current activities and planning for the future.

7

FERTILITY

Trends in Rural–Urban Fertility

R URAL PEOPLE have and always have had more children than urban people. This is one of the oldest, most basic, and valid premises of fertility analysis. Benjamin Franklin noted the pattern in the American colonies in 1751, and Wilson Grabill and associates demonstrated it using the census of 1800, where they showed that the ratio of children to women of childbearing age was more than 50 percent higher in the rural population than in urban places.[1] In many subsequent periods the relative difference was even wider.

The major explanations offered for higher rural fertility in modern times have been the incentive to childbearing provided by the economic usefulness of children on farms and the lower cost of living in rural areas, coupled with social factors that reduce fertility in urban areas, such as higher proportions of single people or broken marriages and greater education. Rural fertility patterns afford a contrast to those in urban areas that is both practically important and, perhaps, theoretically revealing.

From 1810 through 1940 both rural and urban fertility rates steadily

[1]Grabill, Kiser, and Whelpton (1958), pp. 5-17.

declined, despite the near absence of formal birth control methods (Figure 7.1). A majority of the drop in American fertility from 1810 to 1940 resulted from the decline in family size in rural areas, rather than from the gradual urbanization of the nation or from the drop in urban childbearing. In 1810, the ratio of children under 5 years to women of childbearing age implied a mean lifetime fertility of 6.6 children surviving to an average age of 2.5 years for every rural white woman.[2] (Data for blacks are not available.) By 1930, this number had been cut in half. With the onset of the Great Depression of the 1930s, fertility sank to its lowest level. Urban childbearing was well below replacement level during the decade 1930–1940, but fertility still was moderately above replacement in rural areas. Thus, for the first time there was a potential for the United States to be dependent on rural childbearing for its natural increase of population if the patterns of the 1930s continued into the future.

Urban women who were 35–44 years old in 1940 had failed to have enough children to replace themselves, and for the national cohort of that age, all childbearing above replacement needs came from the residents of rural areas.[3]

Childbearing revived, however, during World War II and particularly in the fifteen years or so after the war that became known as the baby boom era. This was especially true in urban areas, where, given the severely limited level of earlier fertility, there was the most potential for increase. In a change that reflected a major shift in social outlook, personal objectives, and economic conditions, marriage rates increased, the age at marriage fell, childlessness dropped, and average family size rose. Figure 7.1 shows that the ratio of children to urban white women of childbearing age fully doubled between 1940 and 1960 to levels not seen for nearly a century.

Rural fertility responded, too, to the pronatalist environment of the postwar period, but in a more limited way. Rural child/woman ratios for whites increased by only 35 percent in the same twenty years that they doubled among urban people, recovering simply to the level of 1920.

---

[2]Ibid., pp. 17-19.

[3]The term "replacement" is here used with respect to whether a given age group of women bears enough children to reproduce itself with daughters in the next generation. The required number of births per 1,000 women needed for such replacement will depend in part on the level of mortality experienced by children before they in turn reach the average age of childbearing and also on the extent of excess of male births over female births in a population. American women 40 years old in 1980 had borne about 5 percent more male children than female, and will lose about 3 percent of their daughters through death before the daughters reach the average age of childbearing. As a result, about 2,100 or slightly more births of both sexes per 1,000 women of that age are necessary for biological replacement of the parental generation. In earlier years replacement needs were somewhat higher because of higher child mortality.

FIGURE 7.1

*Number of Children under 5 Years Old per 1,000 White Women
20–44 Years Old, Urban and Rural, 1800–1980*

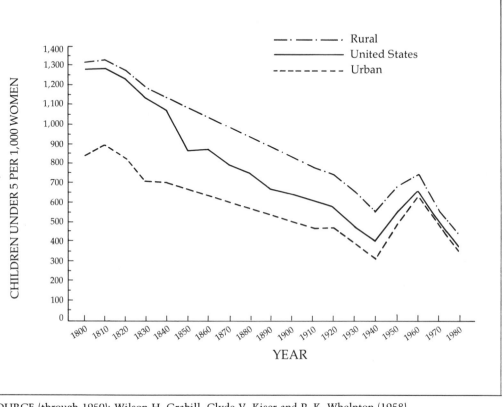

SOURCE (through 1950): Wilson H. Grabill, Clyde V. Kiser and P. K. Whelpton (1958).
NOTE: Rural and urban ratios not available for 1850 through 1900. Previous urban definition used for
1800–1840 and 1910–1950, current definition for 1950–1980.

There was not to be a return to the truly large rural family pattern of
the past.

Although the baby boom was disproportionately an urban phenomenon, it did not raise completed urban fertility levels to rural levels. The
implications of this fact were particularly strong if one considered the
role of urban and rural people in contributing to the excess of childbearing above that needed for parental replacement. In 1960, 27 percent of
women 35–44 years old were rural residents. But this rural minority of
women had contributed an estimated 66 percent of all the children

borne by this cohort who were in excess of replacement need.[4] The urban women of this age had cumulative childbearing only 9 percent above replacement need (2,264 children per 1,000 women, with a replacement need of 2,084 children). Rural women, on the other hand, with 3,004 children per 1,000 women, had 44 percent more births than necessary for replacement. Rural fertility was not extraordinarily higher than that in urban areas (an average of three-quarters of a child per woman), but because urban fertility was still so minimally above replacement, rural childbearing dominated generational growth.

However, among the women who had the largest number of children ever born per woman as a result of the baby boom (the cohort 15–24 years in 1950 and 35–44 years in 1970), urban fertility rose to within 15 percent of that in rural areas, and became significantly higher than replacement needs. The figures were 2,834 children per 1,000 urban women and 3,297 children per 1,000 rural women. In this cohort, urban women had about 65 percent of the number of children above replacement needs. The rural contribution of 35 percent of this number was only moderately above the 25 percent that rural women comprised of the cohort.

As national fertility rates diminished in the 1960s and 1970s, rural childbearing fell somewhat more rapidly than urban. Thus for women aged 35–44 years, the number of children ever born per 1,000 women fell by 10.7 percent for urban women between 1970 and 1980, but by 14.5 percent for rural women. Certain rural populations of relatively high past fertility showed distinct declines in childbearing in this period, such as southern blacks and those in Roman Catholic areas of the agricultural Midwest.

Among women under 35 years of age—most of whose childbearing had occurred in the previous decade—the fall off in urban fertility between 1970 and 1980 somewhat exceeded that in rural areas. For example, among women 25–34 years old, those of urban residence in 1980 had borne 33.3 percent fewer children than had the cohort of that age in 1970. Among rural women of these cohorts the decrease was 29.7 percent. With the rise in the average age at first marriage and in the average age at childbearing that has been taking place, it is possible for some of the drop in cumulative fertility among younger women to be made up in the latter half of their childbearing years. And, the pattern of delayed childbearing may be disproportionately an urban phenomenon. It seems unlikely, however, that the making up of deferred births will substantially alter the relative difference in urban and rural completed fertility.

[4]Beale (1972).

Fertility Differences by Residence in 1980

In 1980, among women 35–44 years old, those in rural areas had borne 2,849 children per 1,000 women, compared with 2,561 children per 1,000 women in urban areas. Cumulative rural fertility was thus 11 percent higher at that age than urban. Under the age-specific birthrates of the early 1980s, these women might expect about 130 additional children per 1,000 women. No urban–rural differences in this pattern are available, but they are not thought to be very large. This additional expected fertility implies that rural women 35–44 years of age in 1980 will finish their childbearing years with nearly 3.0 children per woman, compared with about 2.7 per urban woman. From a replacement point of view (with an allowance for the small amount of childbearing yet to come), rural women of this age have borne 43 percent more children than required for generational replacement, compared with 33 percent childbearing above replacement for urban women.

Metropolitan versus nonmetropolitan location does not distinguish major differences in rural fertility. The metropolitan rural value for women 35–44 years of age in 1980 (2,732 per 1,000 women) is only 7 percent lower than that of nonmetropolitan rural, and the corresponding metropolitan urban value is 10 percent lower than the nonmetropolitan urban value (see Table 7.1). On the other hand, there is even less difference between urban and rural fertility levels within nonmetropolitan areas. Thus completed family size among rural women within the boundaries of metropolitan areas is somewhat lower than that of women in nonmetropolitan urban places. The metropolitan rural category is somewhat diverse in character. On the one hand, it includes a number of people living in sparsely settled territory on the far edge of metropolitan counties who have little economic integration with the urbanized area and who would not have been classed as metropolitan if units smaller than counties had been used in delineation of metropolitan status. On the other hand, there are some millions of people living in densely settled rural territory just beyond the edge of the urban fringe whose communities are incipiently suburban. Such areas tend to be above average in income, social status, and proportion of white population, and their fertility is closer to that of suburban than to that of nonmetropolitan rural populations. If one takes as a proxy for densely settled metropolitan rural areas those counties having 100,000 or more rural people, the number of children ever born per 1,000 rural women 35–44 years of age in such counties was 2,632, compared with 2,503 for all United States metropolitan urban women outside of central cities and 2,940 for nonmetropolitan rural women.

TABLE 7.1

Children Ever Born per 1,000 Women by Residence, Race, and Spanish Origin, 1980[a]

Age, Race, and Hispanic Origin of Women	Total	Metropolitan			Nonmetropolitan		
		Total	Urban	Rural	Total	Urban	Rural
Women 25–34 Years Old							
Total	18,747	14,522	12,507	1,955	4,225	1,603	2,622
Children ever born	27,646	20,319	17,098	3,221	7,357	2,616	4,741
Per 1,000 women	1,470	1,399	1,361	1,648	1,741	1,632	1,808
White	15,503	11,748	9,901	1,847	3,756	1,385	2,371
Children ever born	21,818	15,462	12,462	3,000	6,356	2,164	4,192
Per 1,000 women	1,407	1,316	1,259	1,625	1,693	1,563	1,769
Black	2,268	1,921	1,851	71	346	158	188
Children ever born	4,219	3,447	3,300	147	772	347	425
Per 1,000 women	1,860	1,794	1,783	2,084	2,228	2,200	2,252
American Indian and Alaskan Native	132	76	64	12	56	16	40
Children ever born	256	131	109	22	125	34	91
Per 1,000 women	1,949	1,731	1,708	1,857	2,246	2,140	2,288
Asian and Pacific Islander	433	399	384	15	34	21	13
Children ever born	514	462	440	22	52	31	21
Per 1,000 women	1,186	1,158	1,144	1,513	1,522	1,446	1,651
Spanish Origin[b]	1,266	1,134	1,077	57	132	81	51
Children ever born	2,430	2,131	2,012	119	299	183	116
Per 1,000 women	1,982	1,879	1,868	2,095	2,263	2,268	2,256

TABLE 7.1 (continued)

Age, Race, and Hispanic Origin of Women	Total	Metropolitan			Nonmetropolitan		
		Total	Urban	Rural	Total	Urban	Rural
Women 35–44 Years Old							
Total	13,067	9,982	8,423	1,559	3,085	1,079	2,007
Children ever born	34,491	25,583	21,323	4,260	8,908	3,008	5,900
Per 1,000 women	2,639	2,563	2,531	2,732	2,887	2,789	2,940
White	10,876	8,108	6,636	1,471	2,768	937	1,831
Children ever born	27,655	19,972	16,012	3,960	7,683	2,471	5,212
Per 1,000 women	2,543	2,463	2,413	2,692	2,776	2,638	2,846
Black	1,491	1,261	1,209	53	230	99	131
Children ever born	4,795	3,889	3,704	185	906	360	546
Per 1,000 women	3,216	3,084	3,065	3,510	3,943	3,649	4,164
American Indian and Alaskan Native	94	53	42	11	41	11	30
Children ever born	322	159	124	35	163	39	124
Per 1,000 women	3,441	3,034	2,959	3,330	3,959	3,563	4,103
Asian and Pacific Islander	274	252	242	10	21	13	8
Children ever born	614	563	541	23	50	28	23
Per 1,000 women	2,246	2,235	2,231	2,323	2,373	2,155	2,711
Spanish Origin[b]	824	735	697	38	89	52	38
Children ever born	2,638	2,305	2,158	147	333	184	149
Per 1,000 women	3,202	3,138	3,099	3,853	3,731	3,579	3,939

[a]Numbers of women and children ever born are in 1,000s. Data for total women are based on published numbers from the full 1980 sample. All other data are from 1:100 sample. Rates from 1:100 sample statistics are calculated from unrounded numbers.
[b]Spanish origin independent of classification by race.

One factor contributing to higher rural than urban fertility is the difference in marital status and marital history between urban and rural women. This is also linked to migration patterns. Urban women consistently show higher proportions who either have never married or whose marriages have been broken by divorce or widowhood. In 1980, 14 percent of all urban women 25–44 years of age had never been married, in comparison with 5 percent of rural women. Failure to marry does not totally inhibit childbearing, but unmarried women 25–44 years of age average fewer than 500 children per 1,000 women. Thus differential failure to marry does affect group differences in completed childbearing. Among women 35–44 years of age in 1980, the rate of children ever born to all women was 11 percent higher in rural areas than in urban places. When the comparison is limited to women ever married, rural fertility was 8 percent higher.

In addition to having a higher incidence of single women, urban areas have a somewhat higher percentage of ever-married women who have been divorced or widowed, whatever their current marital status. For ever-married women 35–44 years old, 33 percent of those in urban areas had experienced divorce or widowhood, against 26 percent of those in rural areas.

To some extent the greater representation of single, ever-divorced, or ever-widowed women in urban areas is the result of migration of such women from rural areas. It is not easy to document this precisely, but it is reflected in the sex ratio, where among persons 18–49 years of age there were 102 males per 100 females in rural areas in 1980, but only 97 per 100 females in urban areas. Both economic and social considerations may be involved. Rural areas have clearly had a disproportionate reliance, over the years, on industries that are heavily masculine in employment orientation, such as farming, mining, timber work, and rail and truck transportation. For women supporting themselves, cities have offered more opportunities.

The Fertility of Blacks

The pattern of childbearing among rural black women earlier in the twentieth century was a curious one. There were many large families and overall rates of childbearing were comparatively high, as might have been expected of a poor, predominantly agricultural population. For example, among nonwhite rural women 45–54 years old in 1950 who had ever been married, 20 percent had borne eight children or more and the mean number of children ever born was 4,335 per 1,000 women. By contrast, fewer than 9 percent of white rural women of the same age had eight or more children, and the white average was 3,209 per 1,000 women ever married.[5] The anomaly of the pattern for blacks was that they simultaneously had high rates of childlessness. In the same cohort, 18.5 percent of the ever-married black women were childless, and another 14 percent had just one child. Childlessness was the modal birth parity, and this is quite extraordinary for women whose childbearing averaged four births per woman, as is the fact that one-child fertility was the second most common outcome. The explanation seems to lie in complete sterility or near-sterility associated with the consequences of venereal diseases, rather than with voluntary limitation. Relatively high incidence of sterility from disease was not limited to the black or rural population prior to 1940 in the era before antibiotics. But its effects appear most striking and contradictory in a population that also has large percentages of women with many children.

With the advent of antibiotic drugs during the 1940s, the frequency of fecundity impairments from gonorrhea and syphilis declined dramatically.[6] By 1970, among black rural women 35–39 years old, only 6.6 percent were childless and 8.4 percent had borne just one child. With no significant reduction in the proportion of very large families, the completed childbearing of this population rose substantially. By 1970, black rural women ever-married who were 40–44 years old had borne 5,372 children per 1,000 women, compared with the already high level of 4,335 observed among rural black women who were 45–54 years in 1950. This occurred despite the fact that during the period 1940–1970 rural blacks shifted from being predominantly agricultural to heavily nonagricultural.

All age groups of black farm women traditionally had much higher fertility than rural nonfarm women. Therefore the shift to nonfarm occupations and residence should have lowered fertility. Despite the higher level from which it began, rural black fertility rose more than white rural fertility during the baby boom years—both relatively and absolutely. A comparison of rural ever-married women 55–64 years old in 1970 with those 35–39 in the same year, reveals the number of children ever born for the younger women to be 24 percent higher for blacks and 15 percent higher for whites. The absolute differences were 992 and 428 children per 1,000 women, respectively. The levels of childbearing associated with American rural blacks at that time led to rates of generational growth commonly associated with developing nations rather

[5]Separate data were not shown for blacks in that census, but at that time the nonwhite rural population was overwhelmingly black, and the inclusion of other races in the data had negligible effect on the results.
[6]Shryock, Siegel, and Beale (1955); Wright and Pirie (1984).

than with the United States, and, indeed, educational attainment, income, and levels of living for rural blacks were all far below those of either urban blacks or rural whites. As an example, the median family income of rural blacks in 1959 was only one-half that of urban blacks and less than half that of rural whites.

Comparison of rural black women, who were 35–44 years old in 1980 with those of the same age ten years earlier, however, reveals a sizable recent drop in cumulative fertility. Those who were 35–44 in 1980 and ever married had borne 4,160 children per 1,000 women in 1980, down by one child per woman from the level reported by their counterparts of the same age ten years earlier. The rates for women 25–34 years old also showed a sharp decline from 1970 to 1980, indicating that further reductions in completed fertility are forthcoming. Although the rural black population decreased rapidly in size after 1940 because of outmigration, the high postwar level of childbearing offset some of the outmovement. With the age structure now undercut by the more recent decline in family size, the likelihood of further reduction in the relative presence of blacks in rural areas has grown. From a social point of view, however, the reduced childbearing has contributed to the lowering of black rural poverty rates, for the large size of black rural families has been a major factor contributing to their high incidence of poverty.

Both metropolitan–nonmetropolitan and rural–urban differences in children ever born are relatively larger for blacks than for whites among women 35–44 years old, but that is not true for women 25–34 years old. There is almost no rural–urban difference for nonmetropolitan black women of the younger age group (Table 7.1).

American Indian Fertility

Fertility rates continue to be high in the American Indian population. In 1970, every age group of rural Indian women 35 years old and over had borne more than 4,500 children per 1,000 women. Those in their forties in that year had averaged 5,000 children per 1,000 women. Naturally, such rates have produced a rapid generational growth rate among rural Indians, although in earlier years of the century high infant and child mortality offset some of the potential growth. In the 1960s and 1970s, however, childbearing among Indians began to fall. The extent of the decline is significant, but the growth implications of recent fertility levels are still substantial.

194

In 1980, rural Indian (and Alaska Native) women 35–44 years old showed 3,871 children ever born per 1,000 women, down by one child per woman from the figure of 4,903 children per 1,000 women for those of that age in 1970. Unfortunately the numbers are not fully comparable because of the higher rate of Indian identification in 1980 (see Chapter 5).

If, as seems likely, the people who were newly listed as Indian in 1980 were disproportionately persons of mixed ancestry whose lives and socioeconomic status were more similar to that of the general population, one would expect their childbearing pattern to have been lower than that of poorer, more traditional, and more isolated residents of the reservation areas. Thus the decline in Indian fertility from 1970–1980 for a given cohort is probably exaggerated. In fact, the states lacking reservations or established rural Indian communities and having large percentage increases in rural Indian population typically have rates of cumulative childbearing that are below the national rural Indian figure of 3,871 children per 1,000 women 35–44 years old. However, their rates are usually well above 3,000. Fertility in this population, therefore, is about midway between that of rural Indians generally and the rate for the white population (2,769).

Fertility of about the same level is observed among the large rural Indian population of Oklahoma (3,352 children per 1,000 women 35–44 years old). Many of the tribes forced to relocate there during the nineteenth century were highly mixed with white ancestry and had adopted American forms of government. On the average, educational standards and levels of cultural assimilation have been higher in Oklahoma than in the Southwest or Northern Plains. Thus it is not surprising that Oklahoma rural Indian childbearing is below the national average. An indicated 79 percent increase in the number of rural Indians in that state from 1970–1980 also clearly implies that many people of mixed descent elected to be counted as Indians in 1980 who had been listed as white or black in 1970.

The largest of the reservation Indian tribes, the Navajo, had 4,606 children ever born per 1,000 women 35–44 years old who lived on the reservation. About one-fifth of these women were urban, for whom separate figures are not available. Rural women would almost certainly have had a value between 4,700 and 4,800. Such a level of childbearing is well beyond that required for a doubling of the population in each generation, despite the higher rates of infant and child mortality that still characterize this population.

The 32,000 rural Sioux Indians of the Dakotas have even a somewhat higher rate of children ever born of 4,907 children per 1,000 women. On some of the Sioux reservations the levels exceed 5,000 as they also do among some of the Chippewa and a number of smaller tribes. Collectively, such rates give tremendous impetus to rural Indian population growth in parts of the West and the Upper Midwest, as well as the alternative of substantial outmigration if growth cannot be absorbed in the home communities.

Among rural Indian women 25–34 years old, the drop in childbearing rates from 1970 to 1980 was rather steep, going from 3,177 children per 1,000 women in 1970 to 2,142 in 1980.[7] This is a decline of nearly one-third. Indian rural women of this age in 1980 had still borne sufficient children to replace themselves even if they had no further births, but the implied eventual margin above replacement has been greatly lowered. The rates are about where those of rural white women were ten years earlier.

In sum, there are two points of equal salience to be made about fertility among rural Indians: (1) it is high and has produced a very young and rapidly growing population with large families and much child-related poverty; and (2) it has decreased rapidly in the last two decades, strongly suggesting that a demographic transition is now underway toward a smaller family pattern. But given the continued high rates of poverty and relative isolation of many of the reservation tribes, it seems doubtful that the decline will continue to the levels of childbearing now found in the rural white population.

Eskimos and Aleuts

The fertility of rural Alaskan Eskimos and Aleuts cannot be obtained readily from available sources, but it can be approximated reasonably by considering data for those areas in Alaska that are rural and in which the Alaskan native population is known to be overwhelmingly of these races rather than Indian. One can identify eight such county equivalents, which account for close to 90 percent of the total rural Eskimo and Aleut population of the state and in which Indians collectively account for just 3 percent of the total Alaskan native people. Thus fertility rates for the combined Alaskan native population in these areas

[7]These figures relate total women in the age group to children born to ever-married women. This is the only basis of comparing rates for total women in the two years, because the 1970 census did not show data on children of single women. The actual rates, therefore, are somewhat lower than they would be if all children were included. Because of rising illegitimacy, they may understate the 1980 rates somewhat more than the 1970 rates. Rates for women ever married were also down by a full child per woman, however.

are validly representative of all rural Eskimo and Aleut women. For women 35–44 years old in 1980, the number of children ever born was 4,721 per 1,000 women. This is similar to the higher values found among Indian tribes on reservations in the lower forty-eight states, and much above the figure of 3,871 per 1,000 women for all rural American Indians (including Alaskan natives). For women 25–34 years of age, the Eskimo and Aleut figure was 2,464 children per 1,000 women, which, like that of the next older cohort, was above the level for all rural American Indians (2,142) but not unlike that of the major tribal groups in the West and the Plains.

There is a suggestion that the Aleut population has lower fertility than do the Eskimos. At least, this is true for rural women 35–44 years old. This would be consistent with the higher median levels of income, education, and age that characterize the Aleut areas.

Hispanic Fertility

Another ethnic group of traditionally high rural fertility is the Hispanic population. As an ethnocultural minority of Roman Catholic religion and lower than average income and education, this is not surprising. Because of this population's heavy earlier concentration in five states of the Southwest, the first direct data on Hispanics were limited to persons of Spanish surname identified from the 1950 census schedules in those states. In that census, rural ever-married white women of Spanish surname 35–44 years old had borne 5,169 children per 1,000 women, compared with just 2,864 per 1,000 for other rural white women in the same states, and a nearly similar figure for those in the nation as a whole (2,871). Thus southwestern rural Hispanic fertility was far higher than that of rural whites in both the same region and nationally, reflecting a wide disparity in economic status and cultural values.

Although the decade of the 1950s was the heart of the baby boom, it did not result in larger families among the already prolific rural Hispanics. By 1960, children ever born had declined slightly to 4,943 per 1,000 ever-married rural white Hispanic women, a figure 4 percent below that of 1950, while the value for whites nationally had risen by 4 percent. Both populations had undergone a rapid decline and out-movement of farm people in the decade, the segment with the largest families.

The data for Hispanics in the 1970 and 1980 censuses are not strictly comparable with those for 1950 and 1960, because they are not limited to the white population and are based primarily on direct response to questions on Spanish origin or (in 1970) Spanish language heritage. In the five southwestern states there is undoubtedly a predominant comparability of coverage in the different censuses. Fertility data for rural people of Spanish language or surname in 1970 yield numbers for rural ever-married women remarkably similar to those of Spanish surname in 1960, namely, 4,944 children ever born per 1,000 women against 4,943 in 1960.

The 1980 statistics are somewhat different, too, in that they are based solely on a Spanish-origin question. The numbers of rural people, however, look rather consistent with those of 1970. The data show a drop in fertility to 4,217 children per 1,000 ever-married rural women in the five southwestern states, about 15 percent below the comparable number for 1970. Decreases of 0.5 to 1.1 child per woman were evident in all five states. Thus the process of decline has begun. Cumulative fertility in 1980 for total rural Hispanic women 35–44 (including single) was 4,058 children per 1,000. About 37 percent of rural Hispanic women 35–44 years old were enumerated outside of the five southwestern states in 1980. As discussed in Chapter 5, some of this number is erroneous inclusion of non-Hispanic blacks and whites, especially in the South (outside of Texas) and in the Midwest. The non-southwestern minority of rural Hispanics reported lower childbearing than did those in the southwestern core homeland—3,357 children ever born per 1,000 total women 35–44 compared with 4,058. The combined national rate was 3,800.

An interesting feature that Hispanic rural fertility has in common with the pattern for blacks and Indians is that childbearing among farm residents is marginally lower than that of nonfarm residents. In the minority groups, people in agriculture have sizable families, but the great majority of them live off the farm and are hired laborers. This is not a full explanation, however, for by far most rural nonfarm Hispanics and other minority populations work outside of agriculture altogether.

Regionally, the highest rural Hispanic childbearing is in the southern High Plains, mostly in West Texas. This is an area that contained few Hispanics two generations ago. But the introduction of irrigated farming into the area attracted many of them to work as hired laborers. Farm work is still the dominant single employment there, especially for men. Paradoxically, median Hispanic household income is higher in the High Plains than in the Texas Rio Grande valley counties where farm work is also important, even though educational attainment is definitely lower. Whatever the combination of social and economic influences that determines fertility in this case, there are a number of nonmetropolitan counties in the Lubbock area of the High Plains where children ever born per 1,000 Hispanic women 35–44 years old in 1980 exceeded 5,000, whereas no county values this high are found in the Rio Grande counties, despite the higher percentage of Mexican immigrants among the Hispanics there. In the traditional Hispanic areas of northern New Mexico and southern Colorado, where much of the population is descended from settlers who were already there when American sovereignty began, rates of children ever born had fallen below 4,000 per 1,000 women in most counties by 1980. Such rates are still considerably above those of the Anglo-white population, however.

Among rural Hispanic women 25–34 years of age in 1980, cumulative childbearing was 2,172 per 1,000 women, being 2,095 in metropolitan and 2,256 in nonmetropolitan areas (Table 7.1). This was already sufficient for replacement, but well below the level observed among women of like age in 1970. Hispanic, black, and Indian rural fertility levels all seem to be declining in recent years at essentially similar rates and to similar levels. In 1980, there was less than 5 percent difference between the rate for either rural or nonmetropolitan Hispanic women 25–34 years old and those for blacks and Indians of the same age and residence.

It is possible from the 1980 Public-Use Microdata Sample file to distinguish separately the fertility of Hispanics who reported themselves as white from those who reported other racial identities. Nationally, of Hispanic women 35–44 years old, 60 percent were white, 4 percent were black, Indian, Asian, or Pacific Islanders, and 36 percent gave another, nonconventional racial entry, such as Mexican, Chicano, or Puerto Rican. Among nonmetropolitan Hispanic women 35–44 years, the group who gave an entry other than white proved to have distinctly larger families than those who regarded themselves as white. The other races group reported 4,128 children per 1,000 women compared with 3,482 for the white majority. To some extent, the lower value for whites is influenced by the erroneous inclusion of some non-Hispanic whites in the Hispanic category, alluded to above. But although the exact number of such people is not ascertainable, it is not of a scale to produce a fertility differential of this magnitude. On the other hand, at age 25–34, there is no difference in number of children ever born between nonmetropolitan white Hispanics and those of other race (2,257 per 1,000 women vs. 2,272). Either the higher rates of the other race group at age 35–44 are the result of more prolonged childbearing, or else the 25–34-year-old cohort is substantially lowering its fertility in comparison with the experience of the cohort just ten years older.

In the nation as a whole, Hispanic white women 35–44 years old comprised 2 percent of the total nonmetropolitan white women of that age. Their cumulative fertility of 3,482 children per 1,000 women is one-fourth higher than that of the rest of the white nonmetropolitan women (2,779). The highest representation of Hispanic whites among white nonmetropolitan women is in the West, where they make up 6 percent of the total at ages 35–44. There the white nonmetropolitan fertility rate of 2,859 children per 1,000 women would be reduced to 2,820 without their presence.

White Fertility

In both the rural and the nonmetropolitan populations, the highest completed levels of childbearing among white women in the twentieth century are among those born from 1930–1934, who were thus 45–49 years old in 1980. These women lived all but the latter part of their fecund years in the baby boom period. They averaged 3,246 children per 1,000 women if rural and a slightly smaller rate of 3,217 children per 1,000 if the nonmetropolitan concept is used. These were levels leading to an approximate 50 percent increase of the parental population, achieved with only limited incidence of childlessness or one-child families (about 8 percent each) or of very large families (about 12 percent with six or more children).

For white women 40–44 years old in 1980, cumulative fertility was 3,056 children per 1,000 if rural and 3,049 for nonmetropolitan as a whole. Although there has been some increase in childbearing rates among white women in their thirties since the 1970s, essentially none has occurred among women 40 and over. At 1983 levels of fertility, each 1,000 white women aged 40–44 (rural and urban combined) would bear only 17 to 18 additional children. Thus the difference in 1980 between the cumulative childbearing levels of women aged 40–44 and 45–49 years is real and subject to only minimal future narrowing.

Rates at the county level are available only for 10-year age intervals of women, with the interval most closely approximating completed fertility being 35–44 years, a group that appears to be within 4 percent of its final childbearing. Around the United States nonmetropolitan white average of 2,776 there is considerable geographic variation, ranging from less than 2,250 in about 35 counties to about 20 counties with values of higher than 4,000. In the context of this cohort, anything over 3,500 children per 1,000 women can be considered rather high. Such rates are found primarily in the Mormon West (discussed separately) and parts of the Northern Plains and Upper Great Lakes areas. On the whole, these counties are sparsely settled and agricultural.

At the other extreme, about 295 nonmetropolitan counties had nearly completed white fertility of less than 2,500 children per 1,000 women in 1980. Five-sixths of them are in the South, with the vast majority east of the Mississippi River. A baby boom that raised county rates to levels of childbearing far in excess of replacement needs or far above previous levels never occurred in these areas. They are a curious mixture of counties. Some are Piedmont industrial areas, with labor force participation rates for women above national metropolitan levels. Many are coastal plain farming areas with large black minorities, or even majorities, where the whites are to a certain degree a social and occupational elite. Yet, many others are mountainous highland counties, almost entirely white, with chronic conditions of low income and education, and female labor force participation often well below average. It is noticeable that they do not yet include any of the core of the Allegheny or Cumberland Plateau country, nor much of the Florida Peninsula with its rapidly growing and highly heterogeneous population, nor any of the Roman Catholic enclaves (South Louisiana, Southern Maryland, west-central Kentucky).

In effect, there were many southern rural and small town counties in which populations of modest socioeconomic status limited themselves during the last half of the baby boom and the decade thereafter to families not quite as large as those typical of white metropolitan America. Outside of the South, the most obvious of the occasional instances of low white nonmetropolitan fertility are high-status resort counties— such as those containing Aspen, Sun Valley, or Lake Tahoe—where large percentages of the residents are inmigrants from metropolitan areas.

The Midwest

From 1935–1940, 157 counties in the United States had period net reproduction rates of 1,750 or higher per 1,000 white women.[8] Of these high rates, only 24, or 15 percent, were in the Midwest, and of those eight were in Ozark or other border southern culture areas. By 1970, the locus of high white rural fertility had radically changed. As measured by cumulative fertility of women 35–44 years old, there were 266 counties

---

[8]The period net reproduction rate is the number of female babies who would survive to childbearing age per 1,000 women if the fertility and mortality rates of a specific time were to continue across a generation. The cumulative fertility is the actual reported number of children of both sexes that are born to women of a given age group reported at a particular time.

in that year that had an average of 4,000 or more children per 1,000 rural white ever-married women, and 70 percent of them were in the Midwest.

This change resulted from both the exuberant increase of childbearing in certain Midwest areas during the postwar years and the near absence of response in the white rural South to the national pronatalism of the period. At the state level, rates of children ever born for rural white women 35–44 years old increased from 1950–1970 in all midwestern states from a minimum of 18 percent in Missouri to 37 percent in Kansas. (In the South, the maximum increase was 11 percent in Louisiana, and in seven states the values actually declined, with North Carolina showing a drop of 13 percent.) The Midwest region had emerged as the highest in rural white fertility, other than the smaller and better understood Mormon culture area of the mountain West.

In an effort to better understand the phenomenon, Midwest county fertility data from the 1970 census were manipulated in conjunction with various social variables to obtain conventional measures of ecological association. Each of the counties with high fertility was also examined as a case and subtabulations were made by township to pinpoint where within each county the high fertility prevailed. It soon became evident that religion was closely linked with the rates. The correlation of county church membership estimates[9] with fertility was examined, along with measures of education, female employment, income, population change, farm residence, and ethnicity.

The percentage of Roman Catholic adherents by county had a correlation with white rural fertility of .62, and this was the strongest relationship of any of the factors tested. Comparatively few people may realize the extent of rural midwestern Catholicism, and the notion of ecological county correlations for Catholicism and rural fertility will seem surprising to many readers. Any view of Roman Catholics as an overwhelmingly urban people in the United States is a generally valid one. For example, estimates of religious affiliation from polls show that 86 percent of Catholics live in urban places.[10] This reality is buttressed by the manner in which the urban-based Italian, Irish, and Polish-American populations are portrayed in our culture as the typical Catholic elements. However, the rural Catholic minority is primarily Germanic—a population group with strong Protestant components that is not thus stereotyped as Catholic. In addition, rural Catholics are not evenly distributed over the nation and can reach significant proportions in some areas because they are comparatively absent from others. Some

[9]Johnson, Picard, and Quinn (1974).
[10]Rosten (1975).

of the Catholic settlements began as unplanned collections of individual families; others were planned colonies. The areas of high fertility in the baby boom era included both types, but it is difficult to read the history of Catholic parishes without being impressed by the extent to which those settled as colonies or served by religious orders or by long-tenured, agrarian-minded priests remained as conservative and large-family-oriented communities.

By 1980, there had occurred a widespread and major reduction in the incidence of high fertility among whites nearing the end of the childbearing period. Instead of 186 Midwestern counties in which rural ever-married white women 35–44 years had averaged better than 4,000 children per 1,000 women, as there were in 1970, the number had dropped to just five in 1980.

To determine the degree of continued linkage between Catholicism and rural white fertility under these conditions of reduced high fertility, another correlation was run for 1980. The measure of Catholic strength used was the percentage of Catholics in the total county population, rather than among religious adherents, and the church membership data came from a 1980 survey.[11] The fertility numbers were for all women rather than those ever married. Thus there was not total comparability with the 1970 numbers. The correlation of Catholic presence with number of children ever born per 1,000 rural white women 35–44 by counties was .54, somewhat below the .62 value of 1970. However, this value continued to be well higher than that of four other traditional factors associated with childbearing—income, female labor force participation, education, and employment of men in farming. When each of these factors is examined net of the influence of the others (partial correlation), the value for Catholicism remained at .54. The highest of the others (employment of men in agriculture) had a partial correlation of just .20.

Among women 25–34 years old the picture is rather different. In this age group the correlation of Catholicism with county rural white fertility in 1980 was .19, far below that of .47 found in 1970. To some extent, a lower correlation of religious affiliation with fertility at younger ages is natural enough in that the higher average fertility of Catholics might not express itself until the latter half of the childbearing years. Note that the correlation for the women aged 25–34 in 1970 was .47 compared with .62 for women aged 35–44 in 1980. However, the radically lower correlation obtained for women aged 25–34 in 1980 (.19) would seem to confirm a waning of the importance of Catholicism as a determinant of family size in the rural Midwest. The partial correlations in 1980 for the 25–34 age group show a value of .21 for the percentage

[11]Quinn, Anderson, Bradley, Goetting, and Shriver (1982).

Catholic, below that of .34 for agricultural employment and −29 for college education.

Other religious groups that show high fertility in the Midwest are the Dutch Reformed, the Amish, and the Hutterites. The two predominantly Dutch nonmetropolitan counties in the region were above the average of other Protestant counties, although not as high as the Catholic areas. The Amish are a minority everywhere, but numerous enough in two counties to produce county-level fertility values far above average. The Hutterites are not sufficiently numerous to have major influence on county-level fertility, but the townships where they live show their influence. These generalizations can be reliably inferred from township-level data and knowledge of where the groups are located, but they can also often be directly measured from data on individual families derived from county atlases that list the religious affiliation of families.

Mormon Fertility

One of the major anomalies of American fertility patterns is the high rate of childbearing among members of the Church of Jesus Christ of Latter-Day Saints (LDS), who are more commonly known as Mormons. Mormon theology is supportive of large families and encourages its adherents to feel an obligation to bring into the world as many children as they can properly support.[12] The pattern is particularly incongruent with that of the larger society, because the Mormon population is an overwhelmingly white one and of high education. In contrast, two much smaller white religious groups of high fertility, the Old Order Amish and the Hutterian Brethren, have a low and deliberately limited education. In the predominantly Mormon population of Utah, 44 percent of the population 25 years old and over had completed at least one year of college in 1980, compared with 32 percent in the United States population as a whole.

Although direct measures of Mormon fertility cannot be obtained from the census, it is possible to identify that of counties whose residents predominantly are LDS members. In Utah, all but two counties are estimated to have a Mormon majority and there are ten such counties to the north in eastern Idaho and one in neighboring Wyoming.[13] In these counties, nonmetropolitan women 35–44 years old in 1980 had borne 3,785 children per 1,000 women, compared with the national fig-

[12]Thornton (1979).
[13]Quinn et al. (1982).

ure of 2,887. This is a far cry from unlimited childbearing, but it is nine-tenths of a child per woman above the national average and produces a generational reproduction rate more than double that of the rest of the nonmetropolitan population.

Rural women in the Mormon counties had completed fertility of 3,960 children per 1,000 women, essentially identical with that of United States rural black women (3,952), and higher than that for Indians and Alaskan natives combined (3,871) and Hispanics (3,800). Superior child survivorship among the Mormons adds to their effective fertility, compared with the other groups named, which have higher child mortality.

Furthermore, fertility has shown much more resistance to curtailment in the Mormon heartland in the last two decades than it has elsewhere. Excluding births to single women, the number of children ever born per 1,000 rural white women 25–34 years old dropped by 29 percent between 1970 and 1980 (from 2,391 to 1,689) in the United States as a whole. In Utah the number declined by only 13 percent (from 2,986 to 2,615). Thus the relative gap in fertility between rural Mormon areas of the West and the rest of the American rural population has widened among women still of childbearing age. Among rural women 15–24 years of age, fertility actually rose significantly in the 1970s in Utah, at a time when birthrates were in general decline elsewhere.

As a result of their young age composition and high birthrates, the predominantly Mormon nonmetropolitan counties of the region have very high rates of natural increase. From 1980 to 1986, there were 4.1 times as many births as deaths, whereas in nonmetropolitan America as a whole there were not more than 1.6 births per death. The rate of natural increase for these counties is on the order of 2 percent per year. Like most Western areas, the Mormon region is sparsely settled, with large arid and/or mountainous sections. The .5 million nonmetropolitan population of the area here defined is not large in the national context, but with its high reproductivity the population will either continue to grow rapidly or become a source of considerable outmigration.

If other contiguous counties are added in which LDS members are a majority of all church members and at least one-third of the total population, there are an additional 200,000 people in the Mormon domain. These counties are on average more highly urban, but their rural fertility is nearly as great as that of the area with a predominance of Mormons in the total population (3,895 vs. 3,960 children ever born per 1,000 women 35–44 years old). They had four times as many births as deaths from 1980 to 1983.

The practical local effect of the difference in Mormon and non-Mormon fertility is nicely illustrated in Idaho. The largely Mormon southeastern part of the state has four times as many births as deaths, whereas the rest of the state's nonmetropolitan population has 2.4 births per death (1980–1986). The rural and small town areas of southeast Idaho are growing almost as fast as those elsewhere despite having a much higher rate of net outmovement of people.

Southern Appalachia

It seems fair to say that part of the historic "hillbilly" image of southern Appalachia was that of the large white family. And not without reason. A mapping of family size from the 1900 census shows the largest and most populous concentration of counties with average family size of 5.5 persons or more for whites to be in central and southern West Virginia, eastern Kentucky, neighboring parts of southwest Virginia, and smaller areas along the Blue Ridge border of Tennessee and North Carolina.[14] Further evidence is found in the 1940 census, before the baby boom. From that census, Grabill calculated net reproduction rates for the white population for the period 1935–1940, based on ratios of children under 5 to women of childbearing age.[15] When these data were grouped into nonmetropolitan State Economic Areas, nine of the eleven areas in the United States having white period net reproduction rates of 1,700 or higher in this five-year span were in the southern Appalachians.[16] Thus even at a time of low national white fertility barely of replacement level, most of the southern Appalachian nonmetropolitan territory had birth rates high enough to produce rapid generational growth. In that period the National Resources Committee noted that the highest fertility in the United States was found among "the women of the Southern Appalachians."[17]

In sharp contrast to that pattern, of the twenty-five nonmetropolitan State Economic Areas highest in cumulative fertility for white ever-married women 35–44 years old in 1970, only one was a southern Appalachian area. (These areas all had rates of more than 3,800 children ever born per 1,000 women ever married.) Several of the Appalachian areas of previous very high birth rates had actually fallen below the national nonmetropolitan average. The locus of high childbearing in the white rural and small town population had shifted to the upper Midwest

[14]U.S. Census Office (1903).
[15]Grabill et al. (1958).
[16]State Economic Areas (SEAs) are substate multicounty areas delineated so as to be as homogeneous as possible in social and economic characteristics (Bogue, 1951). SEA delineations were employed in some tabulations of the censuses of 1950 through 1970.
[17]National Resources Committee (1938).

(Wisconsin, Minnesota, North and South Dakota) and to the Mormon West.

The inception of decline in southern Appalachian fertility at a time when family size in most of the rest of the nation was increasing was extensively documented by DeJong. He found that whether measured by general fertility rates (based on births) or child/woman fertility ratios from censuses, the rate of childbearing in the region as a whole dropped from a level 50 percent above the national white average in 1940 to one not larger than the national average in 1960.[18] There was a mild upward Appalachian response to the general recovery of birthrates in the 1940s, but a countercyclical drop in the 1950s occurred during the heart of the baby boom. The high fertility that had previously existed was supported by an exceptional degree of rurality—much of it characterized by isolation, very low education and income, and Protestant religious fundamentalism that was supportive of early marriage and large families and was often negative about birth control.[19] The subsequent decline in the face of national fertility increase is more elusive to understand fully. Education improved and labor force participation of women rose, but this was true elsewhere as well. The hold of fundamentalist "God's will" views of the desired course of childbearing may have weakened, for unlike the Catholic position of the time, there was no formal denominational dogma to impede the individual adoption of family limitation or its public advocacy in this overwhelmingly Protestant region.

A highly indicative measure of increased rationalism in personal and economic behavior by the population of the region at the time was the sudden, large outmovement of people seeking a better life elsewhere. Prior to 1940, the southern Appalachians had experienced a rate of population growth about equal to the rest of the country or, in the case of the Depression years, higher than elsewhere. But, during the national economic boom of the 1940s and 1950s—which contrasted so greatly with the rapid losses in farm and coalmining work that took place within the region—an estimated net outmigration of 1.8 million people occurred. The movement was so heavy, even from the poorest and most isolated counties, that it is difficult to think that any family would not have been exposed to the desire for material gain and enhanced standard of living that impelled it. Increased family limitation by those who elected not to move away may simply have been a behaviorial analog to the outmovement of others.

Fertility was by no means uniform in the southern Appalachians in the past and is not so today. It was commonly higher in areas of the

[18]DeJong (1968).
[19]DeJong (1965).

FIGURE 7.2

Fertility of Selected Rural Groups and Areas, 1980

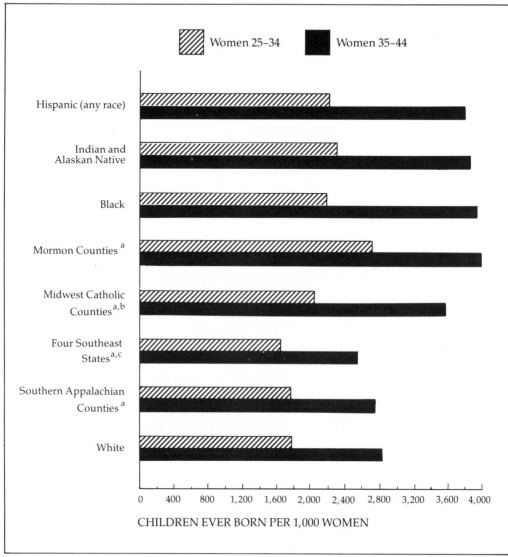

[a]White women.
[b]40% or more Catholic in total population.
[c]Virginia, North Carolina, South Carolina, Georgia.

Allegheny or Cumberland Plateaus than in counties through which the Shenandoah and Tennessee valleys ran or in the Blue Ridge counties. Declines have affected all of these sections, but a lingering echo of the older pronatalist culture is still observable in some of the core areas of the Cumberlands. However, only four counties reported as many as 3,500 children ever born per 1,000 women 35–44 years old in 1980, and the incidence of counties above 3,000 children per 1,000 women is far below that in the much more prosperous Dairy Belt, western Corn Belt, and Great Plains. The overall white rural rate in an area stretching from northern West Virginia to northern Georgia was 2,693, compared with a national white rural nonmetropolitan figure of 2,778.

The fertility of selected rural groups and areas is summarized in Figure 7.2. Hispanics of any race, Indians and Alaska Natives, blacks, and Mormon counties all had between 3,800 and 4,000 children per 1,000 women 35–44 followed by Midwest Catholic counties at about 3,500. The three other white groups are considerably lower at between 2,500 and 2,800. The pattern for younger women is rather different. Mormon counties are outstanding among the groups with more than 2,600 children per 1,000 women aged 25–34. The Hispanic, Indian, black, and Midwest Catholic counties were between 2,000 and 2,300, and the other white county groups were between 1,600 and 1,700. At the younger age, then, there is a definite convergence among all the groups except the Mormon counties. This pattern, of course, may be altered somewhat as these women complete their childbearing years.

Age at Marriage

In an era of increasingly ready access to communications, transportation, and higher education, it is not surprising to witness some convergence between rural and urban people in social practices and ways of life. But, in one of life's major passages—marriage—people living in rural or small urban settlements continue to commit themselves at an earlier average age than do people in metropolitan cities. For fertility, age at first marriage proves to be a key characteristic associated with completed family size. Figure 7.3 shows that among ever-married women 35–44 years in 1980, 39.4 percent of those living in metropolitan urban places had first married before their twentieth birthday. At the other end of the settlement scale, in rural nonmetropolitan territory, 56.8 percent had married in their teens. (Metropolitan rural and nonmetropolitan urban women were rather alike in amount of early marriage and intermediate between the two extremes.) The early marriage

FIGURE 7.3

Distribution by Age at First Marriage of Women Aged 35–44, 1980

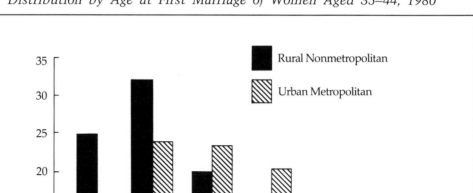

difference was due mostly to the extent of very early marriage for rural nonmetropolitan women, fully one-fourth of whom were less than 18 when married. Women aged 25–34 in the 1980 census, who were born from April 1945 to March 1955, showed some moderation of the propensity to early marriage that characterized those who were born in the late 1930s and early 1940s, but the wide urban–rural difference still persisted. There was a smaller percentage of marriages occurring before age 18 in all residential areas, but the relative difference before age 20 was still intact—54.0 percent of the rural nonmetropolitan women aged 25–34 had married before that age compared with 37.6 percent of the metropolitan urban women.

Few personal characteristics are as highly associated with fertility differences as is age at first marriage. The younger that women marry, the more children they ultimately have as a group. Despite the extent to which childbearing in America has been generally limited and controlled since the late 1960s, differences of only a few years in age at

marriage still are associated with significant differences in fertility out-
comes. In 1980, according to Figure 7.4, among nonmetropolitan women
35–44 years old, those married below age 18 had borne one-sixth more
children per 1,000 women than those married at 18 and 19 (3,643 vs.
3,103), who in turn had 9 percent more than those married at 20 or 21
(2,837), who had 15 percent more than women who waited until they
were 22–24 years to marry (2,465). On average, nonmetropolitan women
marrying under age 18 had nearly one-half more children per 1,000
women than those who married at ages 22–24.

A similar association between fertility and age at marriage is seen
in this figure for metropolitan women. If the extremes of the residential
types are compared, rural nonmetropolitan ever-married women 35–44
years old had borne 357 more children per 1,000 women in the aggregate
than had urban metropolitan women of the same age and marriage status. However, if the fertility rate for rural nonmetropolitan women was
standardized to the age-at-marriage distribution of urban metropolitan

FIGURE 7.4

Fertility of Women Aged 35–44 by Age at First Marriage, 1980

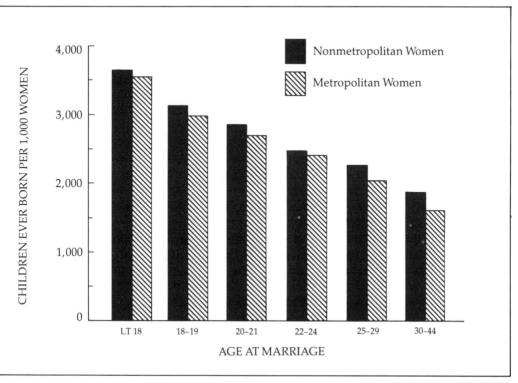

women, the difference would be cut in half to 175 more children per 1,000 women.

In short, the overall rural–urban differential in fertility was not major for women 35–44 years old in 1980, but one-half of it was associated with the sociocultural values that continue to induce a lower age at marriage in the rural setting. The rise in the average age at first marriage that has occurred over the last fifteen years can be instrumental in the decline of cumulative fertility, but need not narrow further the relative gap in rural and urban fertility unless it occurs disproportionately among rural people. Through 1980 there was no evidence of this taking place.

Education

Educational attainment of women continues to be strongly associated with fertility in both urban and rural settings and among all races. Nationally, among nonmetropolitan women 35–44 years old, those with five years or more of college had only one-half as many children ever born per 1,000 women as did those who did not finish high school, and within this range fertility was higher with each lower unit of schooling (see Figure 7.5). Although some women of this age interval will have additional children, it is unlikely that those of five years or more of college will have enough to replace themselves. The differences in fertility by educational status were very similar to those among metropolitan women, but at each educational level nonmetropolitan women had about 200 to 250 more children per 1,000 women than did metropolitan women.

There is also considerable regularity among nonmetropolitan women in the size of childbearing difference by educational group between women 35–44 years old and those 25–34 years old. In each educational group, the older women have about one child per woman more than the younger ones (ranging from 961 to 1,113 children per 1,000 women). But, with 35–44-year-old women of five years or more of college having only one-half of the cumulative childbearing of those who did not finish high school, the relative fertility difference between the 25–34-year-olds and those 35–44 years old is far greater at high education levels than at the lower levels. Nonmetropolitan women 25–34 who did not go through high school would need to have about 46 percent more children in their next ten years to attain the fertility of women already 35–44, but those with five or more years of college would have to bear 171 percent as many children in the next ten years as they had borne by age 25–34. Corresponding percentages for metro-

FIGURE 7.5

Fertility by Residence and Education, 1980

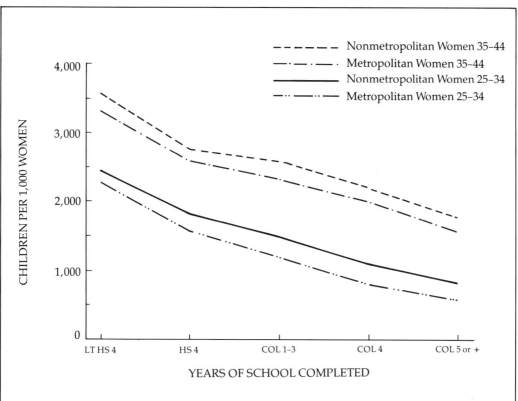

politan women are 46 and 117. To a certain extent, women of advanced education bear more of their children at older ages, but given the low birthrates that have prevailed since 1980, none of the nonmetropolitan educational groups 25–34 in 1980 seems likely to attain completed fertility levels comparable to the cohort ten years older. In addition, the gradual transfer of more women into higher educational levels reduces the influence of the still more-than-ample childbearing of the lower educational groups. Among nonmetropolitan women 35–44 years, 29 percent had not finished high school and 10 percent had been through college, but among those 25–34 years, these percentages were 20 and 15, respectively.

In the younger age group here discussed (the 25–34 year olds), it is the women with higher education who make a disproportionate contribution to the difference in childbearing that exists in the white majority between the extremes of the residential scale, that is, the rural nonmetropolitan women as opposed to urban metropolitan women. At this age, the most rural group had borne an average of over 500 more children per 1,000 women than had the urban metropolitan group. Two-fifths of this higher rate of fertility had occurred among the rural nonmetropolitan white women who had finished at least one year of college, although this well-educated segment comprised only one-fifth of all rural non-metropolitan women who were 25–34. Thus although higher education is associated with markedly reduced family size in both urban and rural settings, its effect on delaying childbearing and/or limiting it is not relatively as great in the most rural communities as it is in the most urban.

The differentials by education are considerably greater among black nonmetropolitan (or rural) women than they are among white women (Figure 7.6). Black nonmetropolitan women aged 35–44 with less than a

FIGURE 7.6

Nonmetropolitan Fertility by Education and Race, 1980

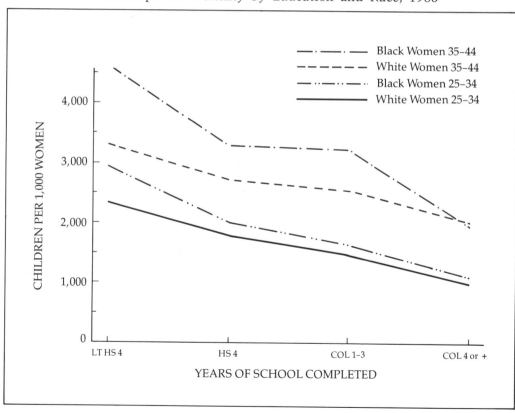

full high school education bore 2.3 times as many children per woman as those who were college graduates, but among white women the ratio was 1.6 to 1. Another way of expressing this is to say that there was essentially no difference in completed family size for whites and blacks among well-educated nonmetropolitan women, but wide differences existed among more poorly educated women. Nonmetropolitan black women actually showed a nominally lower number of children ever born per 1,000 women among college graduates (1,964) than did white women (2,028). (There may be no real difference, because of sampling variation associated with the results for the comparatively small number of black women with this level of schooling.) However, black nonmetropolitan women of age 35–44 without four years of high school had borne 4,592 children per 1,000 women, fully double their replacement needs and 39 percent above the comparable rate for white women (3,302). Improvements in educational attainment among blacks have proceeded very rapidly, though, and the incidence of failure to finish high school dropped from 57 percent among black nonmetropolitan women aged 35–44 in 1980 to 37 percent among those 25–34 years old. The latter percentage level is still far above that of nonmetropolitan white women of the same age (17 percent), but the decline—along with expected further declines—foreshadows further reductions in black rural and small town childbearing. If the black 25–34-year-old women had the same education-specific rates of children ever born, but with the educational distribution of black women 35–44, their childbearing would have been 10 percent higher.

Labor Force Participation

At any given time, women who participate in the labor force have been found to have smaller numbers of children than those who do not. In 1950, for example, of all United States women 40–44 years old, those currently in the labor force had borne 1,806 children per 1,000 women, whereas the comparable figure for other women was 2,679. The childbearing of those not in the labor force was nearly one-half higher than that of the women working or looking for work. At that time, however, labor force participation by women was much less common than it is today, especially in rural areas. For the women 40–44 years old only one-third were employed or looking for work in 1950, and in rural America only one-fourth were.

In the years since then, it has become more customary for women to work at all stages of the childbearing and childrearing period, as noted in Chapter 8. By 1980, at ages 35–44 (a somewhat broader age group), 60 percent of rural women were in the labor force. Those not working were the minority, but the relative split between women currently working and those not working was much more even than it had been thirty years earlier. The completed fertility of women in the labor force today is much higher than it was at that time. Increased labor force participation in and of itself has not been the deterrent to childbearing that might have been presumed from earlier experience. As it has become the norm, families (and society) have accepted the notion of working mothers and child care. One must also keep in mind that working is not a fixed attribute. Many women go into and out of the labor force as economic conditions vary or their stage in the family cycle changes. But, for women of nearly completed fertility (35–44 years), there is still some difference in number of children between those currently working and those not working. The difference is less for rural women than it is for urban women, however. The number of children born to rural women aged 25–34 in 1980 is almost 50 percent higher among those not in the labor force than it is for those in the labor force, but this number is almost 80 percent higher for urban women (see Table 7.2). Corresponding percentages for women aged 35–44 are lower: 14 and 22 percent.

Thus the effect of labor force participation on fertility is less in both residence settings for older women. Though many of the older women no doubt returned to work after a period more fully devoted to childbearing, 1980 labor force participation rates for women in the two age groups examined are almost identical at about 60 percent. In general,

TABLE 7.2

Children Ever Born per 1,000 Women
by Labor Force Status and Residence, 1970, 1980

Age and Labor Force Status of Women	1980		1970	
	Urban	Rural	Urban	Rural
25–34 Years				
In labor force	1,097	1,454	1,590	2,077
Not in labor force	1,979	2,151	2,486	2,730
Percent difference	80	48	56	31
35–44 Years				
In labor force	2,387	2,707	2,517	2,997
Not in labor force	2,903	3,098	3,177	3,591
Percent difference	22	14	26	20

the older pattern of leaving the labor force to raise children, creating a dip in participation rates in the twenties and early thirties, has about disappeared in the United States. Thus, we have either considerably lower prospective completed fertility pending for working women who were 25–34 years old in 1980 than for those of the same age not working, or else the working women of that age will have to have a rather high proportion of their births in the latter half of the childbearing period, and will have a longer mean length of generation than other women.

A look at data for 1970 reveals that in that year—as in 1980—the relative differences in fertility by labor force participation were much greater at ages 25–34 than at 35–44. Whereas rural women aged 25–34 who were not in the labor force in 1970 had a rate of cumulative childbearing 31 percent higher than that of those in the labor force, by 1980 this difference had dropped to 14 percent for the same cohort, by then 35–44 years old. The comparison is not exact, for the composition of the cohort would have altered some through migration and changes in rural–urban status of some places. Nevertheless, the point is almost certainly correct. Thus recent past experience indicates that much of the differential in fertility by labor force status that exists at age 25–34 is not present ten years later among the same women.

It should be noted that in 1980 the relative gap in childbearing by labor force status for women aged 25–34 was greater than it had been among women of that age in 1970. By 1980, rural women of this age not in the labor force had borne 48 percent more children than those who were working, whereas in 1970 the comparable difference was 31 percent. By 1980 we had a situation in which, simultaneously, rural women who had essentially completed their childbearing (ages 35–44) showed a lower difference in fertility by labor force status than did women of that age ten years earlier, but women 25–34 years old showed a considerably wider difference by work status than had been true of women at the same age a decade before. With a majority of rural women 25–34 years old already in the labor force in 1980 (59 percent), compared with just 40 percent in 1970, there is less potential for the labor force fertility differential to narrow in the current decade simply by a shifting of fertile women into the labor force category. More of any future convergence trend would have to result from late childbearing by those already working in 1980. The prospect seems likely that the difference in childbearing by labor force status for women completing the childbearing years is about to widen after having narrowed in the last several decades. Even so, labor force status will probably continue to be less a factor in childbearing levels among rural women than it is in the cities, given the very wide differences that characterize younger urban women.

Occupations of Women

As might be expected, the fertility of employed nonmetropolitan and/or rural women varies by occupation (see Figure 7.7). Those working in administrative, managerial, or professional and technical positions—which typically require higher education—have smaller than average families. The same is true of those in administrative support positions, which are heavily weighted with secretarial, bookkeeping, and other office clerical work, even though this white collar group is not as high in educational requirements as are the others. Fertility in these groups ranged up to one-eighth lower than the average for all nonmetropolitan working women for those 35–44 years old, and up to one-fourth lower among women aged 25–34. The lower relative values for the younger group are consistent with the higher age at marriage and delayed pattern of childbearing that goes with education. Occupations of an industrial, service, or agricultural nature are associated with higher than average childbearing. These include jobs such as food preparation and service, cleaning and building services, health service aides, motor vehicle operators, farmers and farm laborers, and unskilled handlers, helpers, and laborers.

Women in all major occupations consistently have somewhat more children per 1,000 women if they are rural or small town residents. But, the lower the skill level, the less difference there is in fertility between metropolitan and nonmetropolitan, or urban and rural. For example, women in the basically blue collar occupations listed above average (unweighted) just 5 percent higher fertility at ages 35–44 in nonmetropolitan areas than in metropolitan areas. However, those in professional and other white collar positions average 15 percent higher fertility in the nonmetropolitan setting than in metropolitan areas. It is possible that the detailed mix of professional and administrative jobs in metropolitan areas, for example, is not really comparable to those in nonmetropolitan areas. The metropolitan areas may have a higher proportion of the most highly demanding or educationally skilled professional jobs and also more unmarried women in such positions.

Part of the overall higher level of childbearing among nonmetropolitan working women is associated with the fact that the proportion of nonmetropolitan women working in high-status, low fertility jobs is less than that found in the metropolitan areas and, conversely, that lower status, higher fertility jobs are more common in nonmetropolitan communities. Nearly one-half of all employed nonmetropolitan women aged 35–44 years were engaged in administrative, professional, technical, or clerical work, but in metropolitan areas three-fifths were in such work. And, whereas seven high fertility occupations accounted for 12

FIGURE 7.7

Fertility by Occupation of Nonmetropolitan Women, 1980*

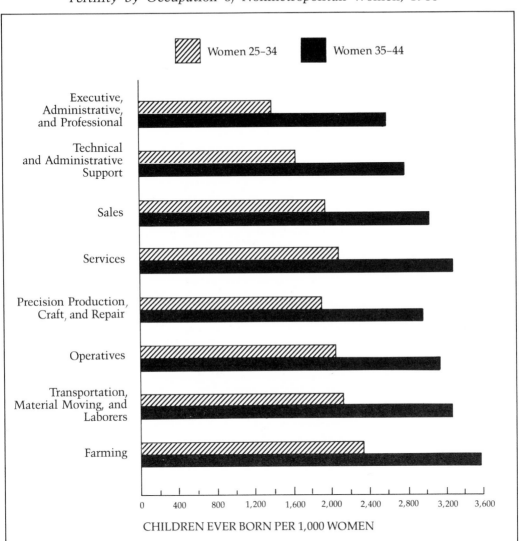

*Including last occupation of unemployed. Data are not shown for several occupation groups employing small numbers of nonmetropolitan women.

percent of the metropolitan employed women, 18 percent were in these jobs in nonmetropolitan areas.

Income and Poverty

In sharp contrast to the strong relationship of fertility to education of women, there was only a modest association with household income levels. For all nonmetropolitan women 35–44 years old, fertility ranged from 3,263 children per 1,000 for households with less than $5,000 of income in 1979 to 2,812 children per 1,000 for those in households with incomes above $35,000.[20] Income intervals above $10,000 all had essentially the same fertility (Table 7.3). Though rural nonmetropolitan women had higher fertility levels than urban within each income category, the relative difference in fertility between low and high income groups was about the same regardless of residence. As was true for other variables, however, this differential was greater for women aged 25–34 than for those 35–44 years old for all residence categories in the table.

Because of the consistently different fertility and income values known to exist by race, separate tabulations were made for whites and blacks. For whites aged 35–44, the differentials by income were narrow, from a high for nonmetropolitan women of 2,951 children per 1,000 women in households with less than $5,000 income to a low of 2,742 in households with $10,000 to $19,999 income. Above that modest income level there was no significant change in fertility. Thus the fertility difference between the intervals with highest and lowest fertility rates was less than 10 percent. For nonmetropolitan black women aged 35–44, the fertility rates at any given income level averaged about one child per woman higher than for white women, but with more of the blacks concentrated in the lower income intervals.

In the nonmetropolitan urban population there is a suggestion of a shallow U-shaped relationship of completed fertility with income for blacks, with both the lowest and highest income households averaging somewhat more children per 1,000 women than the households with income in the $10,000–$19,999 class. However, this effect is absent for white rural women.

It is when income is considered in relation to the concept of poverty that an association with fertility becomes evident. Among white nonmetropolitan women 35–44 years old in 1980, those in families with

[20]Women in households with zero income were omitted from the computation. This group consistently shows aberrant values that suggest some heterogeneous composition or unusual enumerative status. Such women comprise only 1 percent of all women in the age group in households.

TABLE 7.3
Children Ever Born per 1,000 Women by Household Income and Residence, 1980

Age of Women and Income	Metropolitan			Nonmetropolitan		
	Total	Urban	Rural	Total	Urban	Rural
Women 25–34 Years Old						
Under $5,000[a]	1,942	1,873	1,997	2,147	2,106	2,175
5,000–9,999	1,709	1,630	1,897	1,921	1,789	2,009
10,000–19,999	1,523	1,423	1,780	1,795	1,667	1,868
20,000–34,999	1,431	1,379	1,599	1,629	1,539	1,724
35,000 +	1,085	1,035	1,256	1,431	1,365	1,473
Women 35–44 Years Old						
Under $5,000[a]	3,012	2,905	3,027	3,263	3,176	3,309
5,000–9,999	2,936	2,846	2,962	3,147	3,050	3,197
10,000–19,999	2,635	2,544	2,791	2,861	2,667	2,953
20,000–34,999	2,612	2,548	2,690	2,819	2,712	2,879
35,000 +	2,537	2,489	2,682	2,812	2,704	2,880

[a]Includes women in households with zero or negative income.

poverty level incomes had borne 3,418 children per 1,000 women, compared with 2,712 for those in families above the poverty level. In one sense, this is a self-fulfilling statistical difference in that, by definition, the poverty threshold for a given level of income varies by number of persons in the family. For example, a family with $8,000 in 1979 would have been considered not in poverty if it had two adults and two children, but in poverty if there had been three children present. It would be unreasonable to hypothesize no fertility differences by poverty status. On the other hand, it would be foolish not to attach some social significance to the fact that children in larger families are on the average more likely to live in situations where the family income is deemed to be too low to support an adequate level of living.

It does not prove to be true that deep levels of poverty are any more related to higher childbearing than are moderate levels or incomes modestly above the poverty line, at least not for most populations. Thus among white nonmetropolitan women aged 35–44, those in families with incomes less than 75 percent of the poverty threshold had fertility levels about 1 percent lower than those for women whose income was between 75 and 99 percent of the poverty level. These levels in turn were higher than those for women with family incomes that were greater than the poverty line by no more than 25 percent—but they were only 2 percent higher. There is no fully adequate explanation for the lack of difference at these low income levels. It is possible, however, that women in very poor families often have been subject to some aspect of social disability that has an at least a mildly limiting effect on fertility. The lack of substantially higher fertility at the worst poverty level may also be influenced by the presence of a somewhat higher proportion of self-employed people of normally middle income levels who report that they lost income in the year concerned. In this connection, it can be shown that farm families in good farming areas who have poverty level incomes in a given year report larger than average income deficits below the poverty level.

Among nonmetropolitan blacks, fertility of women 35–44 years old was 4,884 for those in families with poverty level incomes, compared to 3,436 for those with incomes above the poverty line. This is a much greater difference than that found among comparable groups in the nonmetropolitan white population. Unlike whites, the black women show a fertility gradient by degree of poverty, with those in the direst financial condition (income less than 75 percent of the poverty threshold) having somewhat higher fertility rates than those with less severe poverty, and the rate for those with income only moderately above the poverty level in an intermediate position. The largest gap between white and black nonmetropolitan fertility by poverty status was for women in the most severe poverty group. In this group, black women averaged 45 percent higher childbearing than white (4,956 vs. 3,407 children per 1,000 women 35–44 years).

The relative difference in fertility by poverty status is consistently greatest among women 25–34 years old. For example, among white non-metropolitan women of that age, those in families with poverty level income had 42 percent more children per 1,000 women than those with higher incomes, whereas at ages 35–44 the rate of the poverty group was just 26 percent higher. To a considerable extent, this may stem from the fact that as children grow up and leave home their departure lowers the size of their family and reduces the likelihood that the family income is inadequate for its size. Some of the women aged 35–44 who have had above average sized families have shifted from the poverty to nonpoverty category because of this factor, and also because income levels in general are higher in families whose heads are approaching middle age than in younger families.

Fertility of Migrants

The unique pattern of metropolitan–nonmetropolitan migration in the 1970s makes it relevant to look at the fertility of migrants. With more people moving into nonmetropolitan areas, were they distinctive in family size? The answer is yes, but not radically so. Both at ages 25–34 and 35–44, women moving into nonmetropolitan communities from metropolitan areas between 1975 and 1980 had borne somewhat fewer children than women who were nonmetropolitan residents at both dates.[21] The greatest difference existed among women 25–34, for whom the fertility rate of 1,807 children per 1,000 nonmetropolitan women of at least five years' residence was more than one-fifth higher than that for metropolitan-to-nonmetropolitan migrants—1,485. However, the women moving into nonmetropolitan areas had more children than those who moved away to metropolitan areas—1,230 children per 1,000 women. Thus the migration exchange of women of this age did add to the presence of children in the rural and small town areas—since the nonmetropolitan inmigrants had more children and women 25–34 years would generally have all of their children with them.

At ages 35–44, there was only negligible difference of fertility for in- and outmigrants, but the inmigrants were still below the longer-term

---

[21]This analysis is based on the special PUMS 1980 Microdata Sample prepared for this project.

nonmetropolitan residents in family size. As a generalization for both ages, it can be said that there was not as much difference in fertility between the two migrant categories as there was between the longer-term metropolitan and nometropolitan groups. The recent inmigrants amounted to nearly one-fifth of the total nonmetropolitan women 25–34 years old, an age group where migration rates are high, but only 13 percent at ages 35–44. The incoming migrant women from metropolitan areas settled somewhat disproportionately in urban nonmetropolitan places rather than in rural areas, and their overall fertility therefore partakes somewhat more of the lower levels of childbearing characteristic of town families than of the higher levels of those living in the countryside.

Abortion

Although most of the metropolitan–nonmetropolitan fertility differences cited in this chapter have been moderate in size, there is one contemporary fertility related event—induced abortion—that is two to three times as frequent among metropolitan women as nonmetropolitan women. It may, indeed, be valid to term the difference in resort to abortion as the largest and most significant social distinction existing between metropolitan and nonmetropolitan residents in the United States today. The conventional measure is the ratio of abortions to live births. Data were available from a thirteen-state reporting area in 1984. These states contain 23 percent of the United States population and are rather well distributed, there being at least one in each of the standard nine census divisions of the country. The data are coded by residence of women and thus are not biased by disproportionate location of abortion facilities in metropolitan places.

In 1984, the ratio of abortions per 1,000 live births was 429 among metropolitan women in these states compared with 168 among nonmetropolitan women.[22] The differences were wide among both whites and blacks, with the metropolitan white ratio (361) being double that in nonmetropolitan areas (165), and the metropolitan black ratio (719) more than triple the nonmetropolitan ratio (213). Within each residence group the abortion ratio was higher for black women than for white, but the nonmetropolitan black ratio was far below the white metropolitan ratio.

The lower incidence of abortion in nonmetropolitan areas may in part result from the lesser availability of facilities in these areas. In

[22]U.S. Department of Health and Human Services (1987).

1980, 69 percent of nonmetropolitan women of childbearing age lived in counties with no abortion facility, whereas the comparable figure among metropolitan women was just 13 percent.[23] In these circumstances, for many nonmetropolitan women the cost and inconvenience of travel to a distant city might prove a deterrent. But, the more conservative attitudes and values of rural and small town society probably in and of themselves create less potential need and/or willingness to resort to abortion. In the thirteen-state reporting area, three-fourths of all abortions were obtained by unmarried women. The much greater incidence of teenage marriage among nonmetropolitan women—discussed earlier—may both reduce the number of unwanted pregnancies among younger women and reflect a greater propensity to culminate an early pregnancy with marriage rather than with abortion.

If the ratios of abortions to births in the reporting states are reasonably representative of the country as a whole, a key implication is the finding that there has been essentially no metropolitan–nonmetropolitan difference in recent years in the combined rate of abortions and live births. The rate of conceptions in 1983 for women 18–44 years of age (exclusive of miscarriages and stillbirths) was about 98.8 per 1,000 metropolitan women and 97.0 per 1,000 nonmetropolitan women. This is estimated by inflating birthrates for women of childbearing age in 1983—derived from the Bureau of the Census fertility survey—by the ratio of abortions to births by residence given in the thirteen-state 1984 abortion report. Metropolitan and nonmetropolitan women appear to have been having a very similar overall incidence of pregnancies resulting in either abortion or live birth. They have differed widely, however, in the extent to which they have chosen to abort the pregnancies or carry them to term.

Recent Trends and Future Expectation

Since 1980, two main features stand out in data on fertility by residence. These are the younger pattern of childbearing among nonmetropolitan than metropolitan women and the minor difference in lifetime births expected by the two groups. Data for 1983 show 130 births in that year per 1,000 nonmetropolitan women 18–24 years old, compared with just 82 per 1,000 among metropolitan women of the same age.[24] The difference was not just one of timing of first births. Half of the

[23]Henshaw, Forrest, Sullivan, and Tietze (1982).
[24]U.S. Bureau of the Census (1983).

births to young nonmetropolitan women were second or higher order births—65 per 1,000 women, compared with 35 per 1,000 for metropolitan women. At ages 25–29 years, the nonmetropolitan women still had more second or higher order births, but the metropolitan women had somewhat higher first order births. Finally, above age 30, the metropolitan birthrate was slightly higher for total as well as for zero parity women. Rural and small town areas obviously continue to be conducive to relatively earlier childbearing in a manner not true of metropolitan society. This is true despite the fact that two groups with the greatest propensity to early childbearing (blacks and Hispanics) are underrepresented in the nonmetropolitan population.

At ages 18–34 in 1986, nonmetropolitan women had already borne better than one-fourth more children per 1,000 women than metropolitan women (1,342 vs. 1,049 per 1,000 women).[25] Yet they did not foresee themselves as bearing significantly more over their lifetimes. Their expected lower future childbearing than their metropolitan counterparts would give them a lifetime rate of 2,150 children per 1,000 women that was only 3 percent higher than the expected total of 2,084 for metropolitan women. Whether rural and small town women and their spouses can sucessfully restrict their future childbearing to the lower levels required to achieve their modest expected completed family size remains to be seen. In any event, if metropolitan and nonmetropolitan completed fertility levels both remained above replacement needs (a prospect that is in doubt) and were equal, the nonmetropolitan population would continue to have somewhat higher annualized growth rates because of the shorter length of generation associated with its earlier childbearing. There would be slightly more turnover of generations within a given time period.

In sum, the following points stand out as most significant in assessing nonmetropolitan and/or rural fertility:

1. Nonmetropolitan women continue to have somewhat higher average fertility than metropolitan women, but not to the extent found in the past.

2. Wide differences characterize the nonmetropolitan fertility rates of black, Hispanic, and American Indian women compared with white women, and the fertility of minority women in the nonmetropolitan setting is much above that in metropolitan areas.

3. Education is inversely associated with nonmetropolitan fertility, especially among younger women.

4. Income levels are also negatively related to fertility rates, although to a somewhat lesser extent than education. At each income

[25]U.S. Bureau of the Census (1987).

level, nonmetropolitan women average about 300 more children per 1,000 women than do metropolitan women.

5. Working women have much lower levels of childbearing than do those who are not in the labor force, but this is much less true of rural women than of city women, particularly at younger ages.

6. One of the major demographic differences between nonmetropolitan and metropolitan women is age of marriage, with well over one-half of all rural nonmetropolitan women aged 25–34 years in 1980 having married before age 20, compared with three-eighths of urban metropolitan women. This pattern contributes heavily to the earlier childbearing of rural and small town women.

7. The ratio of abortions to live births is only 40 percent as high among nonmetropolitan women as it is in metropolitan areas—a major difference in social behavior.

8. Despite bearing many more children at early ages, nonmetropolitan women expect a completed lifetime fertility that is only 3 percent higher than that of their metropolitan counterparts (women 18–34 years old in 1986.) It remains to be seen whether or not they are unrealistic about their future success in curtailing childbearing sufficiently to attain this goal.

9. If birth expectations are achieved, only the nonmetropolitan population would have a fertility level that is marginally above generational replacement level.

8

LABOR FORCE AND EMPLOYMENT

THE CHANGING structure of the American economy, particularly its industrial composition, has reshaped the types of job opportunities and their availability in local economies throughout the nation. In this chapter we focus on making a living in rural and nonmetropolitan America; labor force participation, employment, and unemployment are analyzed. Briefly, we show how rural and nonmetropolitan areas have reflected the major national direction of change in labor force participation and how profoundly national industrial transformations have altered the stability of nonmetropolitan employment and have left rural labor markets increasingly vulnerable to cyclical trends, technological changes, and macroeconomic policies. This focus is extended in the next two chapters, which cover the industrial structure of employment (Chapter 9) and the population associated with farming (Chapter 10).

Gainful employment is the essence of making a living for most persons. Wages and salaries and earnings from self-employment accounted for 83 percent of all income in the United States in 1980. The nonmetropolitan proportion was slightly lower (81 percent), but still the overwhelming majority of persons depend on employment for most of their economic support. Accordingly, the number and types of jobs available in local labor markets are the critical elements contributing to material well-being for most Americans.

A number of societywide demographic and economic trends have affected the supply and demand for labor in rural and nonmetropolitan America in recent years. Perhaps most significantly, labor supply was markedly expanded by the maturation of the baby boom generation into adulthood. As demonstrated in Chapter 4, rural and nonmetropolitan areas have shared in this trend in which the large birth cohorts of the 1950s and early 1960s have reached labor force age.

The effect of this trend has been enhanced by the increased proportion of rural and small town women who work, and by the increased continuity of their labor force participation throughout the life course. Changed attitudes toward the economic role of women are partly responsible for this trend, but economic necessity is the most important determinant. The poverty rate has risen since 1979, and an increasing share of this poverty is among females. Changes in household structure, especially the increased proportion of households maintained by women, are importantly related to the feminization of poverty and to increased need for women to work outside of the home. Labor supply has also been increased by the civil rights movement and by the passage of equal opportunity employment legislation, which have reduced discrimination in the workplace.

In contrast, the growth of retirement programs for persons in their late fifties and early sixties has reduced labor supply, especially among men. An increasing proportion of America's population receives benefits from public and/or private pension programs, reducing their economic need to work. And, because some of these programs permit (or encourage) early retirement, they are reducing labor force participation rates before the traditional retirement age of 65.

The demand for labor in rural and nonmetropolitan America has also been affected by recent economic and demographic trends. The decentralization of economic activities during the 1970s, a trend that accompanied the population turnaround, enhanced labor demand in rural and small town economies. Much of this new demand was in consumer and personal services industries associated with the new population growth. In addition, nonmetropolitan areas competed successfully with metropolitan areas in attracting and/or creating new job opportunities in manufacturing. In fact, the share of all United States wage and salary manufacturing employment in nonmetropolitan areas rose from 19 percent in 1969 to 22 percent in 1984.[1]

The structural transformation of rural and nonmetropolitan America that this represents has had both positive and negative effects for the rural and nonmetropolitan labor force. In the South particularly, the

[1]U.S. Bureau of Economic Analysis, unpublished data (1984).

FIGURE 8.1

Labor Force and Employment Structure

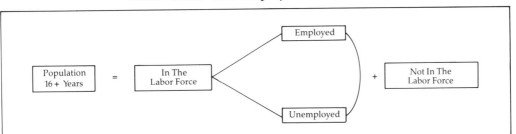

growth of manufacturing jobs helped to elevate many rural households out of poverty. Yet the industrialization of many rural economies has made them vulnerable to cyclical trends and technological changes. The growing rural manufacturing base rests disproportionately on low wage, labor intensive industry, where jobs are declining in the American economy as a whole.[2] Goods producing recessions, such as were experienced during the early 1980s, economywide problems of foreign competition, and technologically induced labor displacement are now deeply felt in rural and nonmetropolitan areas. One indication is that the nonmetropolitan unemployment rate has exceeded the metropolitan rate ever since the beginning of the 1979–1982 recession.[3]

The analytical plan for this chapter is summarized in Figure 8.1. First, we consider the working age population (consisting of labor force participants and nonparticipants) and the factors associated with participation. Labor force participants are then divided into those who are employed and unemployed, to compare their characteristics.

The Nonmetropolitan Labor Force

Labor force participation in the United States has changed in several ways in recent decades. In general, participation by men, especially older men, has declined, and participation by women of all ages has increased and become more continuous across the life course. Reduced male participation is associated with the increased availability and improved coverage of retirement programs and with the decline of some traditionally male-oriented occupations and resource-based industries.

[2]McGranahan (1988).
[3]Brown and Deavers (1988).

Heightened participation by women was facilitated by the transition to a service-based economy and the spread of manufacturing and service jobs across the nation's regions and throughout its settlement structure. Of equal importance are several demographic factors affecting the supply of female labor: increased age at marriage, decreased fertility, increased divorce, a greater proportion of families maintained by women, and increased educational attainment.

The deconcentration of employment opportunities during the 1970s diminished residence as a differentiating factor in labor force activity, and nonmetropolitan areas have shared in significant national trends in labor force participation such as increased women's employment and earlier retirement. However, as demonstrated in Chapters 4 through 7, residential categories still differ in aspects of population composition that are closely linked with labor force participation, especially among women. For example, nonmetropolitan and rural areas generally have an older age composition, a greater proportion of husband-wife-with-children families, higher fertility, and lower educational attainment. And rural people have generally been considered to be more conservative in their views of the role of women and the appropriateness of women's work outside of the home, although more recent evidence supports a growing acceptance of labor force participation for rural women.[4]

Labor Force Status and Participation

About three-quarters of the men and about one-half of the women were in the United States labor force in 1980 (Table 8.1). Labor force participation of males was somewhat higher in metropolitan counties in 1980. This difference is attributable to differences in the proportion of employed men; the proportion unemployed varied only slightly by metropolitan–nonmetropolitan residence in that year. Rural–urban differences are slight—regardless of metropolitan status, participation was a bit higher among rural men. Participation in the armed forces was concentrated in urban areas in both metropolitan and nonmetropolitan counties.

Women's labor force participation was also higher in metropolitan than in nonmetropolitan areas (51.3 and 45.2 percent, respectively). The percentage point difference between male and female labor force participation was slightly greater in nonmetropolitan than in metropolitan counties, and in rural compared with urban areas. However, the residential differences in the male-female gap were not large, ranging from 23.7

---

[4]Glenn and Alston (1967); Willets, Bealer, and Crider (1973).

TABLE 8.1

Labor Force Status of the Population by Sex and Residence, 1980

Labor Force Status	Total	Metropolitan			Nonmetropolitan		
		Total	Urban	Rural	Total	Urban	Rural
Males							
In labor force	75.1	76.4	76.3	77.1	71.3	71.4	71.3
Civilian	73.3	74.5	74.2	76.2	70.0	68.7	70.8
Employed	68.5	69.8	69.5	71.4	64.9	64.0	65.5
Unemployed	4.8	4.7	4.7	4.8	5.1	4.7	5.3
In Armed Forces	1.8	2.0	2.1	0.9	1.3	2.7	0.5
Not in labor force	24.9	23.6	23.7	22.9	28.7	28.6	28.7
Total males 16+	100.0	100.0	100.0	100.0	100.0	100.0	100.0
Females							
In labor force	49.9	51.3	51.9	47.8	45.2	47.7	43.6
Civilian	49.7	51.2	51.7	47.8	45.1	47.5	43.5
Employed	46.5	48.0	48.5	44.8	41.8	44.2	40.2
Unemployed	3.2	3.2	3.2	3.0	3.3	3.3	3.3
In Armed Forces	0.2	0.2	0.2	0.1	0.1	0.2	0.1
Not in labor force	50.1	48.7	48.1	52.2	54.8	52.3	56.4
Total females 16+	100.0	100.0	100.0	100.0	100.0	100.0	100.0
Male Minus Female Participation Rate	25.2	25.1	24.4	29.8	26.1	23.7	27.7

points in urban-nonmetropolitan areas to 29.3 points in rural-metropolitan.[5]

These same residential patterns in participation were evident in 1970 (Table 8.2). The major change between the two dates was a small decline in participation rates among males and a larger increase for women.

[5]The armed forces population accounts for only 1.0 percent of all labor force age persons (1.5 percent of the total labor force), and it is very heavily concentrated among men living in urban areas (82 percent). Accordingly our attention, in the remainder of this chapter and in Chapter 9, will be on the civilian labor force.

TABLE 8.2

Percentage of Population 16 and Over in Civilian Labor Force by Sex and Residence, 1970–1980

Sex and Year	Total	Metropolitan			Nonmetropolitan		
		Total	Urban	Rural	Total	Urban	Rural
Males							
1970	76.6	78.0	78.2	72.1	72.1	73.0	71.5
1980	73.3	74.5	74.2	76.2	70.0	68.7	70.8
Percentage Point Change							
1970–1980	−3.3	−3.5	−4.0	−4.1	−2.1	−4.3	−.7
Females							
1970	41.4	42.6	43.9	37.9	37.3	41.6	34.5
1980	49.8	51.3	51.8	47.8	45.2	47.5	43.6
Percentage Point Change							
1970–1980	8.4	8.7	7.9	9.9	7.9	5.9	9.1

Metropolitan areas had slightly larger percentage point increases in women's labor force participation than nonmetropolitan areas. In contrast, rural areas, regardless of metropolitan–nonmetropolitan location, exceeded urban areas in percentage point growth. Accordingly, while the metropolitan–nonmetropolitan gap in women's participation was maintained during the decade, the urban–rural gap was almost cut in half in both the metropolitan and nonmetropolitan sectors.

Labor Force Participation by Age and Sex

Labor force participation is clearly associated with age. The prime working ages are typically considered to be ages 20–44 with lower participation before and after this age range. However, until recently this age pattern of participation was more characteristic of men than of women. Women's participation was less continuous throughout the life course, including a period of dropout and reentry during the prime child-bearing ages.

Male Participation. Male labor force participation in 1980 exceeded 50 percent in every age group from ages 16–19 through ages 45–64. Over nine of ten males in the prime working ages (25–44) were in the labor force; 80 percent participated at ages 45–64; and even after age 65 almost one-fifth of men were in the labor force (Table 8.3).

Males in metropolitan areas consistently had slightly higher labor force participation rates than men in nonmetropolitan areas, although

TABLE 8.3

Percentage of Population 16 and Over in Civilian Labor Force
by Sex and Residence, 1980

Age and Sex	Total	Metropolitan			Nonmetropolitan		
		Total	Urban	Rural	Total	Urban	Rural
Males 16+	74.7	75.9	75.8	76.9	70.9	70.6	71.1
16–19	51.7	52.4	52.4	52.5	49.7	51.8	48.4
20–24	81.9	82.0	81.4	86.2	81.4	76.1	85.7
25–34	92.7	92.7	92.5	94.0	92.6	91.8	93.0
35–44	94.1	94.5	94.4	95.3	92.8	93.4	92.5
45–64	80.9	82.2	82.4	81.4	76.9	79.1	75.8
65+	19.3	19.8	19.9	18.7	18.3	18.1	18.5
Females 16+	49.8	51.3	51.8	47.8	45.2	47.5	43.6
16–19	45.5	46.9	47.5	43.2	41.2	45.6	38.1
20–24	67.5	69.1	69.9	64.7	62.3	64.0	61.0
25–34	64.6	65.7	66.7	59.3	60.9	65.5	58.1
35–44	64.7	65.3	66.3	60.1	62.7	67.4	60.2
45–64	50.2	51.4	52.2	45.8	46.4	51.4	43.4
65+	8.1	8.2	8.3	7.1	7.8	8.4	7.3

at ages 20–44 the differences were essentially trivial. In contrast, the urban–rural pattern of male participation does not consistently favor more highly urbanized areas. In fact, in both metropolitan and nonmetropolitan counties proportionately more prime working age men are in the labor force in rural areas.

Female Participation. One-half of all women aged 16 and older were in the civilian labor force in 1980. Participation dropped below 50 percent only in the youngest (16–19) and oldest (65+) age groups. Over two-thirds of women participated at ages 20–44, and almost one-half participated in the 45–64 age group. This age pattern of participation differs substantially from 1970 when paid employment outside of the home typically declined in the childbearing ages (25–34) and then increased at ages 35–44 when most of these women's children had reached school age. These trends in aggregate participation rates provide indirect evidence of women's increased attachment to the labor force. The disappearance of the drop in participation during the childbearing years strongly suggests more continuity in labor force participation over the life course. Continuity of female labor force participation during the entirety of adulthood is generally considered to be one of the major gender-based social changes of the 1970s.[6]

[6]Bianchi and Spain (1986).

FIGURE 8.2

*Labor Force Participation by Sex, Age,
and Metropolitan–Nonmetropolitan Residence, 1980*

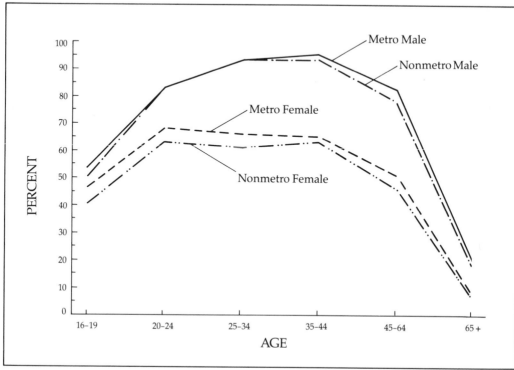

The data in Figure 8.2 and Table 8.3 show that residential differences in women's labor force participation by age are much stronger, and much more consistent by age, than was true for men. At every age a higher proportion of metropolitan women were in the labor force than was true of nonmetropolitan women; similarly, participation among urban women was higher at every age than was true of rural women. Residential differences in women's labor force participation were especially noticeable at the earliest ages. The metropolitan and urban advantage was much smaller during the prime working ages.

Women's Participation by Race and Residence. Similar to the situation for all women regardless of race, black women's labor force participation in the South was higher in more urbanized settings than in nonmetropolitan and rural areas.[7] These residential differences were

---

[7]The analysis by race contained in this chapter is restricted to the South because 93 percent of black labor force age women in nonmetropolitan counties lived in this region in 1980.

somewhat greater for blacks than for the rest of the population. For example, 56 percent of black women in metropolitan areas participated in the labor force, compared with only 47 percent of nonmetropolitan black women. The metropolitan–nonmetropolitan difference for nonblack women was 6 percentage points, 50 and 44 percent, respectively.

Although a higher proportion of black than nonblack women participated in the labor force in all residential settings, the difference was especially marked in metropolitan (especially urban-metropolitan) areas. However, the data in Figure 8.3 show that these differences are mainly in the prime working ages. Younger black women actually had lower labor force participation rates than nonblacks. This was especially true of black women in nonmetropolitan counties, who had the lowest participation rates at ages 16–19 and 20–24 of the four race-residence categories displayed in Figure 8.3. Regardless of these differences, the data in Figure 8.3 do not show a drop in participation during the prime working ages for any of the race-residence groups. In contrast, research for

FIGURE 8.3

Female Labor Force Participation by Age, Race,
and Metropolitan–Nonmetropolitan Residence, South, 1980

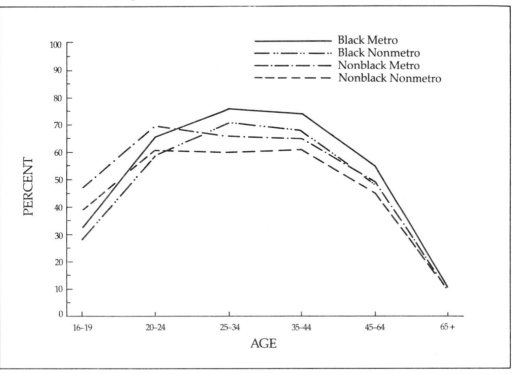

TABLE 8.4

Female Civilian Labor Force Participation by Marital Status and Residence, 1980

Marital Status	Total	Metropolitan			Nonmetropolitan		
		Total	Urban	Rural	Total	Urban	Rural
U.S. Total	49.8	51.3	51.8	47.8	54.2	47.5	43.6
Married	49.0	49.8	50.3	47.7	46.8	49.7	45.2
Single	59.9	62.0	62.7	54.9	51.7	55.3	48.5
Widowed	20.6	21.3	21.3	21.0	18.6	19.1	18.2
Divorced, separated	69.9	70.7	70.6	71.0	66.5	67.9	65.0

1970 demonstrated that such a drop was especially characteristic of white women in metropolitan areas.[8]

Women's Participation and Marital Status. Women's labor force participation is importantly linked to marital status, but traditional patterns—higher participation among single women and lower participation among married women with children—are changing. Indeed, it has been shown that the sharpest increases in participation have been among married women with children.[9] Accordingly, delayed marriage and fertility are not the primary factors explaining women's increased labor force activity. Data previously cited that indicate continuity of labor force participation throughout the life course support this point, as do data on labor force participation by marital status shown in Tables 8.4–8.6.

Regardless of residence, divorced and separated and single women had the highest participation rates (Table 8.4), but over half of married women also participated. Only one in five widowed women were in the labor force. The low participation rate of this latter category is due to its age composition—elderly widows comprise a significant part of this group. The higher rates for divorced and separated women reflect their greater economic needs. Single women are also more economically self-dependent than other women, but their labor force participation rate is lower than that of divorced or separated women because they tend to be younger and hence more likely to be in school and/or to live at home. Differences in female labor force participation by residence were consistent across the marital status categories, but were considerably smaller for married and widowed than for single and divorced or separated women. Although half of married women and one-fifth of widows were in the labor force in all residence categories, participation among single

[8]Brown and O'Leary (1979).
[9]Michael (1985).

women varied from over 60 percent in metropolitan-urban areas to less than 50 percent in nonmetropolitan-rural areas.

Divorced and separated women are overrepresented in the labor force (Table 8.5). While they comprise less than 10 percent of labor force age women, they account for 14 percent of the female labor force. Similarly, single women had the second highest participation rate of the four marital status categories, but they accounted for only about one-fifth of women in the labor force ages, and consequently they comprised only about one-quarter of all women in the labor force (Table 8.5). The data in panels 1 and 2 of Table 8.5 show that single women were slightly overrepresented in the labor force compared with their proportion of the population (25.3 percent and 21.1 percent, respectively). In contrast, widowed women comprised 12.6 percent of the labor force age population but only 5 percent of the labor force. Married women in the labor force were about proportional to their component of the labor force aged population, 55.7 percent and 56.5 percent, respectively. These same patterns hold in all of the residence categories, although married women comprise a much larger proportion of the labor force in rural areas, and conversely divorced and separated women are a relatively smaller proportion of female workers in such settings.

TABLE 8.5

Marital Status Distribution of Labor Force Age Women, 1980

Marital Status	Total	Metropolitan			Nonmetropolitan		
		Total	Urban	Rural	Total	Urban	Rural
Women Age 16+							
Married	56.5	54.9	52.9	68.2	61.3	54.0	66.1
Single	21.1	22.3	3.2	16.4	17.3	20.3	15.4
Widowed	12.6	12.2	12.6	9.3	13.9	16.1	12.4
Divorced, separated	9.8	10.6	11.3	6.1	7.5	9.5	6.1
Total	100.0	100.0	100.0	100.0	100.0	100.0	100.0
Women Age 16+ in Civilian Labor Force							
Married	55.7	53.5	51.3	68.0	63.4	56.3	68.7
Single	25.3	26.9	28.1	18.8	19.8	23.6	17.1
Widowed	5.2	5.0	5.2	4.1	5.7	6.5	5.2
Divorced, separated	13.8	14.6	15.4	9.1	11.1	13.6	9.0
Total	100.0	100.0	100.0	100.0	100.0	100.00	100.0

TABLE 8.6

Female Civilian Labor Force Participation Rates by Marital Status and Presence of Children, 1980

Marital Status/Children	Total	Metropolitan			Nonmetropolitan		
		Total	Urban	Rural	Total	Urban	Rural
Married, Spouse							
Present	49.2	50.0	50.4	48.3	46.8	49.6	45.2
Children LT 6	43.9	43.7	44.2	41.2	44.6	47.7	42.9
Children 6–17	60.1	60.3	60.8	58.4	59.5	63.5	57.6
No children	45.6	47.2	47.6	45.1	40.9	43.7	39.2
Other Marital Status	50.8	53.2	53.7	48.2	42.4	44.8	40.2
Children LT 6	54.6	53.7	53.3	59.3	58.0	59.8	56.2
Children 6–17	74.5	74.9	74.7	76.4	72.8	76.0	69.9
No children	48.2	50.9	51.5	45.1	38.7	41.1	36.6

Women's Participation and the Presence of Children. The presence of minor children in the household has generally been considered to be an impediment to women's work outside of the home. Using 1950 census data, Gertrude Bancroft noted that American women typically retired from the labor force during the prime childbearing ages, and then returned to work after their last child had been enrolled in school.[10] However, as shown earlier, this has changed in recent years. As Bianchi and Spain have commented, "delayed marriage and childbearing are not the real key to labor force increases among women, for the sharpest growth in rates has been among married women with children."[11]

By 1980 over 40 percent of all women living in households containing pre–school-aged children were in the labor force (Table 8.6), but the presence of young children in the household continues to be associated with lower levels of labor force participation. Regardless of residence or marital status, women who live in households with children under 6 years of age had lower labor force participation rates than women in households containing older children.[12] Women in households with no children had participation rates roughly similar to women in households with young children, but this is probably due to the relative preponderance of older women in this group and not the lack of children in their

[10]Bancroft (1958).

[11]Bianchi and Spain (1986), p. 167.

[12]These rates are averages for women of all ages within the same household status. Among women of the same age there could very easily be less variation in participation by the presence of young children.

households. Robinson has shown that older cohorts of women have had lower labor force participation rates at every age than have younger cohorts reaching the same ages.[13]

While the overall rates of participation among married women with a spouse present and women in other marital statuses did not differ much, married, spouse present women had lower labor force involvement than women in other marital statuses when children were present in the household.[14] Residential differences in women's labor force participation by the presence of children were not entirely consistent. Married women with a spouse present and minor children had very similar participation rates in metropolitan and nonmetropolitan counties, although participation was somewhat higher in urban as compared with rural areas within these counties. Women's participation rates for households with no children present were much higher in metropolitan and urban settings. Labor force participation of women with minor children in other marital statuses was not consistently related to the level of urbanization or metropolitan status, but differences were large and consistent across the residence categories for those without children.

Education and Labor Force Participation

The educational attainment of rural and nonmetropolitan persons has been consistently lower than that of persons in more highly urbanized areas. And since educational attainment is positively associated with labor force participation, differences in education between the residential categories might explain differences between their labor force participation rates.

Higher levels of formal education increase an individual's employment options by providing them with a broader range of occupational requisites. And, since more highly educated persons can generally command higher wages, their "costs" of not working are higher. The data in Table 8.7 show that regardless of sex or residence labor force participation is positively associated with education attainment. The major difference is between persons who have not completed high school and those with at least a high school diploma. Differences in participation

---

[13]Robinson (1980).

[14]The similarity of overall participation rates between married and other women is because of the differential size of various components of the two groups. For example, the proportion of nonmarried women living in households with no children is much larger than for married women, which tends to reduce the overall participation rate for nonmarried women. In contrast, the proportion of married women with children 6–17 is relatively large, which tends to increase the participation rate of the category.

TABLE 8.7

Civilian Labor Force Participation Rate by Sex, Educational Attainment, and Residence, 1980

Education	Total	Metropolitan			Nonmetropolitan		
		Total	Urban	Rural	Total	Urban	Rural
Males (16+)	74.7	75.9	75.8	76.9	70.9	70.6	71.1
Not high school grad.	57.1	58.1	58.0	58.8	54.8	54.2	55.0
High school graduate	83.3	83.3	82.4	87.6	83.4	80.2	85.2
Some college	81.4	82.2	81.7	86.2	78.2	73.7	82.2
College graduate	89.2	89.5	89.3	91.3	87.4	87.5	87.4
Females (16+)	49.8	51.3	51.8	47.8	45.2	47.6	43.6
Not high school grad.	32.3	33.3	33.5	31.8	30.0	31.5	29.1
High school graduate	56.1	56.8	57.1	55.0	54.0	56.1	52.6
Some college	60.4	61.6	62.1	57.7	55.6	56.8	54.5
College graduate	67.7	68.5	69.0	64.0	64.1	63.5	64.5

between high school graduates and persons with college education are less dramatic, but important, nonetheless.

Differences in labor force participation associated with educational attainment were more pronounced for women than for men. In fact, women with a college degree were twice as likely to be in the labor force as those without a high school diploma (men were one and one-half times as likely). The average educational attainment of both men and women has increased sharply since 1960, and the gap in overall attainment has narrowed (even though the gender gap in college completion actually increased).[15] Since the principal education-based difference in labor force participation involves high school completion, these data suggest that increased educational attainment of women has been a factor in diminishing the gender gap in labor force activity.

Residential differences in educational attainment do not appear to be a major factor explaining differences in labor force participation between the residence categories. Within each educational level, labor force participation tends to be somewhat higher in metropolitan than in nonmetropolitan areas regardless of sex, and for women in urban compared with women in rural areas. For men, in contrast, rural areas have higher participation rates than urban areas within each educational level.

This section has focused on the effects of residence on civilian labor

[15]Bianchi and Spain (1986).

force participation, with particular emphasis on the participation of women. The analysis has demonstrated that while levels of participation continue to lag somewhat in less urbanized areas, especially for younger women, the population in rural and nonmetropolitan America has participated in the major recent labor force trends and changes. Male labor force participation declined slightly and women's participation increased dramatically in rural and nonmetropolitan areas between 1970 and 1980. Moreover, the aggregate trends presented here provide indirect evidence that women's participation in all residential settings has become more continuous across the life course. Although the presence of young children in the household continued to limit labor force participation, over 40 percent of married (and unmarried) women with children were in the labor force in all residential areas.

Increased labor force participation among women has been shown to be associated with a complex set of economic, demographic, and familial factors. Certainly the deconcentration of employment in nondurable manufacturing and in services during the late 1960s and early 1970s brought employment opportunities to women in small town and rural areas where few existed before. In fact, it has been shown that women accounted for over 80 percent of all nonmetropolitan employment growth in manufacturing in the 1960s.[16] Wages paid to women, especially married women, have also increased, thus increasing labor supply. Rising wage rates, according to Fuchs, are the most important factor explaining increased labor force participation of women during this century.[17]

Other factors have increased the supply of women available for work outside of the home. Rising educational attainment has increased women's preference for work and increased their costs of remaining outside of the labor force. Changing marriage and childbearing patterns are also critical. Postponed marriage and fertility appear in part to be active responses by women to actualize their preferences for increased education and career. In addition, the rising divorce rate and consequent growth in the number of families maintained by women has increased women's needs to support themselves financially. As we have seen in earlier chapters, these changes in household composition and fertility have occurred in rural and small town America as well as in their metropolitan counterparts, although it should be reemphasized that metropolitan areas still exceed nonmetropolitan areas in labor force participation rates.

---

[16]Brown and O'Leary (1979).
[17]Fuchs (1983).

Nonparticipants in the Labor Force

The majority of all labor force age persons is now in the work force, but a substantial proportion remains outside. As shown in Table 8.1, the proportion not participating is higher among women than among men (50 percent vs. 25 percent) and for both sexes it is higher in non-metropolitan than in metropolitan areas. Reasons for not participating are numerous. Census practice typically accounts for being an inmate of an institution, having a work limiting disability, attending school, being of retirement age, and—among women not citing any of these reasons—having minor children at home. These reasons are listed separately in Table 8.8, but some of them (old age and disability, for example) might work together. Accordingly, a more detailed analysis of reasons for being out of the work force would include consideration of some of their possible joint effects.

Reasons for Being Outside of the Labor Force in 1980

About 40 percent of labor force age persons not participating in the labor force stated either that they were unable to work because of disability or that they were attending school. Another 21 percent indicated that they were not in the work force because of advanced age. Only about 5 percent were inmates of institutions. Of the remaining 40 percent of adults outside of the labor force, the majority were women—more than half of whom had minor children in their households. Very

TABLE 8.8

Reasons for Being Out of the Labor Force by Residence, 1980

Reasons	Total	Metropolitan			Nonmetropolitan		
		Total	Urban	Rural	Total	Urban	Rural
Inmate of an Institution	3.7	3.5	3.5	3.7	4.1	5.7	3.1
Work-Limiting Disability	20.6	19.6	19.7	19.0	23.8	22.8	24.3
Enrolled in School	15.8	16.3	16.6	14.7	14.2	16.7	12.7
Age 65 or Older	21.0	21.0	21.5	17.7	20.9	22.6	19.9
Not Included in Above							
Males	5.4	5.5	5.5	5.0	5.1	4.3	5.6
Females—child in home	19.8	20.2	19.5	24.8	18.8	16.0	20.5
Females—no child in home	13.7	13.9	13.7	15.1	13.1	11.9	13.9
Total Not in Labor Force (16+)	100.0	100.0	100.0	100.0	100.0	100.0	100.0

few males who were not inmates, disabled, in school, or elderly abstained from participating in the work force.

The general pattern of reasons given for not being in the labor force is very similar in all of the residence categories, although there are some differences. Work limiting disability, for example, was a somewhat more important reason in nonmetropolitan than in metropolitan areas (probably because of the higher incidence of work-related injuries in farming, lumbering, mining, and some types of manufacturing). Conversely, a higher proportion of metropolitan persons stated that they were unable to work because they were enrolled in school (a difference probably due to younger age composition).

Within the metropolitan and nonmetropolitan categories themselves there were some urban–rural differences, but they tended to be slight and the general pattern of reasons for being outside of the labor force was similar in all categories. School enrollment was somewhat more important in urban areas and advanced age was stated more frequently in rural areas (again probably because of differences in age composition). Also, a higher proportion of rural women who did not state disability, school, or old age as a reason for being out of the work force indicated that they had minor children at home.

In summary, a somewhat larger proportion of nonmetropolitan and rural adults was outside of the work force in 1980 than urban and metropolitan adults. Similarly, although there were some residential differences in reasons for not participating in the work force, they were not very large and the general pattern of reasons was similar regardless of residence. However, there is some evidence that lower levels of rural and nonmetropolitan labor force participation are associated with a greater degree of work limiting disabilities and/or with older age.

Attention to labor force participation should not obscure the fact that productive economic activity also occurs outside of formally organized labor markets. We tend to underestimate the non-labor force contribution to family and community well-being. Women's economic contributions in particular have been undervalued. Housework, community service activities, and roles performed on farms and in private businesses are frequently left out of our economic accounting.[18]

The Employed Population

We now focus on those labor force participants who are employed. Between 1950 and 1970 employment increased slowly in nonmetropol-

[18]Haney (1982).

itan America; job gains in manufacturing and services were offset by job losses in agriculture and resource-based industries.[19] During these two decades, nonmetropolitan growth in the labor force ages exceeded net job growth, resulting in outmigration to metropolitan workplaces (and probably in increased levels of metropolitan-oriented commuting).

Nonmetropolitan Employment Change Since 1970

Nonmetropolitan job growth accelerated greatly during the 1970s, and the now familiar population growth turnaround was accompanied by a decentralization of employment. The data in Table 8.9 show that nonmetropolitan employment grew by 2.4 percent per year during the 1970s compared with 2.0 percent per year in metropolitan areas.

In contrast, post-1980 data indicate that nonmetropolitan employment is growing at a lower rate once again (consistent with the situation for population). The effect of the downturn of the business cycle during the early 1980s is evident in both metropolitan and nonmetropolitan areas—average annual employment growth in both residential categories was lower during the 1980s than in the 1970s. But the downturn was much greater in nonmetropolitan than in metropolitan areas. In fact, nonmetropolitan employment hardly grew at all during the first half of the decade (135,000 jobs, 0.1 percent per year).

TABLE 8.9

Wage and Salary Employment Change by Residence, 1969–1984

Year	United States	Metropolitan[a]	Nonmetropolitan
Wage and Salary Employment (000s)			
1969	78,396	63,656	14,740
1979	96,331	77,611	18,720
1984	101,101	82,246	18,855
Wage and Salary Employment Change 1969–1979 (000s)	17,935	13,955	3,980
Percentage change[b]	2.05	1.98	2.38
Wage and Salary Employment Change 1979–1984 (000s)	4,770	4,635	135
Percentage change[b]	0.97	1.16	0.14

SOURCE: Unpublished data from the Bureau of Economic Analysis, U.S. Department of Commerce.
[a]Metropolitan areas as designated in the 1980 Census used throughout.
[b]Average annual percentage change.

[19]Bluestone and Daberkow (1985).

These employment data (and unemployment data to be shown later) indicate that nonmetropolitan areas have recovered very slowly from the 1979–1982 recession. The poor performance of the nonmetropolitan economy since 1980 is associated with problems in three goods producing industrial sectors—mining, farming, and manufacturing.

Mining employment has been negatively affected by significant price declines, and financial stress in agriculture has led to decapitalization and reduced labor utilization. However, manufacturing, which was the "engine" of nonmetropolitan growth during the 1970s, displayed the sharpest slowdown in employment growth.

Employment growth in manufacturing has remained essentially stagnant since 1980 because of intensified foreign competition, technology induced increases in labor productivity, and a new practice among manufacturers of buying services from specialized firms that they previously produced themselves. In addition, service sector employment growth in nonmetropolitan areas has been disproportionately in low wage consumer and personal services, not in the rapidly growing business and professional services sectors.[20]

Nonmetropolitan Employment and Population Change Compared

The data in Table 8.10 show that patterns of employment change closely parallel those for population in both the 1960–1970 and 1970–1980 decades. In the 1960s metropolitan population growth as measured by percentage change was more than three times the level for nonmetropolitan areas, whereas in the 1970s this pattern was reversed, with the nonmetropolitan growth percentage higher than before and almost one and one-half times the decreased level prevailing in metropolitan areas. The data show a similar pattern for the percentage change in the total number employed, though with higher levels and smaller differentials. Employment levels are higher than population growth for both periods, but particularly for the most recent decade.

An even stronger indication of the parallel between employment change and population change is given by correlations between the change in number employed and population change based on individual nonmetropolitan county data, which are 0.88 in the 1960–1970 period and 0.91 for 1970–1980 Some researchers have taken this as evidence that the population turnaround trend of the 1970s was not new in its underlying basis but reflected and extended decentralization of many

[20]Miller and Bluestone (1988).

TABLE 8.10

Components of Difference Between Employment Change and Population Change by Sex and Metropolitan–Nonmetropolitan Status, 1960–1980[a]

Components	Metropolitan[b]			Nonmetropolitan		
	Total	Male	Female	Total	Male	Female
1960–1970						
Change in:						
Employment	19.5	12.3	32.3	9.4	0.4	27.6
Population	15.7	15.1	17.1	4.2	3.3	5.8
Difference	3.8	−2.8	15.2	5.2	−2.9	21.8
Components of difference:						
Employment rate	0.5	−6.2	12.8	0.1	−8.2	17.6
Proportion employment age[c]	3.3	3.4	2.4	5.1	5.3	4.2
1970–1980						
Change in:						
Employment	23.5	15.2	35.5	26.7	18.8	39.1
Population	9.4	9.2	9.6	14.6	14.2	14.9
Difference	14.1	6.0	25.9	12.1	4.6	24.2
Components of difference:						
Employment rate	6.7	−2.5	19.5	6.0	−2.4	19.0
Proportion employment age	7.4	8.5	6.4	6.1	7.0	5.2

[a]Decennial rates per 100. See Appendix 8.1 for methodology.
[b]Metropolitan status as of 1974.
[c]Ages 15–64.

economic activities formerly found in and around metropolitan cities.[21] Although a rather close association has been shown so far in this chapter between population and employment change, this in itself is insufficient to conclude that the turnaround trend, along with the older trends of the 1960s and before, rested almost entirely on economic development and job opportunities.

Decomposition of Population–Employment Difference. The interrelations between population and employment growth need to be studied more closely. The two, after all, do not have to be closely related. Population growth due to fertility, for example, will add people too young for the labor force over a decade and, other things being equal, cause population growth without employment growth. The same would be true for the migration of retired persons. In contrast, an increased labor force participation rate can increase the number of employed persons with no concomitant increase in population.

We have expressed the interrelation between population and employment change using an accounting or decomposition model, which shows that population change will lead directly to employment growth provided there is no compensatory change in the proportion of people employed or in the proportion of the population in the labor force ages (15–64). Our development of this model is contained in an appendix following this chapter. In general, however, our analysis decomposes the difference between population change into two components—one accounting for changes in the rate of employment and the other expressing changes in the proportion of the population of labor force age. The results are included in Table 8.10.

For 1960–1970 the total change in employment was only slightly above population change, and most of this difference could be attributed to an increase in the proportion of population of employment age. The size of this component was small relative to population change in metropolitan areas, but it was about as large as population change in non-metropolitan counties.

The small importance of change in employment participation was a balancing of a negative effect for males and a positive effect for females. For males, population actually grew more than employment in the 1960–1970 period, with a decline in the ratio of the number of males employed divided by the male population 15–64, overriding the increase in the proportion of employment age. This differential was greater in nonmetropolitan than in metropolitan counties.

For women, on the other hand, change in the employment rate was by far the most important component, and was considerably larger than

[21]Long and DeAre (1982); Estall (1983).

population change in both residence categories. In contrast, the change in the proportion of employment age was slightly less for women than for men.

For 1970–1980, the difference between change in employment and population is much greater than in the 1960s for each of the residence-by-gender categories. In metropolitan areas increase in the level of employment change and decrease in the level of population change made for an increased difference between the two rates. In nonmetropolitan areas an increase in employment change more than offset a higher rate of population change in the later decade. For both types of residence the greater employment change was due both to the proportion aged 15–64 who were employed and the proportion of employment age. Again, for males, the change in the proportion employed was a negative component in both metropolitan and nonmetropolitan areas, though smaller than in the preceding decade. The increased importance of the proportion of males of employment age, reflecting the baby boom entering adulthood, more than offset this male 1970–1980 employment rate decline.

For females in 1970–1980, the most important component for both county groups, as was true in the preceding decade, was the growth in the proportion employed. In both metropolitan and nonmetropolitan counties this component is larger than for 1960–1970, and, as before, at least three times larger than the change in proportion of employment age. These findings are consistent with the analyses in the preceding section, which showed decreased labor force participation rates for men and increased rates for women in all residence categories.

This decomposition model, relating population and employment change, does not directly address the question of the importance of noneconomic factors in the recent nonmetropolitan population trends, but it does indicate that the simple correspondence of population and employment growth rates across areas is insufficient evidence that economic factors were the only important determinants of the population turnaround trend of the 1970s, given the varying magnitude by gender and residence, of the two additive factors; that is, change in the proportion of the population of working age, and change in the proportion of those of working age who are employed.

Attributes of the Employed Labor Force

Class of Employed Workers. The great preponderance of the employed labor force works for wages and salaries (95 percent of women and 87 percent of men) (Table 8.11). Self-employment accounts for almost all of the remainder, and unpaid family work is less than 1 per-

TABLE 8.11

Class of Employed Workers by Sex and Residence, 1980

Sex and Class of Worker	Total	Metropolitan			Nonmetropolitan		
		Total	Urban	Rural	Total	Urban	Rural
Female	100.0	100.0	100.0	100.0	100.0	100.0	100.0
Wage and salary	94.6	95.3	95.6	92.9	92.3	94.0	90.9
Private	74.1	75.6	75.9	73.0	69.0	70.2	68.0
Government	20.5	19.7	19.7	19.9	23.3	23.8	22.9
Self-employed	4.6	4.1	3.9	5.7	6.3	5.1	7.1
Agriculture	.4	.2	.1	.9	1.0	.1	1.6
Nonagriculture	4.2	3.9	3.8	4.8	5.3	5.0	5.5
Unpaid family work	.8	.6	.5	1.3	1.5	.9	2.0
Male	100.0	100.0	100.0	100.0	100.0	100.0	100.0
Wage and salary	87.0	89.2	89.9	84.8	82.1	87.8	78.7
Private	73.0	74.7	75.0	72.8	67.5	70.6	65.7
Government	14.5	14.5	14.9	12.0	14.6	17.2	13.0
Self-employed	12.3	10.6	10.0	14.8	17.5	11.9	20.5
Agriculture	2.1	.7	.2	4.0	6.4	.9	9.6
Nonagriculture	10.2	9.9	9.8	10.8	11.0	11.0	10.9
Unpaid family work	.3	.2	.1	.4	.6	.2	.8

cent. However, a higher proportion of self-employed workers is a traditional attribute differentiating the rural and nonmetropolitan work forces from their more urbanized counterparts. Nonmetropolitan counties had a higher proportion of self-employed workers in 1980 than metropolitan, and within both residence categories rural areas exceeded urban areas. For men, self-employment ranged from 20.5 percent in rural-nonmetropolitan areas to 10.0 percent in urban-metropolitan. The same pattern held for women, but the differences were less pronounced.

Residential differences in self-employment have traditionally been associated with the concentration of farming in rural areas. The data in Table 8.11 show that in 1980 most of the difference in the proportion of workers who are self-employed continued to be in agriculture, although for employed women, and for both men and women residing in metropolitan counties, more rural settings also had a slightly higher proportion self-employed outside of agriculture. Unpaid family work, a minor part of the work force, was consistently greater in less urbanized settings. This is largely associated with unpaid work on farms.

Government jobs have been a major source of employment growth in local rural economies. Even in 1950, Duncan and Reiss noted, government jobs were important in local area development, and Bluestone and Daberkow reported that during 1975–1982 they accounted for 12 per-

TABLE 8.12

The Journey to Work by Metropolitan–Nonmetropolitan Residence, 1980[a]

			Nonmetropolitan		
	United States	Metropolitan	Total	Adjacent[b]	Not Adjacent
Percentage Crossing County Boundary	20.8	21.1	19.8	22.4	15.4
Time Traveled to Work (%)					
Less than 30 minutes	71.5	69.5	78.5	76.7	81.5
30 minutes to 1 hour	22.5	24.3	16.1	17.4	13.9
More than 1 hour	6.0	6.2	5.4	5.9	4.6
Total	100.0	100.0	100.0	100.0	100.0

[a]Population at work at the time of the census, less those working at home and those who did not respond to commuting questions.
[b]Adjacent to a 1980 metropolitan county.

cent of nonmetropolitan job growth.[22] Government jobs accounted for about one-fifth of all wage and salary workers in the United States economy in 1980. The proportion was higher for women than for men, reflecting the greater concentration of their jobs in education. Metropolitan and nonmetropolitan counties did not differ much in the proportion of government workers, although among men within both county groups urban areas had a higher representation.

Commuting Status. The separation of workplace from home is an essential aspect of the development of Western urban-industrialized societies. Although most people work near their homes, a substantial number make longer distance commutes. In census practice this behavior is measured by determining whether a worker crosses county lines to go to work, and/or by the amount of time spent in a one-way journey to work. The data in Table 8.12 indicate that about one worker in five commuted across a county boundary in 1980, and almost one-third of all workers spent at least one-half hour in the journey to work.

It is generally thought that long-distance commuting—crossing county lines and/or spending a long time in the journey to work—is more prevalent in nonmetropolitan areas because of the large distances separating nonmetropolitan places, and because economic opportunities are more abundant in metropolitan areas. The data in Table 8.12 show this not to be true. In fact, the journey to work appears to require less time in nonmetropolitan than in metropolitan counties. Although about

[22]Duncan and Reiss (1956); Bluestone and Daberkow (1985).

the same proportion of nonmetropolitan and metropolitan workers crossed a county boundary to get to work, a greater proportion of nonmetropolitan workers worked very near home (as indicated by a commute of less than one-half hour). Extremely time-consuming commutes were about equal between the two residence categories, but moderate duration commutes, one-half hour to an hour, were notably more prevalent for metropolitan workers.

This makes sense when one considers the multicounty structure of most metropolitan labor markets in 1980. A large volume of surburban workers commute to central city jobs (and vice versa), and commuting between different surburban counties, facilitated by "beltway" type highways, is also common. These metropolitan commutes, especially when measured by time in transit, are frequently quite long.[23]

Differences in commuting were even more noticeable between adjacent and nonadjacent nonmetropolitan counties. The journey to work was much quicker in nonadjacent counties, and only 15 percent of workers in nonadjacent nonmetropolitan areas crossed a county boundary on the way to work, compared with 22 percent of workers in adjacent counties. This indicates the relative self-sufficiency and/or isolation of labor markets in nonadjacent nonmetropolitan areas. In contrast, nonmetropolitan workers in counties adjacent to a metropolitan area have effective access to a greater abundance of jobs in the metropolitan market, and consequently a higher proportion of them commute to another county to work. (See Chapter 12 for an analysis of commuting among metropolitan and nonmetropolitan size-of-place groups.)

Unemployment

The remainder of the civilian labor force is comprised of unemployed workers. Unemployment has both individual and societal importance.[24] Individual unemployment implies that a person's material welfare is impaired. It is generally considered to identify individuals in economic distress. From a societal standpoint, the unemployment rate (unemployed workers as a fraction of the civilian labor force) has become an important social and economic indicator of how well the economy is performing, and of what stage it is at in the business cycle. Unemployment rates are generated for local labor markets (counties or groups of counties) and are used to identify areas with economic dis-

[23]In the 1975 Annual Housing Survey, the journey to work was measured by both time and distance. The data generally showed that metropolitan workers spent more time commuting, but nonmetropolitan workers traveled longer distances.
[24]Wachtel (1984).

tress. Area eligibility for assistance under some public programs is determined by having a high relative unemployment rate.

While there is much controversy surrounding the measurement of unemployment and its meaning, experts such as those on the National Commission on Employment and Unemployment Statistics generally agree that while flawed, it is better than any alternative.[25] The controversy centers on whether the measure underestimates or overestimates unemployment. Proponents of the former position contend that it underestimates unemployment because underemployed workers are counted as employed, and discouraged workers are excluded from the work force. Rural-oriented analysts, for example, have shown that discouraged workers and workers on involuntary part-time schedules are more prevalent in nonmetropolitan areas. Adjusting for this significantly increases the gap between metropolitan and nonmetropolitan unemployment rates. Proponents of the latter position feel that the unemployment rate overstates the problem because it contains unemployed individuals with very weak attachments to the labor force (teenagers, for example). With this caution in mind we briefly review recent trends in the level of unemployment in nonmetropolitan and metropolitan America, and describe some attributes of unemployed workers as of 1980.

Recent Trends in Nonmetropolitan Unemployment

Prior to the 1970s, the nonmetropolitan unemployment rate was lower than the metropolitan rate—remaining below the metropolitan rate throughout recession and recovery. The most recent recession (1979–1982) represents a significant break with that pattern. The nonmetropolitan unemployment rate rose more rapidly than the metropolitan, peaked at a higher level, and has remained above the metropolitan rate throughout the 1980s (Table 8.13). Employment in timber industries fell as new housing starts declined. Many rural manufacturing plants were linked to the struggling auto and steel industries. And mining and other energy extractive industries once again suffered a severe contraction. The textile, clothing, and leather goods industries, which are concentrated in nonmetropolitan areas, also suffered from increased import competition during this period.

Nilsen has demonstrated that changes in the industrial composition of the nonmetropolitan labor force between the 1970s and the 1979–1982 recession made them more vulnerable to the most recent

[25]National Commission on Employment and Unemployment Statistics (1979).

TABLE 8.13

Nonmetropolitan and Metropolitan Unemployment Rates, 1973–1985[a]

Year	Nonmetropolitan[a]		Metropolitan[b]	
	Reported	Adjusted	Reported	Adjusted[c]
1985	8.4	13.0	6.9	9.9
1984	8.1	12.2	7.3	10.4
1983	10.1	14.9	9.4	13.1
1982	10.1	14.9	9.5	13.1
1981	7.9	11.5	7.5	10.3
1980	7.3	10.7	7.0	9.5
1979	5.7	8.5	5.8	8.0
1978	5.8	8.8	6.1	8.4
1977	6.6	9.8	7.3	9.3
1976	7.0	10.2	8.0	10.6
1975	8.0	11.6	8.7	11.5
1974	5.1	7.9	5.8	7.9
1973	4.4	7.1	5.1	7.1

SOURCE: U. S. Bureau of Census, Current Population Survey.
Annual average unemployment rate.
Metropolitan area delineation was updated in 1985 and is not directly comparable with earlier years in data series.
Unemployment rate adjusted to include discouraged workers and half of the workers employed part-time for economic reasons.

economic downturn than to previous recessions.[26] This was a goods-producing recession, and nonmetropolitan economies are now more dependent on such industries. In fact, they are more dependent on goods production than metropolitan areas. Accordingly, nonmetropolitan areas experienced a disproportionately large share of the 1979–1982 unemployment increase.

Nonmetropolitan areas have recovered from the recession less rapidly than metropolitan areas. The nonmetropolitan unemployment rate actually increased between 1984 and 1985 while the metropolitan rate declined. As of 1986, the official nonmetropolitan unemployment rate remained 1.7 percentage points above the metropolitan rate. Most of this difference is explained by the poor performance of the nonmetropolitan manufacturing sector. There is evidence that nonmetropolitan manufacturing subsequently began a recovery from the recession by adopting labor saving, productivity enhancing technology. Accordingly, it is not yet clear whether a revived manufacturing sector will mean more jobs for nonmetropolitan workers.

[26]Nilsen (1984).

Table 8.13 also contains metropolitan–nonmetropolian unemployment rates adjusted for discouraged and involuntary part-time workers. This adjustment raises the rate in both residential sectors, but more so in nonmetropolitan areas. Accordingly, the metropolitan–nonmetropolitan percentage point gap in adjusted unemployment is greater than the difference in reported rates. This is consistent with Lichter's conclusion that nonmetropolitan underemployment was greater than metropolitan.[27] He used a labor utilization framework to estimate that the conventional unemployment rate captured about 40 percent of employment-related hardship in nonmetropolitan areas, compared with 45 percent of the hardship in metropolitan areas.

Attributes of Unemployed Workers in 1979

Unemployment Rates by Age and Sex. The unemployment rate is at its highest among youth, and then declines directly with age. This age pattern is characteristic of both males and females, and regardless of metropolitan–nonmetropolitan or urban–rural residence.

At the time of the 1980 census (April) the nonmetropolitan unemployment rate was somewhat above the metropolitan rate. Higher nonmetropolitan unemployment characterized both sexes, all age groups (especially after age 20), and both urban and rural areas (Table 8.14). Unemployment rates differed very little between the rural and urban parts of metropolitan counties. Unemployment data in the census are recorded at place of residence and not at place of work. Accordingly, greater access to employment opportunities in all parts of metropolitan areas probably provide metropolitan/rural workers some measure of protection from the recession. The same age, sex, and residence patterns characterize black workers in the South, although blacks had substantially higher unemployment rates at each age, for both sexes, and in all residence categories. In most cases the black unemployment rate was at least twice as high as the corresponding rates for nonblacks.

Duration of Unemployment. Only a small proportion of individuals who are unemployed at a given time are in that state for a protracted period. Rather, many workers experience occasional spells of unemployment that last for relatively short periods of time. The 1980 census data displayed in Table 8.15 show that only about one-sixth of the persons who were unemployed at any time during 1979 were unemployed for a half of the year or longer, and about one-third were unemployed for less than five weeks. The duration of unemployment is very similar for both

[27]Lichter (1987).

256

TABLE 8.14

Unemployment Rates by Sex, Age, Race (South Only), and Residence, April 1980

Sex/Age	Total	Metropolitan			Nonmetropolitan		
		Total	Urban	Rural	Total	Urban	Rural
United States							
Male age							
LT 20	15.7	15.7	15.9	14.1	15.8	15.4	16.0
20–44	6.7	6.5	6.5	6.5	7.6	7.2	7.8
45+	4.0	3.9	3.8	4.1	4.5	4.0	4.9
Total	6.5	6.3	6.3	6.3	7.2	6.9	7.4
Female age							
LT 20	13.4	13.0	12.9	14.0	14.6	13.7	15.4
20–44	6.5	6.2	6.2	6.2	7.5	7.1	7.8
45+	4.4	4.3	4.4	4.2	4.8	4.5	5.1
Total	6.5	6.2	6.2	6.2	7.3	6.9	7.6
South Only							
Male							
Nonblack	4.5	4.0	3.9	4.6	5.7	4.8	6.1
Black	9.7	9.3	9.3	9.5	10.4	11.0	10.1
Female							
Nonblack	5.2	4.7	4.6	5.4	6.2	5.6	6.6
Black	10.5	9.6	9.6	9.4	13.0	13.1	12.9

sexes, although women are more likely than men to be unemployed for a very short time. Nonmetropolitan and rural unemployed workers were more likely than metropolitan and urban workers to be unemployed for a long period of time, but the difference is slight. Data by race for the South (not shown) indicate that while the duration of unemployment for black workers was substantially greater than for nonblacks, the great majority of blacks who were unemployed at any time during 1979 were also unemployed for a moderate to short amount of time during the year.

Last Industry of Unemployed Workers. The vast majority of workers who were unemployed at some time in 1979 but who worked for a period during the year, last worked in transformative (principally manufacturing) and in distributive industries (Table 8.16). To some extent this reflects the industrial structure of the economy, but unemployed workers whose last job was in these industries are represented disproportionately. The goods producing recession that began in the last quarter of 1979 clearly affected the stability of employment in

TABLE 8.15

Duration (in weeks) of Unemployment by Sex and Residence, 1979

Sex and Age	Total	Metropolitan			Nonmetropolitan		
		Total	Urban	Rural	Total	Urban	Rura
Male							
1–4 weeks	29.2	29.8	30.2	27.8	27.1	30.8	24.
5–26 weeks	54.8	54.3	53.7	57.7	56.6	54.2	58.
27–52 weeks	16.0	15.9	16.1	14.5	16.3	15.0	17.
Total	100.0	100.0	100.0	100.0	100.0	100.0	100.
Female							
1–4 weeks	35.2	36.1	36.4	33.4	32.1	36.3	28.
5–26 weeks	49.3	49.0	48.7	51.3	50.5	47.5	52.
27–52 weeks	15.5	14.9	14.9	15.3	17.4	16.2	18.
Total	100.0	100.0	100.0	100.0	100.0	100.0	100.

TABLE 8.16

Last Industry of Unemployed Workers, 1980[a]

	Total	Metropolitan			Nonmetropolitan		
		Total	Urban	Rural	Total	Urban	Rur
Last Worked in 1979 (000s) (percentage distribution)	5,487	4,001	3,425	5,766	1,485	547	93
Extractive	4.5	3.1	2.6	6.6	8.0	6.5	8
Transformative	43.8	41.6	39.9	51.1	49.9	44.8	52
Distributive	19.9	21.2	21.7	18.1	16.3	18.8	14
Producer services	6.5	7.7	8.2	4.7	3.3	4.2	2
Social services	11.9	12.3	13.0	8.6	10.9	12.5	10
Personal services	13.4	14.1	14.6	10.9	11.6	13.2	10
Total	100.0	100.0	100.0	100.0	100.0	100.0	100
Last Worked before 1979 (000s) (percentage distribution)	555	434	391	42	121	50	7
Extractive	3.1	2.1	1.8	4.0	6.6	2.2	9
Transformative	29.3	28.0	27.8	31.0	34.3	33.3	35
Distributive	20.3	21.0	20.4	26.7	17.6	18.7	16
Producer services	7.3	8.2	8.4	6.2	4.3	4.2	4
Social services	23.1	23.7	24.3	18.4	20.8	24.5	18
Personal services	16.9	17.0	17.3	13.7	16.4	17.1	15
Total	100.0	100.0	100.0	100.0	100.0	100.0	100

[a]Universe excludes new entrants to labor force.

these two industrial sectors. In contrast, relatively few unemployed workers last worked in producer services, the fastest growing sector of the economy.[28]

The general distribution of last job of workers unemployed for a period during 1979 did not differ much over the residence categories, although the concentration of last jobs in transformative and distributive industries was even more extreme in rural areas than in urban areas. In metropolitan counties, for example, fully 70 percent of unemployed rural workers last worked in these two sectors, compared with 62 percent of urban workers. In addition, a higher proportion of unemployed rural and nonmetropolitan workers last worked in extractive industries (farming, forestry, fisheries, and mining) than was true in urban and metropolitan areas. This reflects the fact that most extractive jobs are in rural and nonmetropolitan economies, as well as a downturn of energy prices that resulted in high unemployment among miners.

The distribution of last job for unemployed workers who did not work at any time during 1979 (about 9 percent of the unemployed) differed from that of unemployed workers who held a job sometime during the year. While the greatest proportion of such workers was still in transformative industries, the concentration was much less marked. In fact, the last jobs of these workers were fairly evenly spread among transformative, distributive, social services, and personal services jobs. The rapidly expanding producer services sector is significantly underrepresented. Again, while the specific proportions of workers in particular industrial categories differed somewhat among the residence categories, the general pattern was much the same for all areas; that is, industry of last employment was spread relatively evenly with the exception of personal services and extractive pursuits. Cyclical factors do not appear to have as large an effect on the long-time unemployed as on individuals who experience periodic spells of job loss.

In summary, coincident downturns during the 1980s in three industrial sectors—agriculture, mining, and manufacturing—have created economic stress throughout rural and nonmetropolitan America. The transforming rural economy is more vulnerable to foreign competition and labor saving technology. Accordingly, rural and small town economy's ability to provide jobs and shield workers from cyclical downturns in the future is questionable if it continues to specialize in goods producing activities.

---

[28]We have defined the extractive category to include agriculture, fishing, forestry, and mining, and the transformative category to include construction and manufacturing (Singelmann, 1978). The service category includes distributive services, such as wholesale and retail trade; producer services, like banking and real estate; social services; and various personal services. This classification is used also in Chapter 9.

Conclusions

Two major themes emerge from this chapter. First, during the 1970s nonmetropolitan and rural areas shared in the nation's major trends and changes in labor force participation. Male participation rates declined slightly during the decade, and women's participation increased dramatically. Moreover, women's participation, especially among white women, was shown to have become more continuous across the life course, and the presence of young children was shown to have diminished as a constraint on women's work outside of the home. Even with these changes, the level of rural and nonmetropolitan labor force participation continued to be somewhat lower than in urban and metropolitan areas. This persistent gap was shown to be associated with older age among the rural labor force age population, and with a greater prevalence of work-limiting disability, a continuing legacy of agriculture, mining, and other types of goods producing industries that are concentrated in rural economies.

Increased women's labor force participation rates were shown to be the principal source of growth in women's employment in nonmetropolitan areas between 1960 and 1980, even though the baby boom cohorts were moving into the labor force ages during these decades. In contrast, because male labor force participation rates were declining during the period, male employment would have actually declined if baby boom age men had not been coming of employment age.

The chapter's second theme reflects the effects of the dramatic industrial transformation of the nonmetropolitan economy on employment stability. This transformation, along with the smaller size of nonmetropolitan labor markets and their greater level of specialization, the deregulation of financial markets, and the internationalization of markets for manufactured and agricultural goods, has made rural and nonmetropolitan economies more vulnerable to cyclical changes in the economy. As a result, nonmetropolitan areas experienced a disproportionate share of employment declines during the 1979–1982 recession, and because goods production is now concentrated in nonmetropolitan areas they have recovered more slowly. Metropolitan economies, in contrast, are larger and more diversified and depend more on services for employment. Persistently high unemployment and slower employment growth in nonmetropolitan areas are almost certainly associated with low nonmetropolitan population growth and net outmigration since 1980.

Appendix 8.1

Decomposition of the Difference
Between Employment Change
and Population Change

We have expressed interrelations between population change and employment change through the following algebraic identity:

$$\frac{E_2}{E_1} = \frac{P_2}{P_1} \cdot \frac{\dfrac{E_2}{S_2}}{\dfrac{E_1}{S_1}} \cdot \frac{\dfrac{S_2}{P_2}}{\dfrac{S_1}{P_1}}$$

Where E is the number employed, P is population, S is population in working ages (here ages 15–64), and the subscripts 2 and 1 identify components at the end and the beginning of the decade, respectively.

From left to right, these four terms represent employment change, population change, change in the employment rate, and change in the proportion of the population of employment age.

This accounting or decomposition model shows how population change may be modified by multiplicative factors to yield employment change. Population growth will lead directly to employment growth provided there is no compensating change in proportion of people employed or the proportion of the age structure that is eligible to be employed. New births, on the other hand, would increase population, but there would also be a corresponding decrease in the proportion of the total population of employment age, and hence no increase in employment. Similarly, increase in employment participation would create employment growth, even if the population were stable or possibly declining. By taking natural logarithms of these components we have the following additive formulas:

$$\ln \frac{E_2}{E_1} = \frac{P_2}{P_1} + \ln \frac{\dfrac{E_2}{S_2}}{\dfrac{E_1}{S_1}} + \ln \frac{\dfrac{S_2}{P_2}}{\dfrac{S_1}{P_1}}$$

These natural logs of ratios, moreover, may be interpreted simply as annualized growth rates. According to the exponential growth function $P_2 = P_1 e^{rt}$ where r is the rate and t the time interval, so $r = \ln (P_2/P_1)/t$. We adjusted these components of employment change to decennial rates per 100 (r times 100 if t is measured in decades), separately for males and females, and by metropolitan–nonmetropolitan county groups over the decade. The rates for employment and population are somewhat below (since they allow for compounding) but generally correspond to percent change values. The age range for S, the employment years, was taken as 15–64, a range that includes more than 95 percent of the employed through this period. No adjustments were made for age distribution variations within the working years. By moving the first term on the right over to the left side we have remaining on the right the two components of the difference between employment change and population. Results in Table 8.10 are presented according to this formulation.

9

INDUSTRIAL STRUCTURE
AND CHANGE

T HE INDUSTRIAL structure of the United States economy has
changed dramatically during recent decades as traditional agricultural and manufacturing pursuits have declined in importance
and service industries have grown rapidly. Despite similarities, this industrial restructuring has proceeded differently in nonmetropolitan and
rural areas than in more urbanized parts of the county. The nonmetropolitan economies have characteristically been more dependent on natural resource-based industries, have had more human and capital resource constraints, and are generally smaller and more geographically
isolated. Changes in the spatial distribution of economic activity over
the past few decades have led to a convergence between metropolitan
and nonmetropolitan areas in the structure of industrial employment,
but the pace and nature of industrial change have differed between these
residential types.

This chapter explores the changing industrial structure of metropolitan and nonmetropolitan employment. The first half of the chapter provides details on the composition and changes in industrial employment
between 1960 and 1980. The trend toward greater reliance on services is
shown to be related to distinct residential trends. Among metropolitan

---

This chapter was written by Max J. Pfeffer, Robert M. Jenkins, and David L.
Brown.

residents, growth in service employment occurred at the expense of manufacturing employment. In contrast, nonmetropolitan manufacturing showed resilience over the two decades, due primarily to a significant increase in employment in that industrial category during the 1960s. The decline in agricultural employment among nonmetropolitan residents stood opposite an expansion of services, not changes in manufacturing. These different trends in employment have brought about an increasing convergence in the structure of industrial employment in metropolitan and nonmetropolitan areas.

Analysis of the nature of residential differences in manufacturing between 1970 and 1980 shows that nonmetropolitan manufacturing growth was broad-based, while growth in manufacturing employment among metropolitan residents was more limited to a core of industries. These rapidly growing types of manufacturing in metropolitan areas were also the fastest growers in nonmetropolitan areas, somewhat dispelling the notion that only slow-growth manufacturing was leading nonmetropolitan manufacturing. And while evidence suggests that the manufacturing core of the North is losing some of its leading position to the South and West, the majority of manufacturing in the nation is still located in the traditional industrial heartland.

The growth of service employment in the economy has been accompanied by the expansion of female labor force participation noted in Chapter 8. This expansion was particularly important to the fastest growing types of industries in the 1970s: producer services, mining, and social services. Residential differences in the structure of female employment in these different types of industries are also detailed in the pages ahead.

Finally, the chapter documents important residential differences in the types of jobs provided and training demanded by different industries. The nonmetropolitan labor force is shown to have consistently lower levels of educational attainment and to be disadvantaged in terms of opportunities for full-time employment. Similarly, metropolitan residents are more likely to be working in white collar jobs than are nonmetropolitan residents. These differences suggest that generalized nonmetropolitan growth may hide important differences in the nature of jobs available to nonmetropolitan residents.

The Changing Composition of Industrial Employment

The transformation or restructuring of industrial employment in the United States has involved two historic shifts. First, there was a shift from predominantly agricultural work to nonagricultural employment. A second shift from producing goods to more reliance on services subsequently affected the mix of nonagricultural jobs. For the first transformation, 1880 has been identified as the pivotal year, when nonagricultural workers first outnumbered agricultural workers.[1] The second transformation can be traced to the immediate post–World War II years, when service industries first accounted for a majority of all employment.[2]

Though the rate of growth of services in recent decades has been faster in metropolitan areas than in nonmetropolitan areas, the latter have also experienced the shift toward service employment. More workers residing in nonmetropolitan areas are now employed in service industries than in goods producing industries, and most of the job growth in nonmetropolitan areas since the late 1960s has been in the service sector.[3] This trend in service employment growth is expected to continue. The Bureau of Labor Statistics projects that total employment in the United States will grow by about 16 million jobs between 1984 and 1995.[4] About nine out of ten of these new jobs are expected to be in the service sector.

The national trend of increasing importance of service industries is apparent in Figure 9.1, where the relative share of employment is shown for three types of industries—extractive, transformative, and services—in each census year from 1960 to 1980.[5] The percentage of the work force employed in extractive and transformative industries has declined over these decades, though the decline in extractive industries did level during the 1970s. Conversely, the percentage employed in service industries continued to increase to the point that by 1980 more than two-thirds of the labor force was employed in services.

There are both similarities and differences between metropolitan and nonmetropolitan residents in the composition of industrial employment over the 1960–1980 period. It is clear from Figure 9.2 that both residential types have similar patterns of change in the percentage employed in extractive and service industries. The share of extractive employment declined, while that of services increased in both decades. The nonmetropolitan work force has also shown a consistently smaller percentage employed in services. The greater relative importance of extrac-

[1]Bogue (1985).
[2]Henderson (1961).
[3]Miller and Bluestone (1988).
[4]This projection utilizes BLS moderate growth projections. The low growth scenario is for 11 million new jobs and the high growth scenario implies 21 million new jobs.
[5]We have defined the extractive category to include agriculture, fishing, forestry, and mining, and the transformative category to include construction and manufacturing (Singelmann, 1978). The service category includes distributive services, such as wholesale and retail trade; producer services, like banking and real estate; social services; and various personal services.

FIGURE 9.1

Percentage Distribution of Industrial Employment, 1960–1980

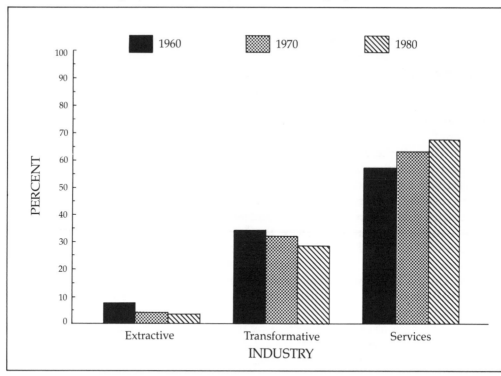

FIGURE 9.2

Percentage Distribution of Industrial Employment
by Metropolitan and Nonmetropolitan Residence, 1960–1980

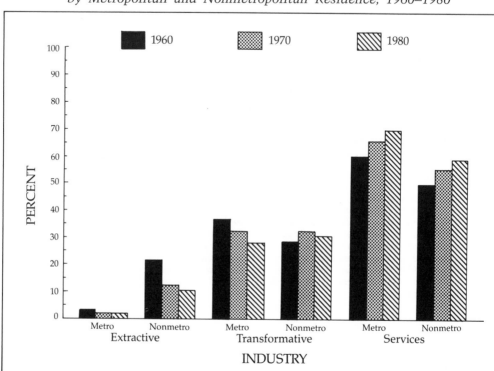

tive employment reflects the traditional role of the natural resource-based economy in rural America.[6]

The major difference between metropolitan and nonmetropolitan residents in industrial composition has been in the relative share of transformative industries. The percentage employed in these industries declined regularly from 1960 to 1980 among metropolitan residents. The trend among nonmetropolitan residents deviated from this pattern, with an increase in percentage between 1960 and 1970 and a slight decrease between 1970 and 1980 that produced a small increase over the two decades. While transformative jobs declined in significance among metropolitan residents, their importance remained relatively constant for the nonmetropolitan work force. These residential differences in transformative employment are analyzed in more detail in subsequent sections of the chapter.

Definitions and Data

The industrial composition of employment and changes in that composition between 1960 and 1980 are the focus of this chapter. Industry refers to the primary activities of firms employing individuals. Industry should not be confused with occupation, which refers to functions, responsibilities, and combinations of skills associated with specific jobs. Particular industries typically employ workers in a wide variety of occupations and will differ from other industries in occupational composition.

For the analyses in this chapter, industries have been grouped into eight main sectors. The extractive industries have been broken into two components—agriculture (including forestry and fisheries) and mining.[7] Goods producing, or transformative, industries have also been divided into two groups—construction and manufacturing. The importance of manufacturing employment in nonmetropolitan economies in recent decades leads us to pay particular attention to this group and disaggregate it in greater detail.

The service industries make up a large and steadily expanding share

---

[6]The importance of natural resource industries has recently been noted by Weber, Castle, and Shriver (1988), who say that these industries account for 20 percent or more of earnings in one of every nine United States counties.

[7]Agriculture, forestry, and fisheries are treated as one category in the remainder of this chapter and are simply referred to as agriculture, a reasonable treatment given the relatively small number of people employed in forestry and fisheries. In 1980, employment in forestry and fisheries accounted for less than two-tenths of 1 percent of total employment and about 5 percent of the agricultural category reported in this chapter.

of total employment and, accordingly, we examine this sector in some detail. We present four reasonably homogeneous types of service employment—distributive, producer, personal, and social service—as they have been developed in other studies.[8] Distributive services provide for the distribution of goods to the ultimate consumer, while producer services are provided to makers of goods and constitute intermediate activities somewhere between primary products and the final output. Personal services share a basic orientation toward the individual consumer. Such industries as hotels, garment services, and beauty shops, as well as employment in private households, constitute personal services. While social services cater to individuals, they tend to be provided by collective entities such as educational institutions, governments, and private medical services, which are increasingly integrated into collective entities such as health maintenance organizations.[9]

Summary census data on employment by county of residence (not by place of employment) are used to examine metropolitan–nonmetropolitan and regional differences in industrial structure and growth.[10] The analysis of differences between metropolitan and nonmetropolitan residents is supplemented with an assessment of trends since 1980 using data from the Current Population Survey (CPS). In addition, comparisons are made among nonmetropolitan counties on the basis of the level of local urbanization and adjacency to metropolitan areas. Finally, the chapter presents characteristics of metropolitan and nonmetropolitan residents employed in different industries using data from the 1980 Public-Use Microdata Sample (PUMS). Characteristics analyzed include full- or part-time employment, educational attainment, and occupation.

Industrial Structure and Change 1960–1980

The conventional picture of rural America is one of domination by agriculture. Data presented in Table 9.1 show that this view was already inaccurate in 1960. In that year, just under one in five nonmetropolitan residents was engaged in agricultural employment. Slightly more than one in five were employed in manufacturing and over one-half of all nonmetropolitan residents held jobs in the services sector.

Nonetheless, the structure of employment in the nonmetropolitan

---

[8]More detail on the makeup of these categories is presented in Appendix Table 9.1.
[9]Browning and Singelmann (1978); Singelmann (1978).
[10]Metropolitan status in 1980 is used to designate counties as metropolitan and nonmetropolitan when working with census data, except the CPS. See Appendix 9.1 for a fuller discussion of the use of the 1980 metropolitan definition.

TABLE 9.1

Employed Population as Percentage of Total Employment
and Percentage of Change by Industry and Residence, 1960–1980

Industry	Percentage of Total Employment			Percentage Change of Employed Population	
	1960	1970	1980	1960–1970	1970–1980
Metropolitan[a]					
Total employed (000s)	46,765	59,555	75,597	—	—
Agriculture	3.0	1.8	1.6	−24.3	12.4
Mining	0.5	0.5	0.6	11.9	62.0
Construction	6.1	5.7	5.6	20.0	24.1
Manufacturing	30.3	26.2	22.2	9.9	7.7
Distributive services	27.1	27.6	28.4	29.9	30.4
Producer services	7.9	9.1	11.3	47.7	58.0
Personal services	7.0	5.3	4.2	−2.6	0.5
Social services	18.2	23.8	26.1	66.8	39.2
Total	100.0	100.0	100.0	27.4	26.9
Nonmetropolitan[a]					
Total employed (000s)	15,266	16,998	22,042	—	—
Agriculture	19.2	10.4	7.8	−39.7	−3.4
Mining	2.6	2.0	2.6	−13.4	63.8
Construction	6.4	6.9	6.9	19.2	29.7
Manufacturing	21.9	25.1	23.3	27.5	20.7
Distributive services	23.6	24.2	25.3	14.5	35.5
Producer services	4.1	4.8	6.4	27.8	74.1
Personal services	7.2	5.8	4.0	−10.0	−10.1
Social services	14.9	20.8	23.7	55.1	47.8
Total	100.0	100.0	100.0	11.3	29.7

[a]Metropolitan or nonmetropolitan as of 1980.

economy in 1960 was distinct from the metropolitan structure. With less than one in thirty workers employed in agriculture, metropolitan residents displayed far less dependence on such jobs. Shares of employment in distributive, producer, and social services were smaller in the nonmetropolitan work force in 1960. Also of note in 1960 was the lesser importance of manufacturing employment among nonmetropolitan than among metropolitan residents.

Changes in the shares of service employment between 1960 and 1980 were similar for the metropolitan and nonmetropolitan labor forces. In both metropolitan and nonmetropolitan areas the relative share of the work force in distributive, producer, and social services increased. Social services showed the greatest increase in relative share among both types of residents. Despite similarities, the percentage employed in these three service types remained over 10 percent greater among metropolitan than among nonmetropolitan residents in 1980.

Manufacturing employment exhibited an important difference in the trend of relative shares by residence type. Between 1960 and 1980, the relative importance of manufacturing declined for the metropolitan work force, while it first increased and then slightly decreased among nonmetropolitan residents. As a result of these divergent patterns, the relative shares of employment in manufacturing converged by 1980, when both residence types had 22 to 23 percent of their employees in manufacturing industries. Construction employment showed a pattern similar to manufacturing employment, declining in share among metropolitan residents and increasing in importance in the nonmetropolitan work force. As a result, construction became more important to nonmetropolitan residents in 1980 than to their metropolitan counterparts.

Changes in relative shares of employment were generated by differential growth rates for both residence and industrial sector. Differences in employment growth by industry for each residence type are also shown in the last two columns of Table 9.1. Employment among metropolitan residents increased strongly in each decade (around 27 percent). The growth in employment among nonmetropolitan residents was much slower in the 1960s (11 percent) but increased to overtake the metropolitan rate in the 1970s (almost 30 percent).

Both similarities and differences between residence types are observable across the two decades. For example, the number employed in agriculture declined in both metropolitan and nonmetropolitan areas during the 1960–1970 period. During the decade of the 1970s, the decline in nonmetropolitan agriculture moderated, but metropolitan residents actually exhibited an increase in agricultural employment. Both the less steep decline in the 1960s and the increase in the 1970s in metropolitan agricultural employment are no doubt due to the growth of nonfarm employment in agriculture. Such industries as veterinary medicine, kennels, and landscaping grew during the two decades and were typically located in metropolitan areas.

Differential growth rates also played a role in bringing about convergence in the relative shares of manufacturing in metropolitan and nonmetropolitan areas. Metropolitan manufacturing employment grew at modest rates during both the 1960s and the 1970s. These growth rates were far below the overall growth rates for jobs in the metropolitan economy as a whole. In contrast, the nonmetropolitan growth rate in manufacturing during the 1960s was well over twice that of overall total nonmetropolitan employment, and the relative share of manufacturing in the nonmetropolitan economy grew sizably by 1970. During the subsequent 1970–1980 period, the growth rate of nonmetropolitan manufacturing was lower than that of overall nonmetropolitan employment. The result was a slight decline in manufacturing's share of nonmetropolitan jobs, but the 1980 share still remained larger than the share in 1960.

During the 1960s, mining employment declined in nonmetropolitan areas, the traditional site of such extractive activities, and increased in metropolitan areas. This latter growth was most likely due to an increase of administrative, technical, and sales activities within the industry. The rapid growth in mining employment in the 1970s stands in stark contrast to the experience of the 1960s and was undoubtedly tied to energy price increases associated with the Arab oil embargo and the resulting energy crisis of the mid-1970s. The energy boom of the 1970s reduced residential differences in mining growth. Both metropolitan and nonmetropolitan areas showed similarly strong growth rates between 1970 and 1980 and far outperformed the growth in overall employment.

In nonmetropolitan areas in the 1960s, growth rates in distributive, producer, and social services lagged behind the growth rates of these industries in metropolitan areas. There was a turnaround in the residential pattern of these growth rates between 1970 and 1980, as nonmetropolitan areas had higher growth rates in the same service sectors as well as in construction. This turnaround is probably associated with the decentralization of population that occurred during the decade, while the enhanced growth of producer and distributive services is likely tied to the decentralization of manufacturing.

The changing location of industrial employment is illustrated in Figure 9.3, which shows the extent to which particular industry groups are located in nonmetropolitan counties. Agriculture and mining show persistent concentration in nonmetropolitan areas, though the level of concentration of each has diminished. Manufacturing employment steadily increased its orientation to nonmetropolitan locations between 1960 and 1980. Producer and distributive services, although related to manufacturing, do not seem to have witnessed a parallel deconcentration. This failure of the two service categories to follow the deconcentration of manufacturing is consistent with ideas of a growing spatial dichotomy in manufacturing-related activities.[11]

---

[11]Noyelle and Stanback (1983) found that functions of management and high-value added production have become increasingly concentrated in large metropolitan centers in recent decades. In nonmetropolitan and small metropolitan areas, it was low-value added production that was gaining in importance. Accordingly, nonmetropolitan areas appear to be missing out on some of the beneficial aspects of manufacturing growth.

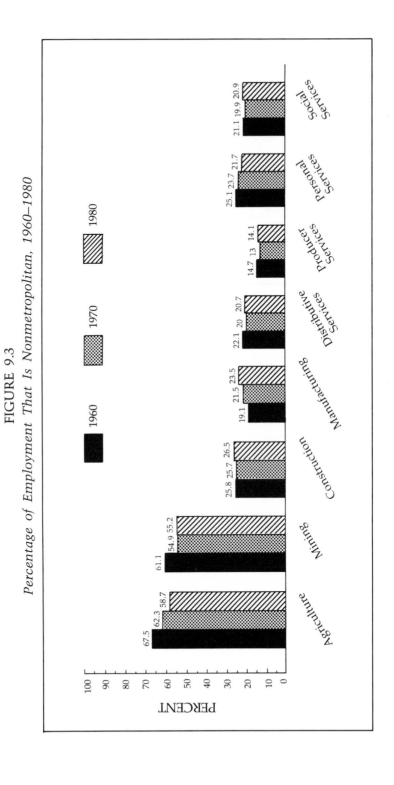

FIGURE 9.3

Percentage of Employment That Is Nonmetropolitan, 1960–1980

TABLE 9.2

Employed Population as Percentage of Total Employment by Industry and Residence, 1976–1984

Industry	1976	1980	1984
Metropolitan[a]			
Agriculture	1.6	1.4	1.2
Mining	0.4	0.6	0.5
Construction	5.4	5.8	5.9
Manufacturing	22.8	20.9	19.8
Distributive services	27.9	27.4	28.3
Producer services	10.2	11.6	13.3
Personal services	5.5	5.0	5.2
Social services	26.2	27.3	25.8
Total	100.0	100.0	100.0
Nonmetropolitan[a]			
Agriculture	9.7	8.3	6.7
Mining	2.0	2.5	2.0
Construction	7.3	7.4	8.0
Manufacturing	23.5	20.9	20.0
Distributive services	24.7	25.2	26.6
Producer services	5.7	6.7	7.7
Personal services	5.1	4.9	5.2
Social services	22.0	24.1	23.8
Total	100.0	100.0	100.0

SOURCE: Machine readable files of Current Population Surveys for October of each year indicated.

[a]Metropolitan or nonmetropolitan as of 1970.

Industrial Composition Since 1980

To assess changes in the composition of industrial employment since 1980, we present data from the Current Population Survey (CPS) for October 1976, 1980, and 1984. Table 9.2 shows the relative shares of each industry type for both metropolitan and nonmetropolitan residents in each year.[12] The data indicate that the changes in relative importance of manufacturing and distributive services in the 1970s continued in the 1980–1984 period. Manufacturing declined in importance at the same

[12]The figures for 1980 presented in Table 9.2 differ slightly from those presented in Table 9.1, because of differences in metropolitan designations. The Current Population Survey used the 1970 metropolitan–nonmetropolitan designation through 1984. The data in Table 9.2 are based on this designation, whereas the data in Table 9.1 reflect the 1980 definition.

FIGURE 9.4

Percentage of Employment That Is Nonmetropolitan, * 1976–1984*

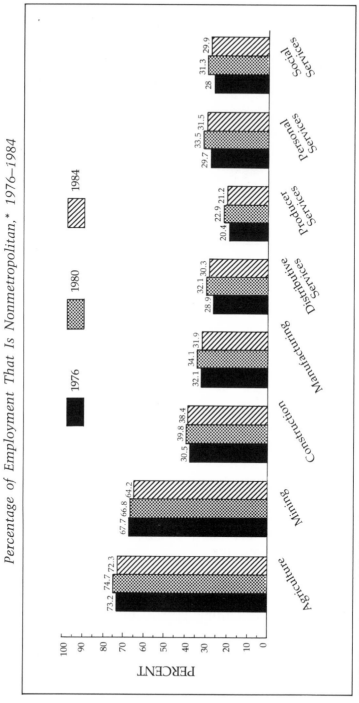

SOURCE: Machine-readable files of Current Population Surveys for October of each year indicated.

*Nonmetropolitan by 1970 designation.

time that distributive services increased in importance among both types of residents.

Key differences between metropolitan and nonmetropolitan residents in changing industrial composition occur with respect to agriculture and producer services. The trend toward convergence in the importance of agriculture seems to have continued since 1980. The importance of agriculture declined among both types of residents, but the decline in importance was greater among those in nonmetropolitan areas. In contrast, the difference in shares of producer services widened in favor of metropolitan residents, even though the relative importance of these activities did increase in nonmetropolitan areas.

The forces underlying these changes in the importance of different industries have also produced changes in the concentration of industries in nonmetropolitan areas. In Figure 9.4 we display the percentage of residents living in nonmetropolitan areas for each industry in the 1976–1984 period using the CPS data.[13] It is clear that in 1984 agriculture and mining continued to be strongly concentrated among nonmetropolitan residents, though the concentration had decreased from 1980. Note that trends toward deconcentration of construction and manufacturing toward nonmetropolitan areas reversed after 1980. These reversals no doubt reflect the fact that all types of industries showed greater metropolitan concentration in 1984 than in 1980. This general trend shows that there are important differences in the 1980–1984 period that distinguish these years from the previous two decades. Unfortunately, a more detailed assessment of these new trends is beyond the scope of this chapter.

Structure and Change in Manufacturing

The convergence in relative shares of manufacturing employment between metropolitan and nonmetropolitan areas has resulted from higher growth rates in manufacturing in nonmetropolitan areas. However, manufacturing activities are very diverse. Overall similarity among areas in the importance of manufacturing employment as a whole may mask substantial differentiation in structure and growth by specific type of manufacturing. Particular types of manufacturing differ in skill and pay levels. Accordingly, labor markets with different types of manufacturing also differ in the amount and quality of employment

---

[13]The figures presented in Figure 9.4 are somewhat higher than those in Figure 9.3, because counties that had been nonmetropolitan in 1970 and became metropolitan by 1980 continue to be counted as nonmetropolitan in Figure 9.4. The trends presented in this graph are, of course, our main focus of interest.

opportunities they provide to the resident population. A number of authors have suggested that there are important differences between metropolitan and nonmetropolitan areas and between regions in type of manufacturing growth. This section explores trends in manufacturing employment in greater detail. By disaggregating into twelve types, we are able to examine these differentials in growth as well as differentials in the structure of manufacturing.

The data in Table 9.3 show that employment in durable manufacturing is more important in metropolitan areas and nondurable manufacturing is more important in nonmetropolitan areas. Every category of durable manufacturing is more important in metropolitan areas than in nonmetropolitan areas, with the exception of manufacturing of furniture, lumber, and wood products.

Manufacturing of timber-based products and textiles and apparel show the largest differences in relative importance between residential categories. Both types of manufacturing are traditionally associated with rural industrialization and have larger shares in nonmetropolitan areas. Food and kindred products and other nondurable manufacturing (which includes such diverse types of manufacturing as tobacco, paper and allied products, petroleum and coal products, rubber and miscellaneous plastic products, and leather goods) also were of greater relative importance to nonmetropolitan employment than metropolitan employment.

TABLE 9.3

Percentage Employed in Manufacturing Type by Residence, 1980

Manufacturing Type	Total	Metro	Nonmetro
Food and Kindred	7.0	6.4	9.0
Textiles and Apparel	10.3	7.9	18.0
Printing and Publishing	7.0	7.8	4.4
Chemicals and Allied	5.8	6.3	4.3
Other Nondurables	9.6	9.3	10.9
Nondurable Subtotal	39.7	37.6	46.6
Furniture, Lumber, Wood	5.6	3.7	11.9
Primary Metals	6.0	6.3	5.0
Fabricated Metals	6.5	6.9	5.3
Machinery, Except Elec.	12.6	13.1	11.0
Electrical Products	10.0	10.9	7.1
Motor Vehicle, Transportation	11.1	12.6	6.0
Other Durables	8.5	8.9	7.1
Durable Subtotal	60.3	62.4	53.4
Total	100.0	100.0	100.0

The types of manufacturing of greatest importance to nonmetropolitan areas tend to be resource-based: food, timber products, other nondurables. Specialization in these types of manufacturing tends to be associated with proximity to resources. An exception to the resource-base orientation in nonmetropolitan areas is textiles and apparel manufacturing. This type of manufacturing is more representative of what some analysts have referred to as mature industries, that is, those industries that have achieved a relative stability in production technique and for which low labor costs dominate competitive concerns. Some observers have suggested that industrial decentralization or deconcentration is a "filtering down of production" in the urban hierarchy by which mature industries search for lower labor costs.[14] This effort of mature industries to reduce costs is hypothesized to have led to the movement of manufacturing from metropolitan to nonmetropolitan areas and from the traditional industrial heartland to the South and Southwest.

Nonmetropolitan industrialization first came to prominence during the 1960s. Manufacturing data for 1970 and 1980 provide an indication of the extent of deconcentration in the 1970s. The change between 1970 and 1980 in the number of persons employed in different types of manufacturing is shown by residence type in Table 9.4. Important residential differences are immediately clear. Nonmetropolitan growth exceeded metropolitan growth in all types except one—furniture, lumber, and wood. Although these categories are highly aggregated, the findings suggest that nonmetropolitan manufacturing growth was not limited to mature industries but also included younger industries. Industries experiencing rapid technological changes, such as chemicals and electrical products, experienced more rapid growth in nonmetropolitan areas than in metropolitan areas.[15] Other industries more typically associated with the mature phase of the product cycle, such as primary metals, fabricated metals, and motor vehicle and other transportation manufacturing, also experienced higher growth in nonmetropolitan areas than in metropolitan areas.

Nonmetropolitan manufacturing growth is frequently assumed to be in slow-growth industries.[16] This thesis is not supported by the data presented here. The fastest growing types of manufacturing in nonmetropolitan areas during the 1970s were precisely those categories that were experiencing the greatest growth at the metropolitan level, that is, nonelectrical machinery, printing and publishing, and chemical and allied products. It is possible that specific industries within these broad

[14]Thompson (1969); Hansen (1979); Norton and Rees (1979); Gilmer (1986).
[15]Norton and Rees (1979).
[16]Petrulis (1979).

TABLE 9.4

Percentage Change in Employment and Percentage Nonmetropolitan by Manufacturing Type, 1970–1980[a]

Manufacturing Type	Percentage Change			Percentage Nonmetropolitan	
	Total	Metro	Nonmetro	1970	1980
Food and Kindred	10.3	5.6	22.8	27.1	30.2
Textiles and Apparel	2.9	−2.3	11.2	38.0	41.1
Printing and Publishing	28.5	25.5	48.8	12.8	14.8
Chemicals and Allied	28.8	27.5	35.7	16.7	17.6
Other Nondurables	−9.8	−13.3	1.6	23.5	26.4
Nondurable Subtotal	7.4	4.6	15.5	25.6	27.6
Furniture, Lumber, Wood	25.7	28.9	22.5	51.1	49.8
Primary Metals	7.9	3.9	28.5	16.4	19.5
Fabricated Metals	−2.7	−6.8	19.2	15.7	19.3
Machinery, Except Elec.	39.0	34.1	61.4	17.7	20.5
Electrical Products	15.4	12.9	30.1	14.7	16.6
Motor Vehicle, Transportation	13.5	11.7	27.8	11.3	12.7
Other Durables	−9.2	−10.2	−5.1	18.7	19.6
Durable Subtotal	12.6	9.6	25.7	18.6	20.8
Total	10.5	7.7	20.7	21.5	23.5

[a]Metropolitan or nonmetropolitan as of 1980.

categories may show support for the hypotheses of mature and slow-growth industry filtering to nonmetropolitan areas, but at this level of detail that position is not supported. Other work has also shown substantial top-of-the-cycle growth in nonmetropolitan economies.[17]

An impact of the greater growth in virtually all types of nonmetropolitan manufacturing between 1970 and 1980 was an increase in the percentage of manufacturing employment that is nonmetropolitan. Nationally, the nonmetropolitan share rose by 2 percentage points between the two census years. Leading the increase was fabricated metals manufacturing. Food and kindred, textiles and apparel, primary metals, other nondurables, and nonelectric machinery also showed increases in their nonmetropolitan shares. Both resource-based and mature manufacturing types became more important to nonmetropolitan economies during this decade (Table 9.4).

[17]Bloomquist (1988).

Regional Variations in Structure and Change

The industrial structure of employment has historically displayed rather pronounced regional variation. Consequently, changes in industrial structure may have distinct regional impacts. Concentrations of certain manufacturing activities, agriculture, and mining have been a critical aspect of regional economic development in the United States. These different industrial profiles have had a major effect on the amount and quality of job opportunities available in the nation's regions.

The Northeast and Midwest have traditionally been the locus of the higher-wage and higher-skill durable manufacturing industries, with the South and the West offering more peripheral manufacturing employment. Such differences have had important social and economic consequences for local areas.[18] While the Midwest has had a greater share of high-wage and -skill manufacturing than the South, both regions have had large concentrations of persons employed in agriculture. Many of the nonmetropolitan areas that are heavily dependent on income from employment in agriculture are remote from urban centers and sparsely settled. In such areas fluctuations in agricultural commodity markets tend to have a large impact on local economies.

Mining employment is relatively small compared with other major industry groups, but it is concentrated in particular areas such as the southern Appalachian coalfields and the West. Although the total number of persons employed in mining is not large nationally, marked changes in this activity can have a large impact on local rural areas with a small employment base.[19] The mining industry is subject to cycles of boom and bust, both of which can have devastating effects on the natural and social environments of local areas. For example, mining activities expanded rapidly during the mid-1970s, creating energy boom towns in some areas; but as the energy crisis eased and economic recession set in in the early 1980s, the economies of many of these towns collapsed.

There has also been regional variation in the importance of service employment. In many parts of the West social services have been an important source of employment. The combination of a high proportion of public lands, military installations, Indian reservations, and other factors have heightened the need for professionals employed in land management, health, education, and welfare.[20] These types of employment are especially important in sparsely settled nonmetropolitan areas.

[18]Ibid.
[19]Beale (1980).
[20]Ibid.

Due to these regional differences in industrial employment, national growth, in particular industrial categories, may have quite different economic development and social welfare implications in each of the nation's regions. Distinct regional variations in industrial structure can be seen in the data in Table 9.5, where the relative employment shares of industries are shown by residence and region in 1960 and 1980. The traditionally strong role of manufacturing employment in the Northeast is evident. This strength was greatest in 1960, when about one out of every three employed persons in the region was involved in manufacturing in both metropolitan and nonmetropolitan areas. In that year, only the metropolitan Midwest approached the same level of employment dependence on manufacturing.

The relative importance of manufacturing employment in the Northeast and the Midwest declined significantly between 1960 and 1980. In fact, manufacturing lost its premier place among industries in the metropolitan areas of these regions as its share of employment dropped by about 10 percentage points. Distributive services became the largest type of employment. This finding is consistent with an overall redistribution of manufacturing away from the metropolitan Northeast. This shift also affected the nonmetropolitan Northeast. Though manufacturing was still the dominant industrial category in the nonmetropolitan Northeast, its share of employment dropped from one in three to one in four during the two decades.

Manufacturing employment was redistributed toward the nonmetropolitan Midwest and South during the 1960s and 1970s. In both regions, the proportion of the nonmetropolitan population employed in manufacturing increased. In the nonmetropolitan South, manufacturing became the largest industrial type in 1980. These changes are consistent with the observation that there has been a deconcentration of manufacturing away from metropolitan areas since 1960.[21]

Important regional variation can be seen in the share of total employment in construction. In the metropolitan areas of the Northeast and the Midwest, construction made up only about 5 percent of the work force in 1960 and dropped even lower by 1980. The metropolitan areas of the South and West had 7 or more percent of the employed population in construction in 1960 and the share also declined by 1980, though it remained higher than in the metropolitan Northeast and Midwest. In the nonmetropolitan areas of the South and West, construction employment held a similar share in 1960—around 7 percent—and this share increased by 1980. These increases in share no doubt reflect the enhanced demand for housing and associated infrastructure related to

[21]Long and DeAre (1982a).

TABLE 9.5

Percentage Distribution of the Employed Population by Industry for Regions, 1960, 1980

Industry	Northeast 1960	Northeast 1980	Midwest 1960	Midwest 1980	South 1960	South 1980	West 1960	West 1980
Metropolitan[a]								
Agriculture	1.5	0.9	2.9	1.4	4.2	1.6	4.3	2.5
Mining	0.3	0.2	0.3	0.3	1.1	1.2	0.6	0.6
Construction	5.2	4.2	5.2	4.5	7.5	7.3	7.0	6.1
Manufacturing	35.3	25.1	35.8	26.9	22.3	18.2	23.7	18.8
Distributive services	25.9	27.0	26.7	28.3	28.5	29.3	27.9	28.8
Producer services	8.5	12.0	6.9	10.1	7.4	11.0	8.8	12.5
Personal services	5.9	3.6	5.6	3.5	9.5	4.7	7.5	5.2
Social services	17.4	27.1	16.6	24.9	19.6	26.8	20.2	25.5
Total	100.0	100.0	100.0	100.0	100.0	100.0	100.0	100.0
Nonmetropolitan[a]								
Agriculture	8.2	3.9	22.6	10.7	20.1	6.3	16.7	8.9
Mining	2.2	1.3	1.4	1.3	3.3	3.4	4.0	4.0
Construction	6.4	5.6	5.7	5.8	6.8	7.7	7.4	8.0
Manufacturing	32.5	26.9	20.6	23.2	22.0	26.2	14.8	11.6
Distributive services	23.0	24.8	24.7	26.0	22.0	24.2	26.5	27.8
Producer services	4.5	6.7	4.3	6.1	3.8	6.1	4.8	7.8
Personal services	6.1	4.0	5.5	3.5	8.8	4.0	7.2	5.4
Social services	17.1	26.8	15.2	23.4	13.1	22.2	18.6	26.5
Total	100.0	100.0	100.0	100.0	100.0	100.0	100.0	100.0

[a]Metropolitan or nonmetropolitan as of 1980.

nonmetropolitan population growth in these regions between 1960 and 1980.[22]

Among nonmetropolitan residents in 1960, agricultural employment was strongest in the Midwest and the South, where it engaged about one in every five workers. In the nonmetropolitan Northeast, agricultural employment represented a much smaller percentage of all employees (only one in about thirteen). In the nonmetropolitan areas of all regions the drop in agriculture's share of total employment between 1960 and 1980 was dramatic and the relative share in 1980 was less than half that of two decades earlier. The drop in share in the nonmetropolitan South was particularly sharp—from one in five involved in agriculture in 1960, to one in sixteen by 1980.

Behind these regional changes in relative shares of employment by industry were differentials in industrial growth (Table 9.6). Regional differentials in the decline of agriculture were evident. All regions and residence types had absolute declines in agricultural employment between 1960 and 1970. The nonmetropolitan South showed the largest rate of decline, nearly 50 percent. The decline in agricultural employment continued to be strongest for the nonmetropolitan South between 1970 and 1980. There was a turnaround in agricultural employment in some regions during the 1970s, principally associated with the growth in the nonfarm agricultural occupations, but this growth was too small to yield an increase in the share of total employment accounted for by agriculture in any region of the United States. Agricultural employment grew in the metropolitan areas of the Midwest, South, and West and in the nonmetropolitan areas of the Northeast and West during the 1970s. The West stands out as the only region where both metropolitan and nonmetropolitan residents experienced growth in agricultural employment between 1970 and 1980.[23] Nevertheless, almost three-fourths of the numerical increase in agricultural employment in the West was captured by metropolitan residents.

Differential regional impacts of the trend in mining can also be seen. While mining was declining in the metropolitan Northeast and South and in all nonmetropolitan areas during the 1960s, this employment grew in all regions and residence types during the 1970s. In both metropolitan and nonmetropolitan areas, the growth in the latter decade

---

[22]Ibid.

[23]It should be noted that 86 percent, or the great majority, of this growth in the nonmetropolitan West occurred in forestry and fisheries rather than in agriculture per se. Large gains in female employment were offset by losses of almost the same magnitude in male employment in agriculture. In contrast, much smaller changes in employment in forestry and fisheries were positive for both males and females, resulting in a larger gain in forestry and fisheries employment than in agriculture proper.

TABLE 9.6
Percentage Change in Employed Population by Industry for Regions, 1960–1970, 1970–1980

Industry	Northeast 1960–1970	Northeast 1970–1980	Midwest 1960–1970	Midwest 1970–1980	South 1960–1970	South 1970–1980	West 1960–1970	West 1970–1980
Metropolitan[a]								
Agriculture	-18.9	-3.0	-29.3	0.8	-30.3	7.9	-13.1	37.0
Mining	-19.0	8.7	6.6	20.0	-34.4	91.6	41.4	55.8
Construction	14.4	-9.6	19.3	4.9	29.1	45.7	14.5	56.8
Manufacturing	-1.7	-6.5	9.6	-1.2	28.1	23.1	17.9	37.9
Distributive services	21.5	11.1	25.6	21.7	35.6	46.4	42.6	48.1
Producer services	37.8	32.3	41.6	48.8	60.0	79.5	58.5	82.2
Personal services	-11.2	-10.2	-3.3	-7.9	-3.5	-2.0	12.5	25.2
Social services	59.7	26.1	62.5	33.3	72.4	53.2	75.9	46.2
Total	18.3	9.4	23.5	16.6	35.7	42.3	38.3	47.8
Nonmetropolitan[a]								
Agriculture	-34.4	4.4	-36.0	-2.9	-47.7	-11.7	-22.4	16.8
Mining	-31.7	23.3	-12.4	42.0	-12.7	71.0	-6.1	81.6
Construction	27.2	0.1	12.6	20.1	26.1	31.3	4.2	78.6
Manufacturing	10.2	8.9	25.4	18.2	40.6	24.8	1.9	30.9
Distributive services	18.8	32.3	11.0	24.5	16.3	39.9	15.5	54.7
Producer services	32.5	62.7	21.1	55.9	32.2	79.9	28.8	113.9
Personal services	-4.6	0.3	-7.1	-10.2	-15.0	-21.6	0.9	25.4
Social services	55.4	46.6	50.4	34.6	59.9	56.4	54.0	57.8
Total	16.5	24.7	8.5	21.3	12.1	31.8	12.2	51.8

[a]Metropolitan or nonmetropolitan as of 1980.

was strongest in the South and West. The nonmetropolitan Midwest showed strong growth in mining in the 1970s as well. Growth in mining employment was especially important in the South, where such activity has historically been concentrated. In 1960, about 52 percent of all persons employed in mining were located in the South. By 1980, this figure had grown to almost 58 percent and was about the same for metropolitan and nonmetropolitan residents considered separately. The energy boom of the 1970s was an important source of growth in employment between 1970 and 1980, and its impact was predictably strongest in the Sunbelt regions. Despite optimism generated by this boom, mining never grew to make up a substantial share of the total work force, and its impact on overall employment was minimal.[24]

The redistribution of manufacturing employment away from the metropolitan Northeast and Midwest and toward the South and West is further demonstrated in the growth rates presented in Table 9.6. In the metropolitan Northeast, there was a negative growth rate for manufacturing in both decades. The metropolitan Midwest also had a negative growth rate during the 1970s. As the industrial heartland experienced losses of its traditional employment base, manufacturing was expanding strongly in the South and West. Expansion of nonmetropolitan manufacturing was particularly strong in the South during the 1960s, where the rate of growth was more than three times the rate of growth of overall employment.

Traditionally, the Northeast and the Midwest have specialized in growth industries, while the South and West have specialized in resource-based and mature, or "bottom of the product cycle," industries. It has been suggested that these traditional specializations are in a process of reversal.[25] The "periphery," the South and West, is increasingly specializing in high-growth industries, while the "core," or North, is beginning to specialize in slow-growth or mature industries.

Nonelectrical machinery, printing and publishing, and chemicals and allied manufacturing have been identified as strong growth industries. The data in Table 9.7 indicate that there are regional differences in growth rates in these expanding industries and that there are variations by residence type within regions as well. In machinery manufacturing, the South and West exhibited the greatest percentage growth during the 1970s and, within these two regions, it was nonmetropolitan areas that exhibited the highest rates of expansion. Similarly, regional variations in the growth of printing and publishing and chemicals and allied manufacturing also favored the Sunbelt, though the South did not

---

[24]Beale (1980); Long and DeAre (1982a).
[25]Norton and Rees (1979).

TABLE 9.7

Percentage Change in Employment in Manufacturing Type by Region and Residence, 1970–1980[a]

Manufacturing Type	Northeast		Midwest		South		West	
	Metro	Nonmetro	Metro	Nonmetro	Metro	Nonmetro	Metro	Nonmetro
Food and Kindred	−7.8	11.9	2.0	21.1	12.9	24.3	21.1	31.8
Textiles and Apparel	−17.9	−13.9	−18.7	1.6	8.4	14.6	61.6	63.6
Printing and Publishing	14.3	41.3	12.4	38.0	42.5	64.0	56.2	66.9
Chemicals and Allied	18.9	54.6	24.4	40.1	32.2	29.1	52.1	46.4
Other Nondurables	−33.7	−11.0	−13.5	1.0	2.6	6.4	21.6	6.5
Nondurable Subtotal	−11.5	0.7	0.5	15.8	15.8	17.1	37.6	33.1
Furniture, Lumber, Wood	6.3	26.8	18.7	33.5	31.9	22.0	54.2	13.3
Primary Metals	−8.6	−1.4	0.6	24.4	28.0	65.6	22.5	25.2
Fabricated Metals	−9.9	30.3	−5.7	8.9	5.5	26.0	−16.4	72.1
Machinery, Except Elec.	25.5	29.1	10.3	44.4	94.4	132.2	32.0	158.4
Electrical Products	11.3	11.5	−4.3	16.1	55.3	52.8	59.7	126.4
Motor Vehicle, Transp.	−1.5	25.6	3.5	21.7	14.4	34.6	40.0	52.1
Other Durables	−10.7	−5.7	−31.1	−12.1	−1.1	0.7	23.9	13.0
Durable subtotal	−2.8	14.6	−1.9	19.6	30.6	36.7	38.0	29.6
Total	−6.5	8.9	−1.2	18.2	23.1	24.8	37.9	30.9

[a]Metropolitan or nonmetropolitan as of 1980.

285

show overwhelming growth rates in chemicals. It is also worth noting that in the Northeast and the Midwest printing and publishing and chemical manufacturing exhibited strong growth among nonmetropolitan residents. This evidence supports the claim that high-growth manufacturing appears to be deconcentrating to the South and West and to nonmetropolitan areas within the North.

In addition to this regional variation in high-growth manufacturing, there are also strong growth rates in the South and West in types of manufacturing that are growing more slowly nationwide. For example, electrical products manufacture grew only slowly in the nonmetropolitan North and actually declined in the metropolitan Midwest. In contrast, the South and West showed a strong growth rate for this type of manufacturing. The metropolitan Northeast also stands out in this category, with a modest gain in employment at the time when overall manufacturing employment was declining. At least in part, this regional growth reflects the impact of the high-technology industries around Boston. In general, the Sunbelt does stand out in its growth in this high-technology category, further supporting the idea of regional restructuring of manufacturing.

Other differences in manufacturing growth are also of interest. Employment in motor vehicle and other transportation manufacturing declined or was sluggish in the metropolitan North while showing average growth in the nonmetropolitan Midwest, the South, and the metropolitan West. Particularly high rates of growth in this category can be seen in the nonmetropolitan areas of the Northeast and West. These trends suggest that this mature industry is expanding more rapidly in areas of traditionally lower labor costs. There was also noticeable nonmetropolitan growth in fabricated metals in the Northeast and West at a time when employment in this category was declining in the metropolitan North, the industrial heartland.

The various trends displayed in this table lend support to the notion that regional restructuring is taking place in the manufacturing sector. The South and West show strong growth rates in many manufacturing sectors, and these sectors are not the resource-based types traditionally associated with these regions. Similarly, the strongest growth in the Northeast and the Midwest occurred among nonmetropolitan residents. These trends indicate a deconcentration within regions as well.

It is still necessary to examine the distribution of manufacturing across different regions and residence types to get a sense of the regional distribution of these activities in the United States. The data in Table 9.8 show that despite the much higher rates of overall manufacturing growth in the West, South, and nonmetropolitan Midwest, the metropolitan areas of the Northeast and the Midwest still retain the greatest

TABLE 9.8

Percentage Distribution of Employment in Manufacturing Type by Region and Residence, 1980

Manufacturing Type	Northeast		North Central		South		West		U.S.
	Metro	Nonmetro	Metro	Nonmetro	Metro	Nonmetro	Metro	Nonmetro	Total
Food and Kindred	15.2	2.6	22.0	11.5	18.1	12.2	14.4	3.9	100.0
Textiles and Apparel	23.3	3.3	3.9	2.5	24.6	34.8	7.1	0.5	100.0
Printing and Publishing	27.1	2.2	23.2	6.3	19.8	4.8	15.2	1.6	100.0
Chemicals	26.3	2.3	20.1	5.1	27.5	9.5	8.6	0.7	100.0
Other Nondurables	20.8	4.0	20.8	8.6	20.6	12.4	11.3	1.4	100.0
Nondurable Subtotal	22.4	3.0	17.0	6.6	22.1	16.4	11.0	1.5	100.0
Furniture, Lumber, Wood	8.4	4.5	10.3	9.0	17.6	26.9	13.9	9.4	100.0
Primary Metals	23.4	3.9	32.8	7.8	15.7	6.5	8.6	1.4	100.0
Fabricated Metals	21.4	2.9	29.6	8.8	16.6	6.8	13.1	0.7	100.0
Machinery, Except Elec.	21.7	3.7	30.0	10.0	14.8	6.0	12.9	0.7	100.0
Electrical Products	24.4	2.6	21.8	6.8	18.3	6.6	19.0	0.6	100.0
Motor Vehicle, Trans.	13.9	1.7	36.8	5.9	14.6	4.6	22.0	0.6	100.0
Other Durables	31.8	3.9	18.0	7.2	15.2	7.3	15.5	1.1	100.0
Durable Subtotal	21.0	3.2	26.6	7.9	16.0	8.1	15.6	1.6	100.0
Total	21.6	3.1	22.8	7.4	18.4	11.4	13.8	1.6	100.0

concentration of manufacturing. These positions as the leading manufacturing locations in the country are generally based on strength in all categories of manufacturing, though there are some exceptions. Concentration in the metropolitan North is particularly strong in the manufacturing of durable goods, printing and publishing, and chemicals. By contrast, the metropolitan areas of the Sunbelt show only a slight concentration in such types of manufacturing (chemicals in the South and transportation and electrical equipment in the West). Both Sunbelt metropolitan areas and all nonmetropolitan areas continue to show concentrations in types of manufacturing that are resource-based. While there is evidence of a deconcentration of manufacturing in the United States, the impact on industrial restructuring has not been dramatic.

Industrial Structure in Different Types of Nonmetropolitan Counties

The economic fortunes of nonmetropolitan counties are often influenced by their degree of urbanization and their proximity to metropolitan areas. These two dimensions provide related but distinct insights into characteristics of nonmetropolitan industrial employment. The economics of local areas can be thought of as part of a system of places. Larger, more complex places serve as trade centers for surrounding areas, and the degree of urbanization is generally considered to be an important determinant of the nature of industries located in local areas. For example, people and businesses in small towns and open areas tend to rely on nearby larger places for services. Consequently, these larger places tend to have a larger proportion of the work force employed in service industries. The population turnaround of the 1970s may have altered the spatial distribution of industrial activity based on the degree of urbanization. Population growth was more dispersed, and nontraditional industries related to recreation and energy development became more important in rural areas.[26] On the other hand, proximity to a metropolitan area tends to counteract the effects of local urbanization on the level of employment provided by service industries. Residents of counties adjacent to metropolitan areas rely more on both employment and services provided by businesses in metropolitan areas.[27] Commuting to metropolitan areas for work is an important option for residents of counties adjacent to metropolitan areas. Particularly because the data

[26]See Chapters 2 and 12; see also Johansen and Fuguitt (1984).
[27]McGranahan, Hessions, Hines, and Jordan (1986).

presented in this chapter are based on place of residence and not place of employment, patterns of industrial employment in adjacent counties can be expected to resemble more closely that of metropolitan counties than is true of the more remote nonmetropolitan counties.[28]

During the 1970s, gains in population and employment, like population growth, permeated all levels of nonmetropolitan areas. In fact, employment growth was observed even in completely rural counties not adjacent to metropolitan areas. Growth also occurred there in a variety of industries not normally associated with rural America.[29] The impacts of these overall changes in industrial employment are magnified in rural areas with small population bases.

The combination of employment and population growth in such areas leads to a variety of demands on local resources. Demands on local infrastructure and services such as sewage disposal, water, refuse collection, roads, fire and police protection, and education are increased by population and economic growth. Many of these services are difficult and expensive to provide on a small scale. Furthermore, the types of industries locating and/or expanding in rural areas will influence the types of services demanded of local governments.

We examine effects of the degree of urbanization and proximity to metropolitan areas by classifying nonmetropolitan counties by adjacency to a metropolitan area and by urban–rural status; that is, whether or not the county includes a place with a population of 2,500 or more.

Growth rates in the employed population by industry for different types of nonmetropolitan counties are displayed in Table 9.9. The overall employment growth rate between 1960 and 1970 was strongest in urban counties adjacent to metropolitan areas. In contrast, rural counties not adjacent to metropolitan areas experienced an overall decline in employment during the decade.

Social service employment displayed the highest growth rates among industries during the 1960s in all nonmetropolitan locations. This high growth demonstrates the gain in employment associated with the expansion of government social programs during this time. Urban counties adjacent to metropolitan areas had the highest rate of growth in social services at 57 percent. The growth of producer and distributive services also was higher in adjacent than in nonadjacent counties in the 1960s.

Manufacturing growth was important throughout most nonmetropolitan areas during the 1960s, but it was most pronounced in rural

---

[28]There is considerable commuting within nonmetropolitan areas as well that tends to make size-of-place differences by residence weaker than corresponding differences by place of employment (see Chapter 12).

[29]Long and DeAre (1982a).

TABLE 9.9

Percentage Change in Employed Population by Industry
and Nonmetropolitan Residence Groupings, 1960–1970, 1970–1980

Industry	Adjacent[a] Largest Place		Not Adjacent[a] Largest Place	
	2,500+	LT 2,500	2,500+	LT 2,500
1960–1970				
Agriculture	−39.7	−42.3	−39.1	−39.4
Mining	−11.8	−8.8	−15.0	−17.8
Construction	21.4	30.6	12.1	20.2
Manufacturing	26.5	33.1	27.4	36.5
Distributive services	17.2	17.2	11.0	6.3
Producer services	30.4	37.3	23.3	17.1
Personal services	−8.7	−9.5	−12.3	−11.2
Social services	57.4	54.0	53.7	42.5
Total	14.6	8.5	8.7	−1.5
1970–1980				
Agriculture	−0.7	−4.6	−6.1	−6.1
Mining	61.1	71.1	67.2	60.9
Construction	28.2	33.9	32.2	27.4
Manufacturing	19.1	25.1	22.7	29.1
Distributive services	37.0	45.4	32.0	31.6
Producer services	74.4	98.3	69.9	69.0
Personal services	−10.6	−0.4	−12.5	−2.7
Social services	48.8	59.3	44.6	43.7
Total	30.1	35.1	28.7	25.4

[a]Counties were classified into four groups according to whether or not they were adjacent to a 1980 metropolitan county and whether or not they included a place having more than 2,500 people in 1980.

counties not adjacent to metropolitan areas. The construction industry displayed the same pattern. These findings lend some support to the argument that such industries tend to be precursors of general population growth. Accordingly, some analysts have contended that nonmetropolitan growth in manufacturing and construction during the 1960s set the stage for the renewed population growth of the 1970s.[30]

Overall employment growth rates during 1970–1980 were higher than in the previous decade for every category of county. Rural counties adjacent to metropolitan centers displayed the highest overall employment growth rates. Residents employed in producer services almost doubled in such counties. These counties also displayed the highest

[30]Ibid.

rates of growth of residents employed in mining, construction, and distributive and social services. The manufacturing industry was an exception to this general pattern. As was true in the 1960s, rural counties not adjacent to a metropolitan area had the highest rate of growth in residents employed in manufacturing.

Industrial Structure and Female Employment

Female labor force participation has grown markedly and women are working over a broader spectrum of the life cycle. This trend was already under way in the 1960s in nonmetropolitan America, as was indicated in Chapter 8. In the past, metropolitan and nonmetropolitan areas typically differed in the types of employment held by women. In part, this difference can be traced to the types of industries that located in nonmetropolitan areas, such as male-oriented extractive jobs. However, over the past two decades women residing in nonmetropolitan America have been able to find employment in a number of other industries, particularly manufacturing and services.[31] Much of this growth in female employment occurred in sparsely populated counties not adjacent to metropolitan areas.[32]

Patterns of industrial growth have an impact on the level and nature of female labor force participation. First of all, despite the pronounced increase in female employment, there is variation in the gender composition of employment across industries.[33] Second, women tend to be disproportionately employed in low wage industries, a point particularly relevant to nonmetropolitan women, who tend to be relegated to employment in peripheral positions in peripheral industries.[34]

Changes in employment by industry and gender for 1970–1980 are presented in Table 9.10. The rate of growth in female employment exceeded that of male employment in every industry, except personal services, in both metropolitan and nonmetropolitan areas. Mining, producer services, and construction ranked highest in the rate of female employment growth regardless of metropolitan–nonmetropolitan residence (largely because few women worked in these jobs at the beginning of the period). Following general trends, the rate of growth in female employment was greater for nonmetropolitan than for metropolitan residents in each of these industries as well as in every other industrial category except personal services.

[31]Beale (1980).
[32]Brown and O'Leary (1979).
[33]Chafe (1976).
[34]Bokemeier and Tickamyer (1985); Lyson and Falk (1986); Bloomquist (1988).

TABLE 9.10

*Percentage Change in Employed Population for Males and Females,
Percentage Female, and Percentage Distribution of
Male and Female Employment by Industry and Residence, 1970–1980*

Industry	Percentage Change 1970–1980		Percentage Female		Percentage of Total, 1980	
	Male	Female	1970	1980	Male	Female
Metropolitan[a]						
Agriculture	3.5	61.9	15.3	22.0	2.2	0.8
Mining	50.5	139.0	13.0	19.2	0.9	0.3
Construction	20.6	75.5	6.4	9.1	8.9	1.2
Manufacturing	2.6	21.0	27.5	31.0	28.0	15.8
Distributive services	22.3	44.5	36.4	40.3	29.6	26.4
Producer services	40.7	81.7	42.3	48.6	10.4	12.8
Personal services	3.2	−4.1	64.1	61.2	2.9	6.0
Social services	21.8	53.5	54.9	60.5	18.1	36.7
Total	16.9	43.1	38.3	43.2	100.0	100.0
Nonmetropolitan[a]						
Agriculture	−10.0	65.1	8.8	15.1	11.0	2.9
Mining	59.6	168.0	3.9	6.3	4.0	0.4
Construction	26.8	97.6	4.1	6.3	10.8	1.0
Manufacturing	15.6	31.4	32.2	35.1	25.6	20.3
Distributive services	25.7	53.4	35.5	40.1	25.8	25.1
Producer services	50.8	114.6	36.5	45.0	5.9	6.9
Personal services	−.4	−13.8	72.4	69.4	2.2	6.7
Social services	29.9	60.7	58.3	63.3	14.7	36.7
Total	20.0	46.9	36.0	40.8	100.0	100.0

[a]Metropolitan or nonmetropolitan as of 1980.

Both metropolitan and nonmetropolitan women made up a larger share of the total work force in 1980 than in 1970. As shown in columns 3 and 4 of Table 9.10, every type of industry except personal services displayed this trend. At both points in time women accounted for the majority of the work force in both personal and social services, regardless of metropolitan–nonmetropolitan residence. These findings are not surprising, given the fact that women have traditionally been disproportionately employed in these industries.[35] Nonmetropolitan women employed in personal and social services and in manufacturing made up a larger share of total employment in those industries than their metropolitan counterparts.

[35]Browning and Singelmann (1978).

Social services were an especially important source of employment for women. Women employed in social services made up a larger share of the total female work force than those employed in any other industry in both metropolitan and nonmetropolitan areas. Distributive services claimed the next largest share among women and the largest share among men.

Some Characteristics of the Employed by Industry

Much of the significance of industrial composition for society rests on the fact that different industries demand different types of workers in terms of degree of commitment and skills and supply different jobs for which workers tend to be rewarded differentially. Using the Public Use Microdata file for 1980, we have examined interindustry differences by metropolitan–nonmetropolitan residence in the extent of full-time employment, educational attainment, and occupational status by sex of worker.

Full-Time Employment

Industries differ in their susceptibility to fluctuations in the production cycle and the demand for full-time workers, and opportunities for full-time employment have important impacts on earnings. That there is some variation across industries in the percent of workers employed full-time during 1979 can be seen in Table 9.11. Agriculture, construction, and personal services generally have lower proportions in full-time employment than other industries. Agriculture employs many seasonal and part-time workers because labor demand is uneven over the growing season. Weather, labor disputes, and problems in securing raw material tend to be associated with uneven construction schedules and lead to more part-time work in construction. Producer services are highest among the services in the percent full-time, and the advantage here is particularly great for women.

There are major gender differences in full-time employment. Regardless of industry or residence, women were considerably less likely to be employed full-time. Overall about two-thirds of the men, but only a little less than one-half of the women, are employed full-time. No systematic differences in full-time employment by metropolitan status are apparent, although among males, those living in rural areas are slightly more likely to be full-time employees and among females those in urban areas are slightly more likely to be full-time.

TABLE 9.11

Percentage of Industry Category Employed Full-Time by Residence, 1980

Industry	Total United States	Metropolitan			Nonmetropolitan		
		Total	Urban	Rural	Total	Urban	Rura
Males							
Agriculture	62.7	55.2	46.1	63.9	67.5	51.2	69.5
Mining	71.5	74.3	74.3	74.4	69.5	71.6	68.3
Construction	56.4	56.8	56.2	59.5	55.1	55.6	54.9
Manufacturing	75.8	76.1	75.7	78.5	74.6	74.6	74.7
Distributive services	67.3	67.1	66.5	70.9	68.1	66.8	69.1
Producer services	70.6	70.7	70.4	73.1	70.3	69.6	70.8
Personal services	52.0	51.6	51.1	55.6	53.8	53.1	54.4
Social services	67.5	68.2	67.9	70.6	64.8	63.2	66.3
Total	68.4	68.5	68.1	71.2	67.7	66.5	68.4
Females							
Agriculture	40.2	36.2	33.7	39.7	44.2	33.3	46.0
Mining	66.7	68.2	68.6	65.2	62.9	66.6	63.0
Construction	50.6	51.9	53.5	43.6	44.7	45.8	43.9
Manufacturing	60.4	61.2	61.0	62.0	58.1	58.6	57.8
Distributive services	41.3	42.2	42.6	39.1	38.2	38.8	37.7
Producer services	56.3	56.6	56.7	55.7	54.9	54.8	54.9
Personal services	31.4	32.2	32.9	26.3	28.7	30.0	27.6
Social services	43.4	44.5	45.1	39.9	39.6	40.2	39.1
Total	46.6	47.4	47.7	45.0	43.6	43.5	43.7

Educational Attainment of Workers

The educational background of workers also differs across the industry types. For males, agriculture has the lowest percentage of persons having 12 or more years schooling, the equivalent of a high school education (Table 9.12). Construction and personal services are also low in education attainment, while producer and social services are at the top. For women, personal services, agriculture, and manufacturing are low, but construction and mining have two of the highest percentages of workers with high school diplomas. Of course, very few women are employed in these industries and those that are employed are typically in white collar pursuits.

Residential differences in educational attainment generally favor urban areas and metropolitan areas within industrial groupings. In manufacturing, for example, 74 percent of the men who live in urban-metropolitan settings have a high school education; but this is true for only

TABLE 9.12

Percentage of Industry Category with 12 or More Years of Schooling by Residence, 1980

dustry	Total United States	Metropolitan			Nonmetropolitan		
		Total	Urban	Rural	Total	Urban	Rural
ales							
Agriculture	57.1	55.3	56.0	54.6	58.3	57.1	58.4
Mining	68.6	76.0	80.6	63.8	63.3	68.7	60.4
Construction	64.8	66.4	66.8	64.6	60.4	64.4	58.5
Manufacturing	71.6	73.4	73.8	71.5	65.7	69.6	63.5
Distributive services	72.5	73.4	73.7	71.6	68.8	71.2	67.1
Producer services	81.2	82.3	82.6	80.1	75.0	78.6	72.2
Personal services	68.2	68.6	69.0	65.1	66.4	68.5	64.5
Social services	87.5	88.5	88.8	86.2	83.5	86.9	80.5
Total	74.1	75.9	76.6	71.8	68.2	73.0	71.7
:males							
Agriculture	65.2	64.4	63.9	65.0	66.0	64.5	66.2
Mining	89.5	91.9	93.1	84.0	83.1	85.5	81.0
Construction	85.2	86.1	86.6	83.4	81.2	81.2	81.1
Manufacturing	66.2	68.1	68.4	66.4	60.8	63.8	59.2
Distributive services	73.4	74.4	74.7	71.7	69.6	71.2	68.4
Producer services	89.3	89.3	89.2	90.1	89.2	90.2	88.4
Personal services	60.2	61.0	60.8	62.6	57.6	57.6	57.6
Social services	87.0	87.8	88.0	86.2	84.1	85.4	83.0
Total	72.8	79.5	79.9	76.9	73.8	76.1	72.1

64 percent of those in living in rural-nonmetropolitan areas, reflecting the greater preponderance of low wage workers in low skill nondurable manufacturing firms in less urbanized economies. In mining, the residential difference is even larger. Management and organizational aspects of mining appear to be located in metropolitan areas, while the extractive activities continue to be concentrated in rural and nonmetropolitan areas.

Educational status patterns are somewhat different for the proportion having a college education or equivalent (16 or more years). Percentages are, of course, considerably lower, but variation among the industries and across residence categories tends to be more pronounced (Table 9.13). Women have a lower proportion of college graduates than do men within almost all of the industry-residence groups. Across residence categories and for both men and women, social services stands out as having the highest proportion with 16 or more years of formal

TABLE 9.13

Percentage of Industry Category with 16 or More Years of Schooling by Residence, 1980

Industry	Total United States	Metropolitan			Nonmetropolitan		
		Total	Urban	Rural	Total	Urban	Rura
Males							
Agriculture	9.5	11.3	14.5	8.3	8.4	14.3	7.6
Mining	14.1	25.0	31.0	9.2	6.4	10.3	4.3
Construction	7.9	8.9	9.6	6.2	5.1	7.0	4.1
Manufacturing	14.6	16.6	17.6	11.9	7.8	11.0	6.1
Distributive services	12.5	13.7	14.2	9.7	8.4	10.3	7.0
Producer services	29.4	31.2	31.9	25.1	19.3	23.7	15.8
Personal services	14.2	14.9	15.2	12.2	11.4	11.1	11.7
Social services	49.7	51.0	51.4	48.2	44.4	48.2	40.9
Total	20.6	22.7	23.8	16.1	13.8	18.4	11.1
Females							
Agriculture	8.7	10.1	11.0	8.7	7.3	11.1	6.7
Mining	16.0	19.7	21.5	7.1	6.6	4.8	8.2
Construction	8.3	8.9	9.5	6.0	5.5	6.4	4.8
Manufacturing	6.1	7.5	8.1	3.8	2.5	3.5	2.2
Distributive services	6.7	7.4	7.8	4.6	4.2	5.0	3.4
Producer services	12.7	13.6	14.1	8.9	6.8	7.7	6.0
Personal services	5.7	6.2	6.5	4.0	3.9	4.1	3.8
Social services	30.1	31.1	31.7	26.6	26.3	27.5	25.4
Total	15.9	16.9	17.5	12.5	12.2	13.8	11.1

educational attainment. For men, producer services has the next highest percentage, but for women mining is ahead of producer services in urban-metropolitan settings. Among nonmetropolitan women, all industry groupings except social services have fewer than 10 percent who have completed college. Social services include traditional women's jobs for those with higher education, such as teaching, social work, and nursing. Almost two-thirds of the women college graduates and almost one-half of the men college graduates are in this industry category.

Occupational Distribution

The occupational distribution of the employed population is dichotomized and shown as percent white collar in the classification by industry and residence in Table 9.14. There are differences across the industry groups by gender that tend to be consistent with those for

TABLE 9.14

Percentage of Industry Category in White Collar Occupations, 1980

Industry	Total United States	Metropolitan			Nonmetropolitan		
		Total	Urban	Rural	Total	Urban	Rural
Males							
Agriculture	6.5	10.3	15.8	5.1	4.0	12.2	3.0
Mining	23.1	37.4	44.9	17.5	12.9	18.9	9.7
Construction	87.3	14.1	14.7	11.3	9.1	11.8	7.9
Manufacturing	30.1	34.2	35.6	26.8	19.9	25.0	17.0
Distributive services	47.8	49.3	50.2	43.4	42.1	45.7	39.4
Producer services	62.7	64.7	65.5	57.5	51.4	58.1	46.0
Personal services	40.0	40.6	40.5	41.6	37.3	39.1	35.8
Social services	68.4	69.5	70.0	66.1	63.7	66.9	60.8
Total	42.5	46.1	48.0	35.1	31.1	39.9	25.9
Females							
Agriculture	23.3	29.7	35.2	22.2	16.9	37.4	13.6
Mining	86.2	90.3	91.4	82.1	75.7	78.9	72.8
Construction	80.0	81.6	81.9	79.9	73.4	71.2	75.0
Manufacturing	38.5	43.8	45.5	34.3	24.1	28.8	21.5
Distributive services	71.6	72.8	73.3	69.3	67.1	67.9	66.5
Producer services	92.4	92.6	92.5	93.1	91.4	92.5	90.6
Personal services	26.1	28.5	28.9	24.9	18.7	19.4	18.1
Social services	76.9	78.5	79.0	74.5	71.2	73.4	69.3
Total	67.1	70.0	71.0	62.8	57.0	61.6	53.6

educational status. Construction is among the lowest in percent white collar for males but among the highest for females. In mining, three-fourths or more of the women have white collar occupations, but among men there is a strong difference by residence. Over four out of ten urban metropolitan males in mining have white collar jobs, but such jobs account for less than 10 percent among rural nonmetropolitan men, who are more apt to be production workers rather than workers in offices performing management jobs. Recall that there has been an increase in employment in agriculture among metropolitan residents, and this rise was particularly among women. Here we see that one-third of the urban women employed in this industry have white collar occupations. Once again, this indicates the essential nonfarm nature of these agricultural jobs.

In general, women are more likely to have white collar occupations and this extends to virtually all of the industry-residence categories. Similarly, urban and metropolitan areas tend to have higher proportions of men and women employed in white collar occupations (heavily weighted with clerical positions). Along with a parallel trend for educational status, nonmanual employment indicates that despite recent deconcentration of many traditionally urban activities into rural and nonmetropolitan areas, administrative functions continue to be more concentrated in urban and metropolitan areas. These results suggest that the seeming convergence of industrial composition between metropolitan and nonmetropolitan areas hides much difference in the nature and quality of actual jobs performed, and in the material rewards accruing to the work.

The data in this part of the chapter have shown that nonmetropolitan workers in each industry type had lower social status than their metropolitan counterparts in terms of education and occupation. These observations are consistent with findings indicating that the differing occupational composition of work between metropolitan and nonmetropolitan areas is a continuing source of differences in income between the residential sectors.[36] The relationship between income and industry is discussed in detail in Chapter 11.

Conclusions

Both metropolitan and nonmetropolitan America are moving toward service-based economies, yet the dynamics of change leading to convergence in industrial profiles have been somewhat different for these two residential areas. Growth in the proportion of metropolitan employment accounted for by services was mostly at the expense of manufacturing, while the increased share of services in nonmetropolitan areas came mostly from the decline of employment in agriculture. In contrast, manufacturing has maintained a relatively constant share of nonmetropolitan employment since 1960.

Some economic development theorists have commented that the deconcentration of manufacturing to nonmetropolitan areas is not particularly beneficial to local workers because the jobs are mostly in low-wage, low-skill "bottom of the product cycle" industries that have filtered down from metropolitan labor markets. Indeed, the manufacturing data presented in this chapter do show that nonmetropolitan counties have a relative preponderance of low-wage manufacturing, but also that a substantial share of new nonmetropolitan jobs has been in high-skill, high-wage manufacturing such as chemicals and electrical products.

The data do not present an optimistic picture for nonmetropolitan

[36]Nilsen (1978).

employment growth in services. While the majority of recent nonmetropolitan employment growth has been in services, nonmetropolitan economies have lagged behind metropolitan areas in gaining jobs in the high-wage producer services category. It appears that United States manufacturers are contracting out for many of the services that they previously performed internally. Accordingly, the geographic linkage between manufacturing and producer services appears to be changing. Job growth in higher skill manufacturing firms does not necessarily guarantee that the same local labor market will also gain employment in allied producer services. Such services may be provided by separate firms located elsewhere.

Our metropolitan–nonmetropolitan comparison of the occupational composition of employment by industry provides additional evidence that the seeming convergence of industrial composition between residence types obscures much difference in the nature of actual jobs performed and in the material rewards accruing to the work. For example, almost two-thirds of metropolitan men employed in producer services held white collar jobs, compared with only one-half of nonmetropolitan men in the same industrial type. Similar large differences were evident in manufacturing and mining for both genders.

Thus, while nonmetropolitan economies recently gained in some top-of-the-cycle manufacturing firms, the data indicate persisting differences in the quality of jobs and in incomes. Much of this lingering difference is undoubtedly associated with the human capital endowment of the nonmetropolitan work force. Regardless of industrial category or gender, employed nonmetropolitan workers had lower educational attainments (particularly college education) than their metropolitan counterparts. Educational upgrading appears as an essential element determining nonmetropolitan America's competitive position in the future.

The data presented here show that United States goods production has become increasingly concentrated in nonmetropolitan economies. This can be beneficial to rural and nonmetropolitan workers, but it can also expose local economies to cyclical downturns in economic activity and increased international competition.[37] Since particular types of goods producing industries tend to be regionally concentrated, structural employment problems may transcend local boundaries to become regionwide problems.

The industrial composition of work is a critical element in the economic future of rural and nonmetropolitan America. The data presented in this chapter indicate a mixed picture—after a decade of more rapid

---

[37]The vulnerability of nonmetropolitan economies to goods-producing recessions is discussed in Chapter 8.

nonmetropolitan than metropolitan growth in most industries there was a reversal in the early 1980s. The optimism of the 1970–1980 period largely evaporated during the 1980s. The transition from heavy reliance on employment in extractive industries to a more diversified economy has not fulfilled the promise of increased employment and better incomes for nonmetropolitan residents in the most recent period. Instead, nonmetropolitan residents have experienced increased rates of unemployment and declining incomes compared with their metropolitan counterparts. It is too early to say whether or not the setbacks suffered in the 1980s will establish a future course for nonmetropolitan America. Taking a longer view, trends of convergence in industrial structure may support a positive assessment of the economic future. Other trends, however, especially the lingering residential differences in educational attainment, suggest that nonmetropolitan areas could have a difficult time competing for high-skill, high-wage employment opportunities.

Appendix 9.1

The 1980 metropolitan–nonmetropolitan county designation is used throughout this chapter because much of our analysis is based on 1980 data or change over the 1970–1980 period. This simplified the presentation of data without compromising the basic conclusions of the analysis. There are, however, some differences in results from what would have been obtained had a "floating" designation of metropolitan status been used, such as the 1960 designation for 1960 or 1960–1970 change, and the 1970 designation for 1970 or 1970–1980 change (see Chapter 2). Among the 704 counties metropolitan as of 1980, 357 were nonmetropolitan in 1960 and 243 were nonmetropolitan in 1970. Consequently, with the 1980 designation, the nonmetropolitan numbers employed are less and the metropolitan numbers employed are greater for both 1960 and 1970 than they would have been had the respective 1960 and 1970 county designations been used.

The impact of using the 1980 metropolitan designation on the relative distribution by industry is to increase the importance of extractive industries in both metropolitan and nonmetropolitan areas for 1960 and 1970 over what they would have been, using the floating approach. There is also a decrease in the importance of the transformative sector for the nonmetropolitan classification but little difference for the metropolitan classification. Complementary percentage decreases in the distributional share of the service sector occur for both residence types in both years.

Using the constant 1980 metropolitan designation also has an impact on the change in employment between decades. Overall, using the 1980 metropolitan designation instead of a 1960 metropolitan designation for change in the decade of 1960–1970 increases metropolitan employment growth and decreases

APPENDIX TABLE 9.1
Industry Classification Scheme

Industry	Industries Included
Extractive	Agriculture, Forestry, Fisheries, and Mining
Transformative	Construction, Manufacturing
Distributive Services	Transportation, Communications, Utilities, Wholesale, and Retail
Producer Services	Finance, Insurance, Real Estate, Business and Repair Services
Personal Services	Personal Services, Entertainment, and Recreation
Social Services	Public Administration, Education, Professional Services, Health, and Welfare

APPENDIX TABLE 9.2

Detailed Manufacturing Categories

Manufacturing Category	PUMS Codes	SIC Codes
Nondurable Goods		
Food and kindred products	100–122	20
Textile and apparel products	132–152	22–23
Printing and publishing	171–172	27
Chemicals and allied products	180–192	28
Other nondurable goods		
Tobacco	130	21
Paper and allied products	160–162	26
Petroleum and coal products	200–201	29
Rubber and misc. plastic products	210–212	30
Leather and leather products	220–222	31
Not specified manufacturing	392	
Durable Goods		
Furniture, lumber, and wood products	230–242	24–25
Primary metal industries	270–280	33
Fabricated metal industries	281–301	34
Machinery, except elec.	310–332	35
Electrical machinery, equipment, and		
supplies	340–350	36
Motor vehicles and other trans. equipment	351–370	37
Other durable goods		
Stone, clay, glass, and concrete	250–262	32
Professional and photographic equip.		
and watches	371–383	38
Miscellaneous manufacturing	390–391	39

growth among nonmetropolitan residents. The results were similar but slightly less dramatic in the decade between 1970 and 1980. During both decades under consideration, the counties achieving metropolitan status between 1960 and 1970 exhibited the fastest growth in employment.

Overall, however, these differences do not change the basic conclusions of our analysis. There is not one correct procedure for metropolitan designation for a study such as this. Although the 1960 and 1970 designations were, of course, actually in use at those times, the counties that were not metropolitan at those dates but became so by 1980 may have had more in common with metropolitan than nonmetropolitan counties at each of these points; and industrial changes in these counties should have more closely approximated processes of change for all metropolitan counties over the 1960–1980 period.

10

THE POPULATION
ASSOCIATED WITH FARMING

MANY PERSONS associated with farming today do not actually
live on farms, and farm residents are an increasingly diverse
group, including a sizable number who have little attachment
to farming as an economic or occupational activity. Although farming
activities concern only a small and declining number and proportion of
the total population, agriculture continues to be one of the major industries of the nation. Consequently, it is important to give attention to
farm-related households and individuals, but this can no longer be ac-
complished by simply distinguishing people who live on farms as a separate residential category.[1]

After a review of the conventional rural farm residence grouping,
we shall present a typology to identify households related to farming on
the basis of residence, occupation, and sources of income. Using the
Public Use Microdata Samples (PUMS) for the censuses of 1980 and
1970 we cross-tabulate households on the basis of (1) rural farm residence; (2) the principal occupations reported by household member; and
(3) farm self-employment income. Results confirm the need to consider
all three elements, as less than one out of five farm-related households

[1]Earlier census monographs concerned with rural America have dealt almost exclusively with farm units or the rural farm population (Truesdell, 1926; Mighell, 1955; Beyer
and Rose, 1957) or made this residence category an intrinsic part of the overall analysis
scheme (Duncan and Reiss, 1956; Hathaway, Beegle, and Bryant, 1968). The situation today calls for a different approach.

303

reported all three and more than one-half reported only one element in 1980. Further, there was a decline in overlap between 1970 and 1980, indicating that such a typology should be even better suited to examine the population associated with farming in the future, especially when new 1990 census data are released.

Using the newly developed typology, we examine types of farm-related households in terms of their metropolitan and regional location and change in number over the 1970–1980 period. We also consider some demographic and economic characteristics of the farm-related population according to these household types and compare them throughout with the population in other households of the nation.

The Rural Farm Population Since 1920

The assumption that rural people were synonymous with people in farming was increasingly recognized as being unrealistic early in this century. Largely though the efforts of C.J. Galpin, the "rural farm" residence grouping was established after the census of 1920, and it has served as a major sorting category in every subsequent census through 1980. The consistent trend since 1920 for the rural farm population so identified has been one of decline in number and in proportion of the total population (Table 10.1). The number of rural farm residents

TABLE 10.1

Change in the Rural Farm Residence Population, 1920–1980

| Year | Rural Farm Population | | | Percent Change from Previous Decade | |
	Number (000s)	% Total Population	% Rural Population	Rural Farm	Total
1980 (1980 farm definition)	5,618	2.5	9.4	−32.2	11.4
1980 (1960 and 1970 farm definition)	7,116	3.1	12.0	−14.2	11.4
1970	8,295	4.1	15.4	−38.3	13.4
1960	13,442	7.5	24.9	−42.4	18.5
1950	23,332	15.5	37.8	−16.1	14.5
1940	27,805	21.1	48.6	−8.7	7.3
1930	30,445	24.8	56.6	−3.7	16.2
1920	31,614	29.9	61.3	—	—

SOURCES: 1960 through 1980 farm populations are from published United States Census figures; 1920 through 1950 are from Leon Truesdell (1960).

dropped from 31.6 to 5.6 million over that time. This was a proportional drop from 30 to less than 3 percent of the total population, and from 60 to less than 10 percent of the rural population.

Two sets of figures are given in the table for 1980 because the farm population definition was changed between 1970 and 1980, and for comparability 1980 counts were given by the 1960–1970 definition as well as for the new one. The new definition removes about 20 percent of the rural farm population in 1980 that would qualify under the old definition.[2] The effect of this is seen in the percent change column for the rural farm population. Without the change of definition the decline is 14 percent, but with the change it is 32 percent for 1970–1980. Percentage changes for some other decades are also affected by definitional changes (see footnote 2) but the table shows that after decades of relative stability major absolute and relative declines in the rural farm population occurred in the post–World War II era. The use of the 1960–1970

---

[2]Leon Truesdell (1949, 1960) has a detailed discussion of definitions and enumeration procedures for the farm population in the censuses of 1920 through 1950. In the census of 1920, the enumerator was instructed to write, for each head of family, in the column primarily used for street number, the symbol "Fm" to indicate residence on a farm. It was also directed that this symbol be entered for families of farm laborers who, while not living on a farm, were living outside any incorporated place. Truesdell (1960:2) estimates that perhaps only 25 percent of the eligible laborers were identified in this way, and this provision was dropped for later censuses. In 1930 a specific question, "Does this family live on a farm?," was incorporated in the schedule, and the inquiry on farm population in 1940 was practically the same. (There was an apparent overcount of the farm population in the census of 1940, according to Truesdell [1960]. He estimated the total farm population to have been 27,805,000 instead of the reported 30,547,000.) In 1950 the basic farm question was "Is this house on a farm?," but the instructions included a paragraph directing that any family or household living in a house for which cash rent was paid should not be counted as a farm resident. These earlier censuses depended largely on the judgments of enumerators in determining whether or not a place was a farm. The essential feature was that the tract of land be "cultivated for pecuniary profit" or "maintained for gain"—not just a garden for home use. More specific instructions were sometimes provided for deciding about places of less than three acres (Truesdell, 1960:1). For 1960 and subsequent censuses, however, more specific criteria were employed throughout, and farm residence became a sample question. The definition of a farm used in the Censuses of Population for 1960 and 1970 was (U.S. Bureau of the Census 1964, 1973a):

> Persons living in rural territory on places of 10 or more acres from which sales of farm products amounted to $50 or more in 1959 (1969) or on places of less than 10 acres from which sales of farm products amounted to $250 or more in 1959 (1969). Persons were also classified as nonfarm if their household paid rent for the house but their rent did not include any land used for farming. (The latter sentence was included in the definition for 1960 but not 1970, but instructions to enumerators accomplished the same purpose.) For 1980 the definition was simplified and made more restrictive (U.S. Census of Population 1983a, Appendix A-2):

> The farm population is identified only in rural areas and includes all persons living on places of one acre or more from which at least $1,000 worth of agricultural products were sold during 1979.

definition for 1960 through 1980 reveals a slowdown in the rate of decline between the 1960s and the 1970s. Post-1980 estimates of the farm population are not directly comparable with census figures, but the Current Population Survey (CPS) estimates (1980 farm definition) were 6.1 million for 1980 and 5.2 million for 1986.[3] If the annualized rate this represents were projected to 1990 the CPS estimate for that year would be 4.7 million, for a 22 percent decline over the 1980–1990 decade.

With the rural farm concept, the fit of farm residence and occupation has never been perfect. In 1920 enumerators were instructed to include in the rural farm population those farm laborers and their families living in the open country but not on a farm. Leon Truesdell, however, was of the opinion that this instruction was not followed consistently, and it was not included in subsequent censuses. In a 1920 census study of eight rural counties across the United States, C. J. Galpin and V. B. Larson showed that over 10 percent of those gainfully employed and residing on farms were engaged in nonagricultural occupations.[4] Since that time we know settlement and occupational trends have considerably lessened the overlap of farm economic activity and farm residence.

Research on part-time farming, beginning in the 1930s, has documented the increasing trend of multiple job holding among persons engaged in farm activities. This research has tended to concentrate on families living on farms, with little attention given to persons with rural nonfarm or urban residence (i.e., not living on farms) who have some involvement in farm activities. T. Lynn Smith, a prominent rural sociologist, pointed out this need in 1938, and proposed that the Census of Agriculture make a complete enumeration of the agricultural population including all those with gainful employment in agricultural pursuits.[5] He noted that in the census of 1930 in selected states as many as 8 to 20 percent of the gainfully employed rural nonfarm workers were in agriculture, while from 2 to 6 percent of the urban workers were also in agriculture. His proposal was not adopted, and the Census of Agriculture has increasingly become a census of economic units called farms with relatively little data collected on the people and workers associated with these farms.

The resurgence of interest in the sociology of agriculture has included some interesting historical accounts of the changing division of

---

[3]U.S. Bureau of the Census (1987).
[4]Truesdell (1949); Galpin and Larson (1924).
[5]Smith (1938).

labor between agricultural and other industrial sectors as well as consideration of farming as an occupation.[6] But it seems fair to say that most of the current empirical research has focused on rural farm operators or at best families who reside on farms, with little attention given to people living in other settings who have some economic identification with farming.

A Typology of Household Farm Involvement

The basic objective of this chapter is to develop a typology of household involvement in agriculture using the 1980 and 1970 United States Census PUMS files. Cross-tabulations of these data sources make it possible to examine a wide range of demographic variables for households classified by measures of their involvement in agriculture.[7]

Specifically, our classification utilizes three farm-related measures—residence, occupation, and farm self-employment income. First, households are cross-classified by the familiar residence categories: urban, rural nonfarm, and rural farm. Second, households are classified by the principal occupations reported by all household members. Farm-related occupations include farmers and farm managers, farm laborers, and farm foremen. Households are classed by combinations of farm operator, farm laborer, nonfarm occupation, or no occupation reported by household members. The third variable considered is farm self-employment income. Respondents for the 1970 and 1980 population censuses were asked to report any net self-employment income from farming, in addition to specifying other income sources. In this way households can

---

[6]See Moore (1984) for an example of the former; Coughenour (1984) for the latter.

[7]For a parallel analysis based on the Current Population Survey, see Banks (1986). Although they were not used in preparing this chapter, subject reports on the farm population were published as part of the Censuses of 1970 and 1980 which included tables cross-classifying these variables (U.S. Bureau of the Census 1973b; 1985). Also, Banks and Kalbacher (1981) have employed Current Population Survey data to examine the characteristics of families reporting farm self-employment income.

Detailed information on the scale and nature of the farm enterprise, as is included in the Censuses of Agriculture, could not be considered here. This is a desirable tradeoff, given our objectives, for the PUMS files provide demographic data unavailable in the Census of Agriculture, not only for people living on farms but also for those with nonfarm residence but with farm employment and/or income.

Another aspect of farm-relatedness which could not be considered is farmland ownership. Harris, McAllister, and Gilbert (1986) have examined social aspects of farmland ownership in the United States, and note that the 1978 Land Ownership Survey found 6.9 million owners of farmland. This is more than twice the number of farm operators and almost twice the number of farm-related households identified here.

be classed according to the contribution of farm self-employment income to total household income.[8]

Measures of Farm Relatedness

In both 1970 and 1980 there were a little more than 2 million households in the rural farm residence category, with a drop of only 31,000 over the decade (Table 10.2). For comparability the 1970 rural farm definition has been used in this table and the analysis to follow. Although the total number has changed little, rural farm households represented a declining share, dropping from 15 to 12 percent of the rural households and from about 4 to 3 percent of the total households. During the 1970s the total number of households grew by 26.8 percent in the United States, a rate considerably above the population growth rate of 11.5 percent. This discrepancy between population and household change is due to the declining size of household, which dropped from 3.2 to 2.8 persons per household. Similarly, while the number of rural farm households declined by only 1 percent, the rural farm population declined about 14 percent over the decade, from 8.3 to 7.1 million (Table 10.1), with the population per household dropping from 3.4 to 3.0.

Household occupational involvement in farming is displayed in Table 10.3. Combinations of principal occupations of one or more employed household members form the basis of this classification. The first category includes those households in which one or more persons reported being a farmer or farm manager, with farm laborer the only other occupation possibly reported by another household member. The second category is like the first except that in addition at least one other household member reported having a nonfarm occupation. This repre-

[8]There are some necessary timing inconsistencies with this approach due to the way questions are asked in the census. For example, farm residence is determined on the basis of the location of the household's dwelling unit, by size of holding, and by the amount of farm products sold during the preceding year. (For comparability, we have used the 1970 farm definition throughout: if less than 10 acres, $250 in farm products sold; or if more than 10 acres, $50 or more sold during the preceding year.) Similarly, farm self-employment income is reported for the year preceding the census (1969 or 1979). Occupation, on the other hand, is reported for "last week" when the census form is completed, presumably during the first week in April of the year in which the census is taken. Thus, a person may have had a farm occupation and farm self-employment income in the year preceding the census, but may have changed into a nonfarm occupation or retired by the time of the census in the following year. Undoubtedly, farm laborers are underestimated, since at the time of the census week not all are involved in farming or report living on a farm. Whitener (1984) estimates this could be as many as two-thirds of the people who do any hired farm work in the course of a year. Nevertheless, our multidimensional analysis gives a more balanced and accurate picture of the place of farm-related households in American society than would be possible with the traditional surveys of farm operators and their families or census comparisons of rural farm, nonfarm, and urban categories.

TABLE 10.2

Distribution of Households by Residence, 1970, 1980

Residence Group	1970 Number of Households	Percent	1980 Number of Households	Percent	1970–1980 Percent Change
Rural Farm[a]	2,395,100	3.8	2,364,300	2.9	−1.3
Other	61,048,600	96.2	78,106,000	97.1	27.9
Rural nonfarm	13,498,000	21.3	17,479,000	21.7	29.5
Urban	47,550,600	74.9	60,627,000	75.4	27.5
Total	63,443,700	100.0	80,470,300	100.0	26.8

[a]Using 1970 definition of a farm.

sents a type of "part-time farming" from the perspective of the household as a unit.[9] Multiple job-holding by an individual is not detected here, since each person may report only one occupation on the census form, whether or not he or she is also pursuing other gainful work.

The third and fourth categories include households with a farm laborer or foreman, but no farm operator. In the third, no other occupation was reported, whereas in the fourth at least one other household member reported having a nonfarm occupation. The two bottom lines in the table identify households in which no one reported a farm occupation. The first of these lines includes households with at least one person employed in a nonfarm occupation, and the second includes those in which no one was employed.

Between 1970 and 1980 the number of households with at least one person reporting a farm occupation dropped from 2.0 to 1.8 million or from 3.2 to 2.3 percent of all United States households. At both dates approximately two-thirds of these farm-related households included a farm operator. Households with farm laborers but no farm operators had a greater rate of decline than those including operators. Households reporting both a farm and a nonfarm occupation gained relative to those with only farm occupations, and the number that included a farm operator and one or more other members having a nonfarm occupation actually gained more than 9 percent over the decade. In 1970, 30 percent of the households with a farm operator also had someone with a nonfarm occupation, and this increased to 37 percent by 1980. Similarly, 44 percent of the farm laborer households included someone else with a nonfarm occupation in 1970, and this was true for 51 percent in 1980. So even with this restricted occupational definition, which does not in-

[9]For a related family definition of part-time farming, see Fuguitt, Fuller, Fuller, Gasson, and Jones (1977).

TABLE 10.3

Distribution of Households by Occupational Involvement in Farming, 1970, 1980[a]

1970–1980 Principal Occupation of One or More Employed Household Members	1970		1980		
	Number of Households	Percent	Number of Households	Percent	Percent Change
Farm Occupation in Household	2,046,100	3.2	1,811,500	2.3	−11.5
(a) Farmer only or farmer and farm laborer	913,900	1.4	746,900	0.9	−18.3
(b) Both farm and nonfarm occupations	399,800	0.7	437,500	0.5	9.3
Subtotal: Households with a farmer	1,313,700	2.1	1,184,400	1.4	−9.9
(c) Farm laborer only occupation	413,200	0.6	304,800	0.4	−26.2
(d) Farm laborer and nonfarm	319,200	0.5	322,300	0.4	1.0
Subtotal: Households with farm laborer but no farmer	732,400	1.1	627,100	0.8	−14.4
Nonfarm Occupation Only	47,783,800	75.3	58,873,600	73.2	23.2
No One Employed	13,613,800	21.5	19,785,200	24.6	45.3
Total	63,443,700	100.0	80,470,300	100.0	26.8

[a]Only one occupation is reported for each individual, and is based on employment in the week preceding the census. "Farmer" includes Census Codes 801–806: Farm and Farm Managers. "Farm Laborer" includes Census Codes 821–846: Farm Laborers and Farm Foremen.

clude individual multiple job-holding, the combination of farm and non-farm occupations within a household is relatively high and on the increase.

The distribution of households by the percentage of 1969 and 1979 who earned income from farm self-employment is given in Table 10.4. Just as with residence and occupations, we see that less than 3 million households in the United States are farm-related based on this measure. The number is larger than for the other two measures of farm-relatedness, and increased more than 5 percent over the decade. Yet this increase was less than the 27 percent gain in the total number of households, so the percentage of all United States households with farm self-employment income declined from 4.0 to 3.3. The table shows also that this absolute increase is in households with farm self-employment as a secondary income source. Households with less than 50 percent of their earned household income from farming increased from 1.3 to 1.5 million, but those with more than 50 percent declined slightly. For only about one in four of the households reporting farm self-employment in-

TABLE 10.4

Distribution of Households by Percentage of Earned Income from Self-Employment in Farming, 1969, 1979

Percent Earned Income That Is Farm Self-Employment Income (FSEI)	1970			1980			1970–1980
		Percent			Percent		
	Number of Households	Total	With FSEI	Number of Households	Total	With FSEI	Percent Change
Farm Self-Employment Income in Households	2,538,700	4.0	100.0	2,680,400	3.3	100.0	5.6
(a) Less than 50% of earned household income[a]	1,347,700	2.1	53.1	1,536,800	1.9	57.3	14.0
(b) 50–99% of earned household income[b]	476,400	0.8	18.8	461,300	0.6	17.2	−3.2
(3) 100% of earned household income[c]	714,600	1.1	28.2	682,300	0.8	25.5	−4.5
No Farm Self-Employment Income in Households	60,904,400	96.0	—	77,789,900	96.7	—	27.7
Total	63,443,100	100.0	—	80,470,300	100.0	—	26.8

[a]Includes a small number of households with farm self-employment income not zero but with total household income less than zero.
[b]Includes a small number of households with farm self-employment income greater than 100 percent of total household income.
[c]Farm self-employment income equal to total household income.

come was this the sole source of income from earnings, and this proportion also declined slightly over the decade.

The three indicators of relation to farming are combined in Table 10.5. Both in 1970 and in 1980 there were about 4 million households with at least one form of farm involvement. This number actually increased slightly over the period, though more slowly than the total number of households, so that the proportion dropped from 6 to 5 percent of all households in the nation. The first combination (top row) is for households with all three indicators, that is, rural farm residence, someone in the household with a farm occupation, and someone who reports farm self-employment income (FSEI). Of the seven combinations, only the first, which includes the traditional family farm operator households situated on their farms, and the sixth, 80 percent of which are farm laborer households, declined in number over the decade. Together their share dropped from 42 to 33 percent of the farm-related households. In contrast, households reporting only farm self-employment income grew almost 50 percent. This growth rate was almost

TABLE 10.5

A Cross-Classification of Three Household Farm Indicators, 1970, 1980

Combinations of Farm Involvement	1970		1980		1970–1980 Percent Change
	Number of Households	Percent	Number of Households	Percent	
Rural Farm					
(1) With farm occupation and FSEI	1,028,300	26.2	771,500	18.3	−25.0
(2) With farm occupation, no FSEI	127,600	3.2	152,500	3.6	19.5
(3) With no farm occupation but FSEI	585,400	14.9	661,100	15.7	12.9
(4) With neither farm occupation nor FSEI	653,800	16.7	779,200	18.5	19.2
Not Rural Farm					
(5) With farm occupation and FSEI	285,100	7.3	292,300	6.9	2.5
(6) With farm occupation, no FSEI	605,100	15.4	595,200	14.1	−1.6
(7) With no farm occupation but FSEI	639,900	16.3	955,500	22.7	49.3
Total Households					
Farm-related	3,925,200	100.0	4,207,300	100.0	7.2
Not farm-related	59,517,900		76,263,000		28.1
All households	63,443,100		80,470,300		26.8
Percent farm-related		6.2		5.5	

twice that of all United States households. Two other combinations grew by almost 20 percent. The first of these has the smallest number of households and includes those that are rural farm with at least one member reporting a farm occupation but no farm self-employment income.[10] The other combination growing at 19 percent over the decade included rural farm residents with no other reported economic association with farming—neither farm occupation nor farm self-employment income.

[10] Three-fourths of this group were farm laborer households in 1970, and these declined in number by 25 percent over the decade, but the farm operator households in this combination gained from 29,000 to 78,000, or by 172 percent. That farm operators reporting no farm income would increase so rapidly, even though the numbers are small, is puzzling. Some may have simply reported that they broke even in self-employment income, and others could have been operators in April 1980 but with no farm activity or farm income in the previous year. This also could indicate an increase in respondent error.

The trend is toward more diversity: the percent of farm-related households with all three elements dropped from 26 to 18, whereas the percent with two elements stayed at about 25, and the percent with only one element increased from 48 to 55. At the same time, the proportion of farm-related households with farm residence among its indicators declined from 61 to 56 percent; those with farm occupation declined from 52 to 43 percent; and those with farm self-employment income were about 65 percent of the total at both times.

The Typology Elaborated

Our next step was to elaborate relationships between the three indicators, simultaneously distinguishing rural farm, rural nonfarm, and urban residence, the six occupational groups already discussed, and percent of household income from farming self-employment (Appendix Table 10.1). There were a number of very small and empty cells, and by making appropriate combinations we set up a working typology for further analysis. We distinguished farm residence from a combination of rural nonfarm and urban residence for five occupational groups, and for the farm operator group we made a further classification by the proportion of total income from farm self-employment.[11]

This classification constitutes the rows of Table 10.6, which are the seven occupational/FSEI categories for the rural farm residence grouping, followed by the seven occupational/FSEI categories for households in all nonfarm (i.e., rural nonfarm and urban) residences. Households

---

[11]The farm operator only and the farm operator and nonfarm occupation groupings were combined for households with less than 100 percent of earned income from farm self-employment, since this distinction added little to the findings beyond that provided by the two income categories. The first type in the new classification, however, includes only households with 100 percent of earned income from farming in which no one reported having a nonfarm occupation. As a consequence about 5 percent of farm operator households having 100 percent of earned income from farming were placed in the 50–99 percent category because some other household member reported a nonfarm occupation. Such a response pattern might be due to having no income from the nonfarm job, or to adding the nonfarm job in the census year since the income variable is for the preceding year, or to an error in filling out the census form. Through this procedure the first type, by all evidence available here, is wholly dependent upon farming for a livelihood. Those with this occupation-income combination and also with rural farm residence may be considered the most traditional type, fulfilling the stereotype of the farm family that is still held by many people.

The smallest number of sample cases in an individual cell of this typology is 580 in 1970 and 537 in 1980, and only four cells for the earlier time and two for the later time had fewer than 1,000 cases. The two smallest groups, farm laborer only and farm laborer and nonfarm, were separated so as to identify households that are more completely dependent upon farm labor for a livelihood. The characteristics data to be presented indicate that farm labor may be of only marginal importance for many households in which some nonfarm occupation was reported.

with no one employed or with only nonfarm occupations in rural non-farm or urban residences (the last two types) can be farm-related only because of some reported farm self-employment income. All other United States nonfarm households with no one employed or with only nonfarm occupations are presented for comparison as "not farm related" households, and are shown on the bottom line of Table 10.6.

The total number of households involved in farming declined about 1 percent in the rural farm residence group but gained over 20 percent

TABLE 10.6

Distribution and Change in Number of Households by Farming Types, 1970, 1980

Household Farming Types	Percent Distribution		Percent Distribution Within Residence Groups		Percent Change
	1970	1980	1970	1980	1970–1980
Rural Farm					
Farm operator					
FSEI 100%	11.9	7.2	19.5	12.9	− 34.7
FSEI 50–99%	7.4	5.7	12.2	10.1	− 18.0
FSEI 0–49%	6.3	6.3	10.4	11.2	5.5
Farm laborer only	2.3	1.5	3.7	2.6	− 30.3
Farm laborer and nonfarm	1.5	1.3	2.4	2.3	− 7.4
Nonfarm occupation only	21.3	22.5	34.9	40.0	13.2
No one employed	10.3	11.7	16.9	20.9	22.4
Subtotal farm-related	61.0	56.2	100.0	100.0	− 1.3
Number: 100s			23,951	23,643	
Rural Nonfarm and Urban					
Farm operator					
FSEI 100%	2.8	2.3	7.2	5.3	− 11.0
FSEI 50–99%	1.9	2.2	4.9	5.0	21.0
FSEI 0–49%	3.0	4.4	7.8	10.1	56.4
Farm laborer only	8.3	5.8	21.2	13.2	− 25.1
Farm laborer and nonfarm	6.7	6.3	17.1	14.5	2.8
Nonfarm occupation only	13.8	18.0	35.4	41.0	39.2
No one employed	2.5	4.8	6.5	10.9	104.2
Subtotal farm-related	39.0	43.8	100.0	100.0	20.4
Number: 100s			15,301	18,430	
Total Farm-Related	100.0	100.0			7.2
Number: 100s	39,252	42,073			
Not Farm-Related					28.2
Number: 100s	595,179	762,630			

in the nonfarm group (subtotals in right hand column of Table 10.6). A comparison of the changes for the separate types shows that in every case gain is greater or loss is less in the nonfarm than in the farm residence classification, and in many cases the difference in the percentage change figures is substantial. Farm laborer only households declined sharply in both residence groups, but the largest percentage loss is for the most traditional family farm household types, those classified as part of the rural farm population, with a farm operator occupation and no nonfarm occupation reported by any household member, and with 100 percent of earned income from farm self-employment. Households of this type declined more than one-third, from about 466,000 to about 304,000 over the decade. These traditional family farm households dropped from 35 to 26 percent of all farm operator households, from 20 to 13 percent of the rural farm households, from 12 to 7 percent of all farm-related households, and from 0.7 to 0.4 percent of all United States households (percentages not shown in Table 10.6 except for rural farm households). The number of households in this first category that were in nonfarm or urban residences also declined but at a lower rate (11 percent) over the decade from about 110,000 to 97,500.

Because nonfarm work by farm operators and by other family members is so prevalent, a less inclusive measure of households that are dependent upon farming should also be considered. The households with a farm operator and more than 50 percent of earned income from farm self-employment, whether in rural farm or nonfarm residence, declined about 22 percent from 942,000 to 732,000 over the 1970–1980 decade. The percentage this subgroup was of all farm operator households dropped from 72 to 62, and the percentage it was of all households with some attachment to farming dropped from 24 to 17 percent over the decade. In the rural farm residence grouping, farm operator households with more than 50 percent of income from farm self-employment dropped from 75 to 67 percent of farm operator households, and from 32 to 23 percent of all rural farm households between 1970 and 1980.[12]

[12]One can determine from Appendix Table 10.1 that another 8 percent of the rural farm and 12 percent of the households that are not rural farm had more than 50 percent of their earned income from farming, but with no one reporting farm operator as principal occupation. Most of these were in the no one employed categories, and further analysis shows most of these have householders of advanced age. Many of these could well have turned the operation of their farm over to a family member living in another household, or could be reporting income from cash rent. The median farm self-employment incomes earned by households with such income is quite low for these types (see Table 10.18), and we believe that if income from all sources were considered rather than earned income the proportions of income from FSEI would be considerably less. We concluded that although extending the farm self-employment distinction to the households without farm operations might reveal some interesting relations, it would also introduce too much additional complexity to the comparisons of this chapter.

TABLE 10.7

Distribution by Residence of Household Farming Types, 1970, 1980

Household Farming Types	Percent Households in Nonfarm Residence		Percent Nonfarm Households That Are Urban	
	1970	1980	1970	1980
Farm Operator				
FSEI 100%	19.0	24.3	25.4	26.2
FSEI 50–99%	20.5	27.6	28.6	28.4
FSEI 0–49%	32.3	41.5	33.0	35.0
Farm Laborer Only	78.5	79.6	27.1	37.5
Farm Laborer and Nonfarm	81.8	83.3	38.4	43.7
Nonfarm Occupation Only	39.2	44.3	51.7	58.7
No One Employed	24.5	29.1	38.3	50.8
Total Farm-Related	39.0	43.8	38.9	47.2
Not Farm-Related	100.0	100.0	78.9	78.4

In notable contrast, those farm-related households with no one reporting a farm occupation increased rapidly over the decade, and in the nonfarm residence setting more rapidly than all United States households. By 1980, 61 percent of the rural farm residence households included no one reporting a farm occupation, and this was true of 52 percent of the nonfarm and urban farm-related households as well.

Between 1970 and 1980 all types became more urbanized. The percentage of farm-related households found in nonfarm settings increased from 39 to 44 percent and within the nonfarm setting the percentage classed as urban increased from 39 to 47 percent (Table 10.7). At each census, the farm operator households, along with households having no one employed, were least likely to be found in rural nonfarm or in urban areas. Among farm operator households the higher the percentage of income from FSEI, the lower the percent nonfarm, or among nonfarm the lower the percent urban. The farm laborer households were least likely to be found on farms, with eight out of ten in rural nonfarm or urban residences. Among households having nonfarm residences, however, those with only nonfarm occupations were most likely to be found in urban areas, with more than 50 percent so reporting.

The Typology by Metropolitan–Nonmetropolitan Location

Although farming is usually considered to be characteristic of rural and nonmetropolitan areas, a substantial proportion of the farm-related population is also found in metropolitan areas, both in rural farm and urban residence locations (Table 10.8). Four out of ten farm-related households are found in metropolitan areas as are three-fourths of all United States households. Metropolitan areas include about 30 percent of the rural farm households and one-half of the farm-related households in other residence settings. These farm-related households are a small proportion of the total within each residence group, however, being about 3 percent of all metropolitan households and 13 percent of non-metropolitan households. Farm-related households not situated on farms are more likely to be urban in metropolitan areas (two out of three) but more likely to be rural nonfarm in nonmetropolitan areas (three out of four).

Just as nontraditional farming types are more likely to be found in nonfarm and urban residences, so too they are more likely to be found in both residence categories of metropolitan areas than in nonmetropolitan areas. Regardless of farm-nonfarm residence, metropolitan households are less likely to be in the types that include a farm operator and more likely to be in the nonfarm occupation only type. Almost one-half of the metropolitan farm-related households have employment only in nonfarm occupations, but this is true for slightly more than one-third of the nonmetropolitan farm-related households. Similarly, a manipulation

TABLE 10.8

Distribution of Households by Farming Types and Metropolitan Status, 1980

| | Percentage Distribution | | | | | |
| | Metro | | Nonmetro | | Percent Metro | |
Household Farming Types	Farm	Nonfarm	Farm	Nonfarm	Farm	Nonfarm
Farm Operator						
FSEI 100%	4.0	1.9	9.2	2.5	20.7	31.7
FSEI 50–99%	3.4	1.8	7.2	2.4	22.5	31.7
FSEI 0–49%	4.2	5.1	7.5	4.1	25.8	42.8
Farm Laborer Only	1.0	6.8	1.7	5.1	25.6	44.5
Farm Laborer and Nonfarm	1.0	8.8	1.4	4.9	30.2	52.4
Nonfarm Occupation Only	20.4	27.6	23.8	11.9	34.4	58.6
No One Employed	8.5	5.5	13.8	4.4	27.1	43.0
Subtotal Farm-Related	42.5	57.5	64.6	39.4	28.6	49.7
Number: 100s	6,761	9,165	16,882	9,265		
Total Farm-Related	100.0		100.0		37.9	
Number: 100s	15,926		26,147			
Not Farm-Related	589,597		173,033		77.3	
Percent of all Households						
Farm-Related	2.6		13.1			

of the percentages in this table shows the combination of nonfarm with farm employment to be associated simultaneously with metropolitan status and with nonfarm residence. Thus the percentage of farm operator households with less than one-half of their earned income from FSEI is highest, 58, for metropolitan nonfarm households, 45 percent for nonmetropolitan nonfarm residence households, 37 percent for metropolitan rural farm households, and only 31 percent for nonmetropolitan rural farm households. A parallel pattern is found for farm laborer households. These associations are tied to the greater array of nonfarm occupational opportunities available for men and women living in rural nonfarm or urban settings and in metropolitan areas of the United States.

Analysis of metropolitan and nonmetropolitan change over 1970–1980 could not be considered, because the 1980 data were for 1980 boundaries and the 1970 data for 1970 boundaries.

Farm Types by Region

Households associated with farming are more likely to be found in the Midwest, followed by the Southern region, and are least likely to be found in the Northeast, according to the bottom line of Table 10.9. The Midwest, furthermore, has a higher proportion that may be considered more conventional farm households. A considerably higher proportion of farm-related households is classified as rural farm rather than nonfarm (rural nonfarm or urban) in this region compared with other regions, and almost one-third of the farm-related households in the Midwest include farm operators in rural farm residence settings, a proportion considerably higher than in any other region. Although the Northeast has the smallest proportion of all households that are farm-related, this region has the second highest percentage (below the Midwest) of such households in rural farm areas that include a farm operator. The West has the highest concentration of farm laborer households, where about 30 percent of the farm-related households include farm laborers but no farm operators.

The preponderance of farm activity in the midwestern states is also indicated by the percentage distributions of the farming types across regions, as shown in Table 10.10. This region has 60 percent of the traditional farmers (top line), almost one-half of the farm-related households living in rural farm areas, and four out of ten of the total farm-related households. The South has almost the same number and a somewhat smaller proportion of all farm-related households as in the Midwest, but, as shown in Table 10.9, these are considerably less likely to be

TABLE 10.9

Distribution of Households by Farming Types for Regions, 1980

Household Farming Types	Northeast	Midwest	South	West	Total
Rural Farm					
Farm operator					
FSEI 100%	5.7	11.5	4.6	4.5	7.2
FSEI 50–99%	5.3	9.1	3.3	4.1	5.7
FSEI 0–49%	6.6	8.2	5.1	5.0	6.3
Farm laborer only	1.1	1.4	1.4	2.2	1.5
Farm laborer and nonfarm	1.0	1.4	1.2	1.6	1.3
Nonfarm occupation only	21.7	23.5	25.1	16.1	22.5
No one employed	7.2	13.0	13.9	6.4	11.7
Subtotal farm-related	48.6	68.1	54.6	39.9	56.2
Rural Nonfarm and Urban					
Farm operator					
FSEI 100%	2.4	2.1	2.3	2.7	2.3
FSEI 50–99%	2.0	1.9	2.3	2.8	2.2
FSEI 0–49%	6.0	2.7	5.2	5.9	4.4
Farm laborer only	5.9	2.2	6.2	13.4	5.8
Farm laborer and nonfarm	9.9	3.4	6.4	12.1	6.4
Nonfarm occupation only	21.9	14.8	19.1	18.8	17.9
No one employed	3.3	4.8	4.9	4.4	4.8
Subtotal farm-related	51.4	31.9	46.4	60.1	43.8
Total Farm-Related	100.0	100.0	100.0	100.0	100.0
Number: 100s	3,006	16,484	16,357	6,226	42,073
Not Farm-Related					
Number: 100s	171,763	192,304	248,738	149,825	762,630
Percent of All Households					
Farm-Related	1.8	8.6	6.6	4.2	5.5

living on farms or to be farm operator households. Four out of ten farm laborer households not living on farms are in the South, followed by the West with about three out of ten. Among farm laborer households in rural farm settings, slightly over one-third are found in the South, with similar proportions in the midwestern states.

The data shown in Tables 10.9 and 10.10 for 1980 were also compiled for 1970. Proportional shifts in distribution were minor, but growth differentials over the decade were sometimes substantial, as indicated in Table 10.11. The bottom row of this table gives the percentage change in number of all United States households by region, with the familiar differential total growth favoring the South and the West. The growth in number of households that are not farm-related is almost

TABLE 10.10

Regional Distribution of Household Farming Types, 1980

Household Farming Types	Northeast	Midwest	South	West	Total
Rural Farm					
Farm operator					
FSEI 100%	5.7	60.6	24.4	9.3	100.0
FSEI 50–99%	6.6	60.5	22.3	10.6	100.0
FSEI 0–49%	7.5	49.2	31.4	11.9	100.0
Farm laborer only	5.5	36.0	36.0	22.5	100.0
Farm laborer and nonfarm	5.6	42.8	33.5	18.1	100.0
Nonfarm occupation only	6.9	39.7	42.8	10.6	100.0
No one employed	4.4	42.2	45.4	8.0	100.0
Subtotal farm-related	6.2	46.1	37.2	10.5	100.0
Rural Nonfarm and Urban					
Farm operator					
FSEI 100%	7.5	37.3	38.0	17.2	100.0
FSEI 50–99%	6.5	36.3	38.4	18.8	100.0
FSEI 0–49%	9.6	25.7	45.1	19.6	100.0
Farm laborer only	7.3	16.1	42.1	34.5	100.0
Farm laborer and nonfarm	11.1	22.2	38.8	27.9	100.0
Nonfarm occupation only	8.8	34.1	41.6	15.5	100.0
No one employed	5.0	42.1	39.2	13.7	100.0
Subtotal farm-related	8.4	30.3	41.0	20.3	100.0
Total Farm-Related	7.1	39.2	38.9	14.8	100.0
Not Farm-Related	22.5	25.2	32.6	19.7	100.0

identical, since farm households are such a small proportion of the total in each region. The farm-related households, which gained more than 7 percent in the United States as a whole, grew almost 20 percent in the West. This region actually had a growth in the total number of rural farm households, with households in this residence that had nonfarm occupations only or no occupations increasing about 30 percent. The other rapidly growing region in terms of total number of households—the South—had the slowest growth (less than 4 percent) in farm-related households.

Within all regions in the rural farm residence category the farm operator households with more than 50 percent of earned income from farm self-employment, and the farm laborer households of both types declined in number, whereas households with farm operators but less than 50 percent dependent on farm self-employment income (FSEI), or

TABLE 10.11

Percentage of Change of Household Farming Types by Region, 1970–1980

Household Farming Types	Northeast	Midwest	South	West	Total
Rural Farm					
Farm operator					
FSEI 100%	−26.2	−32.7	−41.3	−32.4	−34.7
FSEI 50–99%	−14.5	−18.7	−17.5	−16.7	−18.0
FSEI 0–49%	2.6	3.3	4.8	19.8	5.5
Farm laborer only	−40.4	−9.3	−49.4	−2.8	−30.3
Farm laborer and nonfarm	−38.8	5.0	−17.1	2.1	−7.4
Nonfarm occupation only	6.5	10.7	12.9	31.7	13.5
No one employed	24.1	31.8	13.3	31.9	22.4
Subtotal farm-related	−2.9	−3.0	−1.5	8.7	−1.3
Rural Nonfarm and Urban					
Farm operator					
FSEI 100%	−30.5	13.8	−25.7	−2.3	−11.0
FSEI 50–99%	18.1	27.7	17.8	37.6	21.1
FSEI 0–49%	23.4	67.9	58.1	58.9	56.4
Farm laborer only	−23.7	−20.2	−37.4	−5.7	−25.1
Farm laborer and nonfarm	−15.8	16.6	−9.9	26.9	2.8
Nonfarm occupation only	108.2	28.9	36.7	44.3	39.1
No one employed	62.9	121.9	94.9	101.4	104.2
Subtotal farm-related	20.1	31.6	10.9	26.6	20.4
Total Farm-Related	7.7	6.5	3.9	18.8	7.2
Not Farm-Related	13.0	20.3	40.7	40.8	28.1
All Households	12.9	19.0	37.7	39.8	26.8

households with only nonfarm occupations or with no occupations became more prevalent. Types with declining numbers in nonfarm residences included farm operator households totally dependent upon farming for earnings (except in the Midwest), farm laborer only households,
and for two of the four regions also the farm laborer and nonfarm occupation households. The other nonfarm residence types increased in all
regions, and often at a very large rate. Although the proportion of the
nonfarm households that are farm-related but with no one employed is
generally low (6 to 15 percent), regional growth rates for this category
ranged from 60 to 120 percent over the decade. The increase in the number of households reporting some self-employment income from farming, with no other indication in the census of attachment to farming,
has been relatively large and widespread across the regions.

Population, Household, and Family Composition

Approximately 13 million people lived in farm-related households in 1980, of which more than 7 million lived on farms (definition of 1970), and 5.8 million fell in the rural nonfarm and urban residential groupings (Table 10.12). About 2.3 million people lived in households primarily dependent on farm operation for a livelihood; that is, farm operator households with more than 50 percent of their earned income from farm self-employment. Almost 5.5 million persons, on the other hand, are in farm-related households in which no one reported having a farm occupation, and another 1.2 million people were in households with no one employed in any occupation.

The population per household columns of Table 10.12 show that the smallest-sized households tend to be those in which no one is employed. These are often comprised of elderly retired people, as will be indicated from the age and household composition variables to follow. The farm laborer only type, which is the most likely to include children, has the largest number of persons per household. Among farm operator households, household size is smaller for those completely dependent on farming for earned income than for those with both farm and nonfarm income sources. With more than one adult in the household, the likelihood of working in both farm and nonfarm occupations would be increased. Nevertheless, one might expect traditional farm households to be larger, with spouses, young people, and other adults assisting the farm operator. As will be seen, however, such traditional farms today tend to have older householders, and many must be at the "empty nest"

TABLE 10.12

Population in Households and Population per Household for Farming Types, 1980

Household Farming Types	Rural Farm		Rural Nonfarm and Urban	
	Population	Pop./Household	Population	Pop./Household
Farm operator				
FSEI 100%	880,500	2.9	264,400	2.7
FSEI 50–99%	877,600	3.7	312,700	3.4
FSEI 0–49%	896,400	3.4	627,700	3.4
Farm Laborer Only	192,500	4.1	806,200	3.3
Farm Laborer and Nonfarm	222,600	3.3	1,140,300	3.2
Nonfarm Occupation Only	3,161,900	3.3	2,307,900	3.1
No One Employed	934,300	1.9	378,800	1.9
Total Farm-Related	7,168,800	3.0	5,838,000	2.9
Not Farm-Related			208,345,800	2.7

stage of the life cycle. The average household size of the farm-related population in 1980, either in rural farm or rural nonfarm and urban residences, is only slightly larger than that of the United States households that are not farm-related.

The farm-related population, particularly those in rural farm settings, is considerably more likely to be made up of households that include families than is true for the household population that is not farm-related (Table 10.13). A family is two or more persons related by blood or marriage, and most nonfamily households consist of individuals living alone. Among the family households, furthermore, those that are farm-related are more likely to include a married couple, and again rural farm households are highest in this regard. The proportion of family households having children aged 16 and under is lower for rural farm families than for the population that is not farm-related, but it is highest for the farm-related households located in nonfarm or urban residences. For all but one of the individual types the proportion of family households with children is higher in nonfarm than in farm residences. The low rural farm proportions must reflect differences in life cycle stage, since rural farm women of childbearing years continue to have somewhat higher fertility than other women in the United States. Among family households that do not have a married couple, almost 60 percent are female-headed among those that are farm-related, but this is true for over 80 percent of the corresponding households that are not farm-re-

TABLE 10.13

Household Composition Measured by Household Farming Types, 1980

| Household Farming Types | Of Households | | Of Family Households | | | |
| | % Families | | % Married Couples | | % With Children[a] | |
	Farm	Nonfarm	Farm	Nonfarm	Farm	Nonfarm
Farm Operator						
FSEI 100%	88.6	80.8	93.7	92.9	41.6	43.4
FSEI 50–99%	98.1	96.4	95.5	94.5	53.9	57.6
FSEI 0–49%	95.4	91.4	94.8	91.8	45.8	50.9
Farm Laborer Only	84.1	79.2	89.6	83.1	57.0	61.9
Farm Laborer and Nonfarm	90.7	95.6	94.9	86.4	64.7	61.5
Nonfarm Occupation Only	92.7	86.7	91.9	91.9	53.2	48.8
No One Employed	65.4	60.4	89.2	87.9	10.7	19.2
Total Farm-Related	87.0	84.7	92.4	89.9	44.7	50.0
Not Farm-Related		72.9		82.2		48.5

[a]Children aged 16 and under.

lated. In all, almost 5 percent of the farm-related households are female-headed families, and this is true of about 10 percent of the households not farm-related.

Traditional married couple families appear most prevalent for the farm operator type with 50–99 percent of earned income from farm self-employment. Among all farm operator types, this type is highest in proportion of households that are families, and it is highest in the proportion of families with married couples and in the proportion of families with children. The farm laborer only type, on the other hand, is low in percent of households that are families and in the percent of married couples, but this type is the highest, along with the farm laborer and nonfarm type, in the percent of family couples with children. The no one employed type is lowest in the percent of households that are families, and it is lowest in the percent of families with married couples and by far the lowest in percent of families with children.

Age, Race, and Spanish Origin of Householders

A consideration of householder age distribution sheds some light on the observed differences in family composition. The householders tend to be older in the farm-related population than in the population that is not farm-related (Table 10.14). This table shows the percentages of householders at both ends of the age range, under 35 and 65 and over, along with the median age. Differences in 1980 medians are considerable across the household farming types. Together, the households with no one employed have by far the oldest householders, with the medians for both residential categories at approximately 70 years. The two farm laborer categories have the youngest householder age distributions, and farm operator families are intermediate. Consistent with the family structure and household size variables, we see that among the farm operator families, those completely dependent upon self-employment income tend to have older householders. In general, medians are less for the nonfarm and urban populations than for the rural farm population residences. Proportions under 35 and over 64 give results consistent with the medians. Notable is the fact that among the farm operator rural farm types, less than one in five include householders that are young farmers under 35 years of age. The percentages of young householders are higher for farm operator families who do not live on their farms.

Changes in age between 1970 and 1980 are different for the two residence categories. There is virtually no change over the decade in most of the medians for rural farm residence. The exception is for the farm laborer only type, which dropped from 50 years to 39.7 years, sug-

TABLE 10.14

Age Distribution Measures for Householders
by Household Farming Types, 1980, 1970

	Rural Farm				Rural Nonfarm and Urban			
	1980			1970	1980			1970
Household Farming Types	Age % 0–34	Age % 65+	Median Age	Median Age	Age % 0–34	Age % 65+	Median Age	Median Age
Farm Operator								
FSEI 100%	17.8	21.8	55.4	55.3	25.7	24.0	52.3	56.6
FSEI 50–99%	17.6	9.1	50.0	50.1	28.0	7.7	45.6	48.1
FSEI 0–49%	17.7	15.5	51.4	52.8	30.9	11.6	45.1	50.7
Farm Laborer Only	41.6	14.4	39.7	50.3	49.7	13.3	40.2	46.3
Farm Laborer and Nonfarm	22.9	6.3	44.5	48.7	38.7	5.1	44.2	47.2
Nonfarm Occupation Only	20.2	11.3	47.8	48.9	18.6	10.9	49.3	50.1
No One Employed	3.5	70.6	70.6	69.1	5.3	69.3	70.2	66.2
Total Farm-Related	16.5	25.3	53.8	53.7	23.4	17.3	49.1	47.8
Not Farm-Related							46.0	47.5

gesting that many older hired hands who earlier were part of traditional farming in many parts of the country passed out of the picture between 1970 and 1980. In contrast, the farm-related population in nonfarm and urban settings experienced a decline in all the median age categories except for households in which there was no one employed. Unlike the rural farm category, types in nonfarm residence settings grew in number of households between 1970 and 1980. Evidently many of those added have householders in the younger age groups.

Rural farm households are considerably less likely to have black householders than either the farm-related population living in nonfarm areas or the population that is not farm-related, according to Table 10.15. The proportion black in the farm-related households with nonfarm residences was higher than for the population not farm-related in 1970, but it had dropped to a lower level by 1980 (6.2 percent) while the latter group had increased to 10.8 percent. In both 1970 and 1980 the largest black proportions were found in the two farm laborer categories. Generally the lowest proportions are in the farm operator households that reside in rural farm settings. All types in both residence groups, with only one exception, declined between 1970 and 1980 in the percent of black householders.

The proportion of the farm-related population living in nonfarm residences that was of Spanish origin in 1980 is above that of households

TABLE 10.15

Percentage of Householders Black (1970, 1980) or of Spanish Origin (1980)
by Household Farming Types

| Household Farming Types | Percent Black | | | | Percent Spanish Origin 1980 | |
| | Rural Farm | | Rural Nonfarm and Urban | | Rural Farm | Rural Nonfarm and Urba |
	1970	1980	1970	1980		
Farm Operator						
FSEI 100%	1.7	0.4	6.5	3.1	0.4	1.3
FSEI 50–99%	1.1	0.4	5.6	2.8	0.5	1.8
FSEI 0–49%	2.9	1.8	8.4	5.7	0.7	4.1
Farm Laborer Only	13.9	5.4	22.8	14.8	8.2	26.5
Farm Laborer and Nonfarm	9.5	3.6	19.5	12.0	2.8	15.9
Nonfarm Occupation Only	4.3	3.4	3.4	3.4	1.0	1.8
No One Employed	6.4	3.7	7.0	2.3	0.9	1.4
Total Farm-Related	4.1	2.6	11.3	6.2	1.1	7.1
Not Farm-Related			9.9	10.8		5.0

not classed as farm-related, but the proportion in rural farm residences is very low, about 1 percent. Again, as with percent black, the two farm laborer types, and particularly those in the rural nonfarm and urban residence categories, have the highest proportion with Spanish origin. In 1980, one-fourth of the rural nonfarm and urban householders in the farm laborer only type were of Spanish origin, and 15 percent were black.

Occupations of Householders

The occupational distribution of the householders employed in the week prior to the 1980 census is summarized in Table 10.16. The managerial, professional, technical, and support occupations have been combined into what might be termed white collar; and the service, production, craft, operations, operators, and laborers have been combined into a blue collar category. The farm category here includes all the farm occupations as well as those associated directly with forestry and fishing. Almost all of the farm operator households have householders who report a farm occupation. Other such households would be those in which some other family member reported being the farm operator and the

TABLE 10.16

Occupational Distribution of Employed Householders
by Household Farming Types, 1980

	Rural Farm				Rural Nonfarm and Urban			
Household Farming Types	White Collar[a]	Blue Collar[b]	Farm[c]	Total	White Collar[a]	Blue Collar[b]	Farm[c]	Total
Farm Operator								
FSEI 100%	—	—	100.0	100.0	—	—	100.0	100.0
FSEI 50–99%	0.9	0.9	98.2	100.0	2.4	1.1	96.5	100.0
FSEI 0–49%	3.9	3.3	92.8	100.0	6.5	7.4	86.1	100.0
Farm Laborer Only	—	—	100.0	100.0	—	—	100.0	100.0
Farm Laborer and Nonfarm	17.7	27.3	55.0	100.0	16.7	33.0	50.3	100.0
Nonfarm Occupation Only	37.7	62.3	—	100.0	60.0	40.0	—	100.0
No One Employed	—	—	—	—	—	—	—	—
Total Farm-Related	19.2	31.1	49.7	100.0	30.9	24.8	44.3	100.0
Not Farm-Related					51.1	48.9	—	100.0

[a]"White collar" includes managerial, professional, technical, support occupations.
[b]"Blue collar" includes service, production, craft, operators, laborers.
[c]"Farm" includes farm operators and managers, farm laborers and foremen, and workers in forestry and fishing.

householder had another occupation. There are a few of these primarily in the lower farm self-employment income categories. About one-half of the farm laborer and nonfarm householders reported farm employment, and one in six reported a white collar occupation. Among those with a nonfarm occupation only, there is a difference by residence in occupational distribution. Four out of ten of this type in rural farm residence are white collar, but six out of ten are white collar among those households in nonfarm and urban residence settings. The latter proportion is above that for the householders that are not farm-related, which stands at about 50 percent in white collar and in blue collar. All in all, only one-half of the rural farm householders report a farm occupation, and this is true for about 44 percent of those that are farm-related living in nonfarm and urban settings.

Income and Poverty

The farm and rural population is often considered to be disadvantaged economically, and a detailed treatment of this topic is given in Chapter 11. The picture is definitely mixed for the household farming

types considered here. The 1979 median income for rural farm households was slightly below that for all households that are not farm-related (Table 10.17). The median for farm-related households in rural
nonfarm and urban areas, however, is more than $2,000 above both of
these figures and approaches $20,000. This difference is largely due to
households reporting only nonfarm occupations or those including no
one employed. Among farm operator households regardless of residence,
those having nonfarm employment that are more dependent upon farming than other sources of earned income (i.e., 50–99 percent FSEI) are
the types with the highest median incomes. Households that are totally
dependent on farming for income had the lowest medians among the
farm operator families, and the difference between $12,000 and $20,000
in both residence settings is appreciable. Among all farming types the
median income tends to be lowest for farm laborer only households, and
for no one employed households in rural farm settings. That it is not so
low for households with no one employed living in rural nonfarm and
urban settings suggests that many of these have appreciable nonwage
incomes. (Note that these figures are cash income and do not include
income in kind or capital gains.)

The percentage of households classified as in poverty using the
United States Census designation is rather high for a number of the
farm-related types, particularly given the level in 1980 for the population that is not farm-related (12.7 percent). Almost one-fourth of the
farm operator families completely dependent upon farming were classed
in poverty, and this is about the same as that for the farm laborer only

TABLE 10.17

Total Household Income Measures by Household Farming Types, 1979

	Rural Farm			Rural Nonfarm and Urban		
Household Farming Types	Median HHI	% in Poverty	% HHI $25,000+	Median HHI	% in Poverty	% HHI $25,000+
Farm Operator						
FSEI 100%	12,788	22.4	19.8	12,387	24.0	19.8
FSEI 50–99%	20,538	12.7	38.4	20,688	12.8	39.7
FSEI 0–49%	17,679	13.8	31.4	18,229	14.0	32.5
Farm Laborer Only	10,490	22.4	10.3	9,489	28.7	6.8
Farm Laborer and Nonfarm	19,338	8.6	34.0	19,236	9.1	31.6
Nonfarm Occupation Only	20,730	6.6	36.4	28,135	3.8	56.8
No One Employed	8,418	23.3	8.9	14,283	12.1	24.2
Total Farm-Related	16,316	14.0	27.4	19,720	11.3	37.7
Not Farm-Related				16,928	12.7	28.8

category in either residence group, and for those rural farm households in which no one was employed. The lowest poverty rates are for households in both residence group that reported only a nonfarm occupation and for the farm laborer and nonfarm households.

The percentage of households with income greater than $25,000 also varies considerably across the types but generally is consistent with the medians and inversely associated with the percent in poverty. The farm operator households not completely dependent upon farming, the farm laborer and nonfarm, and the nonfarm occupation only households in both residence settings had higher proportions with median incomes over $25,000 than did all households in the country not classed as farm-related. The percentage with high income is particularly high (57 percent) for those households with only a nonfarm occupation and found in rural nonfarm and urban locations. Recall that households in this type are classed as farm-related only because of having some farm self-employment income. Although the farm laborer only type was generally lower on these income measures, the farm laborer and nonfarm types had relatively high income. That the latter type has such high income measures and low proportions in poverty indicates that farm labor, with its very low wage levels, is a small part of the economic activity for this group. In many cases the farm laborers here may well be teenagers or housewives employed on a casual or part-time basis.

Comparable summary measures for farm self-employment income are shown in Table 10.18. The first column under each of the two resi-

TABLE 10.18

Farm Self-Employment Income Measures by Household Farming Types, 1979

Household Farming Types	Rural Farm				Rural Nonfarm and Urban			
		Of Those With FSEI				Of Those With FSEI		
	% With FSEI	Median FSEI	% FSEI LOSS	% FSEI $20,000+	% With FSEI	Median FSEI	% FSEI LOSS	% FSEI $20,000+
Farm Operator								
FSEI 100%	100.0	9,742	10.2	23.1	100.0	9,002	9.6	22.2
FSEI 50–99%	100.0	13,999	7.9	32.7	100.0	13,696	9.0	31.1
FSEI 0–49%	70.5	2,850	24.1	2.8	44.7	2,872	21.6	3.5
Farm Laborer Only	28.1	3,523	16.1	8.1	2.9	3,088	17.1	7.1
Farm Laborer and Nonfarm	44.5	1,078	38.5	5.0	4.7	1,750	22.0	4.2
Nonfarm Occupation Only	51.1	1,052	25.8	2.4	100.0	1,077	21.2	3.1
No One Employed	35.9	2,337	9.0	5.3	100.0	2,798	7.7	6.7
Total Farm-Related	60.6	3,737	17.3	12.4	67.7	1,976	17.2	7.3

dence groupings is the percentage of households that have any farm self-employment income. This by definition is 100 percent for the first two farm operator categories, as well as for the nonfarm occupation only and no one employed categories in nonfarm and urban residence settings. This percentage is quite low for farm laborer only types, as most of these households must depend on wages only for farm income. As was found for total median income, the median farm self-employment income (among those having such income) is highest for farm operators in the 50–99 percent farm self-employment category. These are by far the highest medians in the table, followed by those for households totally dependent upon farm self-employment for earned income.

The farm self-employment income distribution is subdivided further in this table by considering first the percentage who reported a loss in self-employment income, and second the percentage with farm self-employment income exceeding $20,000. The percentage reporting a loss is highest in the nonfarm occupation only category and among the farm operators with 0 to 49 percent of income from FSEI, along with those households reporting both farm labor and nonfarm occupations. These high proportions of losses coupled with the rather high total household median incomes shown in the preceding table suggest that a number of households may be associated with farming for its tax advantages.

The only types with more than 20 percent of the households earning more than $20,000 in farm self-employment income are the top two farm operator categories in both residence groups. About one-third of those dependent upon agriculture but with other earned income (i.e., 50–99 percent FSEI) reported a farm self-employment income of more than $20,000, and this was true whether they were living in rural farm or nonfarm and urban residences.

This typology of farm-related households, based on the Censuses of Population, cannot take into account the size or economic importance of the farming enterprise. A number of these types include households only peripherally involved in farming, and although only a relatively small proportion of the households can be identified as those of traditional farmers, these may still be the ones with by far the preponderant stake in farming as an enterprise. To examine this question, we distributed the total farm self-employment income reported in the 1980 census (over $18 billion) among the household farming types.

This distribution (Table 10.19) shows that nontraditional farming types included households that reported more than one-half of the aggregate farm self-employment income. The traditional types—farm operator households with more than 50 percent of their incomes from farm self-employment and with rural farm residences—reported 45 percent of the income, and such households with rural nonfarm and urban

TABLE 10.19

Aggregate Farm Self-Employment Income by Household Farming Types, 1979

Household Farming Types	Total Percent Distribution		Percent Distribution Within Residence Groups		
	Farm	Nonfarm	Farm	Nonfarm	Total
Farm Operator					
FSEI 100%	22.3	6.8	36.2	17.5	29.1
FSEI 50–99%	22.5	8.6	36.6	22.3	31.1
FSEI 0–49%	3.4	2.1	5.4	5.7	5.6
Farm Laborer Only	0.7	0.2	1.1	0.6	0.8
Farm Laborer and Nonfarm	0.4	0.3	0.8	0.8	0.8
Nonfarm Occupation Only	7.1	13.5	11.6	35.1	20.6
No One Employed	5.1	7.0	8.3	18.0	12.0
Subtotal Farm-Related	61.5	38.5	100.0	100.0	100.0
Total Farm-Related	100.0				
Amount	$18,422,975,000				

residences included another 15 percent. All rural farm household types together reported 62 percent of the aggregate farm self-employment income. The four types of households with no one reporting a farm occupation had one-third of the farm self-employment income, and the highest single percentage except for the traditional types is for households not situated on farms with only nonfarm occupations reported (13.5 percent). We see that some types that might be considered peripheral to farming do not have a trivial share of farm self-employment income as of 1980. This reflects the spread of ownership and control of farm activities into the sectors of American society not traditionally associated with farming. Both types of farm laborer households receive an extremely small share of the total farm self-employment income. Unfortunately, it is not possible to identify farm wages separately from other wages reported in the census so as to consider the distribution and amount of farm wages among the farming types.

The Farm-Related Population: An Overview

Farming remains an extremely important part of our economy. The relation of population to farming activity, however, has changed considerably over the past half-century. With the commercialization of agriculture, farm activity has merged with other parts of the food and fiber industry, and become more closely linked with other sectors of the national and global economies. Use of nonfarm capital has increased, and the population identified as farm-related has become more differentiated. By the mid-1980s there was considerable concern about a crisis in agriculture, shown most dramatically by the numbers of commercial farmers in serious financial trouble or even forced out of business. In addressing such acute problems or dealing with a wider range of farm and rural policy issues, the traditional concepts used to provide basic information may no longer accurately reflect reality.

The rural farm residence category is a case in point. Though never a perfect fit, this concept today has limited value, for not only are the farm residents quite diverse, including many individuals engaged in nonfarm occupational activity, but many others not living on farms are involved in farming. A complex pattern of results was revealed in our analysis when households were identified with farming according to three criteria: rural farm residence, whether or not any household members report a farm occupation, and whether or not household members reported self-employment income from farming. A basic finding from this approach was that the farm-related population is diverse and becoming more so.

The rural farm population, first designated in the Census of Population for 1920, was in its time an effort to introduce a farm-related concept that would be closer to reality than rural residence alone, with the recognition that many rural people were not engaged in farming. By 1980, almost one-half of the households classed as farm-related lived in rural nonfarm and urban areas, a higher proportion than in 1970. Households not classed as rural farm include almost four out of ten of the farm operator households wholly dependent upon income from farming and together earn 40 percent of the aggregate self-employment income from farming.

At the same time, most households (six out of ten) in the rural farm population have no one reporting a farm occupation, and four out of ten have no one reporting self-employment income from farming. Less than one-fourth are farm operator households with more than 50 percent of their earned income coming from farm self-employment, with only one out of seven wholly dependent upon this source of earned income. Clearly, the relation between trends in the rural farm population and recent trends in commercial agriculture must be a tenuous one.

Further analysis showed that the rural farm households are more concentrated in nonmetropolitan than in metropolitan areas, and most highly concentrated in the Midwest. They are more likely than other households to consist of families and married couples, and more likely to have an older age structure, with one quarter of the householders over 65 years old. A very low proportion of rural farm households are black or of Spanish origin. Only about one-half of the employed rural farm householders reported a principal occupation in farming and a wide range of other occupations were represented. The rural farm population ranks lower in median income, higher in percentage in poverty, and lower in percentage with income of more than $25,000 than either the farm related nonfarm or the other nonfarm population. These findings are consistent with or parallel those of many previous studies comparing the rural farm with other residence groups. Though there are exceptions, the farm-related households in nonfarm residences generally stand between the farm-related rural farm and the households that are not farm-related on these measures.

The typology presented here makes further differentiation possible across the residence categories. Consider first the households in which someone reports an occupation of farm operator. Less than one-third of the farm-related households can be classed in this way in 1980, and the proportion declined between 1970 and 1980. At the same time the proportion of these farm operator households not primarily dependent on farm self-employment for earned income increased. Farm operator households, and particularly those more dependent upon farm income, were more likely to be found in rural farm residences, nonmetropolitan, and midwestern locations than most other farm types. The most prosperous farmers, with younger families on which much of the future of farming must depend, are those in which both farm and nonfarm income are combined, with farm income as the major source. "Part-time farming" or "multiple job-holding," the combining of a farm and a nonfarm occupation by an individual or by different family members, has been viewed as marginal, not for the serious farm family, unless as a way out of or into farming. But our findings support the view that combining farm and nonfarm employment is a viable adjustment, evidently being made by more young families today, which is associated both with higher total and farm self-employment income.[13]

Despite the increasing scale of farming in the United States, farm laborer households have declined in number, particularly those households in which this was the only occupation reported. Farm laborer households are concentrated in the West and South, and eight out of ten are in nonfarm residences. They have the highest proportion black and Hispanic, and have the youngest householder age structures of all types. Households that report only farm laborer occupations are larger, but they are less likely to be family or married couple units than other types. They have the lowest income levels and highest proportion in poverty, except for the rural farm households with no one employed. The farm laborer and nonfarm type, however, is similar to the nonfarm

---

[13]See Wimberly (1983) and Fuller (1984) for recent reviews of part-time farming that emphasize both its importance and its relative permanence.

occupation only type in characteristics, suggesting that farm labor is a small contributor to the incomes of many of these households.

The type that included the most households (four out of ten, with the same proportion in each residence group) had members with non-farm occupations but none with a farm occupation. Three-fourths of these had some farm self-employment income, but commitment to farming was such that no one considered it a principal occupation. Households in this category increased between 1970 and 1980, particularly in nonfarm settings, and proportionately they are more likely to be found in metropolitan areas and in the South and Midwest. This type has a younger age structure, larger household size, and a higher proportion of family and married couple households than all farm-related households combined. It also has the highest proportion with white collar occupations, and the highest household income measures among the types—indeed considerably higher than the total population that is not farm-related. The low median farm self-employment income figures and the fact that one-fourth reported farm income losses suggest that a number of households in this type may be engaged in nominal farming perhaps primarily for the tax advantages.

Households in which no one is employed make up almost one out of six of the rural farm and the nonfarm residence farm-related households. In nonfarm residence settings, such households are considered farm-related only if they report farm self-employment income, whereas two-thirds of those in rural farm settings do not report farm income in 1979. This type probably consists primarily of elderly retired persons. On the rural farm side, this type has the lowest level of income and the highest percentage in poverty, but in rural nonfarm and urban residence settings this type stands well above the farm laborers in income level.

This has been a detailed chapter, but the detail is necessary to point out the diversity among the farm-related population. In relating this population to social and economic trends, it is convenient and traditional simply to consider as a unit the people who live on farms. Yet we have demonstrated that an increasing proportion of the farm-related population, including many seriously committed to farming, resides in rural nonfarm and urban areas, and that many farm residents have a tenuous identification with farm activity. The solution is not to make any single definition more stringent in identifying the population associated with farming. Different types, such as those identified here, will be affected quite differently, and perhaps not at all, by trends in agriculture and in the national economy, or by government programs and policies. The fact that households with nontraditional attachments to farming have increased in number should not be ignored but is in itself evidence of the changing structure of agriculture in America.

APPENDIX TABLE 10.1

Cross-Classification of Households by Residence, Farm Occupation of Household Members, and Percentage of Total Earned Household Income from Farm Self-Employment, 1980 (in hundreds)

Residence and Occupations of Any Household Members	Percentage of 1979 Earned Income from Farm Self-Employment				
	None	0–49	50–99	100	Total
Rural Farm					
(1) Farm operator only[a]	534	608	1,165	3,043	5,350
(2) Operator and nonfarm[a]	246	1,253	1,145	89	2,733
(3) Farm laborer only	447	74	41	58	620
(4) Farm laborer and nonfarm	298	213	26	0	537
(5) Nonfarm only	4,624	4,442	365	31	9,462
(6) No one employed	3,168	341	217	1,215	4,941
Total (all farm-related)	9,317	6,931	2,959	4,436	23,643
Rural Nonfarm					
(1) Farm operator only[a]	360	175	265	720	1,520
(2) Operator and nonfarm[a]	281	401	351	38	1,071
(3) Farm laborer only	1,469	27	11	10	1,517
(4) Farm laborer and nonfarm	1,430	72	11	0	1,513
(5) Nonfarm only	—	2,878	214	16	3,108
(6) No one employed	—	188	130	678	996
Total farm-related	3,540	3,741	982	1,462	9,725
Not farm-related	165,065	—	—	—	165,065
Urban					
(1) Farm operator only[a]	181	61	102	255	599
(2) Operator and nonfarm[a]	213	200	143	15	571
(3) Farm laborer only	889	15	2	5	911
(4) Farm laborer and nonfarm	1,129	42	2	0	1,173
(5) Nonfarm only	—	4,122	290	9	4,421
(6) No one employed	—	256	133	641	1,030
Total farm-related	2,412	4,696	672	925	8,705
Not farm-related	597,565	—	—	—	597,565

[a]Another family member may also be a farm laborer.

11

INCOME AND POVERTY

Wealth and poverty coexist in both urban and rural settings. The same characteristics associated with inadequate income in urban areas also predict low income in rural areas, such as low education, lack of a male wage earner in the family, or black, Indian, or Hispanic minority group status. But, average income levels are different for urban and rural people, as are the family composition and work patterns that influence the adequacy of income. Moreover, although urban poverty is usually concentrated in neighborhoods of cities or in individual communities within a metropolitan complex, high rural poverty rates are often endemic enough to characterize entire blocks of counties, extending over some thousands of square miles. The focus of this chapter is first on the comparative levels and sources of urban/metropolitan and rural/nonmetropolitan income, with attention to race. The frequency and nature of poverty are then discussed, both in terms of the characteristics of the poor and the geography of poverty and of income inequality within areas.

It has been more difficult, on average, to generate incomes capable of supporting an acceptable standard of living in rural and small town places than in metropolitan cities and suburbs. Agriculture may have been the objective of the great majority of the immigrants who came to this country in the first 200 to 250 years of settlement. It resulted in comparative comfort, property ownership, and social stability for many, but it was also accompanied by economic failure for others and by poverty for a large class of slaves and their tenant descendants, small farmers on marginal land, and farm laborers. The wealth accruing to professional skills, entrepreneurship, trade, and finance was and still is disproportionately created in cities where centralized, specialized services are located and mass markets exist. In the late twentieth century, nonmetropolitan and/or rural America has diversified its economy and is not nearly as dependent on agriculture, but although great progress in modernization and levels of living has been made, wage rates and availability of work remain lower than in the urban sector. This has resulted in nonmetropolitan personal incomes continuing to be lower overall than those in metropolitan areas, and in a higher incidence of impoverishment in rural and small town communities. Within the rural population there is also wide variation in income levels between geographic areas and between racial groups.

Income

Among families living in nonmetropolitan areas in 1980, the median income in the preceding year was $16,592, some 22 percent below that of $21,165 for metropolitan families (Table 11.1). The average number of persons per family dependent on these incomes was almost identical in metropolitan and nonmetropolitan areas—3.27 vs. 3.26 persons. Among persons not living in families—that is, living alone or with non-

TABLE 11.1

Median Income by Age and Residence, 1979

Family Status and Age of Householder	Total	Metropolitan			Nonmetropolitan		
		Total	Urban	Rural	Total	Urban	Rural
Families	$19,917	$21,238	$21,165	$20,940	$16,592	$17,302	$16,204
Unrelated Individuals[a]	6,695	7,270	7,320	6,713	4,962	4,779	5,213
Family Median by Age of Householder							
15–24 years	12,669	12,901	12,612	14,556	12,229	11,754	12,555
25–34	19,041	19,814	19,691	20,476	17,014	17,200	16,912
35–44	23,162	24,321	24,258	24,595	20,284	21,104	19,867
45–54	25,864	27,388	27,649	26,138	21,376	23,215	20,441
55–64	21,950	23,686	24,186	20,867	17,416	19,516	16,356
65 and older	12,295	13,421	13,775	11,426	10,157	11,165	9,633

[a]15 years old and over.

relatives—the median income disparity was even greater, with the non-metropolitan median of $4,962 lower than the metropolitan median of $7,320 by 32 percent.

In the course of the 1960s, per capita income in nonmetropolitan areas increased somewhat more rapidly than it did in metropolitan communities. On an inflation-adjusted basis, the nonmetropolitan per capita figure increased by 21 percent from 1969–1979, compared with a 14 percent metropolitan rise. This converging trend still left nonmetropolitan per capita income only 77 percent as high as that in metropolitan areas in 1979.

Does it take as much money to live in a rural or small town place as elsewhere? It is commonly assumed that it does not, that things cost less away from cities. Unfortunately, the federal government does not conduct its extensive cost of living surveys in the open country or places of less than 20,000 population—a strange, even cavalier omission given the tens of millions of people who live in such communities. For many years the official federal poverty criteria assumed that the poverty income threshold for farm people was 15 percent above that of nonfarm people, apparently on the premise that farm people raised large portions of their food or perhaps that their cost of housing was reduced by being entwined with the cost of the farm. Eventually in 1980 this provision was abolished. Nevertheless, there is still a general perception that rural and small town costs of living are lower than those of large urban areas. Anecdotally, this most often seems to relate to lower costs of housing and local taxes. On the other hand, rural costs may be commonly higher for retail goods in the absence of discount houses, economies of scale, or competition.

Hoch and associates recently made an effort to infer differences in metropolitan and nonmetropolitan costs of living by an examination of county variations in wage rates for relatively homogeneous occupations.[1] The premise is that "... if wage rates for the same work differ between locations, the differences must be compensatory. Thus, people working in a more costly or more harsh environment must be compensated for those conditions, or they will not work in that location." Wage rates compensate for both good and bad consequences of differences in community size. As a consequence, wage differentials are generally wider than conventional cost of living index differences because they reflect quality-of-life aspects as well as purchased items. Applying this theory to United States county data on per capita income for 1981, Hoch estimated that nonmetropolitan per capita income was 75 percent of that in metropolitan areas in nominal terms but 89 percent in real

[1]Hoch, Hewitt, and Virgin (1984).

terms. If so, then a little more than half of the national metropolitan–nonmetropolitan income differential may be offset and accounted for by cost and quality-of-living differences. The true income difference is considerably narrowed but not eliminated. In practice, these differences vary from region to region. No effort has been made in this chapter to adjust the census data for differences in cost of living, but it should be kept in mind that, on average, such differences exist and that they may be approximately at the level suggested by the work cited above.

The relative deficiency of nonmetropolitan incomes is not serious for young families, but it worsens steadily until retirement age, where it lessens slightly. Thus among family householders 15–24 years old, median nonmetropolitan family incomes were 95 percent of those in metropolitan areas. But there is less progression in nonmetropolitan income levels with further age. The entry level incomes appear to be closer to ultimate achievements than is true in metropolitan communities. Note from Table 11.1 that by ages 55–64 nonmetropolitan family median income ($17,416) was only 74 percent as high as that of metropolitan families with householders of that age ($23,686). In both metropolitan and nonmetropolitan areas income was highest where the family householder was 45–54 years old. But, whereas in metropolitan areas the incomes of such families were 2.1 times as great as those of families headed by people aged 15–24, in nonmetropolitan areas the middle-aged families had median incomes just 1.7 times those of the youngest families.

This pattern is especially pronounced in the rural population. In the nonmetropolitan rural population, which has the lowest educational attainment of any of the residence groups, the median income of families with heads who are 15–24 years old is essentially equal to that of urban metropolitan families with heads of similar age ($12,555 vs. $12,612). However, where heads are 55–64 years old, rural nonmetropolitan families have incomes only 68 percent of the urban metropolitan median ($16,356 vs. $24,186)—a very different situation from that at younger ages. To some extent, the gap at the older age results from the fact that a somewhat higher percentage of nonmetropolitan rural residents are retired or otherwise not in the labor force. Indeed, there is a net movement of retired former urban metropolitan residents into rural communities in their late fifties and early sixties. Although they tend to have good retirement incomes, these incomes are likely to be lower than those of people who continue to work. But this does not explain the disparity in nonmetropolitan rural and metropolitan urban incomes that exists for families with heads in the 35–54 age bracket who are still in prime working years. Many rural nonmetropolitan jobs simply lack the demand, skill, or career ladder aspect necessary to command desirably higher wages or salaries as experience and maturity are acquired. The failure of rural and/or nonmetropolitan people to earn appropriately higher income with advancing age in relation to urban or metropolitan people is particularly found among blacks and American Indians.

Among people living alone or with nonrelatives, the low level of nonmetropolitan income in comparison with metropolitan income is worst among people of working age and does not result from a high presence of widowed older people.

As would be expected in any segment of society, well-educated rural people earn more money than those with less schooling. For example, mean weekly earnings in 1979 of rural men with four or more years of college were much higher than those for men with just four years of high school at all age groups (Table 11.2). This education benefit increased with age. Thus, for men 45–54 years of age the earnings of the college educated group were more than 60 percent higher than those of the high school graduates, compared with a superiority of just a little more than 20 percent among men aged 25–34.

However, the data suggest that there has not been as much payoff to advanced education in rural areas as in urban places. At ages 25–34,

TABLE 11.2

Mean Weekly Earnings for Men by Age, Education, and Residence, 1979

Age and Years of School Completed	Urban	Rural	Percent Difference[a]
25–34 Years Old			
9–11 years completed	$263	$263	—
12 years	304	307	1.0
13–15 years	321	322	0.3
16 or more years	388	374	−3.6
35–44 Years Old			
9–11 years completed	329	323	−1.8
12 years	385	371	−3.6
13–15 years	437	416	−4.8
16 or more years	615	552	−10.2
45–54 Years Old			
9–11 years completed	357	340	−4.8
12 years	409	378	−7.6
13–15 years	472	432	−8.5
16 or more years	701	617	−12.0

[a]Rural minus urban as a percentage of urban.

341

rural men with four or more years of college in 1980 had mean weekly earnings that were 3.6 percent below those of urban men. At ages 45–54, on the other hand, the average rural wages were 12.0 percent below those in urban areas for men of this same level of education. For men with nine to eleven years of school there was a similar decline, but no rural disadvantage at all to begin with. By age 45–54 rural men with incomplete high school education were 4.8 percent below their urban compeers in earnings, compared with the 12.0 percent disadvantage of college graduates. Although rural areas are comparatively short of college trained people, this shortage has not enabled degree-holding rural residents to reap financial benefits commensurate with their formal training and relative scarcity.

Sources of Income

About four-fifths of both metropolitan and nonmetropolitan households received income from earnings in 1979—that is, either wages, salaries, farm or nonfarm self-employment, or a combination of these sources of work income (Table 11.3). The other one-fifth had no work income and depended on investment income, pensions (including Social Security), or miscellaneous sources such as public assistance, child support payments, unemployment or workmen's compensation, and annuities. Although earnings were the main source of support for most families, it was precisely this income source for which the ratio of nonmetropolitan to metropolitan household income was lowest, with the nonmetropolitan mean earnings being only .79 that of the metropolitan mean.

Nonmetropolitan residents came closest to parity with metropolitan incomes in money received from Social Security (including railroad retirement pensions). Mean payments to nonmetropolitan households were .92 as high as those to metropolitan households, and the percentage of nonmetropolitan households receiving this income (31) was higher than the percentage of metropolitan households that did so (24). Thus Social Security income plays a role (albeit modest) in helping to reduce the overall disparity in metropolitan and nonmetropolitan incomes. In part, this stems from the somewhat higher proportion of older people in nonmetropolitan areas. All nonmetropolitan households as a group received $8.65 of Social Security income for every $100 of earnings income, compared with $5.70 of such income for every $100 of earnings income in metropolitan households. Income from interest, dividends, rentals, or other investments was another source of income in which the receiving nonmetropolitan households differed only moder-

TABLE 11.3

Sources of Household Income by Race, Residence, and Spanish Origin, 1979

Percentage of Households with Income from:

Residence, Race, and Spanish Origin	Total	Earnings			Interest, Etc.[a]	Social Security	Public Assistance	All Other[b]
		Wage or Salary	Self-Employment Nonfarm	Farm				
All Races								
Metropolitan	81.9	79.2	8.9	1.7	42.9	24.3	7.8	23.7
Nonmetropolitan	79.2	73.3	10.5	8.4	36.8	30.6	8.6	24.3
White								
Metropolitan	82.4	79.4	9.7	1.9	48.1	25.4	5.6	24.4
Nonmetropolitan	79.5	73.2	11.2	9.0	39.6	30.8	7.0	24.7
Black								
Metropolitan	77.2	76.3	3.4	0.3	11.7	21.1	21.5	20.8
Nonmetropolitan	73.7	72.1	3.6	2.2	7.3	32.3	26.1	19.9
Indian[c]								
Metropolitan	84.8	82.5	7.4	1.3	20.1	15.8	15.6	24.3
Nonmetropolitan	80.8	78.3	6.3	3.3	13.5	21.3	19.7	24.7
Hispanic								
Metropolitan	84.3	82.6	5.8	0.6	17.2	13.8	16.1	18.2
Nonmetropolitan	83.9	81.2	6.5	2.4	13.4	20.3	14.3	19.8

[a]Interest, dividends, rent, and royalties.
[b]Unemployment compensation, pensions, child support, annuities, and veterans payments.
[c]Indian includes Alaska Natives; Hispanics may be of any race.

TABLE 11.4

Percentage Distribution of Aggregate Income
Received by Each Fifth of Families by Residence, 1969, 1979

Quintile	1969			1979		
	Metro	Nonmetro	Total	Metro	Nonmetro	Total
Total	100.0	100.0	100.0	100.0	100.0	100.0
Lowest fifth	5.5	4.8	5.0	5.1	5.1	5.0
Second	12.3	11.6	12.0	11.6	11.4	11.4
Middle	17.4	17.3	17.3	17.3	17.3	17.6
Fourth	23.0	24.1	23.3	23.7	24.0	23.4
Highest	41.8	42.2	42.4	42.3	42.2	42.6
Index of Income Concentration	0.361	0.375	0.371	0.372	0.373	0.376

ately from metropolitan households having such income, obtaining .90 as much per household. However, fewer nonmetropolitan households reported receiving investment income (37 percent against 43 percent in metropolitan areas), thus offsetting any contribution to overall income parity from this source.

The comparative degree of equality of income distribution between metropolitan and nonmetropolitan families can be measured by the index of income concentration. This index has the theoretical potential to run from 0 to 1. The higher the score, the greater the extent of concentration, and thus of inequality of income distribution.[2] As shown in Table 11.4, both metropolitan and nonmetropolitan areas showed a moderate degree of family income concentration in 1969, with the nonmetropolitan index (.375) being slightly above the metropolitan index (.361). By 1979, this difference had been nearly eliminated (.373 vs. .372). The mechanism of change, however, came principally from a rise in metropolitan income concentration rather than through a reduction of the nonmetropolitan level. As the table reveals, the poorest two-fifths of metropolitan families received 17.8 percent of metropolitan income in 1969, but only 16.7 percent in 1979. In nonmetropolitan families, on the other hand, the poorest two-fifths had not lost any share of income during this time (16.4 vs. 16.5).

[2]For computation of this Gini Index of Concentration see Shryock, Siegel, and Associates (1975), pp. 178-186, 367.

Income Levels by Race

Blacks. The largest racial or ethnic group difference in income within the nonmetropolitan population is that between the white and black population. In 1979, the median income of black nonmetropolitan households stood at $8,167, 44 percent below that of $14,663 for white households (Table 11.5). However, black households were larger on average (3.33 persons compared with 2.72 persons for white households), so the per capita income of blacks was only half that of whites. As in the cities, the income position of nonmetropolitan blacks is lowered by the relatively high frequency of female-headed families with children and no spouse. They comprise 19 percent of all nonmetropolitan black families, compared with just 5 percent among whites. Their median income of $5,531 was well below half that of black nonmetropolitan married couples ($12,479). For married couples the median black income was two thirds that of whites.

Despite the higher proportion of families that are headed by women with dependent children, rural and small town blacks are more dependent on income from wage and salary earnings than are whites. Blacks received 4.8 percent of their income from public assistance, whereas such income made up just 0.9 percent of white income. However, blacks had only very small amounts of money coming in from self-employment—either farm or nonfarm—or from interest and other investment

TABLE 11.5

Median Income by Race and Residence, 1979

Household Status and Race	Metropolitan	Nonmetropolitan
Households		
Total	$17,880	$14,040
White	18,969	14,663
Black	11,602	8,167
Indian[a]	13,912	10,575
Hispanic[b]	13,811	11,595
Unrelated Individuals		
Total	7,270	4,962
White	7,710	5,243
Black	5,218	2,929
Indian[a]	5,636	3,569
Hispanic[b]	5,599	3,898

[a]Includes Alaska Natives.
[b]Hispanics may be of any race.

TABLE 11.6

*Median Income of Males and Females Employed Full-Time
Year-Round by Residence, Race, and Spanish Origin, 1979*[a]

Race and Spanish Origin	Metropolitan		Nonmetropolitan	
	Male	Female	Male	Female
Total	$18,239	$10,862	$15,113	$8,688
White	19,062	11,017	15,454	8,826
Black	13,467	10,053	8,378	7,162
Indian[b]	15,313	10,167	12,048	8,299
Hispanic[c]	13,101	9,046	12,065	7,732

[a]Full-time year-round workers were employed at least 35 hours for at least 50 weeks in 1979.
[b]Includes Alaska Natives.
[c]Hispanics may be of any race.

income. Nonmetropolitan whites obtained 17 percent of their income from these sources; blacks obtained less than 4 percent. In the aggregate, nonmetropolitan blacks received 77 percent of their income from the wage and salary labor market, whereas whites received 70 percent.

There is an interesting difference in the relative incomes of nonmetropolitan black men and women who are employed full-time throughout 1979, both in relation to one another and to nonmetropolitan whites.[3] Black nonmetropolitan women who were year-round full-time workers earned 76 percent as much as did similarly employed nonmetropolitan black men, whereas nonmetropolitan white women with full-time jobs received only 57 percent as much as did white men with the same amount of work (Table 11.6). In one sense it can be said that nonmetropolitan black women come much closer to the ideal of equal income with men than do white women (or for that matter Hispanics or Indians). However, they do so not because their income levels are comparatively high, but rather because those of black rural and small town men are so low. (The same phenomenon is found in metropolitan areas.) Yet, one can also argue that the 23 percent superiority in income that white nonmetropolitan women had over black women among the year-round full-time workers was a comparatively minor payoff to them for education in light of the fact that 63 percent of the white female population 18 years and over were high school graduates compared with 42 percent of black women of the same age and residence. Further, differences in income by sex are still so great that nonmetropolitan white

[3]Full-time year-round workers are those employed for at least 35 hours a week and for at least 50 weeks in 1979.

women with year-round full-time work had a median income 6 percent below that of black men of the same work status, despite having a 63 percent to 40 percent advantage in possession of a high school education.

American Indians and Alaska Natives. The median income level of nonmetropolitan American Indians and Alaska Natives ($10,575) was above that of blacks, but somewhat below that of Hispanics and well below that of whites (Table 11.5). There is wide variation, however, among the reservation groups. On the one hand are several reservations with at least 1,000 Indian residents where the median household income is above that of the national nonmetropolitan white population. Warm Springs, Oregon, and Laguna Pueblo, New Mexico, are examples. But, with one exception, all of the reservations containing more than 5,000 people had median household incomes below $10,000. The huge Navajo reservation, with its more than 100,000 nonmetropolitan residents, had a median of $8,342, which was one-fifth below the national Indian figure and more than two-fifths below that for whites. Several of the Sioux reservations were below $8,000, as were the Hopi.

The median income for all reservation Indian households (including those within metropolitan areas) was $9,116, significantly less than that of approximately $11,000 for those Indian households who live in rural areas and small towns but who have left reservations or have never lived on them.

The Indian population has a high percentage of households with earnings from employment (81 percent), despite an abnormally low rate of labor force participation by men (63 percent). Like Hispanics, the young age distribution minimizes the percentage of older people whose households contain no workers. Indians most closely resemble Hispanics in other sources of income, too, such as relatively low receipt of Social Security and investment income. Public assistance income was received by 20 percent of nonmetropolitan Indian households in 1979, but reached 30 percent in some of the poorest areas. There is also an exceptional dependence on employment by government. Fully half of all employed reservation men and two-thirds of women were government workers in 1980—either tribal, federal, state, or local. In part this reflects the special relationship that most reservations have with the federal government; in part the control of tribal resources that many tribes have; in part the large numbers of children to be educated; and in part the lack of availability of private economy jobs in many of these locations. This heavy dependence on public administration employment is fully triple that found in the nonmetropolitan white population or among nonreservation Indians such as those in Oklahoma.

One of the principal factors limiting the income of nonmetropolitan

Indians is the low proportion of employed men who work at full-time year-round jobs. In 1979, only 45 percent of nonmetropolitan Indian men who worked during the year did so full-time (at least 50 weeks and usually for 35 hours or more per week). This compares with 61.5 percent for nonmetropolitan white men. The main problem was lack of year-round work rather than lack of full-time jobs.

Hispanics. The sources and levels of income among nonmetropolitan Hispanics are rather intermediate between those of whites and blacks. Their median household income in 1979 was 21 percent below that of whites, but 42 percent above that for blacks. They have a higher incidence than blacks of receipt of income from nonfarm self-employment and from investments but much lower than whites. They are more dependent than whites on public assistance but less so than blacks. In one respect, however, Hispanics exceed both white and black households, namely, in their very high percentage with earnings from employment (83.9 percent against 79.5 for whites and 73.7 for blacks). In large part this may result from their young age structure. With their continued augmentation by young immigrants and their relatively high fertility, less than 6 percent of the Hispanic nonmetropolitan population had reached 65 years of age by 1980, well below the level for blacks and less than half that of whites. As a result, more of the households had people of working age, and only 20 percent were getting Social Security income, compared with 30 percent or more for both whites and blacks.

Despite the high percentage of earners, the lower overall income of the nonmetropolitan Hispanics in relation to whites is not surprising when one notes that one-fourth of all employed men in this group work as laborers, either farm or nonfarm, compared with one-tenth of white men.

Hispanics show less difference between metropolitan and nonmetropolitan income levels than do the major racial groups. Hispanic median nonmetropolitan household income in 1979 ($11,595) was 16 percent less than that of metropolitan Hispanics. By comparison, median white nonmetropolitan household income was 23 percent below that of metropolitan whites, and the difference for blacks was 30 percent. A major part of the explanation for this pattern may be the low educational attainment of metropolitan Hispanics, fewer than half of whom were high school graduates. Many are relatively recent immigrants.

Occupation and Income

As a means of judging the comparative earnings of various occupations in metropolitan and nonmetropolitan settings, median earnings for 1979 were calculated for selected occupations for persons employed full-time year-round in that year (Table 11.7).[4] For nonmetropolitan men, the most highly paid jobs of those examined were (in order) extractive occupations, managerial and professional work, precision production work (mechanics, craftsmen, etc.), and technical and related positions (health technicians, draftsmen, computer programmers, etc.). Note that although two of these are white collar groups that typically entail a college education, the other two are generally regarded as blue collar occupations involving nonacademic skills. All of the categories noted paid annual median earnings of above $16,000.

Nonmetropolitan precision production workers earned 90 percent as much as their metropolitan counterparts. They enjoyed comparatively high paid work without much of a wage differential associated with their rural and small town location. Although the large managerial and professional group had the second best nonmetropolitan occupational earnings, it had nearly the poorest ratio of parity with metropolitan men of the same broad occupation status (81 percent). There is a wide range of managerial and professional positions. Many of those with the highest levels of responsibility or specialization are located in metropolitan centers (such as corporate executives, and medical and legal specialists), so it is not surprising that the rewards clearly favor the metropolitan group.

Extractive workers (miners, basically) are not a large group compared with most of the others shown, numbering only about 150,000 full-time. But, with their top wages, lack of any nonmetropolitan discount in pay scale, and predominantly rural and small town location, they have been an important source of nonmetropolitan income. The growth of this group in the 1970s contributed to the "rural turnaround," and conversely, the major decline in mining employment thereafter has had a disproportionately adverse effect on nonmetropolitan conditions in the 1980s.

The poorest paid full-time occupations for nonmetropolitan men were farm labor, food service and preparation, health services (excluding professionals), and farm operators. The very low income of farm workers ($8,080) is alleviated to some extent by the fact that most of the regular workers are believed to receive food and lodging or family housing in addition. Nonmetropolitan food workers made over 90 percent as much money as those doing the same work in metropolitan areas, but this is more a commentary on the low pay of metropolitan food workers than on the merits of such work elsewhere. The low median income of farm operators occurred despite the fact that 1979 was to many farmers the

[4]The fit between income and occupation here is not perfect. Income is from all wage, salary, and self-employment earnings in 1979 whereas occupation is the principal occupation during the census week in April of 1980 or, if not employed then, the last occupation held.

TABLE 11.7

Median Income from Earnings for Full-Time Year-Round Workers in Selected Occupations by Sex and Residence, 1979[a]

Sex and Occupation	Total	Metropolitan	Nonmetropolitan	Ratio Nonmetropolitan/ Metropolitan
Male				
All occupations	$17,330	$18,220	$14,780	.81
Managerial and professional	22,380	23,260	18,780	.81
Technical and related	18,320	18,660	16,130	.86
Sales	17,930	18,630	15,270	.82
Administrative support	16,940	17,150	15,890	.93
Protective services	16,950	17,150	13,680	.80
Food preparation and service	9,280	9,410	8,520	.91
Health service occupations	10,470	10,740	9,280	.91
Household, cleaning, and building services	11,220	11,510	10,450	.86
Farm operators and managers	10,410	11,550	10,110	.88
Other farm occupations	8,420	9,010	8,080	.90
Mechanics and repairers	16,580	17,370	14,740	.85
Construction trades	16,920	17,830	15,060	.84
Extractive occupations	20,480	20,610	20,430	.99
Precision products occupations	18,390	18,340	16,350	.89
Machine operators and tenders	15,140	15,210	13,490	.89
Motor vehicle operators	15,670	16,410	13,840	.84
Other transport and moving equipment operators	17,250	17,980	15,720	.87
Handlers, helpers, laborers	12,470	13,090	11,060	.84
Female				
All occupations	10,080	10,500	8,450	.80
Managerial and professional	13,420	13,910	11,400	.82
Technical and related	11,560	12,090	9,840	.81
Sales	8,810	9,360	7,100	.76
Administrative support	10,040	10,300	8,690	.84
Food preparation and service	6,560	6,740	6,140	.91
Health service occupations	7,990	8,440	6,920	.82
Household, cleaning, and building services	6,800	7,040	6,180	.88
Personal services	7,560	7,880	6,620	.84
Farm operators and managers	4,380	4,860	4,210	.87
Other farm occupations	6,690	6,980	6,470	.93
Precision prod. occupations	10,080	10,480	8,740	.83
Machine operators and tenders	8,670	9,080	7,960	.88
Motor vehicle operators	8,110	9,950	8,200	.86
Handlers, helpers, laborers	8,870	9,340	7,920	.85

[a]Occupation is that of chief job activity in the last week of March 1980; earnings are all wage, salary, and self-employment income in 1979. Persons included worked 50 or more weeks and 35 or more hours per week. Those with occupations employing comparatively small numbers of people are excluded from the list but included in the total.

last good farm year before the agricultural recession of the 1980s and despite the widespread supplementation of farm earnings by off-farm work. Farm operator income is somewhat difficult to compare with wage and salary income, for the cost of housing may be subsumed in the cost of farm ownership and there are often opportunities for home production of some food items. However, it must be remembered that farmers do not have benefit packages to pay for insurance, vacation time, or sick leave. There are some prosperous farmers, but the exodus of recent years makes it clear that monetary returns to farming have been widely inadequate. The occupation group in which nonmetropolitan men took the largest relative discount in earnings was protective services. Such workers—police, guards, and firemen—had only 80 percent of the income in nonmetropolitan areas as they did in metropolitan places. In all, full-time year-round male workers, who are usually the main household wage earners, earned anywhere from 80 to 99 percent of the earnings received by metropolitan counterparts in the eighteen occupations examined.

Among nonmetropolitan women, the leading four occupations in earnings for those working full-time year-round were the same as for men, with the substitution of administrative support positions (primarily secretarial, clerical, and accounting) for extractive occupations, in which few women work. The comparatively high rank of administrative support jobs is important because it is still the largest single source of work for nonmetropolitan women. However, the average earnings in such work were 45 percent below those of nonmetropolitan men in the same general category. A higher percentage of the men were supervisors and very few were secretaries. The ratios of nonmetropolitan to metropolitan earnings are fairly similar to those for men in most occupations but with earnings for women always far below those for men. Three of the four most poorly paid nonmetropolitan occupations for women were ones in which their numbers were relatively small—farm operation, farm labor, and household, cleaning, and building services. The fourth was more significant—food preparation and service. Relative to women living in metropolitan areas, nonmetropolitan women accepted the widest earnings differential if they worked as sales clerks or representatives (including real estate), where their full-time earnings were only 76 percent of those received by such women in metropolitan places.

Industry and Income

When nonmetropolitan employment is viewed industrially, the highest paid industry using 100,000 or more full-time year-round men

TABLE 11.8

Median Income from Earnings for Full-Time Year-Round Workers in Selected Industries by Sex and Residence, 1979[a]

Sex and Industry	Metropolitan	Nonmetropolitan	Ratio Nonmetropolitan/ Metropolitan
Male			
All industries	$18,220	$14,780	.81
Agriculture	10,880	9,560	.88
Coal mining	22,300	22,050	.99
Other mining	21,400	18,860	.88
Construction	17,360	13,810	.80
Manufacturing			
Food and kindred	17,460	14,410	.83
Textile mill products	13,180	12,100	.92
Paper, etc.	18,210	18,820	1.03
Miscellaneous nondurables	19,380	16,470	.85
Logging	16,250	12,570	.77
Sawmills, etc.	15,700	14,540	.93
Wood buildings, furniture, etc.	13,600	11,280	.83
Stone, glass, concrete	17,801	15,430	.87
Metal industry and machinery, except electrical	19,080	16,170	.85
Electrical machinery	19,390	15,050	.78
Transport equipment	21,060	16,510	.78
Rail, truck, and water transport	20,370	18,840	.92
Other transportation and communication	20,370	18,840	.92
Utilities and sanitation services	19,220	16,960	.88
Wholesale trade	18,010	14,700	.82
General merchandise apparel and drug	15,670	14,730	.94
Grocery, dairy, and bakery	16,650	13,810	.83
Eating and drinking places	10,950	10,490	.96
All other retail trade	15,160	12,660	.84
Financial, insurance, real estate, and business services	19,010	17,300	.91
Repair services	13,670	11,050	.81
Entertainment and recreation	13,920	10,890	.78
Health services	17,030	14,750	.87
Education and social services	16,270	14,000	.86
Legal, engineering, and other professional services	24,310	20,350	.84
Public administration	19,380	15,420	.80

TABLE 11.8 *(continued)*

Sex and Industry	Metropolitan	Nonmetropolitan	Ratio Nonmetropolitan/ Metropolitan
Female			
All industries	10,500	8,450	.80
Agriculture	7,360	6,010	.82
Manufacturing			
Textile mill products	8,900	8,600	.97
Apparel, etc.	7,680	6,900	.90
Miscellaneous, nondurables	10,950	8,820	.81
Metal industry and machinery except electrical	11,360	10,060	.89
Electrical machinery	10,930	9,100	.83
Other transportation and communication	14,450	12,350	.85
General merchandise apparel and drug	8,550	6,900	.81
Grocery, dairy, and bakery	10,140	7,510	.74
Eating and drinking places	6,950	5,940	.85
All other retail trade	9,270	7,630	.82
Financial, insurance, real estate, and business services	10,280	8,530	.83
Personal services	7,150	6,140	.86
Health services	17,740	8,460	.79
Education and social services	10,930	9,600	.88
Public administration	11,990	10,020	.84

[a]Industry is the group of the chief job activity in the last week of March 1980; earnings are all wage, salary, and self-employment income in 1979. Persons included worked 50 or more weeks and 35 or more hours per week. Industries employing comparatively small numbers of people are excluded from the list but included in the total.

was coal mining, with such men having a median income from earnings of $22,050 in 1979 (Table 11.8). The industry is notorious for strikes, labor violence, pictures of grime-faced miners, victims of black lung disease, and images of poverty—all associated with the southern Appalachian coal fields. But much of the industry has shifted elsewhere to well-paid, above ground operations, and even in the Appalachian area incomes are good when the work is uninterrupted. Jobs in legal, engineering, and miscellaneous professional services comprised the only other industrial group in which full-time year-round male earnings topped $20,000. Several industries offered earnings that clustered at nearly $19,000. These were mining other than coal; rail, truck, and water transportation; paper and allied products manufacturing; other transportation (air, pipelines); and communications. In each of the six well-paid industries listed above except for legal, engineering, and miscellaneous professional services, the nonmetropolitan earnings levels were at least 88 percent of those for the same groups in metropolitan areas. Thus work in these industries did not entail any wage disadvantage for men in nonmetropolitan locations, especially when allowance is made for cost of living differences. Earnings for men in nonmetropolitan paper and allied products work actually were slightly higher than those elsewhere, probably because of a greater proportion in paper and pulp mill work, rather than the lower paid fabricated products work that has a more metropolitan concentration.

The most poorly rewarded of nonmetropolitan industries for men was agriculture, the only one in which median earnings ($9,560) were below $10,000. At 88 percent of the metropolitan level, these earnings were not disparately below those in metropolitan agriculture. The problem for the nonmetropolitan economy, however, is that agriculture is still a major source of employment of men (10% of the total), despite the prolonged drop in farm jobs that has occurred. Thus the low returns to farming disproportionately affect overall nonmetropolitan income. Three other industries yielded incomes of less than $12,000 for male workers: eating and drinking places ($10,490), repair services ($11,050), and the manufacture of wood buildings, furniture, and miscellaneous wood products ($11,280). Note the major contrast between the earnings of the paper and allied products part of the wood products industry and that of wood buildings, furniture, and miscellaneous.

In comparison with metropolitan earnings levels, the lowest relative nonmetropolitan incomes for men come from manufacture of electrical machinery, transportation equipment, logging, entertainment and recreation, construction, and public administration. All of these showed income from earnings of less than 80 percent than found in the same industries in metropolitan areas. Three of these six groups yielded incomes higher than the overall nonmetropolitan median, however, and thus bolstered the economy despite the discount from metropolitan earnings that work in them entailed.

Fewer than half as many nonmetropolitan women as men worked full-time year-round, and thus they did not have significant numbers in as many industries. Their earnings were highest in "other transportation" and communications ($12,350), metal industries manufacturing ($10,060), and public administration ($10,020). Their highest paid industries exceeded only a few of the lowest paid for men in earnings. Women in health services, which is by far the leading single source of work for nonmetropolitan women among the industries examined, had full-time year-round earnings of only $8,460, more than 20 percent below those of metropolitan women in the same industry. Lowest earnings were obtained in eating and drinking places, agriculture, and personal services (all around $6,000). Only one industry—textile mill products—provided incomes for women that were more than 90 percent those of metropolitan women in the same industry.

Parameters and Varieties of Rural Poverty

Rural and small town poverty has a variety of forms, reflecting the diversity of conditions that lead to inadequate income and affect metropolitan and nonmetropolitan areas differently. In this section, we consider how this variety manifests itself and where it is found. From the standpoint of widespread use, the measurement of poverty has surely been one of the most successful statistical concepts introduced into twentieth century American social science. However, both because of spatial differences in the cost of living and changes over time in the provision of noncash benefits to those in need, the official income-based measure of poverty has its limitations. In one sense the poverty rate is neither fish nor fowl. By being based on all cash income received it does not reflect the full number of people who would be poor without public income support. On the other hand, it does not reflect all whose poverty status is alleviated by noncash benefits, such as food stamps, Medicare/Medicaid, or housing subsidies. Nevertheless, it is still a very useful general indicator of the extent and degree of seriously inadequate incomes.

Basically, to be in "poverty" is, in federal statistical terms, to live in a family or other household unit where the annual level of income is less than three times the cost of an economy food budget for that unit. This amount is adjusted annually for changes in the Consumer Price Index as a means of obtaining comparability of results over time. In 1979, a family of four persons that included two children under 18 years was deemed in poverty if its income was less than $7,356; in 1986 the comparable standard was $11,203.

The poverty concept was not originated until 1964, but an application of it to the 1960 census data showed 33.2 percent of the nonmetropolitan population to be poor, based on 1959 income, a rate more than double that of 15.3 percent in the metropolitan population (Figure 11.1). At that time, more than half of the poor lived in nonmetropolitan areas.

FIGURE 11.1

Percentage of Population Below Poverty Level by Residence, 1959–1986

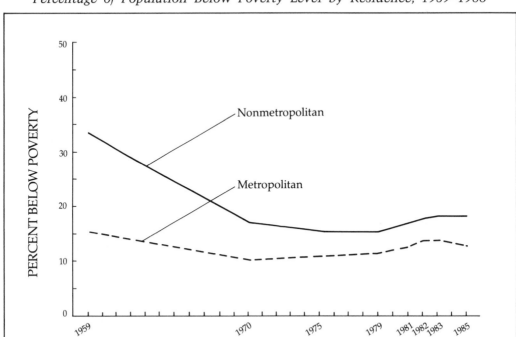

SOURCE: Current Population Reports, P-60, No. 147.

NOTE: Comparison of 1983 and 1985 data is affected by sample redesign.

By 1969, the rates had dropped to 19.2 and 11.2 percent, respectively, in response to improved economic conditions, increased transfer payments, and a lower birthrate. The improvement was major in both groups, but greatest for nonmetropolitan residents.

In the next decade, nonmetropolitan poverty dropped somewhat further, to 15.4 percent in 1979, but there was no reduction in the metropolitan poverty rate, which at 11.4 percent was nominally higher than in 1969. In metropolitan areas, the increasing proportion of black and other disadvantaged populations and of children living in female-headed households stymied further progress in poverty reduction, as did the rise in nonfamily households, which have above average poverty. Nonmetropolitan areas, however, were either unaffected or less affected by these factors and had a decade of comparatively good economic development.

356

TABLE 11.9

Poverty Rates (percentage in poverty) of the Population by Residence, 1969, 1979[a]

		Metropolitan			Nonmetropolitan		
Year	Total	Total	Urban	Rural	Total	Urban	Rural
1979	12.4	11.4	11.7	9.3	15.4	14.8	15.8
1969	13.7	11.2	11.2	11.2	19.2	16.1	21.3

[a]Rates for 1969 and 1979 are reasonably but not fully comparable. The definition of poverty among farm residents was broadened in 1979, serving to raise the 1979 rates somewhat in rural areas. Metropolitan–nonmetropolitan and rural–urban designations are as the time of each census.

In 1964, 25 percent of the rural population was poor, a rate two-thirds higher than that of 14.8 percent in urban areas.[5] The 1970 census showed 1969 rural and urban poverty rates of 18.4 and 12.0 percent, a substantial drop for a short period. By 1979, however, the urban poverty rate (12.1) had no further reduction, but rural poverty fell to 13.2 percent. Thus by this year there was only a minor difference remaining between urban and rural poverty, in contrast with the somewhat wider difference between metropolitan and nonmetropolitan poverty rates—11.7 and 15.4 percent. This pattern is explained by the fact that the 40 percent of the rural population that lives within the boundaries of metropolitan areas is more consistently prosperous than any other residential sector, and is an increasingly large fraction of the total rural population. The metropolitan rural poverty rate in 1979 was only 9.3 percent (Table 11.9). The nonmetropolitan rural poverty rate of 15.8 percent was 1.7 times as high. Within the total nonmetropolitan population there was only minor difference between urban and rural poverty. Rural people in metropolitan settings are less subject to inadequate income than are urban residents in nonmetropolitan locations.

Geography of Poverty

A county map of high nonmetropolitan poverty rates in 1979 subdivides rather readily into five major groups and circumstances.

1. There is a broad sweep of poor counties in the Southern Coastal Plain, extending from southeastern Virginia to northern Florida, then westward to eastern Texas as well as northward through the Mississippi Delta into southeastern Missouri (Figure 11.2). Within this large area of about 300 counties it is the condition of the black population that pro-

[5]President's National Advisory Commission on Rural Poverty (1967).

FIGURE 11.2

Ethnocultural Character of High Poverty Areas, 1980

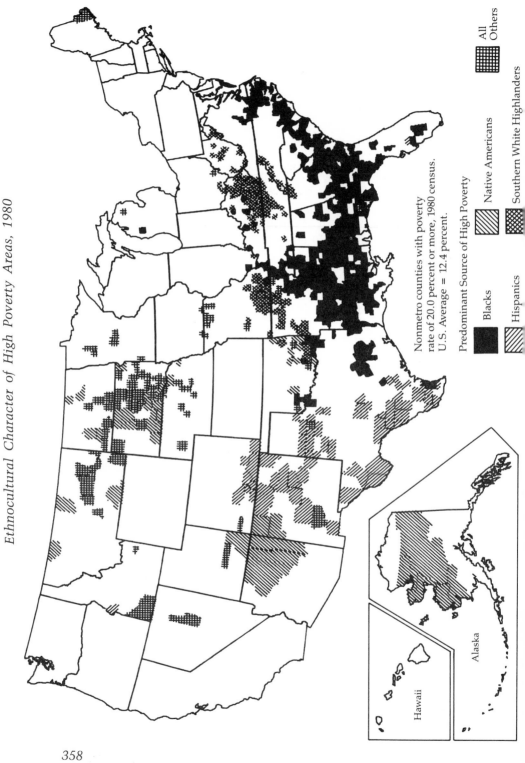

Nonmetro counties with poverty
rate of 20.0 percent or more, 1980 census.
U.S. Average = 12.4 percent.

Predominant Source of High Poverty

Blacks

Hispanics

Native Americans

Southern White Highlanders

All
Others

Hawaii

Alaska

duces the high poverty rates, except in about forty somewhat dispersed counties where the white population also has an incidence of poverty above 20 percent. The area represents the heart of the old agricultural South—once mostly dependent on cotton—into which blacks were brought as slave farm workers and where they remained in later generations. Despite much progress in measures that reduce poverty, such as better education and employment, public assistance, and the onset of lower childbearing, the level of black poverty in this region was rarely as low as 30 percent in the 1980 Census. In more than ninety counties of this region over half of the black residents had poverty level money incomes, including any public assistance. Black poverty rates are especially high where the percentage of blacks in the total population is high. It is noticeable that in the Piedmont South, which has the highest extent of industrialization, not a single county has a black poverty rate as high as 50 percent and rates of 20 to 30 percent (which look poor for whites, but which are among the best for blacks) are common.

2. Two groupings of counties reflect the long-established high incidence of poverty among white people in the highland South. The area of most intense and entrenched poverty consists of the Cumberland Plateau and Highland Rim sections of eastern Kentucky and Tennessee, and smaller areas of Virginia, West Virginia, and southern Ohio. West of the Mississippi, much of the Ozark Plateau and Ouachita Mountains country of Missouri, Arkansas, and Oklahoma has continued to experience relatively high poverty as well. Neither of the two highland regions ever had a golden era of prosperity. Neither was well suited to commercial agriculture, although both were attractive in the settlement period to poorer whites seeking free or cheap land in an environment conducive to subsistence living and free of the competition of slavery. The relatively high material poverty, low education, isolation, and cultural distinctiveness of these areas were already recognized in the nineteenth century. With the exception of coal mining in parts of Appalachia and some metal mining in the Ozarks, the highland areas lacked a modern economy going into the post–World War II years. Major improvements have since been made in highways, schools, medical facilities, and other infrastructure. Dam reservoirs have brought major recreation and retirement development and there has been some acquisition of manufacturing employment. In consequence, poverty rates have greatly diminished, but they remain well above the national average.

Two characteristics that contribute to the frequent occurrence of poverty in the southern highlands are low education and high rates of work-preventing health disability. Lack of a high school education among the middle-aged and older adults of the highlands is commonplace, but more surprising and ominous for the future welfare of these areas is the continued high rate of failure to finish high school among the young. Nationally in 1980, 25 percent of the nonmetropolitan white population 18–24 years old had not completed four years of high school. But, in the southern coal fields and some adjoining areas of Tennessee and southern Kentucky, more than 40 percent had failed to finish high school. In some counties the dropouts were over half of the young adult population, a rate rarely seen elsewhere. Clearly the values and conditions that impel and permit young people to obtain a minimally standard education are still well below national norms in these areas. Early outmovement of many young adults who finished high school probably contributes to the situation but by no means explains it, for the area also had very high rates of teenagers 16–19 years old who were not in school and had not finished high school. Only a small percentage of these teenage dropouts had jobs—less than 20 percent. The continued prevalence of low levels of education among the young also affects the Ozark–Ouachita area, although not to the degree found in the Appalachian core.

In nonmetropolitan America as a whole, 5.5 percent of all noninstitutionalized people 16–64 years of age report themselves as unable to work because of a disability—somewhat higher than the metropolitan rate of 4.0 percent. However, in the southern highlands these rates are usually 10 percent and above. The work-preventing disability rate in the southern coal fields is 13 percent, but rates at the 10 percent or higher level are common in nonmining counties as well. There are additional people who report a work-limiting health condition even though they are employed. But both of the two southern highland regions consistently show a higher proportion of the people reporting any work-limiting health condition as being prevented from working by the condition. The comparatively high incidence of disability among people of working age in southern Appalachia and the Ozark–Ouachita region adds to the burden of dependency and poverty and limits the effectiveness of economic development solutions alone to the income problems of these chronically distressed areas.

Although lifetime fertility is no longer high in most of these counties (as discussed in Chapter 7), childbearing has continued to start at young ages. Thus many counties had 500 or more children ever born per 1,000 women 15–24 years old, compared with a national nonmetropolitan average of 350. This raises poverty rates by enlarging family size before parents have approached their maximum earning capacity.

Another common poverty-related feature of both the Appalachian core and the Ozark–Ouachita highlands is a relatively low rate of labor force participation by men of prime working age, 25–54 years old. In the nation as a whole, only 7.5 percent of men this age were not in the labor force in 1980. However, in the southern highland areas referred to, rates of two and three times this percentage were typical. In the coal counties, disability from "black lung" or mining accidents has contributed to the pattern, but this does not explain the situation in the Ozark–Ouachita area or other noncoal counties which also have high rates of nonworkers and self-reported inability to work. Despite the major improvements in the southern highlands in transportation, health facilities, and education, in the last quarter-century (including the heavy infusion of money into Appalachia through the Appalachican Regional Commission), these regions remain distinctly different from any other rural areas whose population is almost entirely non-Hispanic white. They continue to rank high on a variety of measures of social disadvantage that make solutions to income problems lengthy, complex, and difficult.

3. A third area with high nonmetropolitan poverty includes most of the Rio Grande Valley, from southern Colorado to the Gulf of Mexico, plus adjoining counties of south Texas, the west Texas plains, and eastern New Mexico that have majorities or large minorities of Hispanic Americans. This includes the county with the highest official poverty rate in the entire country—Starr County, Texas (54 percent). The great majority of this population is native-born American of Mexican origin. The Mexican-born minority reaches 20 percent of the Hispanic total in some places along the international border but is as low as 1 percent in the more northern sections where Hispanic presence is very old without recent replenishment. Some of the Hispanic settlement region is very thinly inhabited, suited for little except ranching. Other parts have intensive irrigated farming. Here and there one finds oil activity or work servicing retired populations.

In this approximately 70-county area, Hispanic poverty rates ranged from the upper 20s to more than 50 percent. In about a dozen cases Anglo-white rates also exceeded 20 percent, but otherwise it was Hispanic poverty that gave the counties their abnormally high rates. The contrast between the poverty rates of Hispanics and those of Anglo-whites was consistently greatest in Texas. In that state, whether in the more recently settled Plains farming areas, where Hispanics have become a significant minority, or in the Rio Grande country, where Hispanics are typically the majority of the population, the economic disparity between Hispanics and Anglo-whites is strong. Poverty rates for Hispanics are typically three times those for Anglo-whites. As noted elsewhere in the chapter, poverty rates in Texas tend to be high relative to available per capita income. Hispanics generally do not share in the self-employment or investment income that more of the Anglo-whites have. In northern New Mexico and southern Colorado, on the other hand, there is less general wealth, but poverty rates for Hispanics are usually well below those in Texas. Although they are still at what would be deemed high levels—say 25 to 39 percent—poverty rates in northern New Mexico and southern Colorado are normally less than double the rates for Anglo-whites. The economic class differences between Hispanics and Anglo-whites are distinctly less apparent and serious here than in Texas.

4. Areas of high poverty in the Four Corners region of the Southwest and in parts of the northern Plains in the Dakotas and Montana reflect the low income of many Indian families. The southwestern area is numerically dominated by the Navajo but also includes the Hopi, Pueblo, and Zuni. These people have clung tenaciously to the native language, with over 90 percent using it at home in 1980. But formal educational levels are low, with fewer than three-eighths being high school graduates. Despite the development of some tribally owned mineral wealth, labor force participation rates among southwestern Indians are low, both full-time and part-time unemployment are high, and poverty-level incomes are the lot of nearly half of the people, given the large families and limited incomes. The contrast between white and Indian economic status is very high.

The Sioux have been much more receptive to English, with three-fifths speaking no other language at home. Their educational attainment is only modestly above that of the Navajo and their neighbors, however. The precarious income and employment situation of the reservation Sioux can be illustrated by data for Shannon County, South Dakota, where one-third of their population is located. Here only 55 percent and 39 percent of the male and female populations of labor force age were in the labor force, compared with a national norm of 75 and 50 percent. Of the people employed in the prior year, just 47 percent of the males and 40 percent of the females had worked for 50 weeks or more, compared with national averages of 55 and 51 percent, respectively. There was so little private work available either on the reservation or within commuting distance that almost four-fifths of all workers (78 percent) were employed by government. Nationally, 17 percent of workers were employed by government.

5. In the northern Plains, a number of agricultural counties had high poverty rates in 1979. These were most numerous in South Dakota, but they extended into North Dakota, Montana, and Nebraska. The population is almost all white. In one sense the poverty status of these counties was different from that of the other four types discussed above, for the state of their economy varies with the economic condition of farming and the poverty is not that of a chronically poor region or disadvantaged ethnic minority. In a good year for grain and cattle none of them might be included on a poverty map. However, this is one

of the most frequently troubled parts of the farm belt and it shows up in a somewhat more limited way in the 1969 poverty data. Droughts have been frequent and productivity marginal relative to costs.

Because the area has many self-employed farmers, it has high exposure to absolute losses of income, and not merely low income. Therefore, the average family income deficit for those in poverty is large. The area thus stands out more prominently on a map of counties with relatively high percentages of people in severe poverty (income less than three-fourths of the poverty level) than it does on a map of general poverty. But the area does not suffer from such poverty-inducing conditions as low education among the young, large numbers of female-headed households with children, or high incidence of work-preventing health disability.

Lower Limits of Poverty

Although wide disparities in poverty rates still exist among nonmetropolitan areas, there was substantial convergence and reduction in these differences during the 1970s. In general, in that period the higher an area's initial poverty rate, the greater the relative as well as absolute reduction that occurred. With most high poverty areas in the South, this certainly resulted in part from the widespread economic development of the Sunbelt during this time, as well as the major decline in poverty among the elderly with the growth of transfer incomes, and the further outmovement of rural low income blacks to metropolitan areas.

It has proved very difficult to reduce poverty levels below about 9 percent in any widespread way. It might be unduly pessimistic to characterize this level as an irreducible minimum, but in the 1970s when much rural progress was being made, the 3 percent of nonmetropolitan counties that began the decade with poverty rates of less than 9 percent were as likely to experience increased poverty rates by 1980 as they were to have declines. This was in sharp contrast to the trend among counties with even moderately higher initial rates.[6]

Empirically, at less than 9 percent poverty, we seem to encounter conditions in which the poor are largely people with personal characteristics or misfortunes—such as mental or physical disability, widowhood, or abandonment by spouse—that have prevented them from having a normal income. Transfer payments may be the main public approach to helping them. The state of the local economy may have little to do with their problem or its solution. Higher levels of poverty,

[6]Elo and Beale (1985).

however, are more likely to imply systematic conditions of low economic opportunity (lack of jobs, low wage or seasonal work), or long-standing social and cultural impediments to income earning (such as racial discrimination), or entrenched patterns of poverty-inducing behavior (for example, large families, early and out-of-wedlock childbearing, low regard for education). Many programs have been undertaken to reduce the structural, social, or economic impediments to financial self-support, although the problem of female-headed households with minor children continues to seem intractable. In general, the only nonmetropolitan counties with poverty rates of less than 9 percent are those with concentrations of nonelderly white people in well-paid jobs. These include some mining and resort areas of the Mountain West, several state capitals, a number of the wealthiest midwestern farm areas (in a good farming year), and some northern industrial centers that have become stagnant in growth but which by 1980 still retained adequate, well-distributed incomes.

The total nonmetropolitan poverty rate was 15.4 percent in 1980, although 9 percent may be accepted as the lowest level now attainable before the chance of a regressive subsequent increase becomes just as likely as a further decline. Consequently, about two-fifths of nonmetropolitan poverty (representing the difference between 15.4 and 9 percent) was potentially amenable to broad approaches aimed at reducing the prevalence of inadequate income among people of working age.

The density of nonmetropolitan poor people per square mile is basically the same in the thickly settled industrial states from New Hampshire to Indiana as it is in the more thinly settled Lower South. In some cases it is even marginally higher. For example, Ohio and Pennsylvania averaged 10.1 and 9.2 poor persons per nonmetropolitan square mile in 1980, while the averages in Louisiana and Alabama were 9.6 and 9.0, respectively. But these areas differ widely in the proportion of people with low income and, to a lesser extent, in the typical amount of income deficiency per poor family. Nationally, the density of the nonmetropolitan poverty population is highest in two areas of the Upper South—the coal fields of eastern Kentucky and the tobacco country of the North Carolina central coastal plain, where in both instances the average was above 20 persons per square mile.

Age, Sex, and Poverty

Higher nonmetropolitan than metropolitan poverty rates affect both sexes at each age group (Figure 11.3). For children under 5 there is only about 2 percentage points difference between metropolitan and nonmet-

FIGURE 11.3

Poverty by Age, Sex, and Residence, 1979

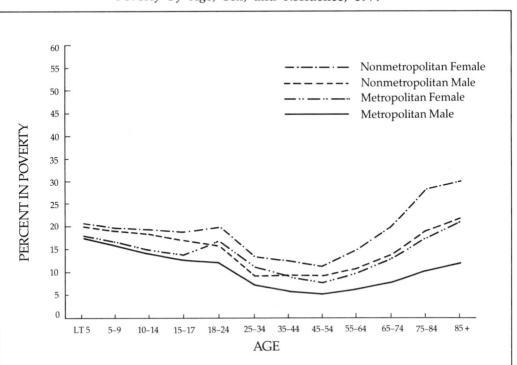

ropolitan poverty. This widens somewhat for older children (through 15–17 years), a fact consistent with the failure of nonmetropolitan parental-age income levels to increase as rapidly as metropolitan levels as people advance into middle age. The metropolitan–nonmetropolitan gaps then narrow again for young adults, but progressively widen after middle age, until they reach 9 and 10 points difference in old age, for each sex. Both metropolitan and nonmetropolitan poverty turn upward momentarily for women at ages 18–24. This is largely produced by the low levels of income received by many college students. It is not uncommon in nonmetropolitan counties with state universities to find poverty rates of 40 percent or more among nonelderly unrelated individuals. This effect is present for males as well, and is evident on a graph of poverty by sex and age for whites. However, it is essentially offset for males by the major reduction of poverty found among young black men as they leave poor female-headed households. Some reduction of poverty is found for 18–24-year-old black women as well, but not nearly as much as for men, given the fact that many of the women move from childhood poverty to the poverty of becoming mothers of young children without a spouse.

Within the nonmetropolitan population, the widest range in poverty by age is that between women aged 45–54 and men aged 25–44, on the one hand, and persons of either sex who are 85 and over, on the other. Despite the progress that has been made in reducing poverty among the elderly, women of advanced age had two-and-a-half times the incidence of poverty as did those of middle age, and men of the same older age incurred poverty level income more than twice as often as did men aged 25–34. Relative differences of this general nature are also found in the metropolitan population but do not reach such high levels for the older people.

Among blacks, poverty rates for nonmetropolitan children under 18 run consistently between 45 and 50 percent, and unlike metropolitan children show no reduction by ages 15–17 (Figure 11.4). As a result, nonmetropolitan–metropolitan disparities in income are greatest for high school age children, and then, at a much later stage of life, are also large for elderly people. By age, nonmetropolitan black poverty rates reach their lowest level among men 25–34 years of age, where they were 22 percent in 1979. The poverty of black nonmetropolitan women was never less than 32 percent, the value at ages 25–34.

In neither the white nor the black nonmetropolitan populations has the vaunted improvement in income levels of the elderly brought poverty rates of older women below those of children. This is a major difference in the patterns of metropolitan and nonmetropolitan poverty. For example, for all nonmetropolitan women 75 years old and over, the poverty rate was over 28 percent, compared with the highest rate for female children of about 21 percent. In contrast, metropolitan men 75 and over had a rate of less than 10 percent compared with 18 percent for metropolitan male children under 5. In short, the poverty condition of children is worse than that of older people as a whole in metropolitan areas, but not in the nonmetropolitan setting.

It is interesting to note that even among children poverty rates are always higher for females than males, regardless of residence. The differences are small for children (typically 1 to 2 percentage points) but consistently present. It may be that in cases of marital separation or divorce a somewhat higher percentage of girls than boys live with their mothers, and thus, on average, in a lower income situation.

In a national longitudinal study of poverty, Ross and Morrissey distinguished between families temporarily poor and persistently poor.[7]

[7]Ross and Morrissey (1986).

FIGURE 11.4

Poverty by Race, Sex, Age, and Residence, 1979

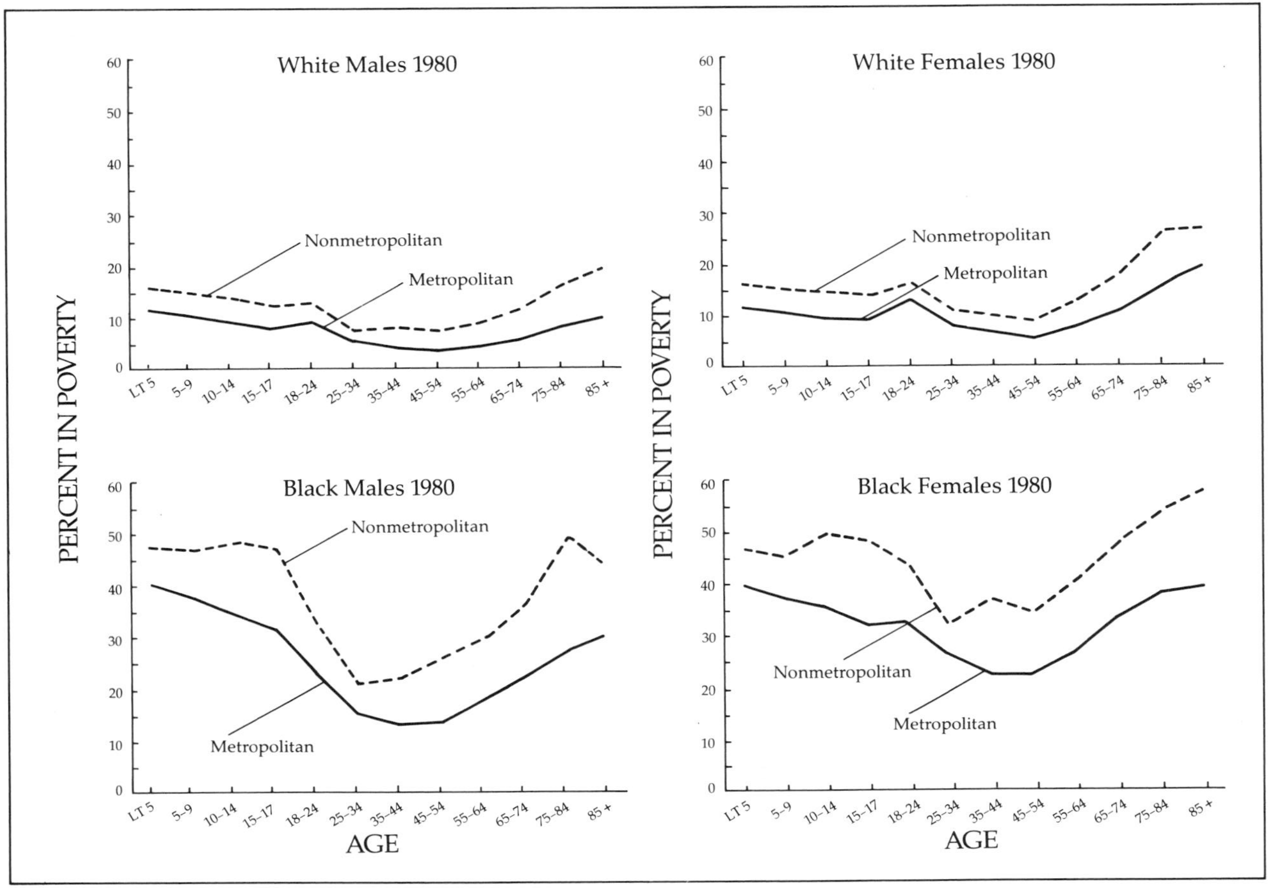

Those with temporary poverty were defined as having poverty level income not more than two years in the five-year period studied (1978–1982). Persistently poor families experienced this condition in at least three of the five years. When characterized this way, those who were persistently poor were three-eighths of the total nonmetropolitan poor, a proportion similar to that in metropolitan areas. The temporarily poor were much more likely to be in husband-wife families, whereas poor families headed by women, blacks, or elderly people most commonly had persistent poverty.

The Elderly

Although the poverty rate among the nonmetropolitan population 65 years old and over was 20.5 percent in the 1980 census, and thus well above the average of 15.4 percent for all nonmetropolitan people, the rate had dropped by over one-third from its level of 31.5 percent in the 1970 census. The condition of the low-income elderly, therefore, is better relative to the general nonmetropolitan population than it was earlier. The role of Social Security income in preventing poverty among the elderly has become substantial. In 1979, almost 1.0 million nonmetropolitan families headed by persons 60 years old and over were not in poverty but would have been without their income from Social Security (Table 11.10). They amounted to one-fourth of all nonmetropolitan fam-

TABLE 11.10

Families with Householder 60 Years and Over
by Receipt of Social Security Income (SSI), Poverty Status, and Residence, 1979

			Not in Poverty			
			With SSI		Without SSI	
	In Poverty		Would be in Poverty Without SSI	Not in Poverty Without SSI		
Residence	With SSI	Without SSI				Total
Families (000s)						
Metropolitan	404	196	1,937	4,360	2,510	9,407
Nonmetropolitan	363	120	995	1,556	792	3,826
Percentage Distribution						
Metropolitan	4.3	2.1	20.6	46.3	26.7	100.0
Nonmetropolitan	9.5	3.1	26.0	40.7	20.7	100.0

ilies with a head of this age. In metropolitan areas, one-fifth of family heads of this age would have been in poverty without their Social Security pensions.

Notwithstanding the disproportionate improvement in the income of the elderly within the nonmetropolitan population in the 1970s, there is still a greater difference between the incomes of the elderly and nonelderly in rural and small town society than there is in metropolitan areas. In consequence, the nonmetropolitan poverty rate among persons 65 years and over was 1.4 times that of the nonelderly, whereas in metropolitan America the elderly had a poverty incidence only 1.1 times that of younger people. The most hopeful interpretation of this difference is that it evidences rapid income progress among young nonmetropolitan people. Whatever the cause, the elderly are more deprived and set apart in income from the rest of the population in nonmetropolitan America than they are elsewhere.

The extensive inmovement of older people into nonmetropolitan areas for retirement in recent decades has introduced a more affluent class of elderly into this population. Among nonmetropolitan residents 60 years old and over in 1980, 19.3 percent of those who had also been in nonmetropolitan areas in 1975 had poverty level incomes, but among the people of this age who had moved in from a metropolitan area in the same period the poverty rate was just 10.2 percent.[8] Furthermore, the incidence of poverty among the metropolitan inmigrants was not appreciably higher for the oldest of the retirees than it was for the younger ones, whereas among the longer-term nonmetropolitan elderly the incidence of poverty rose considerably with increased age.

Unemployment and Poverty

In both nonmetropolitan and metropolitan areas there is a strong association between unemployment and poverty. It would be strange to find it otherwise. Among nonmetropolitan families in which the householder worked 50 or more weeks in 1979 and usually 35 or more hours per week, only 5.4 percent had poverty-level incomes, compared with 25.2 percent in poverty where the householder did no work during the year (Table 11.11). (The latter group includes both persons voluntarily not employed, such as retired people, as well as those involuntarily out of work.) This is a wide disparity. Families without an employed householder in 1979 comprised 45 percent of all nonmetropolitan poverty families, compared with just 18 percent of those not in poverty. Even so, one of the distinguishing features of nonmetropolitan poverty is that

[8]Glasgow and Beale (1985).

TABLE 11.11

Family Poverty Rates (percentage in poverty) by Extent of Employment of Family Head, Type of Family, and Residence, 1979

Employment Status	All Families		Male Heads and Female Heads with Spouse		Female Head, No Spouse Present	
	Metro	Nonmetro	Metro	Nonmetro	Metro	Nonmetro
Full-time[a]	2.7	5.4	2.2	4.9	7.1	12.3
Part-time[b]	17.3	20.2	10.8	15.3	38.6	45.4
Not employed[c]	23.0	25.2	13.1	20.0	48.5	45.4

[a]Worked 50 or more weeks and 35 or more hours a week.
[b]Worked less than 50 weeks and/or less than 35 hours a week.
[c]Either not in the labor force or unemployed.

it is more common among families with a fully employed householder (5.4 percent) than is true in metropolitan areas (2.7 percent). Some 27 percent of nonmetropolitan poor families had a fully employed householder.

One objective of preparing a tabulation on poverty and employment was to assess the extent of poverty alleviation afforded by part-time employment of the head. The conclusion seems to be "very little." In every tabulation made, the poverty rate in families with a part-time employed householder (less than 50 weeks of full-time work) was much closer to that of unemployed householder families than to that of families whose heads worked year-round full-time. For nonmetropolitan families as a whole, those with a part-time worker householder showed a 20.2 percent incidence of poverty, four-fifths as high as that of unemployed householder families and four times as high as that of families with fully employed heads. Almost certainly, the families with householders working part-time would have had a lower average deficit of income than those with no work, but progression from no work to part-time work offered only modest reduction in formal poverty rates. This was true in metropolitan areas also.

This point is especially important for families headed by women with no spouse present, many of whom have minor children. Among these families, 25 percent had heads who worked part-time, whereas only 15 percent of heads of other families did so. Among the part-time worker female-headed families, 45 percent had poverty level income, which was the same rate found among the female-headed families in which the head did no work at all during the year (1979). To make the point is not to denigrate the sense of worth and social value that may derive from part-time work or to ignore the fact that such income makes a contribution to a family's budget. But, it is clear that access to part-time work has not been a solution for the poverty status of female-headed families.

Poverty and Work-Limiting Disability

In the 1980 census a question was asked as to whether each person had a physical, mental, or other health condition that had lasted for six or more months, and which either limited the kind or amount of work the person could do or prevented the person from working altogether. The answers are at least in part subjective, and people with similar conditions might respond differently. Even so, since people act on perceptions, the data have a social reality to them. For persons aged 16–64, work-limiting disability of any degree is somewhat more common among nonmetropolitan than among metropolitan men (11 percent vs. 8 percent), but there is no residential difference for women—9 percent in each case.

The question of concern here is the extent to which disability is associated with poverty. As shown in Table 11.12, poverty rates prove

TABLE 11.12

Percentage of Persons 16–64 in Poverty
by Disability Status, Sex, Race, and Residence, 1979

Disability Status and Sex	Total		Black	
	Metro	Nonmetro	Metro	Nonmetro
Total	9.5	13.0	22.6	33.7
No disability	8.7	11.7	20.8	31.4
Disability not preventing work	13.1	17.4	28.7	38.2
Disability preventing work	24.5	30.2	42.7	53.5
Males	7.8	11.2	17.9	28.2
No disability	7.1	10.0	16.4	26.0
Disability not preventing work	10.6	15.3	22.9	32.3
Disability preventing work	21.2	27.2	35.8	50.5
Females	11.2	14.6	26.5	38.2
No disability	10.3	13.2	24.4	36.0
Disability not preventing work	16.5	20.6	34.5	44.6
Disability preventing work	27.0	32.7	47.3	55.4

to differ substantially by disability status. Among nonmetropolitan people aged 16–64 they range from 11.7 percent for those reporting no disability, to 17.3 percent for those with a work-limiting condition, and 30.2 percent for those prevented from employment by their disability. Women consistently have somewhat higher poverty rates for each disability status (just as they do age-for-age or for other personal characteristics), and the nonmetropolitan poverty rates are higher than the metropolitan rates for each sex and disability group.

In the aggregate, persons with some degree of disability accounted for 19 percent of all nonmetropolitan persons in poverty at ages 16–64, whereas they were just 10 percent of the total nonmetropolitan population of that age. There was no difference between metropolitan and nonmetropolitan areas in the percentage of those in poverty having work-limiting disability conditions, but more severe work-preventing disability was characteristic of a somewhat higher percentage of adult nonmetropolitan poverty (13.1 percent) than of metropolitan poverty (10.4 percent).

Among nonmetropolitan black residents, poverty rates run approximately 20 percentage points higher at each disability status than for the population of all races. This means that poverty level incomes are found among more than half of adult blacks with a work-preventing disability, and that poverty rates among blacks with no disability are as high as those for persons of all races who are unable to work. The percentage of nonmetropolitan poor blacks reporting some disability is very similar to that found in the total nonmetropolitan population in poverty. However, because the adult nonmetropolitan black population is younger than nonmetropolitan adults as a whole, and disabilities are more common among older people, the extent of disability poverty might be higher for blacks than that of the total population on an age standardized basis.

Per Capita Income and Poverty Rate

Per capita income is a commonly used measure of income adequacy and is estimated annually for all counties. It is a mean, however, and areas can have identical per capita incomes while having substantially different poverty rates, because they differ in the distribution of income. One area may have a comparatively egalitarian distribution of income among its residents while another with the same per capita value has more extremes of wealth and poverty. One rarely finds areas with very high poverty rates having above average per capita income, or areas of very low per capita income that are nearly poverty free. But the variations between poverty and per capita income are significant and show some geographic patterns. To identify the areas where there is a marked lack of congruence between rankings on poverty and per capita income, nonmetropolitan counties were arrayed from highest to lowest on poverty rate and lowest to highest on per capita income from the 1980 census. In all counties shown on Figure 11.5 there was a difference of at least 400 ranks in either direction between the poverty rate and per capita income. (There are a total of 2,384 nonmetropolitan counties and county equivalents.)

Several subregion-sized areas are revealed in which there is low poverty in relation to the level of per capita income. One is in the West and clearly reflects most of the Mormon settlement area of Utah and eastern Idaho. Here, despite high birthrates and resultant large families (as discussed in Chapter 7), poverty rates are very low in comparison with per capita incomes. Indeed, in a majority of the Mormon area counties shown, there is a difference of at least 750 ranks on poverty and per capita income. Only four of these 30 counties have per capita incomes in the top half of all nonmetropolitan counties, but three fourths of the 30 have poverty rates that are in the lowest half of counties. There is a relative absence both of racial minorities that are commonly poor or of very wealthy people whose incomes would raise the mean income without reducing the incidence of poverty. The real (if difficult to describe) effect of the values and class structure common to Mormonism seems apparent from the abrupt way in which the existence of the low poverty rate in relation to per capita income ends as one looks at the areas that adjoin the Mormon country in any direction.

In a very different setting, there is a midwestern block of contiguous counties with low poverty in comparison with what might be expected from their per capita incomes. This group stretches across the Upper Peninsula of Michigan, the adjoining northern third of Wisconsin and into northeastern Minnesota, as well as some parts of the northern part of the Michigan Lower Peninsula. Here family size is more modest than in the Mormon area. Family income levels are not typically high, for the region has had a hard time for many decades in finding adequate paying year-around jobs to replace work that vanished with the end of the timber boom and the inexorable decline in metal mining. There is much summer recreation industry, but there are very high winter unemployment rates. However, available income is so distributed that in all but a few counties poverty rates are below the median of all counties, even though in two-thirds of the counties per capita income is below the median, and in most such cases well below. Along with the Mormon country, this is the part of nonmetropolitan America where the widest socially desirable divergences in per capita income and poverty ranks occur.

A somewhat analogous but smaller area is located in the interior of

FIGURE 11.5

Poverty Relative to Per Capita Income, 1979

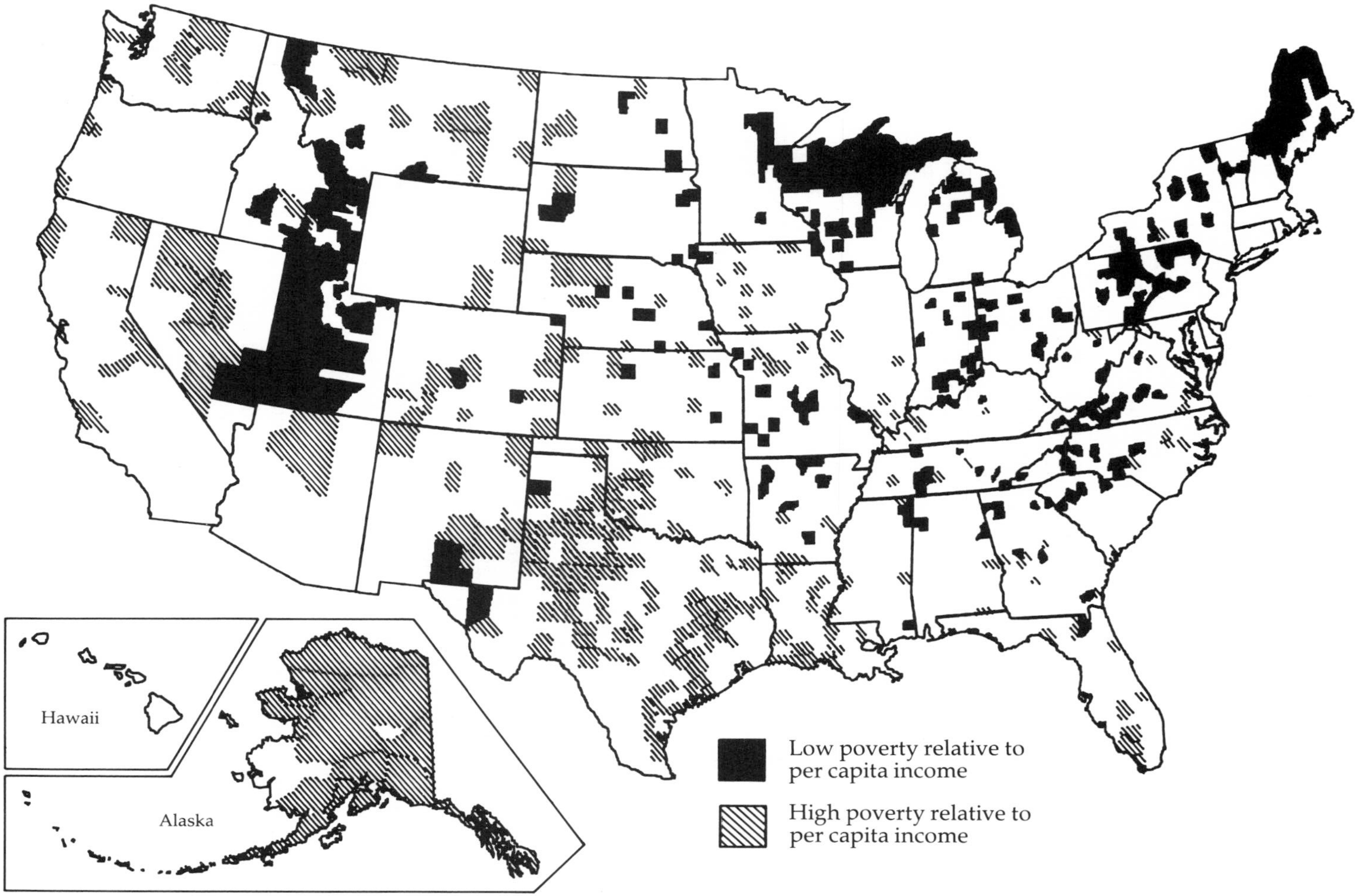

Low poverty relative to
per capita income

High poverty relative to
per capita income

Hawaii

Alaska

Maine and adjoining northernmost New Hampshire. Here, too, there is a dependence on timber industries and summer recreation. A fourth area is found in central and northern Pennsylvania and parts of upstate New York. Most of the counties in this area have been in a state of economic difficulty and demographic stagnation for many years. There is a mixed dependence on older manufacturing, with diminished levels of coal, oil and gas, timber industries, and agriculture.

Few areas of this type appear in the South. It is unrealistic to expect to find them in counties that have much black population, for the income position of blacks is so far below that of whites, and the high incidence of female-headed families is so conducive to poverty, that areas with significant black population usually have both low per capita income and high poverty rankings. The Piedmont South, however, with its more predominantly white population has a section in North Carolina, extending over into South Carolina and Virginia, where a number of populous manufacturing counties have achieved relatively low poverty incidence compared with what might be anticipated simply from their per capita income levels. These counties generally have very high labor force participation rates for women—providing many two earner families—coupled with low (but adequate) levels of child-bearing.

The other side of the ledger is the many counties that have poverty rates much higher than would be expected from their per capita income levels. This phenomenon is heavily focused on Texas, Louisiana, and ajacent areas of Oklahoma and New Mexico. A majority of the affected counties have considerable oil and gas wealth, or are agricultural in character, or have a combination of those industries. Most have large minorities of Hispanics or blacks. In one large block of more than 40 counties on the Texas plains, the great majority of counties have wide, unfavorable disparities in per capita income and poverty. In 14 counties of Texas the rank on poverty is more than 1,000 rankings worse than that on per capita income—a radical difference.

Wide adverse disparities in relative rankings on poverty and per capita income do not typically occur simply from wide differences in wage and salary rates within a population. Rather they most commonly emerge where a significant portion of a population obtains substantial income from self-employment or from investment income (interest, dividends, rents, or royalties) and where many people work at low or modest wages. In Texas, the average amount of investment or royalty income received in all nonmetropolitan counties by persons having such income was much higher than that obtained in the nonmetropolitan United States as a whole ($3,870 vs. $2,762). In the counties with high per capita income in relation to poverty rates the investment income was higher still in most cases.[9] Even without investment income, areas with good farm income that use many hired laborers rather than family labor (such as is common in irrigated areas, for example) often have more poverty than might be expected from overall income. And this, too, is characteristic of parts of the Texas-centered area here referred to.

There are a number of counties eleswhere that show the same effect but without forming much of a geographical grouping, except in the case of Alaska. More than 20 scattered counties with state universities can be identified in which the low income of many students technically elevates the poverty rate beyond what would otherwise be expected.

It should be stressed again that the counties here discussed do not (with very few exceptions) represent the poorest counties in the nation. Rather, they are those having the greatest lack of congruence between the incidence of poverty and the mean level of income per person. In some of the classic long-standing areas of deepest rural poverty there is such a limited amount of money received that the counties rank either about the same or even a little worse on per capita income as they do on poverty. One might say there is a democratization of poverty in such places. Among the 100 poorest nonmetropolitan counties (by poverty rate), this is widely true of the southern Appalachian counties (except those with coal) and of the Sioux Indian counties of the Dakotas. By contrast, in the Delta part of Mississippi, where all 10 counties fall in the poorest 100 nationally, there is plantation-based agricultural wealth. However, the black population, which is in the majority in every county, typically does not share in this wealth and the counties all rank mildly to moderately better on per capita income than they do on poverty.

Post-1980 Trends in Income and Poverty

The recession of the early 1980s fell more heavily on nonmetropolitan areas than it did on large cities and suburbs. The severe agricultural depression, the decline of mining, and a slump in timber industries

---

[9]The most extreme case is just that—extreme—but it is nonetheless instructive. Kenedy County, Texas, is thinly settled ranchland and had just 543 residents in 1980. Nearly 45 percent of all employed people were hired agricultural workers, mostly Mexican American, with modest earnings. However, there is oil in the county and 23 percent of the households received investment income (including royalties) averaging $83,000 per household. As a result, in this county investment income accounted for three-fifths of all personal income, but because of its limited distribution, the county ranked 63rd worst in the nation among nonmetropolitan counties in poverty rate but 30th best in per capita income.

drove down employment and income in the entire traditional extractive sector of the rural economy. Many manufacturing industries had extensive layoffs and closings as well, especially as import competition grew. Unfortunately for rural and small town communities, the widely touted recovery since 1983 has been primarily a metropolitan recovery. By 1986, the metropolitan unemployment rate was only 0.8 above that of 1979 (6.6 vs. 5.8 percent), but the nonmetropolitan rate was still 2.6 higher than that of 1979 (8.3 vs. 5.7 percent; see Chapter 8). In this economic setting, the median income of nonmetropolitan families fell as a percentage of the metropolitan median. As measured in the Current Population Survey (CPS), the nonmetropolitan median was 81 percent of the metropolitan figure in 1979 and 79 percent in 1983, but it had fallen to 73 percent in 1986. It should be stressed that in all likelihood a major part of the drop from 1983 to 1986 was procedural rather than real, resulting from a redesign of the CPS, which shifted a net of about one-fourth of the nonmetropolitan population into the metropolitan category. This was the first updating of metropolitan boundaries in the CPS since before the final delineation of metropolitan boundaries after the 1970 census. Inasmuch as the areas reclassified from nonmetropolitan to metropolitan contained many suburban and exurban people of above average income, the 1983 and 1986 results are not comfortably comparable. However, the .73 to 1 ratio of nonmetropolitan to metropolitan median family income in 1986 is a better and more realistic measure of actual nonmetropolitan–metropolitan income disparity than the earlier values are.[10]

By 1986 the poverty rate was 18.1 percent in nonmetropolitan areas, significantly above the metropolitan rate of 12.3. Both of these values were higher than those of 13.8 and 10.7 reported in the CPS in 1979. As with the median income data, the poverty rates are affected by the redesign of the CPS. The nonmetropolitan rate in 1986 was essentially back to the level of 17.9 percent in 1969, although the existence of the Food Stamp program, in particular, provided a degree of alleviation of poverty in 1986 that was not nearly as available in the earlier year. Despite some increase in income poverty in the 1980s, the nonmetropolitan poverty rate in 1986 was still far below that of 33.2 percent in 1959.

Estimates of poverty that allow for the value of noncash benefits

---

[10]The results of the 1980 census that form the major data base for this volume also show a somewhat larger nonmetropolitan population than they would have if the 1983 metropolitan criteria used in redesign of the CPS sample could have been fully applied to the published reports and data tapes of that census. However, the problem is much smaller than the one that had accumulated in the CPS, representing only about 5 percent of the census national nonmetropolitan figure, and thus having only limited effect on 1980 averages and distributions.

(food, housing, medical care) have been made in recent years and naturally show lower levels of poverty.[11] There are several means of making such estimates, but all show little difference in the extent to which metropolitan and nonmetropolitan poverty are affected. A technique known as the Poverty Budget Share Value gave a nonmetropolitan poverty rate of 15.6 percent in 1983 compared with the standard estimate of 18.3, a reduction of a little less than one-sixth. The adjusted metropolitan rate was 11.7 percent, compared with a standard value of 13.8. In each case, the adjusted rates had increased more since 1979 than had the standard rates.

In effect, all of the net progress made since 1959 in getting nonmetropolitan incomes above the poverty level was achieved by 1970. The nonmetropolitan poverty rate for blacks has edged above 40 percent again. Although they comprised only 9 percent of the nonmetropolitan population, blacks were 21 percent of persons with poverty level incomes in 1985.

The severe downturn in nonmetropolitan economic conditions in the 1980s was unanticipated and illustrates the difficulty of projecting the length or permanence of trends. It is impossible to say how long the relatively depressed state of the rural economy will continue or whether this economy will ever in the meaningful future resume a pattern of job growth more rapid than that in metropolitan areas, as was so surprisingly seen in the 1970s. The loss of farm jobs may be permanent, with a gradual substitution of more modestly paid hired workers for entrepreneurs. The mining industry could bounce back, especially if oil and gas prices again increase, but industrial metal mining is increasingly profitable only at lower wage rates, given the flooding of the market with cheap ores from developing nations desperate for hard currency. Wood products employment, too, is subject to heavy foreign competition and labor-displacing productivity increases. Textiles and finished textile products appear to have slumped rather permanently in employment (in part from technological change), and this is particularly serious for nonmetropolitan areas where this industry has been by far the largest manufacturing group.

Future income from earnings will almost certainly come increasingly from services, just as is true in city and suburban areas. However, some of the best paid and most rapidly growing service industries are disproportionately found in metropolitan locations. This is true of finance, insurance, real estate, business services, and of legal and other professional services.[12] These do not look to be as portable to the rural

[11]U.S. Bureau of the Census (1984).
[12]See Chapter 9 and Miller and Bluestone (1987).

and small town scene as some types of manufacturing proved to be earlier.

Nonmetropolitan manufacturing in general has suffered in this decade from difficulty in competing with foreign wages, even though cheap labor may have been a major incentive for rural industrial location as recently as the mid-1970s. Nonmetropolitan manufacturing is also heavily composed of lower skilled, more routinized industries, and within a given industry it has a lower than average share of the more highly paid professional and managerial jobs.[13] There was major growth in professional service and trade employment in rural and small town areas in the 1960s and 1970s as these areas modernized and, in particular, broadened their medical and educational services. But most of this catching up is over. Growth still continues in recreational and retirement services, but beyond that the transition to the heralded service economy of the future seems vague and elusive as a means of replacing or increasing the income once received in nonmetropolitan communities from extractive industries and manufacturing.

An exception to this generalization can be made for the rural metropolitan population. By 1980, rural metropolitan residents were 40 percent of the total rural population and numbered 24 million people. This population has not been discussed much in the context of this chapter, but as the United States population becomes more metropolitanized, rural metropolitan residents become a larger proportion of the rural total. A minority of them live beyond the effective commuting range of an urbanized area, and are metropolitan only by virtue of the approximations entailed by use of county lines to define metropolitan areas. The majority live in localities that are visually rural and small town but are well within the metropolitan labor market. Still others live within small outlying subdivisions or densely settled rural territory that is incipiently suburban. Rural and urban, after all, are not a discrete dichotomy in reality. With greater access to urban employment or to businesses attracted by proximity to the urbanized area, metropolitan rural people have a wider choice of employment and higher incomes than do nonmetropolitan people—either urban or rural. The median income of rural metropolitan families in 1979 was $20,940, compared with $17,302 and $16,204 for nonmetropolitan urban and rural families, respectively (Table 11.1). The rural metropolitan median was barely less than that of metropolitan urban families—$21,165. A portion of the rural metropolitan population is steadily in the process of being transformed into urban at any given time, as urban sprawl and peripheral infill continue. (The same point can be made about the progression of

[13]McGranahan (1987).

larger nonmetropolitan cities into metropolitan areas.) But in the interim, millions of people combine a preferred rural residence with urban metropolitan income levels. The entire United States rural and small town population cannot acquire metropolitan access—distances in most places are too great for that. The distinctly higher income level of rural metropolitan people, however, makes clear the comparative advantage.

Summary

In several ways it is surprising that income and poverty levels should be worse in nonmetropolitan communities than in metropolitan areas. Nonmetropolitan areas have a distinctly lower presence of three population groups typically afflicted with low income—black and Hispanic minorities, unrelated individuals, and female-headed households with children. With these compositional features one would expect to find the poverty rate higher in metropolitan areas, yet it has always been higher among rural and small town people.

What factors explain this paradox? The reasons are not all clear, nor is there certainty about their relative importance, but they include the following.[14] There is more worker-related family poverty in rural America. The wage and skill structure of rural industries and businesses on average supplies lower paid jobs that in some instances do not yield income above poverty level even with full-time work. And life in a rural setting also more frequently means acceptance of seasonal jobs than is true in cities. To some extent these conditions are inherent in the extractive and recreational industries that will always be a part of the rural economy, and in the economic costs of space that are the antithesis of urban economies of scale. Further, there is a higher incidence of work-limiting health disability among rural people, whose perpetuation is not fully understood but which particularly affects the South. The South as a region generally has lower incomes and higher poverty rates than the rest of the nation—whether urban or rural—and contains a much higher proportion of the national nonmetropolitan population than it does of metropolitan people. So the disproportionate location of nonmetropolitan residents in the South contributes to their income problems. Another factor is the existence of large pockets of chronic white poverty, especially in the southern Appalachian and Ozark–Ouachita highlands, that are not found anywhere in urban America. Low education, lack of

---

[14]This discussion is adapted in part from Elo (1985).

employment, and high rates of disability contribute to conditions in these areas, but there is a residual effect of lengthy former cultural isolation that has not yet been dissipated, even though much progress has been made. In combination, all the factors mentioned have thus far more than offset those aspects of racial composition and living arrangements that would act to give an income advantage to nonmetropolitan people.

12

CHARACTERISTICS OF CITIES, TOWNS, AND RURAL AREAS

IN OUR examination of rural and small town America, primary emphasis has been on population redistribution and the comparison of various social and economic characteristics across metropolitan and nonmetropolitan areas, and between rural and urban residence categories. We extended this set of distinctions in Chapter 3 to consider a size-of-place classification for the study of population redistribution. In the present chapter we again use such a grouping to examine differentials in characteristics of the population living in cities, small towns, and rural areas.

The purpose of such an extension is not just to complete an analysis scheme, although in a sense this chapter represents an elaboration and overview of much that has gone before. From a cross-sectional perspective the settlement structure may be viewed as an array of cities of different sizes and their hinterlands interrelated through a complex division of labor. Though population size certainly does not uniquely determine what a place does, it is an indicator of its position in the settlement hierarchy that has emerged with the process of urbanization. Accordingly, we would expect, and indeed past research has shown, systematic differences in demographic, social, and economic characteristics of communities ordered by population size.[1] Larger places provide a

---

[1]The classic source, and the model for this chapter, is Duncan and Reiss (1956), part 1, Size of Community. Other sources include Thompson and Whelpton (1933), Ogburn (1937), Schnore and Varley (1955), Duncan, Scott, Lieberson, Duncan, and Winsborough (1960), Schnore (1963), and Appelbaum (1978). Work concerned with size differences of rural villages and/or nonmetropolitan places includes Fuguitt and Field (1972) and Johansen and Fuguitt (1984).

more extensive market for goods and services and can more easily support highly specialized activities, hence the overall economy tends to be more diversified. They also tend to attract a greater variety of people from diverse origins than do smaller communities. Organizational complexities related to the greater division of labor, density of settlement and activity, and a more diverse population may lead to different patterns of family and community life that are reflected in the characteristics of the population. We report here the extent to which many such differentials have prevailed in recent years in the United States, for residence categories arranged by size of place and metropolitan–nonmetropolitan status.

In Chapter 3 we saw that recent changes in population redistribution trends included shifts in growth patterns according to size of place. The older pattern was one in which larger places grew more rapidly than smaller ones in a process of urban concentration. This was modified to a more uniform pattern of growth by size among places in metropolitan areas well before the 1970s, evidently reflecting an increasing integration of activities across all places and including their rural peripheries. The concentrated growth pattern favoring larger places was still the rule in nonmetropolitan areas until the 1970–1980 decade, when the pattern became much more like that of metropolitan areas.

Similarly, as part of the shift to a more diffuse settlement, we would expect changes between 1970 and 1980 toward weaker and less regular differences in characteristics by size of place. The increased and widespread nonmetropolitan growth of the 1970s has been associated with various changes in economic activities, such as a deconcentration of manufacturing activity; an increase in service employment, including that associated with resort and retirement communities; and a corresponding further decline in the relative importance of the farm-related population. This renewed population growth, primarily through migration, and transformation in economic activities should have resulted in more population diversity in small towns and rural areas and thus less notable differences among size-of-place groups. A decreasing difference in rural-urban and metropolitan–nonmetropolitan social characteristics, services, facilities, and life-styles, which may tend to make less dense residential settings more attractive, has often been mentioned as one partial explanation for the nonmetropolitan migration gains of the 1970s.[2] In sum, there is reason to expect some convergence in population characteristics among the residence categories between 1970 and 1980. We will investigate this possibility for nonmetropolitan areas, as well as among all of the size-of-place groupings (metropolitan and nonmetropolitan) considered together. Unfortunately, intercensal data on

[2]Wardwell (1980).

population characteristics are unavailable for individual communities, so that it will not be possible to assess the effect of the post-1980 turnaround reversal until the results of the 1990 census can be utilized.

Recent trends in community structure have undoubtedly been strongly influenced by the practice of commuting. Not only does this activity tie together elements of the urban hierarchy but it should also generate different social and economic differentials by size of place for the resident and the working population. To the extent that persons tend to seek out more rural settings for residence than for work, one might expect socioeconomic gradients across size-of-place groups to be stronger by place of work than by place of residence. Using a commuting variable available on our special Public-Use Microdata Sample (PUMS) file for 1980, we give attention to the patterns of commuting among the size-of-place groups, and compare the gradients by place of work with those by place of residence for occupation, industry, and income.

The Comparison Groups

On the metropolitan side, the distinction employed is between (1) central cities; (2) other urban metropolitan territory, including incorporated and unincorporated places and other population in urbanized areas; and (3) metropolitan rural areas. The nonmetropolitan classification includes (1) places 25,000 and over along with the population that lives outside places of 2,500 or more in urbanized areas; (2) places 10,000–24,999; (3) places 2,500–9,999; (4) rural places less than 2,500; and (5) other rural territory.[3] Places here include all incorporated centers and census designated places (CDPs). To be identified, a CDP generally must have at least 1,000 population, a density of 1,000 persons per square mile; and other "urban-like" qualities such as an accepted name and a street pattern.[4]

---

[3]The other rural population includes those living in unincorporated villages of less than 1,000, which are not separately identified by census procedures. Duncan and Reiss (1956) estimated that the population of all rural villages under 1,000 in 1950 was 2.25 times that reported in rural incorporated places of that size. In 1970 the nonmetropolitan population in incorporated places of less than 1,000 was approximately 3.2 million, and it was 3 million in 1980. If we assume that the factor above was approximately 2 in 1970 and 1980, then the other rural population here would include a population in unincorporated places of about 3 million. This is a little more than 10 percent of the other rural component, the remainder being "open country" population and the urban fringe around smaller places not included as urban through an urbanized area delineation.

[4]Minimum size exceptions are made for Alaska where the minimum is 25, for Hawaii where the minimum is 300, and inside urbanized areas having a city of 50,000 or more where it is 5,000. See U.S. Bureau of the Census 1983a, Chapter A, Appendix A.

The sources of data are special PUMS files for 1970 and 1980, which have both metropolitan-nonmetropolitan and urban-rural size-of-place distinctions for the nation and census divisions. The nonmetropolitan population in urbanized areas was combined with the 25,000 and over group because it was too small to separately identify in either census due to the disclosure rules of the Census Bureau, and this preserved the conventional rural-urban distinction. Consequently the third category is the rural metropolitan population, and the last two size categories are together the rural nonmetropolitan population. The nonmetropolitan urbanized area group is altogether about 35 percent of the combined 25,000 up and urbanized area category in 1980. Most of this urbanized area population, however, resides in cities with more than 25,000 people, so that only 15 percent of the category consists of people not actually living in places of this size group in 1980. The nonmetropolitan urbanized area population was smaller in 1970.[5] Each PUMS file has the metropolitan-nonmetropolitan distinction of the census on which it is based, and so we must employ a "floating" metropolitan definition in the analysis.

The distribution of the population by this size-of-place classification is given for 1970 and 1980 in Table 12.1. The metropolitan central city is the category with the largest proportion of people in 1970, but by 1980 the other urban metropolitan category had become the largest. The third largest in importance in both decades was the nonmetropolitan other rural. In comparing the two time periods, metropolitanization is the most apparent trend. That is, all the nonmetropolitan size categories are relatively less important in 1980 than in 1970, and the other urban and the rural-metropolitan categories are more important. Within the nonmetropolitan classification, the other rural category increased from 46 to 48 percent of the total and the 25,000+ category decreased from 12 to 8 percent. This decrease in the largest city category was no doubt due in large part to the shift of counties having larger cities into the metropolitan classification between the two censuses.

The distribution of the population by size of place is shown for regions of the United States in Table 12.2. Differences are considerable, particularly in the proportion of the population in the nonmetropolitan other rural category, which ranged from 8 in the West to 23 in the South in 1970, and from 7 in the West to 18 in the South in 1980. Overall, the regions became somewhat more similar in their distributions by size of place between 1970 and 1980.

[5]The nonmetropolitan urbanized area population was entirely overflow from adjacent metropolitan areas in 1970. In 1980 some complete urbanized areas were nonmetropolitan if they did not have a central city of 50,000 and were in counties having fewer than 100,000 people.

TABLE 12.1

Population by Size of Place, 1970, 1980

Size of Place	1970 Population (000s)	1970 Percentage Distribution	1980 Population (000s)	1980 Percentage Distribution
Metropolitan	139,136	68.5	169,929	74.8
Central city	63,546	31.3	66,409	29.2
Other urban	59,191	29.1	79,466	35.0
Rural	16,400	8.1	24,054	10.6
Nonmetropolitan	63,840	31.5	57,379	25.2
25,000 up and UA[a]	7,532	3.7	4,745	2.1
10,000–24,999	7,817	3.9	7,239	3.2
2,500–9,999	10,902	5.4	9,752	4.3
Rural LT 2,500[b]	8,500	4.2	7,874	3.4
Other rural	29,089	14.3	27,770	12.2
United States	202,976	100.0	227,309	100.0

[a]Places 25,000 and over and other urbanized area population.
[b]Rural places with less than 2,500 population.

TABLE 12.2

Percentage Distribution of Population by Size of Place for Regions, 1970, 1980

Size of Place	1970 North-east	1970 Mid-west	1970 South	1970 West	1970 United States	1980 North-east	1980 Mid-west	1980 South	1980 West	1980 United States
Metropolitan	79.9	66.6	56.0	78.6	68.6	84.9	70.8	66.8	82.4	74.8
Central city	35.1	30.1	28.4	33.1	31.3	31.4	27.5	27.6	31.9	29.2
Other urban	35.9	27.8	19.5	39.4	29.1	42.3	31.9	27.7	43.4	35.0
Rural	8.9	8.6	8.1	6.1	8.1	11.2	11.4	11.5	7.1	10.6
Nonmetropolitan	20.1	33.4	44.0	21.4	31.5	15.1	29.2	33.2	17.6	25.2
25,000 up and UA[a]	4.1	3.7	4.0	2.6	3.7	1.6	2.2	2.2	2.3	2.1
10,000–24,999	2.3	4.1	5.1	3.4	3.9	1.6	4.0	3.9	2.7	3.2
2,500–9,999	3.1	5.7	7.3	4.4	5.4	2.4	5.0	5.5	3.4	4.3
Rural LT 2,500[b]	2.0	6.0	4.9	3.0	4.2	1.7	5.4	3.7	2.3	3.4
Other rural	8.6	13.9	22.7	8.0	14.3	7.8	12.6	17.9	6.9	12.2
United States	100.0	100.0	100.0	100.0	100.0	100.0	100.0	100.0	100.0	100.0

[a]Places 25,000 and over and other urbanized area population.
[b]Rural places with less than 2,500 population.

TABLE 12.3

Percentage Distribution of the Population by Region for Size-of-Place Groups,
1970, 1980

	1970					1980				
Size of Place	North-east	Mid-west	South	West	United States	North-east	Mid-west	South	West	United States
Metropolitan	28.1	27.1	25.2	19.6	100.0	24.6	24.6	29.7	21.1	100.0
Central city	27.1	26.8	28.0	18.1	100.0	23.3	24.4	31.4	20.8	100.0
Other urban	29.6	26.6	20.7	23.1	100.0	26.2	23.7	26.5	23.7	100.0
Rural	26.6	29.7	30.9	12.8	100.0	23.0	28.1	36.2	12.7	100.0
Nonmetropolitan	15.5	29.6	43.3	11.6	100.0	13.0	30.0	43.7	13.3	100.0
25,000 up and UA[a]	26.5	28.0	33.3	12.2	100.0	16.9	28.0	34.0	21.1	100.0
10,000–24,999	14.3	29.5	41.2	15.0	100.0	10.7	32.5	40.9	15.9	100.0
2,500–9,999	14.1	29.8	42.1	14.0	100.0	11.9	30.0	42.7	15.4	100.0
Rural LT 2,500[b]	11.6	39.7	36.2	12.5	100.0	10.9	40.5	35.7	12.9	100.0
Other rural	14.5	27.1	48.9	9.5	100.0	13.8	26.8	48.7	10.7	100.0
United States	24.1	27.8	30.9	17.2	100.0	21.7	26.0	33.2	19.1	100.0

[a]Places 25,000 and over and other urbanized area population.
[b]Rural places with less than 2,500 population.

Table 12.3 gives the regional distribution of the population within each size-of-place group. The South has the highest proportion of all but one group in 1980 and of all but two groups in 1970. Differences among the regions are relatively small on the metropolitan side, but the South clearly dominates as the location of nonmetropolitan size-of-place groups, except for villages, that is, rural places less than 2,500 in size, which are somewhat more likely to be found in the Midwest. This region was settled with an extensive hinterland of small farmers and associated agricultural service centers, and continues to have a large number of small incorporated villages. This village concentration is also a consequence of state differences in incorporation practice, since the data set available to us includes only incorporated places among all under 1,000 in size, and such places are less likely to be separate political units in other regions.

Across the 1970–1980 decade, the Northeast lost its proportional share of all size-of-place groups, and the Midwest lost its share of metropolitan groups and its share of the nonmetropolitan other rural segment. The South gained in all metropolitan but lost in some nonmetropolitan groups, and the West gained in all but the metropolitan rural category. The shift in proportional share was particularly large for the 25,000 and over (including urbanized area) nonmetropolitan group, which dropped from 27 to 17 in the Northeast and gained from 12 to 21 percent in the West.

Demographic Characteristics

Age

The age distributions by size of place generally show a regular gradient (Table 12.4). Within metropolitan areas the proportion of the population aged 18–34 is greatest in central cities followed by the other urban and then the rural segments. The proportion aged 65 and over is highest for central cities. Differentials in the proportion under 18 are in the opposite direction, however, being highest for the rural population. Similarly, among the nonmetropolitan groups the larger the place size the higher the proportion of ages 18–34 and the lower the proportion of ages 5–17. The proportion over 65 is largest for the rural less than 2,500 (village) group and is less for successive larger sized groups. The other rural population, however, has the smallest proportion 65 and over of all the nonmetropolitan groups. These differentials hold for both time periods. For all size-of-place groups the 1980 distributions have higher proportions of the elderly and of the population 18–34 and lower proportions in the other groups than do the 1970 distributions. These overall shifts reflect the aging of the population and the effects of the baby boom.

The age distributions are summarized in the first two columns of Table 12.5, which give the medians for 1970 and 1980. The results generally are consistent with the percentage aged 65 and over discussed above in that for metropolitan size-of-place groups the medians are higher the more urban the group, whereas for nonmetropolitan size-of-place groups above the other rural, the medians are lower the more urban the group.

Except for the higher proportion 65 years old and over in the metropolitan central cities, these findings are quite comparable to those reported by Duncan and Reiss (1956) for 1950. The greater concentration of young adults in cities has long been recognized and attributed largely to rural–urban migration. Similarly, the concentration of the elderly in American rural villages has been noted and examined by a number of authors.[6] The new population distribution trends of the 1970s appear to have had little impact on these size-of-place gradients for age.

---

[6]For example, Johansen and Fuguitt (1984).

TABLE 12.4

Percentage Distribution of the Population by Age for Size-of-Place Groups, 1970, 1980

Size of Place	1970						1980					
	LT5	5–17	18–34	35–64	65 up	Total	LT5	5–17	18–34	35–64	65 up	Total
Metropolitan	8.4	25.9	24.3	32.1	9.3	100.0	7.1	20.8	30.1	31.2	10.8	100.0
Central city	8.2	23.8	25.1	32.0	10.9	100.0	7.2	19.3	31.9	29.6	12.0	100.0
Other urban	8.5	27.1	23.9	32.5	8.0	100.0	6.9	21.1	29.6	32.2	10.2	100.0
Rural	8.7	29.5	22.2	31.6	8.0	100.0	7.5	24.1	26.9	32.4	9.1	100.0
Metropolitan	8.3	27.0	22.2	31.1	11.4	100.0	7.6	21.8	27.3	30.1	13.2	100.0
25,000 up and UA[a]	8.2	24.7	26.8	30.3	10.0	100.0	7.3	19.3	32.5	28.1	12.8	100.0
10,000–24,999	7.9	24.5	25.6	30.3	11.7	100.0	7.6	19.1	31.7	28.1	13.5	100.0
2,500–9,999	8.0	25.5	22.5	30.8	13.2	100.0	7.6	20.2	27.2	29.2	15.8	100.0
Rural LT 2,500[b]	7.9	25.8	19.6	31.3	15.4	100.0	7.6	21.1	24.7	29.3	17.3	100.0
Other rural	8.7	29.2	20.7	31.6	9.8	100.0	7.8	23.6	26.0	31.5	11.1	100.0
United States	8.4	26.2	23.6	31.8	10.0	100.0	7.2	21.1	29.4	30.9	11.4	100.0

[a]Places 25,000 and over and other urbanized area population.
[b]Rural places with less than 2,500 population.

TABLE 12.5
Age, Sex, Race, and Hispanic Composition by Size of Place, 1970, 1980

Size of Place	Median Age		Sex Ratio		Percent Black				Percent Hispanic
					South		Non-South		
	1970	1980	1970	1980	1970	1980	1970	1980	1980
Metropolitan	28.0	30.0	93.6	93.1	20.0	20.4	10.6	11.6	7.6
Central city	28.9	29.6	90.3	90.0	27.5	29.4	17.8	19.8	10.7
Other urban	27.4	30.4	95.2	94.2	9.0	11.5	3.6	5.3	6.4
Rural	26.7	29.8	100.5	100.7	13.3	10.4	1.4	1.2	3.0
Nonmetropolitan	28.1	30.2	95.9	95.4	18.1	16.3	1.5	1.2	3.2
25,000 up and UA[a]	26.5	29.0	94.0	93.6	18.6	22.1	3.9	3.3	4.8
10,000–24,999	27.4	29.0	90.7	89.6	20.3	22.3	2.6	2.3	5.2
2,500–9,999	29.2	31.1	91.0	89.3	18.8	21.3	1.3	1.3	4.7
Rural LT 2,500[b]	31.7	32.4	91.2	90.5	16.4	16.9	0.6	0.6	2.7
Other rural	27.4	30.0	101.2	101.0	19.4	16.5	0.9	0.5	2.0
United States	28.0	30.0	94.3	93.9	19.0	18.6	7.5	8.4	6.5

[a]Places 25,000 and over and other urbanized area population.
[b]Rural places with less than 2,500 population.

Sex Composition

The sex ratio (number of males per 100 females) also is shown for the total population in Table 12.5. Among the metropolitan groups there is a regular gradient, with 90 males per 100 females in central cities, about 95 males per 100 females in other urban areas, and an even balance between males and females in rural areas. The ratios for the nonmetropolitan other rural group is highest of all at about 101 in both years, but the other size-of-place groups are irregular, with the 25,000 and over category showing higher ratios than the intermediate sized places. It is not clear why urban places over 25,000 should have higher ratios. Perhaps it is because they are disproportionately found in more sparsely settled parts of the country (West North Central, West South Central, and Mountain divisions), where a higher male percentage may be typical even in more urban places.

Sex ratios also were calculated for the population 65 and over (not shown). As expected they are all much lower than corresponding ratios for the total population, due to the greater longevity of women. Ratios for 1980 are somewhat lower than those for 1970, whereas for the population of all ages they are little different across the decade. The metropolitan and nonmetropolitan patterns by size of place are, however, similar to those for the total population of all ages.

The higher sex ratio for the nonmetropolitan other rural population is a common finding. Duncan and Reiss (1956) reported this difference, with almost identical ratios for the other size-of-place groups. This has been related to differential migration of women from rural areas to cities, and the greater prevalence of traditional families in more rural settings. We will consider family composition variables further on in this analysis.

Race and Ethnic Composition

Because there are very few rural and small town blacks living outside the South, the percent black is shown separately in Table 12.5 for the South and the remainder of the country. In both areas the percent black is highest in metropolitan central cities, and increased there between 1970 and 1980, as well as in the metropolitan other urban category, although it decreased for the metropolitan rural group. Almost one in five nonmetropolitan residents is black in the South, whereas that is true of less than 2 percent of nonmetropolitan residents elsewhere. This percentage dropped slightly over the decade in both areas, but in the South there was an increase in the black proportion for places over

2,500, showing urban concentration there as well as in metropolitan areas.

In general, among the nonmetropolitan size-of-place categories, larger size groups have higher percentages black. In their 1950 census monograph, Duncan and Reiss found a regular gradient by size of place for the population outside all urbanized areas in 1950.[7]

The Hispanic population is over 10 percent of the population in metropolitan central cities in 1980, and over 6 percent of the metropolitan other urban segment. Proportions are lower in metropolitan rural and all nonmetropolitan size-of-place groupings. Except for the 25,000 and over category, which is slightly lower than the next smallest group, the larger the size-of-place group, the higher the proportion of the population classed as Hispanic.

Family and Household Composition

The results of Chapter 6 included evidence that rural areas continue to have a higher proportion of people living in traditional household arrangements, that is, in families, in husband-wife families, and in families that include children. Duncan and Reiss (1956) identified family organization and functions as a major complex differentiating places by community size. In explaining this association, they noted that although homes generally are better equipped in large than in small places, they carry a higher price, are more frequently in multiple unit structures, are less frequently owned by the occupants, and may be less suitable for use by large families. As the size of the community increases, more and more specialized agencies offer competition to the family in the performance of traditional functions. A higher proportion of women work in more urban settings, and urbanization reduces the economic return from children and increases the cost of child-rearing.[8] More recent observers have emphasized the concentration of disadvantaged groups in major urban areas as associated with less traditional family arrangements.

The detailed distributions by size of place of some summary measures of family structure and fertility are given in Tables 12.6 and 12.7. The first is the percent of population in family households. (Those not in family households include persons living alone or with unrelated individuals and those in group quarters.) Although there is little difference between metropolitan and nonmetropolitan areas as a whole, there are

[7]Duncan and Reiss (1956), p. 59.
[8]Ibid., (1956), p. 4.

TABLE 12.6

Family Household Variables by Size of Place, 1970, 1980

| Size of Place | Percent Population in Family Households | | Of Population in Family Households, Percentage in Households with | | | |
| | | | Husband-Wife | | Children LT 18 | |
	1970	1980	1970	1980	1970	1980
Metropolitan	89.3	85.7	86.8	82.8	68.0	64.4
Central city	86.2	81.3	82.0	75.3	64.1	62.4
Other urban	91.5	87.5	90.2	86.1	71.0	64.6
Rural	93.2	92.0	92.0	90.6	72.7	66.2
Nonmetropolitan	90.2	87.8	88.1	86.7	67.7	64.8
25,000 up and UA[a]	85.9	81.3	86.8	83.9	67.0	63.5
10,000–24,999	85.1	80.8	86.7	83.0	65.7	63.4
2,500–9,999	87.5	84.4	86.3	83.4	66.3	63.2
Rural LT 2,500[b]	89.8	87.0	87.5	86.4	64.9	63.6
Other rural	93.7	92.1	89.8	89.1	69.7	66.2
United States	89.6	86.2	87.2	83.8	67.9	64.5

[a]Places 25,000 and over and other urbanized area population.
[b]Rural places with less than 2,500 population.

regular gradients in the expected direction within both residence categories in 1970 and in 1980. That is, the larger the place, the lower the percentage in families. Evidence of the general decline in the prevalence of traditional family arrangements is seen by the decline in the total percentage for this variable from 90 in 1970 to 86 in 1980. Every size-of-place category had a corresponding drop, but relative declines were larger, the larger the community size. Consequently, differences among the size-of-place groupings were greater in 1980 than in 1970.

The next two variables in Table 12.6 are concerned with family households. The first is the percentage of the population living in family households that are in those households having both a husband and a wife. Again there is a regular gradient in the expected direction. Further, the proportions are less in 1980 than in 1970 for each group and again the decline in the proportion is greater in more urban settings, making for an increase in the differentials by size of place. The second of these variables is the percentage of the population living in family households that are in households including children under age 18. There is the expected gradient among the three metropolitan size-of-place groups, with more rural categories more likely to have family households with

TABLE 12.7

Percentage in Husband-Wife Families by Age and Mean Number of Children Ever Born by Size of Place, 1970, 1980

| Size of Place | Percentage in Husband-Wife Families | | | | Mean Number Children Ever Born | | | |
| | Of all LT 18 | | Of All 65 + | | Females 25–34 | | Females 35–44 | |
	1970	1980	1970	1980	1970	1980	1970	1980
Metropolitan	84.3	78.6	55.6	56.8	2.1	1.4	2.8	2.6
Central city	77.8	68.4	49.1	50.0	2.0	1.3	2.8	2.6
Other urban	88.7	83.1	57.8	60.9	2.1	1.4	2.8	2.5
Rural	90.5	89.0	61.5	66.1	2.4	1.6	3.2	2.8
Nonmetropolitan	85.8	83.6	56.5	59.6	2.4	1.7	3.2	2.9
25,000 up and UA[a]	83.9	79.1	50.2	57.2	2.1	1.5	3.0	2.6
10,000–24,999	81.9	78.5	50.6	52.8	2.2	1.6	3.0	2.7
2,500–9,999	83.4	78.7	51.0	54.3	2.4	1.7	3.1	2.8
Rural LT 2,500[b]	85.5	83.0	53.4	56.7	2.5	1.8	3.2	3.0
Other rural	87.9	87.1	64.3	65.9	2.5	1.8	3.4	3.0
United States	84.7	79.9	54.6	57.6	2.2	1.5	3.0	2.6

[a]Places 25,000 and over and other urbanized area population.
[b]Rural places with less than 2,500 population.

young children. On the nonmetropolitan side, however, there is no clear gradient. Although the other rural category has the highest proportion of such families at both times, the next highest in 1970 is the 25,000 and over category, and in 1980 all of the other size-of-place groupings are about the same and a little less than 3 percentage points below the other rural.

Much concern about recent trends in family life has focused on children and on the elderly.[9] The first variable in Table 12.7 includes only persons under 18 and is the proportion of these who live in husband-wife families. There is a gradient for both 1970 and 1980, with children in more rural areas more likely to live in such traditional families. The exception to a regular gradient is the 25,000 and over category, which is somewhat larger than expected. Generally, however, the decline in this percentage between 1970 and 1980 is greater in more urban settings, consistent with several of the preceding family variables, increasing the size-of-place gradient over the 1970–1980 decade. Overall, the percentage of children living in husband-wife families dropped from 85 to 80 percent between 1970 and 1980.

The next variable is concerned with people over 65 years old and is the percentage of these individuals who live in husband-wife families. Elders are more likely to be in husband-wife families in more rural settings with the exception again of the 25,000 and over group for 1980. This discrepancy for these and other family variables may be due to the inclusion of the nonmetropolitan urbanized area population within this category and/or regional differences in the distribution of places by size. In contrast to the situation for children, the proportion of the elderly population living in husband-wife families increased slightly between 1970 and 1980. This may be due to increased longevity, so that married couples are more likely to have survived intact by the later census. For whatever reason, this increase is greater for more rural metropolitan size groups, so that the metropolitan gradient is somewhat greater in 1980.

Fertility

Fertility is measured here as in Chapter 7 by the number of children ever born per woman aged 25–34 or per woman aged 35–44. That rural areas tend to have higher fertility than urban areas is a well-established generalization, though differences have been lessening in recent years (see discussion in Chapter 7). In elaborating the rural-urban distinction, Duncan and Reiss (1956) reported a regular gradient by size of place for

[9]Preston (1984).

the fertility ratio in 1950.[10] Similarly, our analysis shows a regular gradient by size of place in the expected direction for both censuses and both age groups of women. The more rural the area, the larger the number of children ever born. Differences between groups are small, however, and the overall level of fertility has declined over the 1970–1980 decade.[11]

Migration

Migration between metropolitan and nonmetropolitan areas was considered at length in Chapter 2, with attention given to the relative importance of these moves, and the finding that movement from metropolitan to nonmetropolitan areas was greater and movement from nonmetropolitan to metropolitan less in the 1975–1980 period than in the 1965–1970 period. In Table 12.8 we show the distribution of intercounty migrants by origin for the 1970 and 1980 population ordered by size of place. The "between metro and nonmetro" migrant group includes those moving from nonmetropolitan to metropolitan areas for the metropolitan size-of-place groups, and those moving from metropolitan to nonmetropolitan areas for the nonmetropolitan size-of-place groups. Among the metropolitan size groups, in both decades the rural category had the highest proportion of all intercounty movers who were nonmetropolitan five years before, followed by the central cities and the other urban, in that order. For nonmetropolitan size groups, the proportion of intercounty movers from metropolitan areas is highest in the 25,000 and over category, followed by the other rural category. Other size-of-place groups follow a gradient from high to low. That the largest nonmetropolitan places (along with other population in urbanized areas) should have the highest proportion of metropolitan origin intercounty migrants shows that these places are more likely to share in the intermetropolitan migration system than are other nonmetropolitan areas. That the other rural population has the second rank, however, is consistent with the findings of Chapters 2 and 3 that much of the new nonmetropolitan growth was outside any city, with former metropolitan residents moving not only to adjacent counties in the extension of the commuting field but to more remote locations, particularly those with retirement and recreation potential.

[10]Duncan and Reiss (1956), pp. 48-51.

[11]Our findings should not be interpreted as necessarily reflecting a difference in fertility behavior between size-of-place groups. Slesinger (1974), to cite one example, has shown differences in children ever born by residence to be largely explained by residential differences in duration of marriage, religious status, work experience, and education.

TABLE 12.8

Percentage Distribution of Inmigrants by Size of Place, 1965–1970, 1975–1980

Size of Place of Residence 1970, 1980	1965–1970				1975–1980			
	Between Metro and Nonmetro	Other Inter-county	From Abroad	Total	Between Metro and Nonmetro	Other Inter-county	From Abroad	Total
Metropolitan	24.5	66.0	9.5	100.0	16.3	73.2	10.5	100.0
Central city	26.8	60.4	12.8	100.0	17.7	67.0	15.3	100.0
Other urban	21.4	70.6	8.0	100.0	14.2	76.7	9.2	100.0
Rural	29.0	66.1	4.8	100.0	20.6	76.0	3.4	100.0
Nonmetropolitan	50.4	45.8	3.8	100.0	57.7	38.5	3.8	100.0
25,000 up and UA[a]	56.2	38.4	5.4	100.0	62.2	31.5	6.3	100.0
10,000–24,999	48.2	47.5	4.3	100.0	56.8	37.4	5.8	100.0
2,500–9,999	49.5	45.7	4.7	100.0	55.9	40.1	3.9	100.0
Rural LT 2,500[b]	43.7	53.6	2.7	100.0	51.3	45.5	3.2	100.0
Other rural	51.6	45.4	3.0	100.0	59.4	38.0	2.6	100.0
United States	32.7	59.6	7.7	100.0	26.7	64.4	8.8	100.0

[a]Places 25,000 and over and other urbanized area population.
[b]Rural places with less than 2,500 population.

Another notable feature of the table is the very high proportion of nonmetropolitan intercounty movers coming from metropolitan areas— about one-half—whereas only about one in five intercounty movers residing in metropolitan areas came from nonmetropolitan areas. Again this reflects the dominance of intermetropolitan movements today in a nation that is more than two-thirds metropolitan, but it shows as well the greater impact of metropolitan origin people on nonmetropolitan areas than the impact of nonmetropolitan origin people on metropolitan areas.

The change in migration patterns over the two decades is indicated by the considerable decline in the importance of migrants from nonmetropolitan areas among the metropolitan size categories and an increase in the importance of migrants from metropolitan areas among the non-metropolitan categories. Since the largest nonmetropolitan size class has the smallest relative increase in this percentage, there is some diminution of differences among the nonmetropolitan size-of-place groups over time.

Another migration gradient of note is the proportion of intercounty migrants coming from abroad. This is a completely consistent high-to-low gradient for 1975–1980 and almost so for 1965–1970 within both metropolitan and nonmetropolitan areas. The higher proportion of people coming from abroad in more urban places reflects a classic property of rural-urban differences—the greater heterogeneity of urban life. The proportion of migrants coming from abroad has increased for larger places across the two censuses, so that this differential appears to be becoming more pronounced.

Socioeconomic Characteristics

Educational Status

Educational status is an important indicator of the quality of the population. Community or size-of-place differences in completed schooling may reflect not only available educational opportunities but also the nature of the economic opportunities in the area. Migration tends to be selective of those having more education, and so areas having positions that require a greater degree of training may gain such migrants on balance and so tend to show higher educational levels. Further, there has been a marked increase overall in the amount of schooling obtained by young people. Since for almost everyone schooling ends in early adulthood, communities with higher proportions of older persons will tend to have lower educational standing.

TABLE 12.9

Percentage of Population 25 Years and Over Completing 12 or More or 16 or More Years of School by Size of Place, 1970, 1980

Size of Place	Not Standardized by Age				Standardized by Age[a]			
	1970		1980		1970		1980	
	12 or More	16 or More	12 or More	16 or More	12 or More	16 or More	12 or More	16 or More
Metropolitan	55.3	12.0	68.9	17.9	55.2	12.1	68.4	17.8
Central city	50.8	10.9	64.9	17.4	51.8	11.2	65.0	17.4
Other urban	61.5	14.2	73.2	19.8	60.1	12.9	72.4	17.7
Rural	50.8	8.8	65.5	13.2	49.9	8.7	63.9	12.8
Nonmetropolitan	46.0	7.8	58.8	11.2	47.9	8.1	60.3	11.5
25,000 up and UA[b]	56.4	12.8	67.8	17.2	57.2	13.1	68.7	17.4
10,000–24,999	52.1	10.4	63.2	15.0	54.1	10.9	65.1	15.5
2,500–9,999	49.4	9.2	59.7	12.4	52.1	9.7	62.7	13.2
Rural LT 2,500[c]	45.4	7.2	56.8	9.9	49.6	7.8	60.8	10.6
Other rural	40.5	5.4	56.4	9.1	41.7	5.5	56.7	9.2
United States	52.4	10.7	66.4	16.2				

[a]The standard is the 1980 United States total population.
[b]Places 25,000 and over and other urbanized area population.
[c]Rural places with less than 2,500 population.

400

Urban areas have tended to have better educational opportunities, and more job opportunities requiring greater educational attainment, along with a higher proportion of young adults either completing or having recently completed their schooling. The consequent advantage in educational level is a well-established rural-urban difference. The measures of educational status used here are the percentage of the population 25 and over having completed 12 or more years of schooling, and the percentage having 16 or more years of schooling. In order to adjust for differences in age structure, the percentages also were directly standardized by age, using the 1980 United States total population as a standard.[12]

Results given in Table 12.9 show quite consistent gradients from larger to smaller nonmetropolitan size-of-place groups for both schooling measures, whether or not standardized by age. Indeed age standardization has very little effect on the results. For metropolitan areas the other urban category shows the highest education levels, and this is generally followed by the central city and the rural, in that order. There seems to be a little less difference among the groups in 1980 than in 1970. On the metropolitan side, the central city and the rural segments increased more than the other urban across the decade, and by 1980 the proportion with 16 or more years schooling is as high in the central city as the other urban segment after standardizing for age. On the nonmetropolitan side, the other rural segment gained at a higher rate than the others across the decade although it still has the lowest levels in the table after the age adjustment.

Labor Force Participation

Characteristics relating to economic activity are of major importance both in differentiating communities by size and in understanding the basic community structure underlying the urban hierarchy. The extent to which individuals are in the labor force, the types of occupations they pursue, and the industrial composition of communities are interrelated with most other demographic and family characteristics. We have examined and reported here the size-of-place differentials by labor force participation, principal occupation, and industry of the employed population.

The percentage of persons 16 and over in the labor force is shown by sex and size of place in Table 12.10. Since labor force participation is highly associated with age, generally peaking between 25 and 44, these

[12]Shryock and Siegel (1971), pp. 289-291.

TABLE 12.10

Percentage of Persons in the Labor Force by Sex by Size of Place, 1970, 1980

| | Not Standardized by Age | | | | Standardized by Age[a] | | | |
| | 1970 | | 1980 | | 1970 | | 1980 | |
Size of Place	Male	Female	Male	Female	Male	Female	Male	Female
Metropolitan	78.1	42.7	76.3	51.3	75.9	42.4	74.2	51.9
Central city	75.5	44.4	73.0	51.1	74.6	45.0	72.0	52.8
Other urban	81.0	42.1	78.8	52.4	77.5	41.0	76.0	52.7
Rural	77.5	37.3	76.9	47.7	74.6	36.2	74.0	46.8
Nonmetropolitan	72.8	38.0	71.2	45.2	73.2	38.8	71.8	47.7
25,000 up and UA[b]	75.8	42.6	72.3	51.0	75.1	42.9	72.6	53.5
10,000–24,999	72.8	42.2	72.1	47.7	73.5	43.5	72.7	51.2
2,500–9,999	72.8	40.3	70.1	46.1	74.1	42.4	72.0	51.1
Rural LT 2,500[c]	71.1	38.1	68.9	43.0	74.1	40.9	72.5	48.5
Other rural	72.3	34.4	71.8	43.6	72.2	34.2	71.3	44.2
United States	76.4	41.2	75.0	39.8				

[a]The standard is the 1980 United States total population.
[b]Places 25,000 and over and other urbanized area population.
[c]Rural places with less than 2,500 population.

percentages have also been standardized by age. For males labor force participation is highest for the metropolitan other urban population. Among the nonmetropolitan groups there is little difference in male rates from large places to the other rural segment, except that the 25,000 and over group is somewhat higher than the others in 1970. Before standardizing by age, rural villages have the lowest rates, but after standardizing the other rural is lowest. Recall that villages have the highest proportion of all groups in the advanced age categories, where labor force participation would be low, so that adjusting for age should increase the rate. For women, on the metropolitan side female participation rates are slightly higher in the central city than in the other urban category in 1970. The rates for these two residence groups are about the same in 1980, however. The female nonmetropolitan labor force participation gradient is regular, being higher for more urban places, and shows more differences between the groups than is true for the males.

As discussed in the preceding chapter on the labor force (Chapter 8) changes over the 1970–1980 decade were quite different for males and females. The unadjusted rates for males in Table 12.10 increased very slightly and those standardized by age all declined across the 1970–1980 period. Labor force participation rates for females all increased substantially, however, and were from one-sixth to one-third larger in 1980 than in 1970. Among females, these increases were largest in metropolitan areas outside central cities and within nonmetropolitan areas in places 25,000 and over and in the other rural category. Except for places 25,000 and over, these groups were low in 1970, so that the gradient for females is less pronounced in 1980.

Occupation

Occupation continues to be an important basis of distinction among communities ordered by size. Table 12.11 gives the occupational distribution of the employed population in six broad categories by sex for the size-of-place groups in 1980. Note that this is by residence rather than by place of work. Because the occupational classification was extensively revised before the 1980 census, comparable data for 1970 are not available. Strong gradients are evident across most occupations for both males and females, with a general pattern of decline in the proportions in higher status occupations going from the larger to the smaller size-of-place groups. The metropolitan other urban segment, however, tends to rank somewhat higher than the central city, having a higher proportion of administrators and other white collar workers. The first two occupational categories, together making up the white collar occupations,

TABLE 12.11

Percentage Distribution of Employed Persons by Major Occupation Groups and Sex by Size of Place, 1980

	Male							Female						
	White Collar		Blue Collar					White Collar		Blue Collar				
Size of Place	Adm. Prof.	Clerks Sales	Skilled	Less Skilled	Service	Farms	Total	Adm. Prof.	Clerks Sales	Skilled	Less Skilled	Service	Farms	Total
Metropolitan														
Central city	22.2	20.8	17.6	24.6	13.1	1.7	100	20.1	45.6	2.4	11.4	20.1	.5	100.0
Other urban	25.6	20.8	20.3	21.8	9.6	1.8	100	20.9	49.0	2.2	10.2	17.1	.6	100.0
Rural	17.7	14.6	24.4	27.4	7.6	8.3	100	17.2	41.8	2.5	15.7	19.9	2.8	100.0
Nonmetropolitan														
25,000 up and UA[a]	22.2	18.5	19.4	24.6	11.6	3.6	100	19.1	43.6	1.9	11.8	22.7	.9	100.0
10,000–24,999	20.4	16.9	20.5	27.7	10.6	4.0	100	18.1	41.0	2.2	13.7	23.9	1.1	100.0
2,500–9,999	18.2	15.3	22.4	28.4	10.6	5.2	100	17.0	37.9	2.4	16.1	25.4	1.3	100.0
Rural LT 2,500[b]	14.7	12.8	23.7	31.2	9.0	8.6	100	16.7	32.9	2.7	17.4	28.1	2.2	100.0
Other rural	12.4	10.6	22.8	29.1	6.9	18.3	100	15.4	34.2	2.6	20.9	21.8	5.1	100.0
United States	21.3	18.2	20.5	24.9	10.1	5.0	100	19.3	44.3	2.3	12.8	19.8	1.4	100.0

[a]Places 25,000 and over and other urbanized area population.
[b]Rural places with less than 2,500 population.

range from 46 to 23 for males and from 70 to 50 for females across the size-of-place groups. Skilled workers are more likely to be found in smaller places or rural areas, as are the less skilled, except that for males there is a lower proportion for the other rural than for villages in both occupational categories. The proportion of males employed in service occupations is positively associated with community size, as is the proportion for females within metropolitan categories. For nonmetropolitan groupings, however, this proportion for females is negatively associated with size of place, except for the other rural category. As expected, the proportion employed in farming, for both males and females, is inversely associated with the community size-of-place groups.

Distinctions between various size-of-place groups in their occupational distributions may be summarized by indexes of dissimilarity.[13] These scores contrasting the metropolitan central city with the nonmetropolitan other rural segments, for example, are 26 for males and 16 for females. This means that 26 percent of the males and 16 percent of the females would have to change occupational categories for these two size-of-place groups to have the same occupational distribution. The indexes for the largest and smallest nonmetropolitan categories are 23 for males and 14 for females. Although the occupational categorization is different, we arranged the results reported by Duncan and Reiss into approximately the same six occupational categories shown in Table 12.11.[14] The 1950 indexes of dissimilarity comparing places outside all urbanized areas that were over 25,000 with those less than 2,500 were 10 for males and 7 for females. For 1980, indexes comparing the largest nonmetropolitan category (25,000 and over) and places less than 2,500 are 16 and 13. This at least suggests that occupational differences among communities distinguished by size have not diminished in recent years.

As indicated, indexes of dissimilarity for the size-of-place differentials in Table 12.11 are somewhat less for men than for women. Traditionally, women have predominated in clerical, sales, and service occupations, and this pattern is reproduced for all the size groups considered.

---

[13]The index of dissimilarity indicates the degree of nonoverlapping of two distributions. Its computation may be illustrated as follows:

Occupation	Metro Central City	Nonmetro Other Rural	Overlap
A	10	30	10
B	15	25	15
C	55	10	10
D	20	35	20
Total	100	100	55

Index of dissimilarity = 100 − 55 = 45.

[14]Duncan and Reiss (1956), p. 96.

Perhaps the smaller differences for women between types of community indicates that they have not been able to take advantage of the differential opportunities represented by the size-of-place groups.

To consider further occupational differences by sex, we calculated indexes of dissimilarity between males and females within each of the size groups in Table 12.11. Results show that differences between males and females for any size group are substantial. The index for the United States as a whole is 36, and there is a regular gradient by size of place, from 32 for metropolitan central cities to 42 for nonmetropolitan other rural.[15] We conclude that although substantial differences between male and female occupational structures remain everywhere, the more urban the setting the greater the likelihood that women will hold jobs comparable to those of men. Since it is also true that for men, the proportion employed in white collar and service occupations is greater in larger community size groups, that is, the broad occupational groups in which women predominate, there is a lower differential among the size groups for women than for men.

Industry

An important aspect of the urban hierarchy is the differential participation of places of various sizes in the industrial activity of the nation. Communities differ in their economic functions, and in this regard there are characteristic differences by size. At the same time, this structure has changed markedly over time, moving from an overall dominance of extractive, rural-based activities prior to extensive urbanization to a dominance of manufacturing and now increasingly services. Manufacturing began as an urban function, but much manufacturing activity has moved to more rural and nonmetropolitan settings in recent years. Service activities are more heterogeneous, but traditionally they have also been associated with more urbanlike settings. Here we want to examine the distribution of the employed population by industry for size of place of residence in both 1970 and 1980.

Table 12.12 shows the distribution of the employed population by four broad industry groups across the community types. The proportion employed in agriculture and mining, construction, and manufacturing was less and the proportion employed in services was greater with increasing community size in both 1970 and 1980. The traditional identi-

---

[15]The indexes are: metropolitan central city: 32; other urban: 36; rural: 40; nonmetropolitan 25,000 + : 36; 10,000–24,999: 37; 2,500–9,999: 37; less than 2,500: 41; other rural: 42.

TABLE 12.12

Percentage Distribution of Employed Persons by Major Industry Groups by Size of Place, 1970, 1980

Size of Place	1970					1980				
	Ag. Mining	Constr.	Mftg.	Serv.	Total	Ag. Mining	Constr.	Mftg.	Serv.	Total
Metropolitan	2.0	5.6	25.7	66.7	100.0	2.2	5.6	22.2	70.0	100.0
Central city	1.1	4.9	23.6	70.4	100.0	1.4	4.7	19.6	74.3	100.0
Other urban	1.4	5.7	27.1	65.8	100.0	1.6	5.6	23.1	69.7	100.0
Rural	8.1	8.1	29.4	54.4	100.0	6.9	8.0	26.5	58.6	100.0
Nonmetropolitan	10.8	6.7	26.2	56.3	100.0	10.1	6.7	23.4	59.8	100.0
25,000 up and UA[a]	1.9	5.2	26.0	66.9	100.0	3.0	5.5	19.7	71.8	100.0
10,000–24,999	3.0	5.3	25.0	66.7	100.0	3.7	5.4	21.7	69.2	100.0
2,500–9,999	4.7	6.3	24.4	64.6	100.0	5.5	6.1	21.9	66.5	100.0
Rural LT 2,500[b]	6.9	7.1	24.7	61.3	100.0	7.4	7.0	22.7	62.9	100.0
Other rural	19.2	7.7	27.8	45.3	100.0	15.5	7.5	25.3	51.7	100.0
United States	4.5	5.9	25.9	63.7	100.0	4.0	5.9	22.5	67.6	100.0

[a]Places 25,000 and over and other urbanized area population.
[b]Rural places with less than 2,500 population.

fication of manufacturing with more urban locations makes the orderly gradient in the opposite direction somewhat unexpected.[16] As shown in Chapter 9, however, nonmetropolitan areas now have a higher proportion employed in manufacturing than do metropolitan areas, and there has been much decentralization of manufacturing activity in recent years. Indexes of dissimilarity for the four industry groups between metropolitan central city and nonmetropolitan other rural segments are 25 in 1970 and 23 in 1980. Overall there is little evidence of convergence among the size-of-place categories. Also the proportional distributions did not change very much over the ten-year period. There was a consistent shift, however, in that the manufacturing proportion declined and the service proportion increased for each residence grouping.

The service component is quite heterogeneous, yet it is a large and increasing proportion of the employed population, ranging from 50 to 75 percent of the total in 1980. We have subdivided this category into the four components used in Chapter 9, with the results given in Table 12.13. Although wholesale and retail trade is usually considered to be an urban function, the proportion of those employed in services who are in distributive industries is inversely associated with size-of-place at each time. In 1970 personal services were more important in the nonmetropolitan size-of-place groups under 2,500, but by 1980 there is no consistent association for this smallest service industry category. Social services, however, including health, welfare, education, and public administration, are more or less positively associated with size, and producer services, which include finance, insurance, real estate, and business services, show a stronger association in the same direction. Compared to the overall industry distribution shown in Table 12.12, however, differences in this table are quite small. The indexes of dissimilarity between the metropolitan central city and the nonmetropolitan other urban are 5 in 1970 and 6 in 1980.

Income and Poverty

Given the differences reviewed here in demographic characteristics, in educational status and occupation, and in industrial structure, it should not be surprising that there are patterns of difference among

[16]For example, Duncan *et al.* (1960, p. 60) showed a positive gradient in 1950, with 25 percent employed in manufacturing in nonfarm rural territory and 31 percent so employed in urbanized areas of 3 million or more. They also showed, however, that when types of manufacturing were split into what they termed processing and fabricating, there was an inverse gradient for the processing component. Differences between the major residence groups by type of manufacturing is shown here in Chapter 9.

TABLE 12.13

Percentage Distribution of Persons Employed in Service Industries by Service Industry Groups by Size of Place, 1970, 1980[a]

Size of Place	1970					1980				
	Distributive	Producer	Personal	Social	Total	Distributive	Producer	Personal	Social	Total
Metropolitan	42.0	14.0	8.3	35.7	100.0	40.2	16.2	6.2	37.4	100.0
Central city	40.4	14.5	9.4	35.7	100.0	37.8	16.3	7.0	38.9	100.0
Other urban	43.2	14.0	7.0	35.8	100.0	41.3	16.8	5.7	36.2	100.0
Rural	45.0	11.4	7.9	35.7	100.0	43.7	13.7	5.8	36.8	100.0
Nonmetropolitan	43.2	9.1	10.2	37.5	100.0	42.5	10.9	6.8	39.8	100.0
25,000 up and UA[b]	41.2	10.3	9.4	39.1	100.0	40.9	12.3	6.0	40.8	100.0
10,000–24,999	41.4	9.0	10.5	39.1	100.0	41.2	10.2	7.1	41.5	100.0
2,500–9,999	44.0	8.5	10.5	37.0	100.0	41.8	10.7	7.5	40.0	100.0
Rural LT 2,500[c]	43.5	8.4	10.3	37.8	100.0	43.8	9.7	7.3	39.2	100.0
Other rural	44.4	9.1	10.2	36.3	100.0	43.2	11.2	6.4	39.2	100.0
United States	42.3	12.7	8.8	36.2	100.0	40.7	15.1	6.3	37.9	100.0

[a]See Chapter 9 for explanation of the service industry categories.
[b]Places 25,000 and over and other urbanized area population.
[c]Rural places with less than 2,500 population.

types of communities in income and poverty. A considerable number of studies have shown larger communities to have higher levels of income. Such differences have been shown to persist even after controlling a number of other variables, including personal characteristics of age, education, and employment as well as cost of living differentials.[17]

The measure used here is the percentage of the population 25 years of age and over and reporting income in the year prior to the census that had an income above the United States median. The results in Table 12.14 show almost regular gradients for both males and females in 1980 and 1970, except that the metropolitan other urban is the highest figure in each case. The same pattern prevails after standardization by both age and level of education. The differences are quite substantial between the high and low size-of-place groups, though they are somewhat less so after standardization. For males this is 17 percentage points in 1980, dropping to 11 after controlling for age and education. Corresponding figures for females are 16 and 12 percentage points. Although in general absolute differences among the size-of-place groups are less for females, relative differences are greater, because percentages for females are so much smaller than for males. From one-half to two-thirds of the males are above the median among these size-of-place groups, whereas for females less than one-third are above the median.

The percentage of persons in poverty is given by sex for the size-of-place groups in Table 12.15. In 1970 there was a regular gradient for the nonmetropolitan size-of-place groups for both male and female, with the more rural groups having the higher proportions in poverty. Rates for metropolitan areas were intermediate, except for the other urban segment, which was the lowest of all. By 1980 there was no regular nonmetropolitan gradient, although the 25,000 and over group continued to be lowest and the other rural group highest. For males the metropolitan central city category had become second only to the nonmetropolitan other rural in the extent of poverty, and for females the metropolitan central city was highest of all groups. Over the decade nonmetropolitan categories declined in percentage in poverty except for a very small increase for the 25,000 and over. Declines were greater in the smaller size groups so that there was not much difference between nonmetropolitan groups in 1980. The metropolitan rural category also declined, but the other two metropolitan categories increased in propor-

---

[17]See Fuchs, 1967; Alonso and Fajans, 1970; Hoch, 1972. The significance and reason for this difference has been debated. For example, it has been contended (Hoch, 1972) that the higher income in big cities is a sort of compensation for urban disamenities, but such an interpretation has been called into question by those who contend that larger places are still more efficient (Alonso, 1975).

TABLE 12.14

Percentage of Population 25 Years and Over with an Income Above United States Median, 1970, 1980[a]

Size of Place	Not Standardized				Standardized by Age and Education[b]			
	1970		1980		1970		1980	
	Male	Female	Male	Female	Male	Female	Male	Female
Metropolitan	79.1	35.0	76.5	39.3	77.8	38.9	73.8	39.7
Central city	74.8	34.8	70.2	38.6	75.2	40.7	68.9	40.4
Other urban	84.6	36.8	81.4	41.3	81.2	38.6	77.7	40.7
Rural	76.4	28.8	76.6	33.5	75.6	32.9	74.5	34.7
Nonmetropolitan	64.8	22.3	66.4	26.3	69.6	28.7	68.3	30.2
25,000 up and UA[c]	75.6	28.9	72.7	32.9	74.5	32.9	71.6	34.4
10,000–24,999	70.1	25.2	70.3	29.2	72.2	30.6	70.2	32.2
2,500–9,999	67.2	22.5	66.4	25.7	71.3	28.5	68.3	29.8
Rural LT 2,500[d]	63.2	19.8	65.1	23.2	70.5	27.4	69.2	28.7
Other rural	60.5	20.1	64.9	25.5	66.9	27.1	66.9	29.2
United States	74.6	31.2	73.9	36.1				

[a]The 1980 median is $8,089; the 1970 median is $4,108.
[b]The standard is the United States total population for 1980.
[c]Places 25,000 and over and other urbanized area population.
[d]Rural places with less than 2,500 population.

411

TABLE 12.15

Percentage of Persons in Poverty by Sex and Age by Size of Place, 1970, 1980

Size of Place	Total				Less Than 18 Years				65 Years and Over			
	Male		Female		Male		Female		Male		Female	
	1970	1980	1970	1980	1970	1980	1970	1980	1970	1980	1970	1980
Metropolitan												
Central city	12.9	14.5	16.7	18.3	18.4	23.6	19.0	24.5	18.9	10.4	28.1	17.6
Other urban	6.2	6.6	8.4	8.9	7.7	10.0	8.0	10.5	13.5	5.9	21.5	11.8
Rural	10.3	8.4	12.3	10.5	11.8	11.2	12.2	11.7	24.1	12.0	31.5	18.1
Nonmetropolitan												
25,000 up and UA[a]	11.5	11.9	15.1	15.3	14.0	16.9	14.3	17.6	19.6	9.5	30.9	18.0
10,000–24,999	14.5	12.9	18.6	17.4	17.9	18.7	17.7	19.7	24.7	11.6	36.5	22.0
2,500–9,999	14.9	12.9	19.5	17.3	18.0	18.7	18.4	20.1	27.5	13.1	39.7	22.7
Rural LT 2,500[b]	16.1	12.6	20.8	17.0	18.7	17.6	18.2	18.5	30.6	14.6	43.7	25.5
Other rural	20.8	15.1	23.0	17.5	24.4	19.4	24.3	20.2	35.4	19.4	41.7	24.9
United States	12.1	10.9	15.2	13.9	15.3	16.2	15.6	16.9	22.4	10.8	30.8	17.5

[a]Places 25,000 and over and other urbanized area population.
[b]Rural places with less than 2,500 population.

412

tion in poverty, the other urban very slightly and the central city by 1.6 percentage points for both men and women.

The other two sections of the table give the percentage in poverty for persons under 18 and 65 years old and over. For the less than 18, 1970 gradients are similar to those for the total population, though percentages are somewhat larger. By 1980, for both males and females there is less evidence of the nonmetropolitan gradient and a general increase in poverty proportions, except in the metropolitan rural and nonmetropolitan other rural segments, which declined.

The 65 and over population shows a considerable gradient in the 1970s, with very high proportions (one-third or more) in poverty in the nonmetropolitan rural segments. There continues to be a gradient for 1980, but all the percentages declined by a large amount. On the metropolitan side, unlike both the total population and the youth, the highest 1970 and 1980 percentage in poverty is in the rural rather than the central city segment.

Change in Size-of-Place Differentials

Throughout the discussion of Tables 12.1 through 12.15 we made a number of comparisons between the differences among the size-of-place groups for 1970 and 1980. These trends will be examined more systematically here using a measure of dispersion, the coefficient of variation, for the median age, sex ratio, and all single percentage variables. Similarly, for the age and industry percentage distributions, indexes of dissimilarity between the various size groups in a given year are compared across the decade.

In comparing the coefficients of variation for 1970 and 1980 (Table 12.16) the direction of the shift (more or less variation over time) for all size classes is generally consistent with that for the nonmetropolitan size classes alone. The direction of the shift is not consistently downward, however, which would indicate a convergence in the differentials. In fact, almost one-half of the coefficients are larger in 1980 than in 1970. The ones that increased include the sex ratio, percent black in and out of the South (with continuing concentration in more urban settings), several household variables, and the poverty rate for males 65 and over. One reason for the increased variation among groups for the household variables appears to be the greater increase of nonfamily living arrangements in metropolitan central cities and larger nonmetropolitan cities than in other categories. The increased variation for males 65 and over in poverty, however, appears to be the result of a greater relative disper-

TABLE 12.16

Coefficients of Variation for Selected Variables by Size of Place, 1970, 1980[a]

Variable	All Size Classes		Nonmetro Size Classes	
	1970	1980	1970	1980
Median Age	5.73	3.54	6.51	4.31
Sex Ratio	4.38	4.82	4.24	4.71
Percent Black South	28.20	31.16	6.91	12.98
Percent Black non-South	132.98	141.15	65.98	66.61
Percent in Family HHs	3.58	5.05	3.51	4.87
Percent Families HW	3.26	5.15	1.43	2.70
Percent Families with Children	4.28	2.05	2.46	1.75
Child. Percent in HW Fams.	4.52	7.36	2.42	4.12
Elder Percent in HW Fams.	9.83	9.54	9.87	7.93
Number born to 25–34	8.15	10.65	6.94	6.94
Number born to 35–44	6.31	6.30	4.77	5.64
Migration Metro/Nonmetro	30.07	46.05	8.23	6.38
Education 12+ (USD)	11.73	8.42	11.22	7.03
Education 12+ (STD)	9.92	6.92	10.77	6.92
Education 16+ (USD)	27.16	24.81	28.39	23.96
Education 16+ (STD)	25.69	21.57	28.93	23.99
Labor Force M (USD)	4.09	4.25	2.33	1.86
Labor Force M (STD)	1.90	1.90	1.35	0.75
Labor Force F (USD)	7.75	6.85	8.13	6.28
Labor Force F (STD)	8.53	6.16	8.72	6.68
Income M (USD)	10.29	7.67	7.85	4.56
Income M (STD)	5.42	4.73	3.42	2.32
Income F (USD)	22.07	7.67	14.63	12.43
Income F (STD)	14.64	13.17	7.44	6.93
Poverty Male	30.18	23.05	19.45	8.21
Poverty Female	26.51	21.85	13.45	4.84
Poverty 0–17 Male	29.05	24.42	17.94	4.88
Poverty 0–17 Female	27.97	24.30	17.35	5.26
Poverty 65 up Male	26.89	30.58	19.35	24.47
Poverty 65 up Female	20.64	21.29	11.64	11.73

[a]The coefficient of variation is the standard deviation of the value for the different size-of-place groups divided by the mean times 100.

sion in 1980 following a rather uniform lowering of the poverty rates for all size groups by about one-half in the preceding decade. On the other hand, the education, labor force (except males for all size groups), income, and other poverty variables were generally consistent in showing declines in the coefficients of variation.

The 28 indexes of dissimilarity between each pair of size-of-place groups for the age distributions displayed in Table 12.4 averaged 5.0 in 1970 and 5.8 in 1980. Those for the ten nonmetropolitan comparisons averaged 5.0 in 1970 and 5.6 in 1980, also indicating that the age distributions were slightly more diverse at the latter time. All but four of the individual indexes were larger in 1980 than in 1970, and generally the overall differences in age distribution patterns for 1970 seem to have been accentuated by 1980.

The seven industry categories of Tables 12.12 and 12.13 were put together in single percentage distributions for each size group and indexes of dissimilarity were calculated. The mean of the 28 indexes between each pair of size-of-place groups dropped slightly from 10.3 to 9.8 and the mean for the ten indexes between the nonmetropolitan groups declined from 10.5 to 9.5. Among both sets of indexes there was convergence, particularly for pairs that included the other rural nonmetropolitan category. This residence declined particularly in the proportional importance of agriculture (3.7 percentage points) and somewhat less so in manufacturing, and gained in all services except personal service, becoming as a consequence more like the other residence groups in industry structure.

We can conclude that the socioeconomic differentials among the size-of-place groups tended to decline, but several demographic and family variables showed increasing difference by size of place between 1970 and 1980.

Commuting and Size of Place

Commuting undoubtedly has had an important influence on recent trends in population distribution and community structure. The separation between location of residence and location of work is a basis for greater interdependence among communities, and preferences for low density residential settlement have led to a decentralization of residences that appears to have outstripped any decentralization in the location of employment. Chapter 3 showed that a dominant recent trend, even in nonmetropolitan areas, has been a greater relative population growth among smaller sized places and rural areas. To the extent that this trend may be due to commuting it could underlie some decline in the size-of-place differentials noted in the preceding section. For 1980, consequently, there would be good reason to expect larger size-of-place differentials, particularly for economic variables, if the population were classified by place of work rather than by place of residence.

We are able to consider this issue using our special 1980 public use (PUMS) census file, and will present highlights of the analysis here. A variable in this file gives place of work by metropolitan–nonmetropolitan and size-of-place categories. Because it is not possible also to distinguish place of work by whether it is inside or outside urbanized areas, a census rural–urban classification could not be made, so we employed an abbreviated five-group size-of-place distinction by which the working population could be cross-classified by place of work and place of residence.[18]

Commuting represents a very important aspect of the interrelation among units of the size-of-place hierarchy. Table 12.17 shows the distribution of the 88 million employed workers represented in the 1980 PUMS file by place of residence and by place of work according to the five size-of-place groups. (The individual commuting streams among the five groups are given in Appendix Table 12.1.) The net interchange in numbers is as anticipated, with net gains of workers in central cities and in the urban nonmetropolitan size-of-place groups from the metropolitan other and nonmetropolitan less than 2,500 categories. Metropolitan areas overall had a net gain of almost 1 million commuters from

---

[18]The reference population here is 88,088,000 as estimated from the PUMS file. This includes persons 16 and over at work during the census week in April 1980 (approximately 96.6 million according to published census reports) less those whose place of work was in an outlying area or foreign country, abroad or at sea, or who did not report a place of work. In addition, we dropped 436,000 persons who lived in nonmetropolitan Urbanized Areas in the Middle Atlantic, South Atlantic, East South Central, and Mountain census divisions. As noted previously, because of disclosure rules the Bureau of the Census combined the nonmetropolitan population in urbanized areas with that in living places of 25,000 or more in the residence code of our special 1980 PUMS file. Since the place of work question allowed designation by metropolitan status and size of place but not by urbanized area status, this created a small discrepancy in the cross-classification of place of work with place of residence for identifying commuting streams. For example, a person living in a nonmetropolitan urbanized area outside any place and working in the same setting would be shown as commuting from a place of 10,000 or more to an area outside places of 2,500 or more. The urbanized area population was identified separately on the file, however, for the census divisions noted above. By dropping these people, we reduced the universe by 0.5 percent and the nonmetropolitan 10,000 and over class by 9 percent. Of the urbanized area component of the reference population remaining (approximately 203,000 people in the other census divisions) about three-fourths actually lived in places over 10,000 population, and hence would not be inconsistent in the place of work–place of residence cross-classification in any event. The remaining inconsistent population is thus estimated at about 55,000, which is a little over 1 percent of the 4.2 million workers living in nonmetropolitan places over 10,000 in size.

TABLE 12.17

Place of Residence and Place of Work by Size-of-Place Groups, 1980[a]

	Size of Place					
	Metropolitan		Nonmetropolitan			
Residence/Work	Central City	Other	10,000 UP	2,500– 9,999	LT 2,500	Total
Population (000s)						
Residence	25,396	42,173	4,167	3,514	12,403	87,653
Work	35,918	32,604	5,731	4,254	9,146	87,653
Difference	10,522	−9,564	1,564	740	−3,257	0
Commute in	15,416	5,748	2,604	2,180	2,198	28,146
Commute out	4,894	15,317	1,040	1,440	5,455	28,146
Percent						
Residence (distribution)	29.0	48.1	4.7	4.0	14.2	100.0
Work (distribution)	41.0	37.2	6.6	4.8	10.4	100.0
Workers who commute in	42.9	17.6	45.4	51.2	24.0	32.0
Residents who commute out	19.3	36.3	25.0	41.0	44.0	32.0
Commuting efficiency[b]	51.8	−45.4	42.9	20.4	−42.5	0

[a]Population 16 and over at work and reporting place of work in the United States. See footnote 18.
[b]Number who commute in minus number who commute out divided by sum of in- and out-commuters times 100.

nonmetropolitan areas, so that the population at work in metropolitan areas was 68.5 million, but that residing in metropolitan areas was 67.5 million. Conversely, the working population in nonmetropolitan areas was 19.1 million and that residing in nonmetropolitan areas 20 million. The differences in the percent distribution by residence and work are marked, particularly for the two metropolitan categories. Less than 30 percent of the working population lived in central cities in 1980, but more than 40 percent worked there. Conversely almost one-half of all the workers in the nation lived in metropolitan areas outside central cities, but only 37 percent worked there.

The number of in- and out-commuters indicates that the importance of commuting is not adequately reflected in the net distribution differences given above. Overall 28 million, or one-third, of the 88 million workers were employed in a different size class location than the one in which they lived. Of the population working in a given size group, from one-half to about one in six lived in other groups, and similarly of the population living in a given size group from 20 up to 44 percent worked in some other group location. The interchange is particularly large for the 2,500–9,999 group, which had a positive net balance of in- and out-commuters of about 750,000, based on more than 2 million in-commuters and 1.4 million out-commuters. The importance of the interchange is summarized in an efficiency index, which is computed in the same way as a migration efficiency index. That is, the difference between the number of in-commuters and out-commuters is divided by the sum of these two numbers and multiplied by 100. This measure indicates, for example, that for the 2,500–9,999 category 100 in- and out-commuters are required to result in a net gain of 20 workers. The highest index, or most efficient interchange, is for the metropolitan central city category, for which 100 commuters are required for a net gain of 52.

This massive interchange among the size-of-place groups, however, has resulted in relatively small differences between place of work and place of residence for economic variables. Table 12.18 gives the results

TABLE 12.18

Occupational Distribution of Working Population by Size of Place of Residence and by Size of Place of Work, 1980[a]

| | Occupational Groups | | | | | | |
| | White Collar | | Blue Collar | | | | |
Size of Place	Adm. Prof.	Clerks Sales	Skilled	Less Skilled	Service	Farms	Total
Distribution by Place of Residence							
Metropolitan							
Central city	24.4	33.4	10.6	16.5	14.4	0.7	100.0
Other	24.9	32.2	13.3	16.5	11.2	1.9	100.0
Nonmetropolitan							
10,000+	23.0	29.3	12.2	18.9	15.1	1.5	100.0
2,500–9,999	20.4	26.6	14.0	21.3	15.5	2.3	100.0
LT 2,500	15.9	21.0	15.3	24.6	12.2	11.1	100.0
Total	23.2	30.5	12.8	18.0	12.6	2.9	100.0
Distribution by Place of Work							
Metropolitan							
Central city	25.8	34.5	11.4	15.4	12.3	0.6	100.0
Other	23.1	30.4	13.6	18.2	12.3	2.4	100.0
Nonmetropolitan							
10,000+	21.4	30.2	12.5	20.3	14.5	1.0	100.0
2,500–9,999	19.6	26.6	13.0	23.6	15.7	1.5	100.0
LT 2,500	16.2	17.8	15.5	23.0	12.1	15.4	100.0
Total	23.2	30.5	12.8	18.0	12.6	2.9	100.0

[a]Population 16 and over at work and reporting place of work in the United States. See footnote 18.

418

for the six occupational groups. Gradients across the size-of-place groups are very similar by place of residence and place of work, though, as expected, the proportions in the higher status occupations in metropolitan central cities are somewhat greater by place of work than by place of residence and conversely less by place of work than by residence in the metropolitan other and nonmetropolitan less than 2,500 categories.

The distributions of employment by industry similarly do not show a great deal of difference between place of work and place of residence (Table 12.19). The small differences that do exist, however, tend to be larger in more rural settings. As would be expected, agricultural employment is more likely to be found in smaller sized nonmetropolitan categories, particularly the less than 2,500 group, with 12 percent of the population working there found in this industry but with only 8 percent of the residents there. The reverse is true in this location category, however, for manufacturing, the industry of more than 26 percent of the

TABLE 12.19

Industrial Distribution of Working Population by Size of Place of Residence and by Size of Place of Work, 1980[a]

				Industry Group				
Size of Place	Agric.	Const.	Mftg.	Dist. Serv.	Prod. Serv.	Per. Ser.	Soc. Ser.	Total
Distribution by Place of Residence								
Metropolitan								
Central city	1.3	4.5	19.5	28.1	12.3	4.9	29.3	100.0
Other	2.6	5.9	24.0	27.9	11.1	3.7	24.8	100.0
Nonmetropolitan								
10,000+	3.2	5.2	21.3	28.5	7.5	4.7	29.6	100.0
2,500–9,999	5.4	5.9	22.0	27.6	7.2	4.9	27.0	100.0
LT 2,500	14.0	7.2	24.8	23.3	5.8	3.5	21.4	100.0
Total	4.0	5.7	22.6	27.3	10.3	4.1	26.0	100.0
Distribution by Place of Work								
Metropolitan								
Central city	1.1	4.8	19.7	28.2	13.1	4.1	29.0	100.0
Other	3.2	6.1	25.7	27.6	9.8	4.2	23.4	100.0
Nonmetropolitan								
10,000+	1.9	5.1	23.1	28.7	7.9	4.1	29.2	100.0
2,500–9,999	3.0	5.0	25.7	27.6	7.1	4.4	27.2	100.0
LT 2,500	19.9	8.1	21.3	21.6	4.9	4.0	20.2	100.0
Total	4.0	5.7	22.6	27.3	10.3	4.1	26.0	100.0

[a]Population 16 and over at work and reporting place of work in the United States. See footnote 18.

419

employed residents but of 23 percent of those working there. Evidently a number of people living in the less than 2,500 location category commute to nonmetropolitan cities (as well as to MSAs) for employment in manufacturing, since these cities have a higher proportion of their working population in manufacturing than their resident population. The metropolitan other category also has a slightly higher concentration in manufacturing by place of work than place of residence. In comparing industry distributions by place of work and place of residence for each size-of-place category, only two differences other than for agriculture and manufacturing are greater than 1 percent.

Finally, the median income from earnings by men and women are compared by residence and by work for the five size-of-place groups in Table 12.20. (Earnings includes only wage and salary and self-employment income). For men the metropolitan population outside central cities has the highest median by residence, which is consistent with the parallel analysis shown in Table 13.14. As a result of commuting patterns, however, the central city median is highest by place of work, making the overall gradient consistent in a positive association by size of place. At the same time the net interchange of commuters led to lower medians by place of work for the metropolitan other and nonmetropolitan less than 2,500 categories.

For women there is a positive association of medians by size of place both by residence and by location of work. This is similarly not inconsistent with the findings of Table 13.14 for women, given that the

TABLE 12.20

Median Income from Earnings for Male and Female Workers by Size of Place of Work and by Size of Place of Residence, 1979[a]

Size of Place	Male		Female	
	Residence	Work	Residence	Work
Metropolitan				
Central city	$13,980	$15,820	$8,110	$8,440
Other	16,700	15,560	7,890	7,390
Nonmetropolitan				
10,000+	13,230	13,320	6,440	6,600
2,500–9,999	12,840	12,430	6,170	6,190
LT 2,500	12,400	11,810	6,240	5,810
Total	14,990	14,990	7,530	7,530

[a]Population 16 and over at work and reporting place of work in the United States. See footnote 18.

metropolitan other urban and metropolitan rural groups are combined in the present table. Again the effect of income on commuting levels is as expected, with a higher income by place of work in the central city and a lower income by place of work in the metropolitan other and the nonmetropolitan less than 2,500 categories.

All in all, these commuting effects of income levels are not great for either sex. The largest percentage difference in median income between place of residence and place of work in the table is 13 for males in metropolitan central cities, with other corresponding percentage differences at one-half of that figure or less. Further work should include a more detailed examination of the income, occupation, industry, and other characteristics of the individual commuter streams among these size-of-place groups which together produce the aggregate differences reviewed in this section.

Conclusion

In this chapter we have compared a variety of demographic, social, and economic characteristics for groups of metropolitan and nonmetropolitan cities, towns, and rural areas. Once more size of place has been confirmed as an important source of community variation. Such a result is hardly surprising. Indeed, more than thirty years ago Duncan and Reiss noted that the sheer physical contrast between a large urban center and a town of 2,500 is so striking that we would be amazed if there were not also important social contrasts.[19] Our findings for 1980 and 1970 tend to be quite consistent with theirs based on the 1950 census. Though there must be some qualifications, in general larger places have an excess of young adults, more women relative to men, a higher proportion of racial and ethnic minorities, lower proportions in more traditional family situations, and generally higher socioeconomic measures, including educational attainment, occupation, and income.

These results may have been expected, but it is important to underscore the fact that such differentials between communities of different size continue to be found despite the fact that many recent demographic and organizational changes over the past thirty years have contributed to a blurring of rural-urban distinctions. Although there have been greatly increased contacts across types of community through innovations in transportation and communication, and a high degree of cultural standardization now exists throughout the nation, the orderly so-

---

[19]Duncan and Reiss (1956), p. 3.

cial and economic differences reflected by the census measures considered here indicate that the urban hierarchy is still alive and well.

A systematic look at changes in the size-of-place differentials between 1970 and 1980 indicates that there has been a move toward convergence among the community size groups in most socioeconomic differentials but a divergence for most other variables, notably those relating to family structure. An important component of both these trends has been a relative deterioration in the overall status of residents of larger cities, especially metropolitan central cities. For example, the percentage of the population in family households, though generally declining, declined more in large cities, thus increasing the differences among size-of-place groups. The percentage of males having income above the national median similarly declined in large cities, but it increased in rural areas, lessening the differences among the groups. For better or worse, such trends of both convergence and divergence may help to make small towns and rural areas more attractive to many people.

At least some of the convergence in economic variables may be due to an increased prevalence of commuting across these size-of-place groups, though data are not available for an interdecade comparison. An examination of commuting streams for 1980 showed this practice to be extremely important today in tying together communities at all levels of the urban hierarchy. Commuting among the size-of-place groups is not primarily in one direction. At least figuratively speaking, many people must pass each other on the way to work in the other person's home community. The net result is a small difference between a classification by place of residence and one by place of work in employment and income size-of-place differentials, although as expected the place of work classification does show stronger gradients.

Distinctions by size of place have often been explained in part by currents of selective migration. Large cities have typically been the recipients of higher status and more long-distance movers who are primarily economically motivated. The migration trends of the 1970s, however, favored smaller nonmetroplitan communities to a greater degree than previously, and this too may help to explain some of the 1970–1980 changes in the size-of-place differentials.

APPENDIX TABLE 12.1

Population by Place of Work and Place of Residence for Size Groups, 1980[a]
(in thousands)

Size of Place of Residence	Size of Place of Work					
	Metropolitan		Nonmetropolitan			
	Central City	Other	10,000 Up	2,500– 9,999	LT 2,500	Total
Metropolitan						
Central city	20,502	4,668	49	47	130	25,396
Other	14,557	26,856	185	149	425	42,172
Nonmetropolitan						
10,000+	100	134	3,127	104	703	4,168
2,500–9,999	108	125	269	2,074	939	3,515
LT 2,500	651	821	2,102	1,880	6,948	12,402
United States	35,918	32,604	5,732	4,254	9,145	87,653

[a]Population 16 and over at work and reporting place of work in the United States. See footnote 18.

13

THE PERSISTING IMPORTANCE
OF RESIDENCE

D URING the latter half of the twentieth century, the American population has undergone gradual but profound changes in demographic composition, socioeconomic attributes, and residential distribution. These changes have been pervasive, affecting people in rural and small town settings as well as those who live in more highly urbanized and densely settled locales. Nevertheless, residential differences persist in the 1980s, structuring the lives people live and the opportunities available to them.

We have shown that rural and nonmetropolitan areas figured importantly in the recent deconcentration of the American population, but we have also shown that population distribution trends affecting rural and small town America have been significantly different from those affecting urban and metropolitan areas. The American population has become less concentrated during recent decades. Suburban growth characterizes most metropolitan areas, and the regional trend has been from the densely settled North to the less densely settled South and West. The dramatic reversal of the decades-long pattern of metropolitan population concentration experienced during the late 1960s and the 1970s also contributed to this trend. Since then, however, there has been a resumption of more rapid metropolitan growth and nonmetropolitan net outmigration. Clearly, residential differences in population growth and migration continue to be important demographic issues in the 1980s.

We have demonstrated the persistence of residential differentiation in social, demographic, and economic characteristics, while at the same time noting that nonmetropolitan and rural areas have participated in recent societal trends and changes. Continuing low fertility, population aging, increased women's labor force participation, the transformation of traditional household structures—these and many other secular demographic trends are characteristic of communities at all levels of the urban hierarchy. Yet our analyses show that while urban influence has spread into rural areas, blurring residential distinctions, the economic and social organization of communities and their demographic structures continue to vary along an urban hierarchy.

Synthesis of Principal Findings

Our comparative research has had three interrelated foci—population growth and distribution, demographic and socioeconomic characteristics, and the economic activities of the population. Key findings from each part of our study are synthesized below. A discussion of the implications of these trends and changes for public policy follows.

Population Growth and Distribution

Throughout most of this century, the twin processes of urbanization and metropolitan development have predominated. Organizational and technological changes in traditional, resource-based, rural industries such as agriculture and mining have resulted in reduced labor demand, while growth of industrial employment was relatively concentrated in larger cities and their immediate environs. The rural population has been relatively stable at between 50 and 60 million persons since 1900. In contrast, urban areas have increased sevenfold, resulting in a radical diminution in the rural share of the nation's population.

The structure of economic activities and their geographic location have changed markedly since the late 1960s, resulting in unprecedented and unexpected shifts in the urban–rural and metropolitan–nonmetropolitan distribution of population. During the 1960s and 1970s, rural and small-town areas competed successfully with more highly urbanized areas in attracting or creating jobs. Even though many of these jobs were relatively routine and low paid, they provided economic opportunities in areas where few nonagricultural activities had previously existed. This employment growth helped rural and small-town areas attract labor force age population from other areas and retain their own workers. As a result, net outmigration of working-age persons from non-metropolitan areas in the 1970s was substantially reduced compared with earlier decades. At the same time, nonmetropolitan areas attracted newcomers outside the young adult ages.

The decentralization of industrial and service-based employment was a critical factor in the nonmetropolitan population turnaround, but other economic and noneconomic factors also affected the flow of mi-gration and consequently the relative rates of population growth be-tween metropolitan and nonmetropolitan areas. These factors, when considered together, reflect the changed status of small towns and rural areas in the national settlement structure as well as their changed eco-nomic activities. Other economic factors affecting population distribu-tion included: an equilibrium in the supply and demand of agricultural labor stemming the flow of rural workers from areas heavily dependent on this sector of the economy, price-induced increases in labor demand in mining and energy extraction, and the development of a widespread recreation and retirement industry throughout rural America. Noneco-nomic, or at least nonpecuniary, factors included community moderniza-tion, greater residential sprawl in the far peripheries of metropolitan areas, and a generalized public preference for living in smaller scale communities. In sum, these changes portray a heightened set of social and economic linkages between rural areas and more highly urbanized locales. Rural and small town America has come to be an integral part of the highly urban and metropolitan society that is the United States today. Accordingly, national (and global) events now have a more direct impact on present-day life there.

These heightened linkages have made rural and nonmetropolitan economies more sensitive to changes in the business cycle, global com-petition, and macroeconomic policy. These factors, combined with long-standing weaknesses in the rural economy, have had an unmistakable effect on the reduced population growth experienced by nonmetropoli-tan areas since 1980. The return to slower nonmetropolitan population growth during this period, and indeed widespread decline and migration loss, is surely associated with a delayed recovery from the 1979–1982 recession, financial stress in agriculture and its linked industries, and slow growth or decline of employment in rural and nonmetropolitan manufacturing and resource-based industries.

Our analysis of variation in population growth among nonmetro-politan counties, however, indicates that the turnaround period of the 1970s signaled a fundamental modification of the United States popu-lation distribution process which is continuing in the 1980s. Thus, there has not been a reversion to the factors associated with growth and decline in the 1960s or before. In comparing the 1960s and the turnaround period of the 1970s, we found a decline in the importance of variables associated with local urban development, a weakening of the positive effects of employment in manufacturing and of median family income, a decline in the negative effect of employment in agriculture, and a substantial increase in the strength of the positive association of population growth with recreation activities and climatic conditions. The post-1980 period saw a further decline in the importance of local urban development, employment in agriculture and median family income, a maintenance of the positive growth effect of recreation and climate, and a switch from positive to negative in the effect of manufacturing employment. Accordingly, we conclude that there has been a modification of the population distribution process. The turnaround appears to have involved a shift in the determinants of population distribution patterns that continues in the 1980s even though the relative rates of population growth have switched in favor of metropolitan areas.

Another indicator that slackened nonmetropolitan population growth since 1980 does not necessarily indicate a full resumption of population concentration to the extent that it occurred in the 1950s and 1960s is that population deconcentration continues to be the dominant pattern *within* the nonmetropolitan sector itself. That is, the rural parts of nonmetropolitan counties continued to grow faster than urban parts during the 1980s, as they did in the 1970s (prior to which time declining nonmetropolitan counties typically experienced the opposite pattern, that is, rapid losses in rural population with accompanying urban growth). Improvements in transportation and communication have permitted population and economic activity to be more dispersed than previously.

Finally, while metropolitan areas are gaining migrants from nonmetropolitan areas once again, and are growing somewhat more rapidly, it should be noted that nonmetropolitan net outmigration is only one of the sources of this metropolitan growth resurgence. International immigration, an increasingly important factor in United States population growth, for example, is almost entirely oriented toward metropolitan destinations. And, even though almost one-half of nonmetropolitan counties have lost population since 1980, their rates of decline are less than they were in the 1960s.

Demographic and Socioeconomic Characteristics

Our monograph has compared major aspects of demographic and socioeconomic characteristics between residence categories. The analytical framework compared rural-nonmetropolitan versus urban-metropolitan areas now and in previous decades, and compared the direction and rapidity of sociodemographic and economic change among these various residential categories over time. In each instance, whether the focus was age–sex composition, household structure, fertility, race and ethnicity, or income distribution, we found evidence of residential convergence, but we also identified persisting residential differences that support the continued importance of considering residence in social scientific analysis and in policy and program development. Some specific examples of persisting differences in the context of residential convergence follow.

Age Composition. Rural and nonmetropolitan areas retain a higher proportion of children, relatively fewer young adults and middle-aged persons, and a larger proportion of the elderly. Dominant secular trends such as persistent low fertility, the movement of large baby boom cohorts into adulthood, and increased longevity have shaped age composition in all residence categories, but the nonmetropolitan population has aged more than the metropolitan population because of aging in place and net inmigration of elderly persons. The working age population grew somewhat more rapidly in metropolitan areas because the baby boom was more dramatic there and because metropolitan areas were gaining labor force age migrants from abroad during the 1970s.

Persisting differences in age composition continue to impose on rural and small town areas a greater dependency burden, on average, than more highly urbanized areas. This is particularly important with regard to the elderly, because much of the residential difference in the dependency ratio is accounted for by a higher proportion of nonmetropolitan persons at the very oldest ages where issues of economic support and specialized service needs are most critical. Moreover, not only are the elderly a greater proportion of the rural and small town population, but they are less well off in terms of objective economic measures than older persons living in more highly urbanized environments.

Fertility. Residential differences in fertility have narrowed, but rural and small town residence continues to be socioculturally conducive to earlier (and greater) childbearing in a way not true of metropolitan society. This is true despite the fact that blacks and Hispanics, two of the groups with the highest propensity for early childbearing, are underrepresented in the rural and nonmetropolitan population.

With the exception of the post–World War II baby boom period, American fertility has declined in both urban and rural settings since the eighteenth century, yet the higher fertility of rural and nonmetropolitan women persists. Our analysis demonstrated that this difference is *not* completely accounted for by rural and small town women's earlier age at marriage or by their lower levels of formal educational attainment. From a generational replacement point of view, rural women at the end of their childbearing years (ages 35–44) have borne 43 percent more children than required for replacement compared with 33 percent more for urban women.

Household Composition. Changes in household composition have been societywide, but rural and small town areas have tended to lag behind the trends. This persistence of residential differences may be associated with more traditional rural attitudes toward marital stability, premarital sex, labor force participation of married women, and geographic isolation and small community size.

Rural and small town areas continue to be characterized by a more traditional household structure. A higher proportion of rural and small town family households contain a married couple, and a smaller proportion is comprised of single parents. A smaller proportion of rural and small town persons live alone, and a higher proportion of those who do are elderly persons, not young adults, as is more likely to be the case in more highly urbanized areas.

Racial and Ethnic Minorities. Minority-related social issues are not as generally salient in rural and nonmetropolitan areas as in more urban locales, but they are immediately pressing in many local and regional areas. Racial and ethnic groups are underrepresented in rural and nonmetropolitan areas. Only American Indians are predominantly (51 percent) nonmetropolitan, while the proportion of blacks, Hispanics, and Asian and Pacific Islanders living in nonmetropolitan areas is much smaller than is true of the total nonmetropolitan population. Looked at somewhat differently, these four groups combined accounted for 12 percent of the nonmetropolitan population, whereas they comprised almost one-quarter of the metropolitan population. The disparity is growing as the number of blacks living in rural and small town areas continues to decline. Hispanics and Asians are increasing in rural and small town areas, but at a much slower rate than in more highly urbanized environments. So, the proportion of all of the major racial and ethnic minorities living in rural and small town areas can be expected to decline further in the future.

Racial and ethnic groups are not evenly distributed across the rural and nonmetropolitan landscape. In most of the South, for example, blacks still comprise large fractions and even majorities of the rural and small town population. In contrast, they are almost totally absent in rural and nonmetropolitan areas outside of this region. This situation is exacerbated by the fact that racial and ethnic minorities tend to be concentrated in rural and nonmetropolitan areas that are socially disadvantaged and are experiencing slow economic growth or decline.

Income and Poverty. Residential differences in income and poverty have converged over time. On an inflation adjusted basis, the nonmetropolitan per capita income increased by 21 percent from 1969–1979 compared with a 14 percent increase in metropolitan areas. This still left nonmetropolitan per capita income only 77 percent as high as that in metropolitan areas, though substantially higher than in the past, and this comparison does not include a consideration of cost of living, which has been shown to be somewhat lower in rural and small town communities. In addition, some of the principal demographic factors associated with poverty are similar regardless of residence. For example, rural and small town poverty has become more concentrated among youth in recent years, a fact that is related to changes in household and family structure, and especially the increase in families maintained by women with no spouse present.

In contrast, rural and urban poor are clearly differentiated on other social and demographic characteristics. The rural and nonmetropolitan poor are more likely to be elderly and white and to reside in the South. Also, the rural and small town poor are more likely to be in the work force. Over two-thirds of poor nonmetropolitan families had at least one worker in 1985, and one-fourth had two or more workers. In metropolitan areas only 54 percent of poor families had even one worker.[1] As a result, the structure and performance of rural and small town labor markets have an important bearing on rural poverty.

Lower rural and small town income and higher poverty is partly attributable to the lower human capital possessed by rural workers, but some of the difference is due to the occupational composition and wage levels of rural economies. For example, our analysis showed that rural workers receive a much lower payoff from each year of higher education than their urban counterparts. And we also showed that rural and small town workers receive lower wages than urban workers with jobs in the same industrial categories.

In summary, these persisting residential differences in demographic and socioeconomic characteristics indicate that the urban hierarchy still matters in the 1980s. Thirty years after Duncan and Reiss did their pioneering work, our analysis of 1980 census data shows many similar socioeconomic and demographic differences between small towns and rural areas and more urbanized environments.[2] Enhanced contacts across community types, facilitated by modern communication and transportation, and the increased cultural homogenization of our society

---

[1]Brown and Deavers (1988).
[2]Duncan and Reiss (1956).

have blurred residential differences but have not abolished them. These persisting differences have important implications for public and private decision making in all types of communities.

Economic Activities

The industrial structure of the United States economy has changed dramatically during recent decades. These changes have affected the number and types of employment opportunities available in local economies throughout the nation, as well as the pecuniary rewards associated with employment. Our analysis of industrial change in rural and small town areas in comparison with changes in metropolitan areas shows parallel transformations toward service-based activities, but also identifies persistent differences.

Industrial Transformation. Both metropolitan and nonmetropolitan areas are moving toward service-based economies, but the path to this similarity has differed in the two residential categories. Growth in the share of metropolitan employment accounted for by services was mostly at the expense of manufacturing, while the increased proportion of services in nonmetropolitan areas came largely from the decline of employment in extractive industries. The share of nonmetropolitan employment accounted for by manufacturing has been relatively stable since 1960. Employment in extractive industries declined in all areas but is still a much larger component of employment in nonmetropolitan counties.

Our analysis showed that nonmetropolitan counties have a preponderance of low wage manufacturing, but we also demonstrated that some new manufacturing jobs in nonmetropolitan areas are in high-wage industries. Nonmetropolitan employment growth in services, in contrast, was mostly in routine, lower wage jobs. This indicates that nonmetropolitan manufacturers are obtaining producer services outside of their local economies, in metropolitan areas.

The occupational composition of employment by industry provides additional evidence that the seeming convergence between metropolitan and nonmetropolitan economic structures masks much difference in the types of jobs actually performed. Almost two-thirds of metropolitan men holding jobs in producer services were white collar workers, for example, compared with only half of nonmetropolitan men working in the same industrial category.

The analysis indicated that United States goods production has become increasingly concentrated in nonmetropolitan economies. This is a mixed blessing. Manufacturing provides relatively high-wage jobs for rural and nonmetropolitan workers, but it also exposes them to the vicissitudes of the business cycle and makes them more vulnerable to foreign competition. This was clearly demonstrated during the 1979–1982 recession when the nonmetropolitan unemployment rate rose more rapidly than the metropolitan rate, peaked at a higher level, and has remained above the metropolitan rate during the 1980s.

One method of increasing industrial competitiveness is to adopt technology that enhances productivity. Since this technology generally reduces the demand for labor, however, such adjustments can hardly be expected to help retain population or attract newcomers. On the other hand, mixing more productive "leaner" manufacturers with high-technology producer services in a more diversified local economy may provide the economic basis for population growth and/or stability in the future. The success of such strategies would seem to be enhanced if several local areas cooperated in economic ventures. This would provide sufficient size to benefit from scale economies and would support the provision of necessary technical assistance in the public and private sectors.

Agriculture will doubtless continue to be the mainstay of many rural economies, especially in the Midwest. Even outside of this farm-dependent region, farming is an important element of the rural and small town economy. This is especially true when farming is viewed from the perspective of the activities to which it is linked. However, even from this perspective it is clear that agriculture provides far fewer jobs and much less household income than was previously true. Although there will be a need for farm-dependent areas to continue to diversify their economies, the technological and organizational changes that gave rise to the massive outmigrations of the 1950s and 1960s are largely completed.

The farm residence category, traditionally the most common way of identifying the "farm population," is now of little use in identifying the farm-related population. We demonstrated that many farm residents are now engaged in nonfarm occupations, and conversely many persons who work in agriculture do not live on farms. The overall trend is toward increasing diversity in the farm-related population. Accordingly, different types of farm-related individuals and/or households will be affected quite differently by different types of trends in agriculture and the national economy. This makes them an exceedingly difficult group to target for assistance.

Women's Labor Force Participation. Increased women's labor force participation was the second major economic theme to emerge from our analysis. Almost 50 percent of nonmetropolitan women worked outside of the home in 1980 and participation was relatively continuous throughout the life course. Participation dipped below 50 percent only before age 20 and after age 65. Even the presence of young children in the home was shown to be a diminished constraint to labor force activity.

Increased women's labor force participation rates were shown to be the principal source of women's employment growth in nonmetropolitan areas between 1960 and 1980, even though the baby boom cohorts were reaching labor force age during these decades. In contrast, because male participation rates were declining, male employment would have declined if baby boom age men had not been reaching employment age.

In summary, although the main economic parameters of metropolitan and nonmetropolitan labor markets have been converging lately, our research shows substantial residential differences in the types of jobs performed and their pecuniary rewards. These differences in economic structure are critically important to the future viability of rural and small town economies, their competitive position in the overall United States economy, and their ability to maintain a stable (or growing) population base and labor force.

Implications of Demographic Change for Rural Economic Growth

Sociodemographic and economic change has blurred residential differences, but it has not abolished them. Regardless of whether we focus on population change and distribution, sociodemographic characteristics, or the economic activities of the population, residence makes a difference in the 1980s. Moreover, the different economic paths now being followed imply that such differences will persist long into the future.

In discussing the implications of these changes and possible policies, it is important to emphasize residential differences particularly because rural needs are easily ignored in a metropolitan society. But our findings also showed clearly that rural and small town America is an integral part of this metropolitan society. Basic demographic and socioeconomic trends often paralleled those for urban and metropolitan areas, and there also was evidence of convergence and increased interdependence that cannot be ignored in policy considerations.

Until a decade ago, rural policy and farm policy were often considered to be synonymous. Such congruency was never entirely defensible, and today it lacks any validity at all. Even in areas that are heavily dependent on agriculture, influences besides those related to farming now exert important effects on the functioning of local economies and the well-being of rural people. Policies focusing on specific industries are not likely to provide a basis for rural economic prosperity.

The transformation of the national economy to greater dependence on services, and the enhanced linkages among local economies throughout the urban hierarchy (and throughout the world) sets the overall context for considering the main dimensions of rural policy in our metropolitan society. How can rural areas and small towns maintain and/or improve their social and economic viability within this changed context? What types of development strategies have the best chance of succeeding in this changed environment? What differentiates successful rural communities from those in economic distress?

Rural Characteristics and Policy

The demographic analysis reported here identifies some critical considerations for assessing these questions and for conceptualizing rural policy.[3] While this research indicates diminishing rural–urban differences, it has also identified a number of limiting characteristics of rural areas and small towns that constrain their development options, which suggests important development strategies.

Small Size and Geographic Isolation.   Rural areas and small towns tend to be characterized by small size, geographic distance from each other and from metropolitan centers, and thin technical, administrative, and managerial capacity in local institutions, especially local government. This suggests that "go-it-alone" development strategies will not succeed. Pooling resources, including human resources, will enable rural communities to benefit from scale economies and develop the necessary capacity in local institutions so that they can manage population and economic growth (or decline) more effectively. The critical mass they achieve will enhance their competitive position in today's interdependent economy.

Economic Specialization.   Many rural and small town economies continue to be highly specialized, even in the midst of the significant industrial restructuring that is occurring. Specialized economies tend to have erratic growth rates that are difficult to predict and manage. In contrast, diversified economies tend to grow moderately but steadily.[4] Rural communities (preferably cooperating together) could enhance

---

[3]U.S. Department of Agriculture (1987).
[4]Killian and Hady (1988).

their economic viability by attempting to retain and attract a diversified mix of economic activities.

Limited Human Capital. The demographic characteristics of rural areas and small towns reflect the often limited human capital available there. Education, training, and other human resource development activities are needed by three distinct groups of rural persons if rural economies are to become/remain competitive in today's information-based economy. Human resource development programs must be sensitive to the differing needs of new generations joining the work force for the first time, current workers who wish to maintain or enhance their employability and standard of living, and farm and industrial workers dislocated in the current industrial restructuring who must be able to make a transition to new jobs.

Dependency and Disadvantage. Rural areas and small towns were shown to have a relatively high dependency burden and more than their relative share of economically disadvantaged persons. Both of these factors indicate the need for special assistance programs, and for publicly provided services and facilities. Elderly inmigrants to rural areas, for example, tend to be relatively well off, but they have specific service needs. Accordingly, both the public and the private sectors will have to adjust to meet this demand. And, as they age in place, these elderly inmigrants are likely to become less well off and more dependent, reducing their initial economic benefits to the community.

Poverty and disadvantage are not evenly spread across the rural and nonmetropolitan landscape, but rather are concentrated in particular areas. Poverty is frequently situated in the context of slow growth or decline and a high level of economic distress. Such communities often are least able to provide assistance to disadvantaged citizens.

Rural Diversity and Policy

The diversity of rural and nonmetropolitan conditions indicates diverse paths to economic viability. No single development model or growth strategy fits across rural and small town America. Some areas will consolidate their economic development efforts around current activities; others will seek to transform and diversify their economies with a mix of goods production and services. Some areas will specialize in residential and consumer-based activities facilitated by commuting to nearby towns or metropolitan areas. The larger and more varied labor markets achieved by multiple community efforts might enhance the range of feasible development options. And, if effectively organized, many services and facilities can be provided more efficiently if their costs are spread over larger population bases.

Much of the responsibility for implementing a rural strategy will depend on the leadership of rural communities and small towns themselves, but other actors may also have important roles to play. Rural business and government, the church, and voluntary associations can all contribute to building effective communities. There is need to strengthen and support the organized institutional and leadership base in many rural communities.

Rural areas now have a major stake in federal macroeconomic policies that promote economic growth and create jobs and income. Such an economic climate contributes to attracting and retaining rural population and enhances the economic well-being of rural persons. Federal and state education and human resource development policies and infrastructure programs also contribute to helping rural communities remain economically viable in our highly urban society.

Concerning the Future

In recent decades there have been unanticipated demographic changes in rural and small town areas of the United States. First the turnaround to widespread and relatively rapid nonmetropolitan growth and migration gain in the 1970s, and then the shift to slower growth and decline in the 1980s, have each been accepted reluctantly at first and then often justified and embraced as the new trend for the future. If one thing can be learned from this experience, it is that demographic *change*, not stability, is the normal state of affairs. We cannot assume that the experiences of any decade, including the current one, have established the destiny of rural and small town America.

Our demographic research has shown that the population of rural areas and small towns continues to be differentiated from their urban and metropolitan counterparts in ways that justify particular attention in policy. At the same time, these areas are by no means isolated or unique, for in many ways they are changing along with the rest of the nation, and increasing their economic and social interdependence with urban and metropolitan areas. More than ever it is true that future changes in the demographic, economic, and social structure of rural and small town America are associated with the ties that bind such areas to the rest of the national economic and social structure, and to the global system beyond our nation's borders.

Yet there is another theme running throughout this work—that of regional and local variability. Regional differences in demographic and economic trends have strengthened in recent years, and our analysis has revealed continued local variations in population structure and change and in economic conditions. Although the desire to explain and make policy prescriptions often leads to broad generalizations, there can be no *one* future for rural and small town America. Moreover, at the local level, by acting on preferences for rural living and working toward common community goals, people can and do make a difference.

Bibliography

Alonso, William City Sizes and Quality of Life: Some Observations. Berkeley: University of California. Department of City and Regional Planning Working Paper 245, 1975.

———— **and Michael Fajans** Cost of Living and Income by Urban Size. Berkeley: University of California. Department of City and Regional Planning Working Paper 128, 1970.

Andrews, Frank M., J. M. Morgan, and J. A. Sonquist *Multiple Classification Analysis*, 2nd ed. Ann Arbor: University of Michigan Institute for Social Research, 1973.

Appalachian Regional Commission Settlement Patterns Study Preliminary Results. Unpublished memorandum, 1980.

Appelbaum, Richard P. *Size, Growth and U.S. Cities.* New York: Praeger, 1978.

Bancroft, Gertrude *The American Labor Force: Its Growth and Changing Composition.* New York: Wiley, 1958.

Banks, Vera J. "Who Make Up the Farm Population." *Rural Development Perspectives* 3(1986):18–21.

———— **and Judith Z. Kalbacher** *Farm Income Recipients and Their Families: A Socioeconomic Profile.* Washington, D.C.: Economic Development Division, Economic Research Service, U.S. Department of Agriculture, Rural Development Research Report 30, 1981.

Beale, Calvin L. "Natural Decrease of the Population: The Current and Prospective Status of an Emergent American Phenomenon." *Demography* 6(1969):91–99.

———— "Rural and Nonmetropolitan Population Trends of Significance to National Population Policy." In Sara Mills Mazie (ed.) *Population, Distribution and Policy.* Vol. V of Research Reports of U.S. Commission on Population Growth and the American Future. Washington, D.C.: U.S. Government Printing Office, 1972.

———— "The Recent Shift of United States Population to Nonmetropolitan Areas 1970–75." *International Regional Science Review* 2(1977):113–122.

———— "The Changing Nature of Rural Employment." In David L. Brown and John M. Wardwell (eds.) *New Directions in Urban-Rural Migration.* New York: Academic Press, 1980.

———— "Poughkeepsie's Complaint." *American Demographics* 6(1984):28–31, 46–48.

———— **and Glenn V. Fuguitt** "Metropolitan and Nonmetropolitan Population Growth in the United States Since 1980." In Joint Economic Committee of Congress, *New Dimensions in Rural Policy: Building upon Our Heritage.* Washington, D.C.: U.S. Government Printing Office, 1986.

Bealer, Robert C., Fern K. Willits, and William P. Kuvlesky "The Meaning of

'Rurality' in American Society: Some Implications of Alternative Definitions." *Rural Sociology* 30(1965):255–266.

Bender, Lloyd, Bernal Green, Thomas Hady, John Kuehn, Marlys Nelson, Leon Perkinson, and Peggy Ross *The Diverse Social and Economic Structure of Nonmetropolitan America.* Washington, D.C.: U.S. Department of Agriculture, Economic Research Service, Rural Development Research Report No. 49, 1985.

Beresford, John C. and Alice M. Rivlin "Privacy, Poverty and Old Age." *Demography* 3(1966):247–258.

Berry, Brian J. L. "The Geography of the United States in the Year 2000." *Transactions of the Institute of British Geographers* 51(1970):21–53.

Beyer, Glenn H. and J. Hugh Rose *Farm Housing.* New York: Wiley, 1957.

Bianchi, Suzanne M. and Daphne Spain *Household Composition and Racial Inequality.* New Brunswick, N.J.: Rutgers University Press, 1981.

———— *American Women in Transition.* New York: Russell Sage Foundation, 1986.

Bloomquist, Leonard "Performance of the Rural Manufacturing Sector." Chap. 3 in David L. Brown, J. Norman Reid, Herman Bluestone, David A. McGranahan, and Sara M. Mazie (eds.) *Rural Economic Development in the 1980's: Prospects for the Future.* Rural Development Research Report No. 69. Washington, D.C.: Agriculture and Rural Economy Division, Economic Research Service, U.S. Department of Agriculture, 1988.

Bluestone, Herman and Stan Daberkow "Employment Growth in Nonmetro America: Past Trends and Prospects to 1990." *Rural Development Perspectives* 1(1985): 20–37.

Bogue, Donald J. *State Economic Areas: A Description of the Procedure Used in Making a Functional Grouping of the Counties of the United States.* Washington, D.C.: U.S. Bureau of the Census, Government Printing Office, 1951.

———— *The Population of the United States.* New York: Free Press, 1959.

———— *The Population of the United States: Historical Trends and Future Projections.* New York: Free Press, 1985.

Bokemeier, Janet L. and Ann R. Tickamyer "Labor Force Experiences of Nonmetropolitan Women." *Rural Sociology* 50(1985):51–73.

Bourne, Larry S. "Alternative Perspectives on Urban Decline and Population Deconcentration." *Urban Geography* 1(1980):39–52.

Bowles, Gladys K. "Contributions of Recent Metro Migrants to the Nonmetro Population and Labor Force." *Agricultural Economic Research* 30(1978):15–22.

Brown, David L. "Spatial Aspects of Post-1970 Work Force Migration in the United States." *Growth and Change* 12(1981):9–20.

———— **and Calvin L. Beale** "Diversity in Post-1980 Population Trends." In Amos Hawley and Sara M. Mazie (eds.) *Nonmetropolitan America in Transition.* Chapel Hill: University of North Carolina Press, 1981.

Brown, David L. and Kenneth L. Deavers "Rural Change and the Rural Economic Policy Agenda for the 1980s." Chap. 1 in David L. Brown et al. (eds.) *Rural Economic Development in the 1980s: Prospects for the Future.* Rural Development Research Report No. 69. Washington, D.C.: Agriculture and Rural Economy Division, Economic Research Service, U.S. Department of Agriculture, 1988.

Brown, David L., Tim B. Heaton, and Benjamin L. Huffman "Sociodemographic Pressures on Farmland Values in Nonmetropolitan America." *Social Science Quarterly* 65(1984):789–802.

Brown, David L. and Jeanne M. O'Leary *Labor Force Activity of Women in Metropolitan and Nonmetropolitan America.* Washington, D.C.: Economic Research Service, U.S. Department of Agriculture, Rural Development Research Report No. 15, 1979.

Browning, Harley and Joachim Singelmann "The Transformation of the U.S. Labor Force: The Interaction of Industry and Occupation." *Politics and Society* 3–4(1978):481–509.

Carlino, Gerald A. "Declining City Productivity and the Growth of Rural Regions: A Test of Alternative Explanations." *Journal of Urban Economics* 18(1985):11–27.

Chafe, William H. "Looking Backward in Order to Look Forward: Women, Work, and Social Values in America." In Juanita Kreps (ed.) *Women and the American Economy: A Look to the 1980s.* Englewood Cliffs, N.J.: Prentice-Hall, 1976.

Cherlin, Andrew *Marriage, Divorce, and Remarriage.* Cambridge, Mass.: Harvard University Press, 1981.

Christenson, Bruce and Doris Slesinger "Effects of Race, Ethnicity and Poverty on Living Arrangements of Widows in the United States." Paper presented to the Population Association of America, San Francisco, April, 1986.

Cleveland, Harlan "The Twilight of Hierarchy: Speculations on the Global Information Society." *Public Administration Review* 45(1985):185–195.

Coale, Ansley J. "How a Population Ages or Grows Older." In Ronald Freedman (ed.) *Population: The Vital Revolution.* Garden City, N.Y.: Doubleday-Anchor, 1964.

Coughenour, C. Milton "Farmers and Farm Workers: Perspectives on Occupational Complexity and Change." In Harry K. Schwarzweller (ed.) *Research in Rural Sociology and Development,* Vol. 1. Greenwich, Conn.: JAI Press, 1984.

Coward, Raymond T. and William M. Smith (eds.) *The Family in Rural Society.* Boulder, Col.: Westview, 1981.

DeAre, Diana and Larry Long "Did the US Undergo Ruralization in the 1970s?" *Intercom* 10(1982):8–10.

DeJong, Gordon F. "Religious Fundamentalism, Socio-economic Status, and Fertility Attitudes in the Southern Appalachians." *Demography* 2(1965):540–548.

—— *Appalachian Fertility Decline.* Lexington: University of Kentucky Press, 1968.

Duncan, Greg J., Martha Hill, and Willard Rogers "The Changing Fortunes of Young and Old." *American Demographics* 8(1986): 26–33.

Duncan, Otis Dudley and Albert J. Reiss, Jr. *Social Characteristics of Urban and Rural Communities, 1950.* New York: Wiley, 1956 .

Duncan, Otis Dudley, W. Richard Scott, Stanley Lieberson, Beverly Duncan, and Hal H. Winsborough *Metropolis and Region.* Baltimore: Johns Hopkins University Press, 1960.

Economic Research Service *Economic Indicators of the Farm Sector: Income and Balance Sheet Statistics 1983.* Washington, D.C.: United States Department of Agriculture, Economic Research Service ECIFS3-3, 1984.

Elo, Irma T. Poverty in Rural America. New York: Ford Foundation, 1985 (unpublished).

—— **and Calvin L. Beale** *Natural Resources and Rural Poverty: An Overview.* National Center for Food and Agricultural Policy. Washington, D.C.: Resources for the Future, Inc., 1985.

Estall, R. C. "The Decentralization of Manufacturing Industry: Recent American Experience in Perspective." *Geoforum* 14(1983):133–147.

Fielding, A. "Counterurbanization in Western Europe." *Progress in Planning* 17(1982):1–52.

Ford, Thomas R. (ed.) *Rural USA: Persistence and Change.* Ames: Iowa State University Press, 1978.

Frey, William H. "Migration and Depopulation of the Metropolis: Regional Restructuring or Rural Renaissance?" *American Sociological Review* 52(1986): 240–257.

Fuchs, Victor Differences in Hourly Earnings by Region and City Size, 1959. New York: National Bureau of Economic Research Occasional Paper 101, 1967.

———— *How We Live.* Cambridge, Mass.: Harvard University Press, 1983.

Fuguitt, Glenn V. "The Nonmetropolitan Population Turnaround." *Annual Review of Sociology* 11(1985):259–280.

———— **and Calvin L. Beale** *Population Change in Nonmetropolitan Cities and Towns.* Washington, D.C.: Economic Development Division, Economic Research Service, U.S. Department of Agriculture, Agricultural Economics Report No. 323, 1976.

Fuguitt, Glenn V. and Donald R. Field "Some Population Characteristics of Villages Differentiated by Size, Location, and Growth." *Demography* 9(1972): 295–308.

Fuguitt, Glenn V., Anthony Fuller, Heather Fuller, Ruth Gasson, and Gwyn Jones *Part-Time Farming: Its Nature and Implications.* Ashford, Kent, England: Wye College Centre for European Agricultural Studies Seminar Papers No. 2, 1977.

Fuguitt, Glenn V., Daniel T. Lichter, and Calvin L. Beale *Population Deconcentration in Metropolitan and Nonmetropolitan Areas of the United States, 1950–1975.* Madison: University of Wisconsin, Applied Population Laboratory. Population Series 70–15, 1981.

Fuguitt, Glenn V., Max Pfeffer, and Robert Jenkins Gross Migration Trends for Nonmetropolitan Counties. Madison: University of Wisconsin Center for Demography and Ecology Working Paper 85–19, 1985.

Fuller, Anthony M. "Part-Time Farming: The Enigmas and the Realities." In Harry K. Schwarzweller (ed.) *Research in Rural Sociology and Development,* Vol. 1. Greenwich, Conn.: JAI Press, 1984.

Galpin, C. J. and V. B. Larson *Farm Population in Selected Counties.* Washington, D.C.: U.S. Bureau of the Census, 1924.

Gilmer, Robert W. "Cyclical and Structural Change in Southern Manufacturing: Recent Evidence from the Tennessee Valley: Note." *Growth and Change* 17(1986):61–69.

Glasgow, Nina L. *The Nonmetro Elderly: Economic and Demographic Status.* Washington, D.C.: USDA-ERS, Rural Development Research Report No. 70, 1988.

———— **and Calvin L. Beale** "Rural Elderly in Demographic Perspective." *Rural Development Perspectives* 2(1985):22–26.

Glenn, Norval and Jon Alston "Rural-Urban Differences in Reported Attitudes and Behavior." *Southwestern Social Science Quarterly* 47(1967):381–400.

Glenn, Norval D. and L. Hill "Rural-Urban Differences in Attitudes and Behavior in the U.S." *Annals of the American Academy of Political and Social Science* 429(1977):36–50.

Grabill, Wilson H., Clyde V. Kiser, and Pascal K. Whelpton *The Fertility of American Women.* New York: Wiley, 1958.

Greenwood, Michael J. "Human Migration: Theory, Models, and Empirical Studies." *Journal of Regional Science* 25(1985):521–544.

Hagood, Margaret J. "Rural Population Characteristics." In Carl C. Taylor et al. (eds.) *Rural Life in the United States*. New York: Alfred C. Knopf, 1949.

Haney, Wava "Women." In Don Dillman and Daryl Hobbs (eds.) *Rural Society in the U. S.: Issues for the 1980s*. Ames: Iowa State University Press, 1982.

Hansen, Niles "The New International Division of Labor and Manufacturing Decentralization in the United States." *Review of Regional Studies* 9(1979):1–11.

Harris, Craig K., Jim McAllister, and Jess Gilbert "Social Dimensions of Farmland Ownership in the United States." In Joint Economic Committee of Congress, *New Dimensions in Rural Policy: Building upon Our Heritage*. Washington, D.C.: U.S. Government Printing Office, 1986.

Hart, John Fraser "Population Change in the Upper Lake States." *Annals of the Association of American Geographers* 74(1984):221–243.

Hathaway, Dale E., J. Allan Beegle, and W. Keith Bryant *People of Rural America*. Washington, D.C.: U.S. Government Printing Office, 1968.

Henderson, John P. *Changes in the Industrial Distribution of Employment, 1919–1959*. Urbana: University of Illinois, 1961.

Henshaw, Stanley K., Jacqueline Darroch Forrest, Ellen Sullivan, and Christopher Tietze "Abortion Services in the United States, 1979 and 1980." *Family Planning Perspectives* 14(1982):5–15.

Hines, Fred K., David L. Brown, and J. M. Zimmer *Social and Economic Characteristics of the Population in Metropolitan and Nonmetropolitan Counties, 1970*. Washington, D.C.: Economic Research Service, U.S. Department of Agriculture, Agricultural Economic Report 272, 1975.

Hoch, Irving "Urban Scale and Environmental Quality." In Ronald G. Ridker (ed.) *Population Resources and the Environment*. U.S. Commission on Population Growth and the American Future. Vol. 3 of Commission Research Reports. Washington, D.C.: U.S. Government Printing Office, 1972.

———, Julie Hewitt, and Vicky Virgin *Real Income, Poverty, and Resources*. National Center for Food and Agricultural Policy. Washington, D.C.: Resources for the Future, 1984.

Hugo, Graeme J. and Peter J. Smailes "Urban–Rural Migration in Australia: A Process View of the Turnaround." *Journal of Rural Studies* 1(1985):11–30.

Johansen, Harley E. and Glenn V. Fuguitt *The Changing Rural Village in America: Demographic and Economic Trends Since 1950*. Cambridge, Mass.: Ballinger, 1984.

Johnson, Douglas W., Paul R. Picard, and Bernard Quinn *Churches and Church Membership in the United States 1971*. Washington, D.C.: Glenmary Research Center, 1974.

Jones, Maldwyn A. "Scotch Irish." In Stephen Thernstrom, Ann Orlov, and Oscar Handlin (eds.) *Harvard Encyclopedia of American Ethnic Groups*. Cambridge, Mass.: Harvard University Press, 1980.

Kasarda, John D. "The Implications of Contemporary Distribution Trends for National Urban Policy." *Social Science Quarterly* 61(1980):373–400.

Killian, Molly Sizer and Thomas F. Hady "The Economic Performance of Rural Labor Markets." Chap. 8 in David L. Brown et al. (eds.) *Rural Economic Development in the 1980s: Prospects for the Future*. Rural Development Research Report No. 69. Washington, D.C.: Agriculture and Rural Economy Division, Economic Research Service, U.S. Department of Agriculture, 1988.

Klaff, Vivian and Glenn V. Fuguitt "Annexation as a Factor in the Growth of U.S. Cities 1960–70 and 1970–80." *Demography* 15(1978):1–12.

Kobrin, Frances E. "The Fall of Household Size and the Rise of the Primary Individual in the United States." *Demography* 13(1976):117–139.

Lang, Marvel "Redefining Urban and Rural for the U.S. Census of Population: Assessing the Need and Alternative Approaches." *Urban Geography* 7(1986):118–134.

Larson, Olaf F. "Values and Beliefs of Rural People." In Thomas R. Ford (ed.) *Rural U.S.A.: Persistence and Change.* Ames: Iowa State University Press, 1978.

Lee, Gary R. "Rural Families: Sterotypes and Realty." In Joint Economic Committee of Congress. *New Dimensions in Rural Policy: Building upon Our Heritage.* Washington, D.C.: U.S. Government Printing Office, 1986.

Leven, Charles L. (ed.). *The Mature Metropolis.* Lexington, Mass.: Lexington Books, 1978.

Lichter, Daniel T. "Measuring Underemployment in Rural Areas." *Rural Development Perspectives* 3(1987):11–14.

Lichter, Daniel T. and Glenn V. Fuguitt "Demographic Responses to Transportation Innovation: The Case of the Interstate Highway." *Social Forces* 59(1980):492–512.

_____ "The Transition to Nonmetropolitan Population Deconcentration." *Demography* 19(1982):211–221.

Lichter, Daniel T., Glenn V. Fuguitt, and Tim B. Heaton "Components of Nonmetropolitan Population Change: The Contribution of Rural Areas." *Rural Sociology* 50(1985):88–98.

Lichter, Daniel T., Glenn V. Fuguitt, Tim B. Heaton, and William Clifford "Components of Change in the Residential Concentration of the Elderly Population." *Journal of Gerontology* 36(1981):480–489.

Lichter, Daniel T., Tim B. Heaton, and Glenn V. Fuguitt "Convergence in Black and White Population Redistribution in the United States." *Social Science Quarterly* 67(1986):21–38.

Long, John F. *Population Deconcentration in the United States.* Washington, D.C.: U.S. Bureau of the Census Special Demographic Analyses CDS-81-5, 1981.

_____ "Migration and the Phases of Population Redistribution." *Journal of Development Economics* 17(1985):29–42.

Long, Larry H. and Diana DeAre Economic Base of Recent Population Growth in Nonmetropolian Settings. Paper presented to Association of American Geographers, San Antonio, Texas, 1982a.

_____ "Repopulating the Countryside: A 1980 Census Trend." *Science* 217(1982b):1111–1116.

Lyson, Thomas A. and William W. Falk "Two Sides of the Sunbelt: Economic Development in the Rural and Urban South." In Joint Economic Committee of Congress, *New Dimensions in Rural Policy: Building upon Our Heritage.* Washington D.C.: U.S. Government Printing Office, 1986.

Masnick, George and Mary Jo Bane *The Nation's Families: 1960–1990.* Boston: Auburn House, 1980.

McCarthy, Kevin F. and Peter A. Morrison *The Changing Demographic and Economic Structure of Nonmetropolitan Areas in the 1970s.* Santa Monica, Calif.: Rand Corporation, Rand Paper Series P-6062, 1979.

McGranahan, David "Changes in Age Structure and Rural Community Growth." *Rural Development Perspectives* 1 (1985):21–25.

444

—— "The Role of Rural Workers in the National Economy." Chap. 2 in David L. Brown et al. (eds.) *Rural Economic Development in the 1980s: Prospects for the Future.* Rural Development Research Report No. 69. Washington, D.C.: Agriculture and Rural Economy Division, Economic Research Service, U.S. Department of Agriculture, 1988.

McGranahan, David, John C. Hession, Fred K. Hines, and Max F. Jordan *The Social and Economic Characteristics of the Population in Metro and Non-metro Counties, 1970–80.* Washington, D.C.: Economic Research Service, U.S. Department of Agriculture, Rural Development Research Report No. 58, 1986.

Michael, Robert T. "Consequences of the Rise in Female Labor Force Participation Rates: Questions and Problems." *Journal of Labor Economics* 3 (1985):S117–146.

Mighell, Ronald L. *American Agriculture: Its Structure and Place in the Economy.* New York: Wiley, 1955.

Miller, James P. and Herman Bluestone "Prospects for Service Sector Employment Growth in Nonmetro America." Chap. 6 in David L. Brown et al. (eds.) *Rural Economic Development in the 1980's: Prospects for the Future.* Rural Development Research Report No. 69. Washington, D.C.: Agriculture and Rural Economy Division, Economic Research Service, U.S. Department of Agriculture, 1988.

Moore, Keith The Household Labor Allocation of Farm-Based Families in Wisconsin. Unpublished Ph.D. dissertation, University of Wisconsin, Madison, 1984.

Morrill, Richard L. "Stages in Patterns of Population Concentration and Dispersion." *Professional Geographer* 31(1979):55–65.

National Commission on Employment and Unemployment Statistics *Counting the Unemployed.* Washington, D.C.: U. S. Government Printing Office, 1979.

National Resources Committee *The Problems of a Changing Population.* Washington, D.C.: U.S. Government Printing Office, 1938.

Nilsen, Sigurd R. "How Occupational Mix Inflates Regional Pay Differentials." *Monthly Labor Review* 101 (1978):45–58.

—— "Recessionary Impacts on the Unemployment of Men and Women." *Monthly Labor Review* 107 (1984):21–25.

Norton, R. D. and J. Rees "The Product Cycle and the Spatial Decentralization of American Manufacturing." *Regional Studies* 13:(1979)141–215.

Noyelle, Thierry J. and Thomas M. Stanback, Jr. *The Economic Transformation of American Cities.* Totowa, N.J.: Rowman & Allanheld, 1984.

Ogburn, William F. *Social Characteristics of Cities.* Chicago: International City Managers Association, 1937.

—— **and Otis Dudley Duncan** "City Size as a Sociological Variable." In Ernest W. Burgess and Donald J. Bogue (eds.) *Contributions to Urban Sociology.* Chicago: University of Chicago Press, 1964.

Olson, Lawrence *Costs of Children.* Lexington, Mass.: Lexington Books, D. C. Heath and Co., 1983.

Petrulis, M. F. *Growth Patterns in Nonmetro-Metro Manufacturing Employment.* Washington, D.C.: Economic Research Service, U.S. Department of Agriculture, Rural Development Research Report 7, 1979.

President's National Advisory Commission on Rural Poverty *The People Left Behind.* Washington, D.C.: U.S. Government Printing Office, 1967.

Preston, Samuel H. "Children and the Elderly: Divergent Paths for America's Dependents." *Demography* 21(1984):435–458.

—— **and John McDonald** "The Incidence of Divorce Within Cohorts of American Marriages Contracted Since the Civil War." *Demography* 16(1979):1–25.

Quinn, Bernard, Herman Anderson, Martin Bradley, Paul Goetting, and Peggy Shriver *Churches and Church Membership in the United States, 1980.* Atlanta, Ga.: Glenmary Research Center, 1982.

Richter, Kerry "Nonmetropolitan Growth in the Late 1970s: The End of the Turnaround?" *Demography* 22(1985):245–263.

Robey, Bryant "A Guide to the Baby Boom." *American Demographics* 4 (1982):16–21.

Robinson, J. Gregory Labor Force Participation Rates of Cohorts of Women in the United States: 1890–1979. Paper presented at the annual meeting of the Population Association of America, Denver, Colo., 1980.

Robinson, Warren C. *Metropolitan and Urban Growth in the U.S.A.: 1900–1960.* University Park: The Pennsylvania State University Institute for Research on Land and Water Resources, 1968.

Ross, Heather and Isabell Sawhill *Time of Transition: The Growth of Families Headed by Women.* Washington, D.C.: Urban Institute, 1975.

Ross, Peggy J. and Elizabeth S. Morrissey Persistent Poverty Among the Nonmetropolitan Poor. Paper presented at the annual meeting of the Southern Sociological Association, Orlando, Fla., 1986.

Rosten, Leo (ed.) *Religions in America.* New York: Simon & Schuster, 1975.

Ryder, Norman B. "Components of Temporal Variations in American Fertility." In Robert W. Hiorns (ed.) *Demographic Patterns of Developed Societies.* London: Taylor & Francis, 1980.

Salamon, Sonya "Ethnic Communities and the Structure of Agriculture." *Rural Sociology* 3(1985):323–340.

Schnore, Leo F. "Some Correlates of Urban Size: A Replication." *American Journal of Sociology* 69(1963):185–193.

—— **and David W. Varley** "Some Concomitants of Metropolitan Size." *American Sociological Review* 20(1955):408–414.

Shryock, Henry S. "The Natural History of Standard Metropolitan Areas." *American Journal of Sociology* 63(1957):163–170.

—— **and Jacob S. Siegel and Associates** *The Methods and Materials of Demography.* Washington, D.C.: U.S. Government Printing Office, 1971.

Shryock, Henry S., Jacob S. Siegel, and Calvin L. Beale "Future Trend of Fertility in the United States." Proceedings of the World Population Conference, 1954, Vol. 1. New York: United Nations, 1955.

Singelmann, Joachim *From Agriculture to Services: The Transformation of Industrial Employment.* Beverly Hills, Calif.: Sage Publications, 1978.

Slesinger, Doris P. "The Relationship of Fertility to Measures of Metropolitan Dominance: A New Look." *Rural Sociology* 39(1974):350–361.

Smith, T. Lynn "The Agricultural Population: Realism vs. Nominalism in the Census of Agriculture." *Journal of Farm Economics* 20(1938):679–687.

Sweet, James A. and Larry L. Bumpass *American Families and Households.* New York: Russell Sage Foundation, 1987.

Taeuber, Conrad and Irene B. Taeuber *The Changing Population of the United States.* New York: Wiley, 1958.

Taeuber, Karl E. and James A. Sweet "Family and Work: The Social Life Cycle of Women." In Juanita Krebs (ed.) *Women in the American Economy: A Look at the 1980's.* New York: The American Assembly, Columbia University, 1976.

Teachman, Jay D., Karen Polonko, and John Scanzoni "Demography of the Family: A Review of Recent Trends and Developments in the Field." In M. Sussman and S. Steinmetz (eds.) *Handbook of Marriage and the Family*. Boston: Plenum, 1982.

Thompson, Warren S. and P. K. Whelpton *Population Trends in the United States*. New York: McGraw-Hill, 1933.

Thompson, Wilbur R. *A Preface to Urban Economics*. Baltimore: Johns Hopkins University Press, 1965.

—————— "The Economic Base of Urban Problems." In Neil W. Chamberlain (ed.) *Contemporary Economic Issues*. Homewood, Ill.: R. D. Irwin, 1969.

Thornton, Arland "Religion and Fertility: The Case of Mormonism." *Journal of Marriage and the Family* 41(1979):131–142.

Tisdale, Hope "The Process of Urbanization." *Social Forces* 20(1942):311–316.

Truesdell, Leon E. *Farm Population of the United States*. Census Monographs VI. Washington, D.C.: U.S. Government Printing Office, 1926.

—————— "The Development of the Urban–Rural Classification in the United States: 1874 to 1949." *Current Population Reports*, Series P-23, No. 1. Washington, D.C.: U.S. Bureau of the Census, 1949.

—————— *Farm Population: 1880 to 1950*. U.S. Bureau of the Census Technical Paper No. 3. Washington, D.C.: U.S. Bureau of the Census, 1960.

Tucker, C. Jack "Changing Patterns of Migration Between Metropolitan and Nonmetropolitan Areas of the United States: Recent Evidence." *Demography* 13(1976):435–444.

U.S. Bureau of the Census *U.S. Census of Population: 1960*, Vol. 1. *Characteristics of the Population*. Part 1. United States Summary. Washington, D.C.: U.S. Government Printing Office, 1964.

—————— *Census of Population: 1970*, Vol. 1. *Characteristics of the Population*. Part 1. United States Summary. Washington, D.C.: U.S. Government Printing Office, 1973a.

—————— *Census of Population: 1970*. Subject Reports PC(2)-8C, *Income of the Farm-Related Population*. Washington, D.C.: U.S. Government Printing Office, 1973b.

—————— *Historical Statistics of the United States Colonial Times to 1970: Bicentennial Edition Part 1*. Washington, D.C.: U.S. Government Printing Office, 1975.

—————— "Characteristics of the Population Below the Poverty Level: 1979." *Current Population Reports* Series P-60, No. 130. Washington, D.C.: U.S. Government Printing Office, 1981.

—————— *1980 Census of Population*, Vol. 1. *Characteristics of the Population*. PC80-1-C1. U.S. Summary. Washington, D.C.: U.S. Government Printing Office, 1983a.

—————— "Fertility of American Women: June 1983." *Current Population Reports*. Series P-20, No. 395. Washington, D.C.: U.S. Government Printing Office, 1983b.

—————— "Estimates of Poverty Including the Value of Noncash Benefits: 1983." Washington, D.C.: U.S. Government Printing Office. Technical Paper 52, 1984.

—————— *1980 Census of Population*. Subject Reports PC80-2-9C. *Characteristics of the Rural and Farm-Related Population*. Washington D.C.: U.S. Government Printing Office, 1985a.

—————— "Provisional Estimates of the Population of Counties: July 1, 1984." *Cur-*

rent Population Reports, Local Population Estimates. Series P-26, No. 84-52-C, 1985b.

―――― "1984 Population and 1983 per Capita Income Estimates for Counties and Incorporated Places." *Current Population Reports, Local Population Estimates.* Series P-26, No. 84, 1986.

―――― "Fertility of American Women: June 1986." *Current Population Reports.* Series P-20, No. 421. Washington, D.C.: U.S. Government Printing Office, 1987.

―――― **and U.S. Department of Agriculture** "Farm Population of the United States 1986." *Current Population Reports, Farm Population.* Series P-27. No. 60, 1987.

U.S. Census Office *Statistical Atlas 1900* 12th Census of the United States. Washington, D.C.: U.S. Census Office, 1903.

U.S. Bureau of Economic Analysis. Unpublished Data, 1984.

U.S. Department of Agriculture "Rural Development in the 1980s: A Summary." Agriculture Information Bulletin No. 533. Washington, D.C.: Economic Research Service, U.S. Department of Agriculture, 1987.

U.S. Department of Health and Human Services, National Center for Health Statistics "Induced Terminations of Pregnancy: Reporting States, 1984." *Monthly Vital Statistics Report*, Vol. 36, No. 5, Supplement 2. Washington, DC: U.S. Government Printing Office, 1987.

Vining, Daniel R., Jr. "Migration Between the Core and the Periphery." *Scientific American* 247(1982):45–53.

―――― **and Thomas Kontuly** "Population Dispersal from Major Metropolitan Regions: An International Comparison." *International Regional Science Review* 3(1978):49–73.

Vining, Daniel R., Jr. and A. Strauss "A Demonstration That the Current Deconcentration of Population in the United States Is a Clean Break with the Past." *Environment and Planning* 9(1977):751–758.

Voss, Paul R. and Glenn V. Fuguitt *Turnaround Migration in the Upper Great Lakes Region.* Madison: University of Wisconsin, Department of Rural Sociology, Applied Population Laboratory Population Series 70–12, 1979.

Wachtel, Howard M. *Labor and the Economy.* Orlando, Fla.: Academic Press, 1984.

Wardwell, John M. "Equilibrium and Change in Nonmetropolitan Growth." *Rural Sociology* 42(1977):156–179.

―――― "Toward a Theory of Urban–Rural Migration in the Developed World." In David Brown and John Wardwell (eds.) *New Directions in Urban–Rural Migration: The Population Turnaround in Rural America.* New York: Academic Press, 1980.

―――― The Resurgence of Rural Growth in the 1980s: Trends and Explanations. Unpublished Paper, Washington State University, Pullman, 1987.

Weber, Adna F. *The Growth of Cities in the Nineteenth Century.* New York: Macmillan, 1899.

Weber, Bruce A., Emory N. Castle, and Ann L. Shriver "The Performance of Natural Resource Industries." Chap. 5 in David L. Brown et al. (eds.) *Rural Economic Development in the 1980's: Prospects for the Future.* Rural Development Research Report No. 69. Washington, D.C.: Agriculture and Rural Economy Division, Economic Research Service, U.S. Department of Agriculture, 1988.

Weed. James "National Estimates of Marital Dissolution and Survivorship." *Vi-*

tal and Health Statistics, Series 3, No. 19. Washington, D.C.: U.S. National Center for Health Statistics, 1980.

Weller, Robert and Leon Bouvier *Population: Demography and Policy.* New York: St. Martin's Press, 1981.

Whitener, Leslie A. *Counting Hired Farmworkers: Some Points to Consider.* Washington, D.C.: Economic Research Service, U.S. Department of Agriculture, Agricultural Economic Report 524, 1984.

Willits, Fern K., Robert C. Bealer and Donald Crider "Leveling of Attitudes in Mass Society: Rurality and Traditional Morality in America." *Rural Sociology* 38(1973):25–36.

Wilson, Franklin D. "Aspects of Migration in an Advanced Industrial Society." *American Sociological Review* 53(1988):113–126.

Wimberly, Ronald C. "The Emergence of Part-Time Farming as a Social Form of Agriculture." In *Research in Sociology of Work: Peripheral Workers,* Vol. 2. Greenwich, Conn.: JAI Press, 1983.

Wright, Paul and Peter Pirie *A False Fertility Transition: The Case of American Blacks.* Papers of the East-West Population Institute, No. 90, Honolulu, 1984.

Zuiches, James J. "Residential Preferences in Migration Theory." In David L. Brown and John M. Wardwell (eds.) *New Directions in Urban–Rural Migration: The Population Turnaround in Rural America.* New York: Academic Press, 1980.

_____ **and David L. Brown** "The Changing Character of the Nonmetropolitan Population, 1950–75." In Thomas R. Ford (ed.) *Rural USA Persistence and Change.* Ames: Iowa State University Press, 1978.

Name Index

A

Alonso, William, 410
Alston, Jon, 232n
Anderson, Herman, 203n
Andrews, Frank M., 43n
Appalachian Regional Commission, 69n
Appelbaum, Richard P., 383n

B

Bancroft, Gertrude, 240n
Bane, Mary Jo, 178n
Banks, Vera J., 307n
Beale, Calvin L., 24n, 36n, 42n, 44n, 65n,
    77n, 102n, 130, 188n, 193n, 279n, 284n,
    291n, 363n, 369n
Bealer, Robert C., 4n
Beegle, J. Allan, 303n
Bender, Lloyd, 122n
Beresford, John C., 173n
Berry, Brian J. L., 2n
Beyer, Glenn H., 303n
Bianchi, Suzanne M., 174n, 178n, 235n,
    240n, 242n
Bloomquist, Leonard, 278n, 291n
Bluestone, Herman, 246n, 247n, 251–252,
    265n, 378n
Bogue, Donald, 107, 108, 110n, 111, 115,
    123n, 206n, 265n
Bokemeier, Janet L., 291n
Bourne, Larry S., 2n
Bouvier, Leon, 108, 137n
Bowles, Gladys K., 49n
Bradley, Martin, 203n
Brown, David L., 36n, 48n, 49n, 55n, 102n,
    106n, 112n, 119n, 231n, 238n, 243n,
    263, 291n, 431n
Browning, Harley, 268n, 292n
Bryant, W. Keith, 303n
Bumpass, Larry L., 165n, 173n

C

Carlino, Gerald A., 2n
Castle, Emory N., 267n

A

Chafe, William H., 291n
Cherlin, Andrew, 158
Christensen, Bruce, 170n
Cleveland, Harlan, 2n
Clifford, William, 125n, 126
Coale, Ansley J., 108n
Coughenour, C. Milton, 307n
Coward, Raymond T., 159n

D

Daberkow, Stan, 246n, 251–252
DeAre, Diana, 15n, 65n, 249n, 280n, 284n,
    289n
Deavers, Kenneth L., 231n, 431n
DeJong, Gordon F., 207
Duncan, Beverly, 383n
Duncan, Greg J., 137n, 251, 303n
Duncan, Otis Dudley, 9, 110n, 383n, 385n,
    389, 392, 393, 396–397, 405, 408n, 421,
    431

E

Economic Research Service, 30n
Elo, Irma T., 363n, 380n

F

Fajans, Michael, 410n
Falk, William W., 291n
Field, Donald R., 383n
Fielding, A., 29n
Ford, Thomas R., 158n
Forrest, Jacqueline Darroch, 225n
Frey, William H., 2n, 58n, 59n
Fuchs, Victor, 243n, 410n
Fuguitt, Glenn V., 36n, 40n, 48n, 56n, 63n,
    65, 69n, 77n, 78n, 95, 102n, 125n, 126,
    161n, 288n, 309n, 383n, 389n
Fuller, Anthony M., 309n, 333n
Fuller, Heather, 309n

G

Galpin, C. J., 304, 306
Gasson, Ruth, 309n

R

Rees, J., 277n, 284n
Reiss, Albert J., Jr., 9, 110n, 251, 303n, 383n, 385n, 389, 392, 393, 396–397, 405, 421, 431
Richter, Kerry, 45n
Rivlin, Alice M., 173n
Robey, Bryant, 136n
Robinson, J. Gregory, 241n
Robinson, Warren, 20n
Rogers, Willard, 137n
Rose, J. Hugh, 303n
Ross, Heather, 178n
Ross, Peggy J., 122n, 366
Rosten, Leo, 155n, 202n
Ryder, Norman B., 158n

S

Salamon, Sonya, 155n
Sawhill, Isabell, 178n
Scanzoni, John, 172n, 178n
Schnore, Leo F., 383n
Scott, W. Richard, 383n
Shriver, Ann L., 267n
Shriver, Peggy, 203n
Shryock, Henry S., 6n, 20n, 31n, 67n, 126, 193n, 401n
Siegel, Jacob S., and Associates, 31n, 67n, 126, 193n, 401n
Singelmann, Joachim, 259n, 268n, 292n
Slesinger, Doris, 170n, 397n
Smailes, Peter J., 58n
Smith, T. Lynn, 306
Smith, William M., 159n
Spain, Daphne, 174n, 235n, 240n, 242n
Stanback, Thomas M., Jr., 59n, 271n
Strauss, A., 2n
Sullivan, Ellen, 225n
Sweet, James A., 157n, 165n, 173n

T

Taeuber, Conrad, 107
Taeuber, Irene, 107
Taeuber, Karl E., 157n
Teachman, Jay D., 172n, 178n
Thompson, Warren S., 383n
Thompson, Wilbur R., 277n
Thornton, Arland, 204n

Tickamyer, Ann R., 291n
Tietze, Christopher, 225n
Tisdale, Hope, 14n
Truesdell, Leon E., 303n, 304, 305n
Tucker, C. Jack, 48n, 49n

U

University of Michigan, Panel Study of Income Dynamics (PSID), 137
U.S. Bureau of Economic Analysis, 230n, 246
U.S. Bureau of Labor Statistics, 265
U.S. Bureau of the Census, 5, 7, 15n, 16, 31, 107n, 178n, 225n, 226n, 305n, 307n, 378n, 410n; *Current Population Reports*, 45, 66, 356; Current Population Survey, 255, 268, 273–275, 306
U.S. Census Office, 206n
U.S. Department of Agriculture, 435n
U.S. Department of Health and Human Services, 224n

V

Varley, David W., 383n
Vining, Daniel R., Jr., 2n, 29n
Virgin, Vicky, 339n
Voss, Paul R., 69n

W

Wachtel, Howard M., 253n
Wardwell, John M., 2n, 29n, 58n, 384n
Weber, Adna F., 63
Weber, Bruce A., 267n
Weed, James, 157n, 158n
Weller, Robert, 108, 137n
Whelpton, Pascal K., 185n, 187, 383n
Whitener, Leslie A., 308n
Willits, Fern K., 4n
Wilson, Franklin D., 58n
Wimberly, Ronald C., 333n
Winsborough, Hal H., 383n
Wright, Paul, 193n

Z

Zimmer, J. M., 112n
Zuiches, James J., 2n, 49n, 106n

Subject Index

Italicized numbers refer to figures and tables.

A

abortion, 224–225

administrative occupations: distribution by size of place, *404, 418*; fertility of nonmetropolitan women in, 218, *219*

administrative support occupations: fertility of nonmetropolitan women in, 218, *219*; income from, *350*

age: and children ever born per 1000 women, 189, *190–191, 192*; composition, *see* age composition of population; distribution by size of place, 389, *390, 391, 414*; and family life course, *175,* 175–176, *176*; farming householder types by, 324–325, *325*; at first marriage, *see* age at first marriage; and labor force nonparticipation, 244, 244–245; and labor force participation, 234–237, *235, 236, 237*; and median family income, 134, *135, 338,* 340–341; and migration, 47, 48–49, 57; of nonfamily householders, *168, 169, 171,* 171; and poverty, 364–366, *365, 367, 414*; and sex ratio, *122,* 122–123; and unemployment, 256, *257*; and weekly earnings for men, *341,* 341–342

age at first marriage, 158; and fertility, 209–212, *210, 211,* 227

age composition of population: changes, 107–109, *109,* 123, *123,* 136; determinants, 105–106, 108–109; economic effects, 136; elderly, *123,* 123, *124,* 125, *133*; importance, 105; median age by urban-rural residence, 110, *111*; median age of nonmetropolitan population, 113; median age of U.S. population, 107, *108*; metropolitan and nonmetropolitan populations: 1960–1980, 119, *120,* 429; metropolitan and nonmetropolitan populations by urban and rural residence, 113, *114–115,* 116; nonmetropolitan population: 1960–1970, 1970–1980, 117, *118,* 119; summary of

findings, 429; and urban/rural-metropolitan/nonmetropolitan concepts, 112–113

agricultural employment, 265, 427, 433; and educational attainment, *295, 296*; full-time, 293, *294*; and Hispanic population, 145; median income from; *352, 353, 354,* 355; and metropolitan adjacency, *290*; and nonmetropolitan county population growth, *37–39,* 41, *60*; and nonmetropolitan turnaround, 29; percentage nonmetropolitan, 271, *272, 274,* 275; percentage of change in, 269, *269,* 270; as percentage of total employment, 268, *269,* 273, 275; percentage of workers in white collar occupations, 297, *297*; regional variations, 279, *281, 282, 283*; by residence, 251, *251*; sex differences, 251, *251, 292, 294, 296, 297, 297, 352, 353*; by size of place, 406, *407, 408, 419, 419*; *see also* farming-related households by residence, occupation, and self-employment income

Alabama, 150

Alaska Native population; income sources, *343*; median family income, *346, 347,* 347–348; and poverty, *358*; *see also* Aleut population; Eskimo population

Aleut population; distribution, *142,* 147; fertility, *190–191,* 196–197, *208*; *see also* Alaska Native population

American Indian-combination ancestry population, 152, *153*

American Indian population: distribution, *142,* 145–147, 154, 430; fertility, *190–191,* 194–196, *208,* 226; income sources, *343*; median family income, *346, 347,* 347–348; and poverty, *358,* 362; size, *142,* 145

"American" population, 148–150, *149*

Amish population, 204

annexation, 69